WHERE CHILDREN RUN

Karen Emilson

WHERE CHILDREN RUN
Copyright © Karen Emilson 1996

Perpetual Books
Box 918
Grunthal, Manitoba
R0A 0R0 Canada

All rights reserved. No part of this book may be reproduced or transmitted in any form or by any means—graphic, electronic or mechanical—without the prior written permission of the publisher, except by a reviewer who may quote brief passages in a review.

Written in cooperation with David and Dennis Pischke based on childhood recollections. Former neighbors, teachers, friends and acquaintances also provided information for the book. Whenever possible, facts have been substantiated through government files, records and other documentation.

Design by Ninth and May Design Co.
Author photo by Kate Pentrelli.
Printed and bound in Canada by Friesens Printing.

LIBRARY AND ARCHIVES CANADA CATALOGUING IN PUBLICATION

Emilson, Karen, 1963-, author
    Where children run / Karen Emilson.

Originally published: Ashern, Man : Nordheim Books, ©1996.

    1. Pischke, Dennis--Childhood and youth. 2. Pischke, David--Childhood and youth. 3. Child abuse--Manitoba--Grahamdale (Rural municipality). 4. Pischke family. 5. Abused children--Manitoba--Grahamdale (Rural municipality)--Biography. 6. Grahamdale (Man. : Rural municipality)--Biography. I. Title.

HV6626.54.C3E47 2017   362.76092'271272   C2017-900382-8

Dedicated to

Gus and Emma Harwart
Jim & Ruby (Ratz) Deighton
Leon & Anna Koch

for their kindness

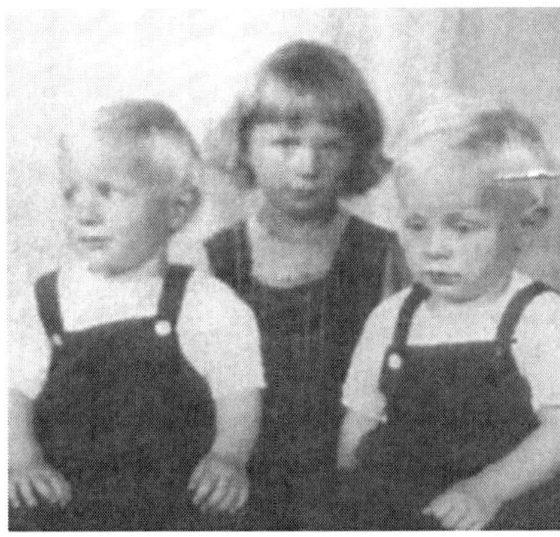

"I taught for 30 years, so a lot of kids have passed through my classroom. Sometimes the only ones you remember are the ones who stand out for some reason. I can still picture those poor Pischke children in my mind."

—LEAH GASPER

"The Pischke kids weren't bad kids at all. They were never bad in school. They were excellent as far as behavior was concerned . . . I knew it wasn't a happy home, but I had no idea of the cruelty. I didn't like the stepfather at all. He made my skin crawl."

—MARION GERING

"I remember those kids coming to my place in the middle of the night. These are awful things to remember—they were all beat up and starving. It was a crying shame that Domko was allowed to get away with it for so long."

—JIM DEIGHTON

"I know exactly who you're talking about when you say the Pischkes. I remember my mother mentioning that family. It was a pretty sad situation."

—LOUISE COLLIER

"I was just a little boy, but I remember the night Dave and Dennis came to our house as clear as if it happened yesterday. In my entire life I've never seen sheer terror as what I saw then. It's something I'll never forget."

—ALVIN KOCH

"The Pischke kids are survivors. So many times I've seen them knocked down but they get right back up again and brush themselves off. And in spite of everything, they've always kept their sense of humour."

—MARJORIE HARWART

FOREWORD

THIS INCREDIBLE STORY ABOUT THE PISCHKE TWINS NEEDED A WRITER who was determined not only to lay out the basic who-what-where-when facts of the case, but a person who could be relied upon to probe the mysteries of so many unanswered questions; somebody not scared to ask the infamous "why?"

Karen Emilson has accomplished this mission, with style, truth, emotion, caring and because I know this lady, not without much personal foreboding.

As such, she has proved again she is a skilled craftsman both as a writer and as a reporter. There is a vast difference. Combined, those two talents have produced for us—as individuals and as a society—a remarkable end product in the book now in your hands.

Here you will find a story of behavior which in places defies human explanation; a strength of love as once defined only by the old poets; serious questions that still have to be answered by churches, social agencies and law enforcement officials.

Here you will also find a true story about rural mid-western life that exposes the dark side to those tales about quilting bees and love-thy-neighbor reports which were paraded out by Hollywood in programs like "Little House on the Prairie."

For this is truth in all stark nudity.

It is not pretty and heart-warming but it is factual.

David and Dennis Pischke appeared on my radio program (CJOB, Winnipeg) in April of 1995. After 35 years as a print and electronic journalist, I thought I had heard and seen it all.

These two gracious survivors from *Where Children Run* did not need raised, angry voices or challenges of revenge to make us all understand very quickly how 12 years of torment had shredded parts of their very souls.

But what struck me during that particular broadcast, were the number of on-air calls to the Pischke twins from people in Saskatchewan, Manitoba, northwestern Ontario, North and South Dakota—radio listeners who sympathized and ended with simple sentences like: "Thank God you have spoken out," and "It happened to us, too."

Thus, what the Pischke boys suffered and what Karen Emilson has given us in book form is historical fact, social history and a gut-wrenching story that still begs answers.

Someone, somewhere once said: "Suffer little children to come unto me."

Perhaps only He has an explanation about why it was allowed to happen—and why it is still happening.

—PETER WARREN, *formerly of CJOB Radio, Winnipeg, Canada*

JUNE 1953

"Shhh, Eunice whispered as she pulled her little sister close. Clasping her hand over three-year-old Rosalie's mouth, she shot her a stern look. Rosie was trying to be brave, but she couldn't stop sobbing because her parents were yelling in the kitchen.

Eunice was six years old now, old enough to understand that it was best not to draw attention to themselves. She watched silently as their brother Norman quietly slipped out of the big bed they all shared. He tiptoed across the floor to the bedroom doorway then pulled the curtain back. He could see their mother arguing with her common-law husband, Boleslaw Domko, who came to their farm as a hired hand just over a year ago. Now they had a baby together, and that's who they were arguing about this time.

Norman couldn't understand everything they were saying since they spoke mostly in Polish, but he could tell by their anger and the occasional English word that Domko was accusing their mother of something. They argued furiously, prompting Norman to let go of the curtain, then tiptoed to the bedroom window. He carefully lifted the metal rungs, pausing at the sound of the loose window panes rattling.

Once the window was open, warm summer air filtered into the stifling hot bedroom. Feeling the breeze, he noticed how serene it was outdoors. The sun shone golden-pink from behind the forest as it set slowly in the western Manitoba sky. Mosquitoes buzzed loudly while the family's cows stood grazing the damp grass in the nearby pasture. A dog barked excitedly somewhere in the distance.

As he slid back on the crowded bed, the smell of urine wafted up and he could feel the warm dampness of the mattress on his bare legs. He shot a disapproving look at his twin brothers.

"R-r-rosie did it," David whispered.

"Uh-huh," Dennis nodded.

Norman rolled his eyes. Probably one of them did it, but it didn't matter. The bed had been peed in so many times it was still wet from the night before. It wouldn't take long and he would warm up, and soon the smell wouldn't bother him either.

"Shhh," Eunice whispered again.

Norman looked at the twins whose bright blue eyes pleaded for help. Physically they were identical—big boned and healthy, but too thin. Their wild blonde hair was bleached white from the sun. David was aggressive with lots of energy and an independent thinker who often made their mother laugh. Dennis was quiet and always went along with whatever David did. He was sensitive and soft-spoken, preferring to sit on an adult's knee rather than play with the older boys. Dennis seemed to annoy their mother who was not very generous with hugs and kisses.

Eunice was the family interpreter since she was the only one who understood the twins' strange language—a jumbled combination of Low German and fabricated words. Nobody cared what they said except Domko, who was oddly preoccupied with their jabbering. If he were in a good mood, he would chase them out of the house, so he didn't have to listen to them. But if he were in a bad mood, he would beat whichever one he could catch.

That afternoon Norman had worked alongside Domko and watched him grow increasingly irritated as they picked rocks out of a field and stacked them in a pile. His older brothers, Walter, 11, and Steven, 10, were beaten the day before for not milking the cows properly, so they had run away. That might be what annoyed Domko this time, but he couldn't be sure. Norman wondered if his older brothers felt as bad as he did about leaving the younger ones behind.

The children listened as their mother calmed Domko, and soon everyone began to relax. Rosie stopped crying, and Eunice dozed off while the Twins shifted their bodies in unison, causing the bedsprings to creak. As the house grew quiet, Norman fell asleep with one leg dangling off the bed, his foot resting on the floor.

It wasn't long afterward that baby Kathy started to cry. At first, the sound was muffled, but soon turned to wailing, and the fighting started again. This time, though, Domko was instantly angry. He complained that the baby made too much noise. Their mother picked Kathy up and began pouring water into a washtub for a bath. She argued that the baby's stomach was cramping because she needed whole milk to drink, but that all he would allow her to have is skim milk.

The children cowered in the bed, expecting Domko would come raging into the bedroom any moment. He hollered that the children cost too much money to support and their mother shot back that the farm was hers and that he was the intruder. They could hear her trying to give the baby a bath. Kathy's little arms and legs thrashed in the basin, splashing water onto the worn linoleum floor. The baby's wails were far beyond her father's tolerance level, and everyone knew it except her.

The twins sat up and clasped their arms around one another. Eunice drew a protective arm across Rosie's chest while Norman slid out of bed and crept to the window. The younger children began to weep as he glanced back at them for a moment, then swung his legs over the sill and disappeared outside.

"I's be showink them soneebeech bastards!" Domko roared. His English was difficult to understand, and his vocabulary consisted mostly of obscenities.

The children heard their mother's tactic change as she began patiently reasoning with him. Violently his voice shook as he screamed at her to make the baby stop crying.

Muttering something about the child not being his, Domko suddenly grabbed the baby from the wash basin. Their mother screamed, and the children braced themselves for what would come. Their mother's voice raised to an agonized pitch as the sickening thud of the baby's body slamming against the wall echoed throughout the house.

"Boleslaw!" she screamed as she ran across the floor. "What have you done now? Get out, get out of my house!"

The sound of Domko's heavy boots crossing the floor caused the children to hold their breath until the kitchen door slammed shut and the house grew quiet. The only sound was their mother's voice whispering to the baby and her prayers to God that Kathy would live.

Knowing they were finally safe, the children began to cry and moan. No one dared get out of bed to comfort their mother, though, just in case he came back.

Pulling the sheet up over his head, Dennis hummed softly, trying to block out the sound of his mother crying. He squeezed his eyes tight, wanting to remember his father. It had been almost two years since his father's death, and each time Dennis searched his memory for his father's smiling face, one memory returned over and over again. It was the cold, February day that Domko arrived at the farm.

His mother had been preparing supper in front of the old wood cook stove, and he'd gotten her attention by tugging on her dress. She looked down at him and frowned because his boots had made a wet mess across the clean floor.

"Dennis, why are you crying now?" She asked, walking past him to a burlap bag on the floor near the door. She pulled out three large potatoes and snapped off the long white eyes that had grown over the winter.

"When's daddy comin' home," he sobbed, rubbing his eyes.

"I told you before," she answered. "Daddy died. He won't be coming home no more."

"I want daddy now," he cried, needing to tell her what had just happened.

"I know you do, but he's not coming," she said. "Now go outside and play until supper is ready."

Dennis turned and left the warm kitchen. Stepping into the late afternoon air, he walked towards his twin who was playing in the snow alongside the house. Dennis looked up at the roof and was disappointed there were no doves perched on the peak. His mother had pointed out a pair of white doves on the roof the day of his father's funeral. She said that the birds were a sign that their father was at peace. Dennis didn't know where Peace was, but he wanted to go there. He hoped the doves would return to show him the way.

Noise in the barnyard caused him to look in that direction. His older brothers Walter and Steven were watching the new farm hand give water to the horses and fresh hay to the cows. The man was irritated, and he said something that made the boys hurry into the barn.

By then, Dennis' hands were cold because he'd lost his mittens. Too frightened to look for them, he went to David and Eunice.

"Eunice," he cried. "My hands are cold."

Looking down at her brother, Eunice took off her mittens and handed them to him. "You can wear 'em 'til my hands get cold then we'll trade back," she said. "Where are yours?"

"T-t-they're in the barn," he stammered.

Both looked toward the gray, shanty-style building. A makeshift fence of old posts and planks that their father built surrounded the barnyard. Eunice would have offered to find the mitts, but the anger Domko displayed earlier that morning was still fresh in her mind.

Domko had hauled a large load of hay into the barn, then returned to the field for more. While he was gone, they all jumped from the loft into the hay. Dennis could never remember being scolded for this before, so he was stunned when Domko returned and flew into a rage. Domko said they were going to have to obey him now, and he lined them up along the hay rack and strapped each one with his belt.

Dennis cringed at the remembrance of how the stiff leather had stung his cold legs. Big, red welts made it hard to sit down afterward. As he drifted off to sleep, he remembered how Domko's eyes flashed when he warned them not to tell anyone.

TWO VERY DIFFERENT MEN

Caroline struggled to keep her eyes open as the rising sun sent a jagged orange stream of light through the kitchen window. The night before was the worst she'd endured since Domko came to the farm.

Sitting on a chair with the unconscious baby swaddled on her lap, she replayed the drama that unfolded the day before.

"You's be seeink your boyfriend again, huh?" Domko accused after she returned home that afternoon. She was careful not to answer immediately, knowing he might misinterpret her reply. She told him that she was looking for her two older sons who were likely hiding at a neighboring farm.

"Lazy bastards," he muttered. His eyes blazed as he leaned in. "Who's be helpink me with some fence? Dennis? David? Those soneebeech bastards be some goot for nuthink."

Caroline had wanted to scream at him that the twins were just little boys, but he'd already kicked over a full can of milk in anger. He was obsessing again in his odd, one-track way about the amount of work that needed doing and the lack of manpower to get it done. She knew when he was having one of his "spells" it was best not to argue and stay out of his way. But as evening approached, he continued to bait her, pressing for a fight. She had seen the signs before when he taunted her children to the breaking point, never satisfied until he hurt someone. Last night, it was his child.

Caroline had hoped that a new baby would make Domko feel like a part of the family. Instead, he chose to believe that the child was fathered by someone else, and berated her about this constantly. Because she had spent time picking berries near a neighboring farm the spring before, it occurred to him that someone else could be the father. Domko spent enough nights in her bed that they both knew who sired the child, but no matter what she said to him, he refused to hear the truth.

How different he was from her first husband, Bill Pischke.

Bill was a kind, gentle man born to German immigrants who had settled in this small farming community near the town of Moosehorn, Manitoba. Bill had lived in the area his whole life, buying this farm in the Bayton District, seven miles northeast of Moosehorn.

Remembering the day she met Bill sent a wave of sadness through her. She had been working at the store in the hamlet of Grahamdale when he came in to purchase a few items. Fifteen years her senior, she knew he was quite smitten with her. She remembered being impressed that he had a car that meant he could take her to dances in town. Anxious to get away from her father, it didn't take long for a romance to blossom. They married and moved to the farm. Not long afterward, Walter was born.

Caroline had switched from Catholicism to the Jehovah's Witness faith a few years before Bill's death. She became disillusioned with the Catholic doctrine after she and Bill caught the Priest of their congregation in a compromising situation. She liked the ideology of the Jehovah's Witnesses who seemed kind and forgiving. Unfortunately, she had kept one Catholic tradition—the rhythm birth control method. She bore seven children by her twenty-seventh birthday.

Bill's most appealing trait was his kindness. He seldom raised his voice and never hit the children. Mostly everyone criticized his leniency because people here believed that children should be seen, and not heard. If children did disobey, most parents in this region strapped them with a belt or willow switch. But not Bill, and because of this, his children were considered naughty—especially the rambunctious twins who always had their hands in something. Bill indulged the boys who were astonishingly cute and smarter than people realized. The Twins called him "Tatoosh" in their odd, indecipherable language. He nicknamed David "Tush" and Dennis "Tushie."

One time she told Bill that Dennis was going to have to toughen up. He had scolded her for it, and she wondered if Dennis was his favorite child. He had a particular way of looking at Dennis that showed a closeness he didn't share with the other children. Bill's death was especially hard on him.

At first, she was unhappy about her eighth pregnancy. She worried about the reaction from members of her church and what they might say about her. After all, she and Domko weren't married, and their relationship was a secret. She believed the news would send the local Jehovah's Witnesses into an uproar. As it was, she had difficulty meeting the standards set by her religion.

To avoid confrontation, she decided to tell only a few people that she was pregnant. The fact she carried discreetly made it easy to hide. She gave birth in a different town and simply left the hospital by bus with Kathy in a shopping bag. However, Kathy began to cry the moment she stepped off the bus in Moosehorn, and within a few hours, all the busybodies in town were speculating that Domko was the father.

Kathy was a good baby but cried at night because she had her days and nights turned around. Soon she would outgrow this, but until then, Caroline had to work extra hard to keep her quiet while Domko was sleeping. He had no tolerance for noise, especially from children.

Now, what was she going to do? The baby had barely moved all night. Her breathing was shallow, and she was limp to Caroline's touch. Watching Kathy's pale face, she wiped away a tear from her own.

Domko had gone too far this time. It was one thing to discipline the older children, but a four-month-old baby? Something wasn't right with him. The headaches and violent outbursts were increasing. Since fall, he no longer bathed and let his beard grow for many weeks before shaving. Also, he enjoyed prowling the neighborhood at night, never explaining where he went or why. He blamed her for his odd behavior, saying she was a terrible wife who purposely tried to make him miserable. She was beginning to fear him more every day.

Quietly, she got up and padded softly past the open bedroom door. Domko had come in hours after their fight and had fallen asleep without a word. She was relieved to see his back was to her—she didn't want to speak to him after last night.

Holding Kathy to her chest, she went to check on the children. She sighed at the sight of Eunice, Rosie and the twins snuggled on the bed. But the empty mattress on the floor meant there would be no one to help with chores that morning.

She shook her head. The children deserved better than this. Looking at their stark room in a new morning's light just reinforced how very little they had. There were no pictures on the wall or rugs to cushion their feet. Everything they did own, even clothing, came from the secondhand store. There were no toys except for a few small things the children hid from Domko.

Oh, how she had hoped her life would be better than this! Hydro and indoor plumbing were luxuries she couldn't afford, and she seldom went anywhere. The occasional trip to the city only reinforced the feeling that they were hillbillies or "bushed" as the local folks would say. Her family was the poorest of the poor, barely accepted in Moosehorn and misfits everywhere else.

Where Children Run

Now Domko was in her life, and she wasn't sure how to get rid of him. She didn't have the energy to decide if leaving would be worth the shame and effort.

Little Dennis stirred then he turned to face his mother, his young eyes searching for answers. Caroline moved to the side of the bed and leaned in close to him. Her words betrayed the hopelessness she felt.

"Everything is going to be all right," she whispered, "justice is right around the corner." Then she smiled and left the room.

Dennis turned onto his side and fell back asleep.

David awoke to the sound of his mother's footsteps. He listened to the peaceful sound of morning—chickens clucking quietly in the yard and the daily wake-up call of the rooster. Shifting slightly, he was stiff and uncomfortable but couldn't move without waking everyone else. Even though Dennis and Rosie peed the bed when they were nervous, he still liked having them close. Forgiving them was easy since he'd peed the bed a few times, too.

A mosquito buzzed aggressively overhead then landed somewhere in his matted hair. He smacked his head then listened as it buzzed away, returning a few moments later, settling on Dennis' arm. David watched as it's stinger prodded, then stopped, and its abdomen began to swell. Blood. The sight of it caused his stomach to roll. He'd seen too much blood since Domko came to the farm.

David remembered how in the beginning Domko would come in the morning, do the chores, eat, and then leave by nightfall. Some days he wouldn't come, and life was easier. Soon, though, Domko started sleeping in the barn and then on the chesterfield. His gruff yell and swinging arms sent them in all directions, and they learned how to avoid him. Unfortunately, once he moved into their small house, that became impossible.

David noticed that Domko didn't seem to mind Walter and Steven, probably because they were old enough to help with chores. Although he occasionally mistreated them, it was the younger ones who he called "useless" and sought out when angry. Domko had an clear dislike for Norman, Dennis and Rosie.

Of all the children, his older brother Norman was the most defiant. He was a thin boy with a crop of thick brown hair and possessed an irresistible charm that most people loved. He smirked in a way that drove Domko crazy, and while Norman feared him, it didn't curb his defiance. Domko despised the fact that he couldn't break his spirit.

Dennis was the opposite. He had a gentle way and preferred drawing to rough and tumble activities. Domko considered his quiet mannerisms a sign of weakness and took advantage of his gallant nature at every opportunity. David wished, for both their sakes, that Dennis could be tough like Norman.

Remembering Rosie's first beating made David feel sick. Rosie was only two years old when Domko came to the farm. She was a bright, inquisitive girl who was too small to jump out the window, and not a very fast runner, so she was by far the most vulnerable of them all.

After supper one evening, Domko stormed into the children's bedroom, yelling in Polish. The children couldn't understand what he was saying, but because of the whippings they'd all received over the past few months, everyone ran toward the door. David remembered how close Domko was behind him, but then there was a small scream. He turned in time to see him grab Rosie. For an instant, David was surprised. Usually, Domko caught Dennis, but this time his twin made it to the doorway, and he stopped to watch.

Holding Rosie by one arm, Domko slipped off his belt and began strapping her.

"Choklit bar? Choklit bar?" he screamed, the force of the blows lifting Rosie off the ground. "I's be showink you choklit bar."

David remembered how it looked as if Domko were beating a rag doll and as each blow struck Rosie's small body, the terror in her eyes grew. She screamed for their mother who was not in the house. David thought that Domko would stop, but he continued until Rosie began bleeding, and each time he'd strike her, blood splashed in tiny droplets across the room.

And then Dennis stepped forward. "I d-did it, I did it," he yelled, waving his arms. "I took the chocolate bar!"

Startled, Domko paused for a moment to look in their direction. A look of pleasure crossed his face as he dropped Rosie's limp body and lunged at Dennis who braced himself and closed his eyes.

Each time the strap stung his brother's skin, sharp pains seared across David's backside and legs. Hearing Dennis scream felt like a dagger in his gut. Then with one final blow, Dennis was thrown against the wall. David couldn't remember what happened after that, but he would forever remember the look in Domko's eyes.

That night Rosie learned to hide under the bed and David discovered that every time Domko caught Dennis, he would feel his brother's pain.

They named their tormentor Satan and from that day forward, he and Dennis never once again called him by his real name.

Caroline spent the day tending to Kathy who hardly moved and didn't respond to voice or touch. The other children sensed the gravity of the situation and did their best not to irritate Domko, who barked commands, as usual, oblivious to the pain he caused.

Caroline's thoughts were interrupted as the kitchen door opened as her eldest son walked in.

"Where have you been?" she asked.

Walter looked sheepishly at his mother then shrugged his shoulders. The bruising around his eye was beginning to fade.

"Where's Steven?" she asked, still holding Kathy in her arms.

Walter just stared at the floor without answering. Almost a teenager, he was the image of his father—tall and thin, with a long nose and slightly bucked teeth. Walter was at the horribly awkward age of twelve—not a boy, but not yet a man. He still preferred playing with the younger children, rolling a toy truck through the mud, to roughhousing or playing sports with older boys. Walter always shared whatever he had and was likely the kindest of her children. Unfortunately, he inherited Bill's stuttering problem, and it seemed to be getting worse.

It wasn't the first time one of the boys refused to say where the other was hiding. She knew that Steven would come home soon. He always did.

"Go help Norman milk and stay out of Domko's way," she said.

Walter nodded. He loved his mother more than anyone in the world but wasn't sure he could trust her anymore. If he told her that neighbor, Jim Deighton, had taken him in, she might tell Domko, and that would cause problems all around. It was best to say nothing.

Walter slipped outside and began walking toward the barn. He suspected Domko would be supervising the milking and dreaded seeing him. As he passed by the water trough, he remembered the time he and his father had spent an entire January morning trying to thaw out the square, cement cubicle. It had been a particularly cold night in 1951. His father was ill and had asked Walter to stoke the fire under the box before bed so that the water wouldn't freeze overnight. This was a big responsibility for a nine-year-old, but Walter accepted it willingly. Unfortunately, in the excitement of having his father home from the hospital, he forgot to make the fire. They awoke the next morning to the sound of bawling cattle standing in front of the frozen trough.

Walter's father had been annoyed at first, but within a few moments, patted him on the back and told him it was all right. Together they thawed the waterer by dousing it with many kettles of boiling water and building a roaring fire underneath.

A lump rose in Walter's throat whenever he thought about his father.

Gently he rubbed his left cheek, still sore from the beating. He had tried to do a thorough job milking, but it didn't take much to irritate Domko.

He couldn't understand why his grandfather Kolodka had brought him to the farm in the first place. He and Steven were obviously old enough to do the chores since they were the ones working while Domko just stood and watched. It was he and his brothers who had slept in the pump house to catch thieves after their father had died. But Grandfather Kolodka said many times that Domko was a good man.

"G-good for n-nothing," Walter whispered as he pulled open the barn door.

Domko stood at the far end of the barn leaning against a pitchfork. He didn't stand taller than Walter but was a gorilla of a man. His dirty face and hands were almost as black as the clothes he wore, and he stunk horribly of body odor and cow manure. On the left side of his forehead was a depression and scar which appeared to turn white when he was angry. His thin, dark hair hid beneath a dirty beige cotton hat which sat sloppily on his head; its greasy peak rolled tightly towards the ceiling.

As he watched Walter pick up a milking pail, his lips pressed together. His short, thick fingers tightened around the pitchfork handle. The stub of a homemade cigarette hung loosely in one corner of his mouth. One sinister-looking gold tooth flashed when he spoke.

"Vere yous be, Valter?" Domko cooed. "At your mommy and daddy's?"

Walter shrugged and quickly sat on a milking stool beside the cow farthest from Domko. Reaching under the animal, he squeezed a stream of warm, creamy milk into the metal pail. Norman, who'd spent the night in the loft, was busy milking on the opposite side of the barn. A dozen cows were waiting patiently in their stalls which lined the east and west walls. Their tails swung from side to side, lazily swishing pestering flies from their backs.

"Fraa," Domko grunted, dropping the pitchfork. Now that Walter was home, the milking would get done without him. He strode toward the barn door, pausing for a moment. Walter sensed him standing very close and froze, trying hard not to cower, as he stared silently into the milk pail. Domko grunted, then disappeared out the door, banging it shut behind him.

Walter relaxed. He knew that Domko wouldn't be back for at least thirty minutes—it took that long for him to drink a cup of coffee and smoke another cigarette.

Just then, Norman jumped up.

"Hey, Valter," he yelled, picking up a small stick and tucking it in the corner of his mouth. "Fraa!" Norman pushed his cap back and puffed out his chest. He stooped slightly, then clenching his fists, swung his arms back and forth. Strutting up and down the center of the barn, he turned his head slowly from side to side.

"Yoooou soneebeeeech," he hollered, pointing at Walter. He narrowed his eyes, grunted, picked up the pitchfork then strode towards his brother. "You's be at your mommy and daaaaaddy's?"

Walter smiled. Norman always made him feel better.

"They's be yittink ant sheetink ant peesink all day long," Norman mimicked, reciting one of Domko's favorite sayings. He often said this when their mother complained the children weren't fed enough.

Their laughter was interrupted by the unexpected opening of the barn door. Norman dropped the pitchfork and stood paralyzed as he struggled to adjust to the afternoon sunlight shining on his face. Walter's heart jumped to his throat as he slowly looked towards the door.

Their mother stepped inside carrying a milk pail. Walter smiled and let out a sigh of relief. Norman relaxed and began laughing.

"What are you two doing now?" she asked, curious, her mood a little brighter.

"Nothin'," Norman said. "Just playin' around."

"The cows won't get milked that way," she scolded as she grabbed a stool and sat beside a large uddered cow. "Hurry up before he gets back."

Caroline was anxious to finish so she could get back to check on Kathy. She wanted to take her to the doctor but knew that Domko would refuse. She decided if the baby wasn't better by morning, she would sneak out of the house early and take the baby to town.

Caroline wasn't yet thirty years old, but she'd been to see this same doctor many times. She cringed at the thought of having to tell him what had happened. She needed a convincing lie since Dr. Gordon Steenson had a strange, unsettling way of knowing her thoughts before she even knew herself. He might guess who was responsible for Kathy's injury and could blame her, too.

Caroline sighed. She preferred to keep domestic problems to herself, and she was so embarrassed by Domko's behavior, that she found herself making excuses. If the police knew about his violence, they would expect her to press charges against him, and that was something she was much too frightened to do.

The following morning Caroline awoke to the patter of rain on the roof. The children were all asleep, and Domko snored loudly beside her. Getting out of bed, she shivered at the dampness in the house. She slipped a cotton print dress over her underwear and pulled on a sweater.

Glancing out the bedroom window, the beginnings of the day were dull and gray. Water streamed off the roof, puddling on the ground below. She could see it had been raining most of the night.

Kathy stirred in the crib along the far wall. As her little arms and legs began to move, she started to cry. Caroline hurried across the floor and lifted her up, cradling her and cooing as she went to the kitchen. She ladled milk from the can sitting on the floor in a baby bottle, and when the nipple was placed in Kathy's mouth, she drank hungrily.

Pacing across the floor, Caroline said a quiet prayer of thanks and began sobbing with relief. It looked as though Kathy was going to be fine.

HIDING IN THE NIGHT

Summer came and went. Good weather meant the children worked long days outdoors. The cows were milked twice a day by Caroline and the older boys while Eunice kept Rosie and Kathy out of harm's way. The twins had daily chores that included feeding the chickens and pigs, picking vegetables from the garden and carrying in wood for the stove.

The older children spent most afternoons in the hay field—cutting, raking and stacking hay. It was important that enough be harvested by fall, as this is what they fed the cows and horses over the long, cold winter.

They stayed mostly on the farm since there was little time for socializing. Few people came by to visit because Domko had alienated most of their friends and neighbors. He only enjoyed seeing his friends who lived on farms ten miles away, near the hamlets of Grahamdale and Faulkner.

Caroline looked forward to occasional trips to Moosehorn, the area's largest town, where she bought groceries and picked up the mail. Since the family didn't have a car, they traveled by wagon or sleigh. Occasionally she would continue south on the highway for an additional seven miles to the town of Ashern, the same size as Moosehorn, but in addition to the usual amenities, Ashern had a hospital, lawyer, and police detachment.

Most of the time, though, Domko would not allow her to go, preferring to travel alone while Caroline and the children stayed home to work. He would sell the week's accumulation of cream to the local creamery and buy farm supplies and a few household staples but refused to discuss with Caroline what he did with the rest of the money.

It was pointless for her to complain about their finances since he had bought the majority of the cattle with money he'd earned elsewhere. He always reminded her of this, adding that she and the children were lucky to have him around.

Domko's moods began to worsen once autumn arrived. At times, the steel plate in his head caused him excruciating pain. Trips to the doctor did nothing to help. Pounding headaches sent him into blinding rages, causing him to beat anyone within arm's reach. The children learned to stay out of his way, but as winter approached, they began spending more time indoors and underfoot.

Eight children under one small roof were hard on Caroline's nerves, but it had a devastating effect on Domko's troubled mind. The fact they were struggling financially and behind in their municipal tax payment, added to his stress. He was deathly afraid of authority figures and didn't trust the local government district. He worried that someone would steal the farm out from under him if he didn't pay the tax bill.

Late one October evening, the family had just finished supper when the twins began playing with a small toy truck on the floor in the front room. They chattered to themselves in their strange language, sliding the truck back and forth, lost in their make-believe world. Their gibberish particularly annoyed Domko who thought they spoke that way so he couldn't understand them. Without warning, he flew from the kitchen into the front room, grabbed both boys and flung them onto the chesterfield. David landed on top, while Dennis slid between the side of the couch and the wall. Domko began beating them with his fists, punching one and then the other.

The other children scattered. Rosie and Eunice slid under a bed while the three older boys bolted out the kitchen door.

"Mommma," David wailed, as he put his arms up over his head and tried to crawl across the cushions.

Caroline hurried from the kitchen into the living room.

"Boleslaw," she screamed. "Leave them alone!"

The past few weeks had been unbearable watching him beat each of the children. Poor little Dennis had received two beatings already that week.

"You're going to kill them," she said, grabbing his arm as she tried to pull him away from them.

Caroline was a strong woman who had worked hard her entire life, but she was no match for Domko. Spinning around, he slammed his fist into her face, and the sound of her nose shattering exploded in her head. Her neck snapped back, and the force of the blow lifted her feet off the ground. Her mind whirled as she landed on her back. She felt fists pummeling her head and chest and tried to raise her arms for protection, but they seemed to no longer belong to her body.

She could hear the children screaming and crying somewhere in the house. As she lay on the floor, she wanted to die. She had endured enough beatings in her childhood to last a lifetime.

Caroline awoke some time later to the sound of Domko's guttural snickering. She didn't have to open her eyes to know that he was sitting on his chair in the kitchen, drinking coffee and smoking a cigarette. Between puffs, he would snicker—a slow, satisfied grunt that they'd all grown accustomed to hearing.

She had no idea how long she lay unconscious. Slowly opening her eyes, she found herself near her bedroom doorway. The house was unusually silent. Her thoughts turned immediately to the children, and she tried to sit up. The sudden movement caused her head to start throbbing. There was blood drying on her hands and the front of her dress. A gentle touch to the nose sent sharp pains across her forehead. Once her eyes refocused, she slowly stood up and walked past him, through the kitchen to the door. The older children's jackets and shoes were gone, but the Twins' coats still hung from the hooks on the wall. Domko snickered again as he looked up from what he was reading. Without a word, she lowered her head and slipped outside.

The bitter north wind cut through her light dress, but strangely, the cold came as a relief. It took a few moments for her eyes to adjust to the dark, starless night. A sprinkling of fresh snow covered the ground. Snowflakes swirled around her legs as she rounded the corner of the house toward the road. Crossing her arms, she wondered which direction the children went. They couldn't have walked very far since the twins were without their jackets and they were carrying the baby.

Fortunately, her own feet were calloused and tough, so she barely felt the stones poking through her thin, homemade slippers. The light that lit their closest neighbor's yard was less than a quarter mile away. Gus and Emma Harwart were good friends who had helped her out many times.

Domko would be mad if he knew that's where they went. She clenched her jaw and balled her hands into fists as she hurried past the Lutheran church that sat cold and dark alongside the road.

"I don't know why she puts up with him," Emma said in a thick, German accent. She shook her soft, white curls. The heavy-set woman was leaning over David, applying a warm cloth to his battered face. Her words were thickly accented in German.

"She should kick him out, that's what she should do," she said. "The house is hers for goodness sake, and it's her quarter of land."

Gus stood in the center of the kitchen with his arms crossed. He was a tall, thin man with a beakish nose and gentle blue eyes. He had large, farmer hands with oversized knuckles and ragged nails. Gus didn't talk much—he left that job to Emma. There were some subjects that the old farmer would discuss, though, and Bob Domko was one of them.

Gus had tried to get along with Domko but found him impossible to like. Domko was selfish and spiteful and thought only of himself. Even though he had a healthy herd of cattle, he was always comparing his farm to everyone else's in the community. He bought another quarter section of land that year from a neighbor, Arthur Betker, and acquaintances were speculating how he was able to expand his herd at such a fast rate. But Gus remembered the children saying Domko brought a suitcase of money to the farm, and he knew how hard the children labored for free.

He looked at the twins sitting at the kitchen table, then to the boys on the chesterfield in the front room. Eunice was standing in the kitchen holding Kathy, while Rosie hid quietly behind her sister's legs.

"Where did you say your Momma was?" Gus asked.

"H-he was punching her on the floor," Walter stammered. "Us guys ran out."

"I think he killed her," Norman said, chin wavering.

Gus and Emma's nine-year-old daughter, Marjorie, was leaning against the living room wall, listening. Marjorie was a pretty girl whose blue eyes danced when she spoke. Soft blonde curls framed her round, gentle face. The youngest of Gus and Emma's seven daughters, she was pleasingly bright. She did well in school and enjoyed helping her father with the chores. She loved to socialize and spent most of her free time playing with the Pischke children.

Her eyes widened at Norman's words. Looking at her mother, she opened her mouth to speak, but her mother interrupted.

"Hush now," Emma said to them all, but mostly to Dennis who started sobbing. "Your Momma will be all right."

Marjorie looked at her playmates. It wasn't the first time they had come to her house in the middle of the night. She had overheard her parents talk about Domko many times, mostly when they thought she wasn't listening, and he sounded like a monster. She was frightened of him but tried not to let it show.

"Auntie Em-ma," David said. "You gots something to eat?"

Emma looked at the youngster who was nearly the cutest thing she'd ever seen, but she couldn't understand a word he said.

"What did you say, darling?" she asked gently.

Where Children Run

"They're askin' for somethin' to eat," Eunice interrupted. "Domko don't let us eat nothin', 'cause he eats it all himself."

Emma looked at the twins who were waiting, their bright blue eyes wide. Their tattered clothes were much too small, and their hair was dirty and matted. Neither had on socks, having walked through the snow in bare feet.

"I most certainly do," she said. "As soon as I get these boys cleaned up, you can have some fresh bread and Saskatoon jam."

Walter and Norman looked at each other. Walter's eyebrows raised high while Norman smiled. Marjorie noticed their reaction and smiled, too. These were her friends. Norman was the same age as she and Walter was only two years older. Both boys made the best of every situation and were fun and outgoing in spite of the turmoil at home. Marjorie pretended not to notice when Walter stuttered at school even though some of the other kids made fun of him. She never did, though, not ever.

"You come and help me get the lunch ready," her mother called.

Marjorie hurried to the kitchen and pulled two fresh loaves of bread from the cupboard and given a chance; she'd be sure to let Norman know that she was the one who baked the bread.

The wind whistled through the trees surrounding the old log house, but inside, they were kept warm by two wood stoves—one used for cooking and the other in the middle of the front room.

The faint smell of roasted meat lingered in the kitchen. This room was the life force of the home, centering around an old wooden table and chairs. The floors were sanded oak planks, painted a natural brown color and mostly hidden by large, braided throw rugs strategically placed in doorways, in front of the large green chesterfield and their metal, spring beds. Quilted and crocheted blankets added warmth to thin, cotton-stuffed mattresses and thick brocade drapes covered the windows to keep out the draft. There were sepia pictures of ancient relatives in smooth oval frames and a prized aerial photo of the homestead on the front room wall.

Gus and Emma came here shortly after the district was settled in the early 1920s, to find most of their neighbors were also Eastern European immigrants. While the land was full of bush and stones, a man could make a living if he was willing to work hard. On the whole, this was poor farm land, but pockets near Lake Manitoba proved adequate for grazing cattle and growing some crops.

The Harwarts were respected in the community but not admired. They had too few possessions to be considered well off, but Gus always did a full day's work and was careful to pay his bills on time, earning what he could with two, quarter sections of land. Raising seven children left little money for luxuries, especially since two of their daughters had Polio at a young age, and one of them spent many years in a Winnipeg hospital. Frequent trips to visit the bedridden youngster put a substantial drain on the family's savings, although the Harwarts never let their daughter feel their strain. Gus was nearing retirement age and dreamed of building a new house for his wife.

The Pischke children were spread throughout the house when the Harwart's two-year-old dog, Sandy, began barking outside. She let out three quick barks and then another more cautious growl. Gus listened as the dog moved alongside the house and then to the back door. Sandy was a small dog of mixed parentage with brown hair, floppy ears, and a thick tail. Although she was short on good looks, she had been Marjorie's favorite pet for years. Sandy slept underneath her bedroom window year round. On winter evenings when food was scarce, Marjorie slipped table scraps through the window, ensuring that Sandy always got plenty of food and lots of love.

Gus went to the door and wedged his foot across the bottom. With his right hand on the knob, he braced his shoulder against the door.

"Who is it?" he asked gruffly.

"It's Caroline. Are the kids here?" she said.

Gus relaxed and opened the door, stepping back. "Come in," he said. "Your kids are all here."

Emma stopped cutting bread and bustled toward the door.

"My Lord Caroline, what did he do to you?" she gasped.

"I'm all right," she answered, eyes fixed on the floor. "How are David and Dennis?"

"They're fine," she said. "Banged up but nothing that won't heal."

"And the baby?"

"Eunice has her. Come in and sit down, we were just about to give them all something to eat."

Caroline flinched as she lowered herself onto a chair. Her body was beginning to throb now, as large, dark bruises began showing on her arms and chest. She slowly pulled her cold feet up onto the chair and rubbed them with her hands. Gradually, the children emerged from the living room.

"We thought you was dead," Walter said while Norman and Steven stood and stared.

"Well, I'm not dead," Caroline replied, reaching up to pat her eldest son on the back. The twins pushed their way past the older boys to their mother.

"Momma," Dennis said, chin wavering, "did you bring my truck?"

Caroline smiled. Then her shoulders slumped. She brought her hands up to her face and began to sob. "I can't take this anymore Emma; I just can't take it anymore."

Putting the plate of bread on the table, Emma guided the children by the shoulders to the kitchen chairs. Obediently, each found a seat except the twins who shared a chair. Gently, Emma took Caroline by the arm and led her into the front room.

"You sit here while I get these children fed," she said. "I'll be back in a few minutes."

Emma gave a few quick instructions to Marjorie. The children had already each taken a piece of bread and were spreading thick globs of wild berry jam on top. They ate greedily, and each drank a full glass of milk. Emma was accustomed to feeding a large family, so caring for the Pischke children was easy.

Caroline sat on the chesterfield and stared at Gus and Emma's wedding photo on the wall. Her children's tattered jackets hung across the small indoor clothes line over the wood stove.

She shook her head in disbelief at her situation. Lately, she'd spent a lot of time daydreaming how easy her life could have been if she hadn't married so young and had so many children. She wondered how other women managed while she had such a hard time.

Bad luck. It was the only way to explain it.

After Bill had died from Tuberculosis, she went to her father, Walter Kolodka, for help. Her father didn't approve of Bill and never hid the fact. In his opinion, Bill was lazy and unsuccessful. The fact he was German just made matters worse. After Bill's death, he was quick to match-make.

"What more could a woman want?" he asked her, referring to Domko's physical appearance, the suitcase full of money and war medals. He was very pleased when Domko moved into her house and thrilled that they had a child together.

"Now she has a good man," he said on many occasions in front of her and the children. She was raised to believe that women were of little value without a husband, and now she had one that met her father's approval.

Her initial impression of Domko was favorable. At thirty-eight years old, he was clean and reasonably attractive. Domko looked at her with a passion and longing that set her heart racing, something she'd missed long before Bill died. Domko made her feel like a girl again—giddy and hopeful. His piercing stare cut into her soul, and within a few weeks, they found themselves locked in a passionate love affair. It didn't take long until Domko was dominating her life as her father once did.

As the novelty began to wear off, she noticed that he became less tolerant of the children, who she believed were good kids, but were noisy and misbehaved occasionally. Domko's response was to beat them whenever they disobeyed, and this was encouraged by her father.

She quickly realized part of the problem was that the children were half-German. Domko harbored great resentment towards German people because he was a veteran of the Polish army who was forced to work in labor camps after Germany and Russia invaded Poland. Only eight years had passed since the end of the Second World War—not enough time to forgive and certainly not enough time to forget.

She was already pregnant with Kathy when she learned a disconcerting fact about Domko—the injury to his forehead and the scars across his back were not from the war as he had claimed. She stumbled upon the truth while talking to relatives living in Poland.

They told her that Domko spent his teen years in and out of jail and lashed as punishment. As a young man, he was beaten by a group of people and left to die alongside the road. A good Samaritan took him to the hospital where doctors inserted a metal plate in the front of his forehead to repair a caved-in skull.

It was after that he spent time in a Russian labor camp, then enlisted in the army in 1942. During his four years of service he was awarded six medals for bravery, and initially, Caroline was impressed. But when the Polish relatives told her that Domko left behind a wife and children when he immigrated to Canada, she found it hard to trust his word.

Neighbors always said that her farm was cursed, and now she was beginning to wonder if it might be true.

Emma watched Caroline staring off into space and wondered what she was thinking. She couldn't understand how such a sweet woman became tangled up with a man like Domko.

Caroline had dark wavy hair that framed a handsome face—high cheekbones and soft blue eyes that danced when she spoke. She carried her weight well, and her figure was only just beginning to show the signs of having supported eight pregnancies. It was disconcerting to see the turmoil of Caroline's life showing on her lovely, young face.

Emma handed her a piece of bread with jam then sat down on the chesterfield beside her.

"Am I a good mother?" Caroline asked, taking a bite of the bread. She looked squarely at Emma, something she didn't often do. Her lips were swollen, and her eyes were purple, nearly as dark as the Saskatoon jam she was licking from her lips. Her neck was bruised and no doubt she'd feel the effects of the beating tomorrow. Although she had tried to scratch it off, there were bits of crusted blood on her face and neck.

She is beautiful, Emma thought. *In spite of everything she has been through she is still more beautiful than I've ever been. But a good mother? Not really.*

"You do the best you can," Emma said. She wasn't lying. Caroline didn't know any better. Rumors were that her younger years were abusive and hard. It seemed that now she was rejecting adulthood trying to relive her younger years. Everyone in the community knew that she would sometimes put on a fancy dress and high heels, then disappear for days at a time, leaving the children with Domko. Where she went, nobody knew.

During those times, the children would show up on Emma's doorstep looking for food. Emma knew the children were neglected, so she fed them. It was then she began hearing unbelievable stories about Domko, and at first, she thought they must be telling tales.

She remembered how in early March Eunice had brought eggs to the house and was reluctant to go home afterward. This surprised Emma who knew that Caroline had arrived home the day before with a new baby—a big event for a country family. Later that afternoon, Emma overheard Eunice and Marjorie talking and was horrified to learn that she was frightened to go home because Domko had locked her in the crawl space under the house for most of the previous day. Emma's heart wrenched as the tiny, sweet girl described Domko's brutality. Apparently, he didn't want to take her along to Moosehorn when it came time to pick up Caroline at the bus depot, so he grabbed Eunice by the hair and dropped her in the crawl space.

After hearing this, Emma began hiding the children from him. She stood many times in the doorway facing him while the children hid in the bedroom. He was the only person she could look directly in the eye and tell a bold faced lie. For some reason, lying to Domko about those children didn't feel like lying at all.

Emma hoped that after this incident Caroline would muster the courage to send Domko away permanently. If he refused to go, then possibly Caroline could move to town and apply for welfare. It was an embarrassing thing to do, but it appeared she had little choice. Caroline was on welfare periodically when Bill was too sick to work—how hard could it be asking now? Surely easier than living with Domko.

"What are you going to do?" Emma asked, hoping Caroline would seek her advice.

"I don't know," she said, caressing her fat lip. "I can't go anywhere looking like this."

"What about your father?" Emma asked. "Have you told him what Domko does to you and the children?"

Caroline chuckled. Then a sad expression came over her face. She lowered her eyes and began twisting the edge of her dress around her index finger.

"He wouldn't believe me anyway," she said. "He always sides with Domko. The kids are too noisy, and of course, he hates the twins. I see how he looks at them. He was so glad when me and Domko got together that I can't disappoint him now."

"What about Bill's family? The Pischkes are decent folk. I'm sure they'd help if they knew the kids were in danger," Emma pressed.

Caroline grimaced, staring vacantly at the wall. Emma sensed that there was history between the families she wasn't willing to discuss.

Suddenly, the dog began barking again, but this time in a frantic, almost vicious way. Caroline looked at Emma who turned to Gus. He was standing at the edge of the kitchen, listening to the women's conversation. He moved quickly, dimming the oil lantern hanging over the table. The children were oblivious to the dog, busily eating the last pieces of bread and jam.

Caroline sat upright, feeling her heart begin to quicken. Gus walked cautiously to the front room window and lifted his finger to his mouth, motioning to the women to be quiet. Pulling back the thick curtain edge, he peered outside. The snow was falling heavily now, whipping furiously against the glass. Gus hoped the dog had simply overreacted to a rabbit running through the yard or a deer at the edge of the bush. Glancing out, he could see Sandy sitting under the window, bristling at something moving near the trees at the front of the house. Squinting, he tried to make out the figure and as the shadow moved closer, could see the outline of a man walking in a wide circle around the dog. Sandy barked furiously, then lunged forward trying to keep him away. There was only one person who she barked at with such hatred.

"It's Domko," Gus rasped, as he turned to them. "And that crazy bastard has a gun."

GUILT

The word "Domko" sent the children running in all directions. Within moments, the older boys slid under the table while Eunice picked up Kathy and scurried between the cook stove and cupboard.

The twins jumped off their chair and ran, one behind the other, toward their mother. Ignoring Caroline's outstretched arms, David ran past her, then squirmed into the small space between the back of the couch and wall. His little arm reached out and grabbed Dennis' shirt, pulling him in behind him. Rosie ran straight to her mother and wrapped her young arms around her mother's waist as Caroline struggled to stand up.

For a moment, she confused feelings of fear with satisfaction and pride that Domko was coming to find her. She felt ashamed of these feelings but excited as well.

Marjorie stood by her bedroom door. "Momma," she called out, "Domko's not going to shoot Sandy, is he?"

"Don't you worry about that," Emma said firmly. "Now you go and climb onto your bed and don't come out until I say so."

"Yes, Momma," she said, turning into her room.

"Where is he now?" Emma asked.

"From what I can tell, he's circling the house," Gus said quietly.

"Circling the house? What's he doing a fool thing like that for?"

"Maybe the dog is keeping him away," he said. "Or maybe he's trying to see in one of the windows. Either way, I don't like it."

Gus went quickly into the bedroom and emerged holding a rifle.

"Gustav!" Emma whispered. "What are you thinking?"

Giving his wife a stern look, Gus loaded a bullet into the chamber.

Unsure how she should be feeling, Caroline looked at Gus and the gun. "What should I do?" she asked.

Annoyed, he motioned for her to be quiet. Caroline's face reddened as she realized she had, once again, put the Harwarts in the position of having to defend her.

"Get Caroline and the children into the cellar and do it quickly before he sees them," he said. Emma could feel her heart in her throat as she motioned for them to follow her to the cellar door in the middle of the kitchen floor.

"What if he asks if they're here?" she said, lifting the heavy hinged door. "What are you going to say?"

Gus didn't answer as he walked past his wife to the back door. Sandy was sporadically barking while circling the house. Within a few minutes, she was protecting the back stoop.

A cool draft blew against Emma's legs as she stood holding the cellar door open. "Caroline, get those children of yours into the cellar while I get the twins," she said, letting the door fall flat on the floor as she hurried to the chesterfield. It took a few moments to coax them from their hiding place but soon returned with a boy in each hand, in time to see the older boys lower themselves into the dark hole. She was momentarily surprised that they did not fear the cold, dark place. Caroline followed, carrying Rosie and handed her to Walter once she was inside. She reached up for Kathy who was in Eunice's arms. Emma lowered the twins then offered Eunice, her hand.

"Can I go to Marjie's room instead?" Eunice asked.

"No, you come down here with us," Caroline said. "We've caused the Harwarts enough problems without you being in full view."

Eunice stood staring at the hole in the floor. The boys had already found themselves potato bags to sit on. Walter saw his sister's reluctance and went to the opening.

"C'mon Beanie, grab my hand, and I'll help you," he said, calling her by her pet name. Reluctantly, she reached out and gave a fearful squeal as she put one leg over her brother's shoulder. Walter held her tight then set her down on a bag of onions.

"I'm going to close the door now," Emma said. "Will you be okay?"

Caroline nodded as she ducked out of the way.

Emma looked at the sad, dirty faces below. She felt bad having to put them in such an uncomfortable place but had no choice.

"I'll let you know when he's gone," she whispered, lowering the door.

Emma turned to see Gus pulling on his work boots. Lifting his coat from its hook by the door, he quickly put it on.

"You sit here and pretend like nothing is happening," he said pointing to the kitchen table. "Get your knitting."

Emma gathered up the new pair of gray wool mittens she was making for Marjorie then sat in her usual spot. She reached across the table and turned on their old, battery-operated radio. Gus nodded. She gave him a nervous smile.

Opening the door, he stepped out onto the stoop with the gun hanging loosely at his side. He shielded his face from the wind with his other hand.

"Sandy, come here girl," he called. "Who's there?"

Sandy slowly approached the stoop, glancing suspiciously over her shoulder. Her lip quivered back, showing a row of sharp, white teeth.

Gus strained to see into the darkness. The wind was cold, as hard snow whipped his cheeks. "Who's there?" he called out again. A few moments passed, and then a figure appeared from around the corner of the house.

"Domko," the familiar voice replied. "Vere's be Carlorka?"

Gus could see his neighbor clearly now although the darkness shadowed his face, making the short, dirty man look even more sinister. He carried a rifle in one hand.

"Caroline isn't here, so you can stop walking around my house," Gus said.

Domko came toward the stoop and smirked, nodding at the gun Gus held. "You's be shootink me?"

"I didn't know who I'd find out here," he said, raising the gun slightly to make a point. "The dog doesn't usually bark like that."

Domko tried to peer over Gus' shoulder as he moved closer to the door, but Sandy's threatening growls caused him to stop. Her small body pressed against the front of Gus' leg.

"I said, Caroline isn't here," he lied again. "Did you check anywhere else?"

Domko shrugged his shoulders, then his eyes narrowed. "They say it be goot here at Harvarts."

Gus chuckled. "By jimminy, they don't come here because they like my farm," he said. "They come here for something to eat. If you'd feed them more often, the kids might like you better."

"Yit, yit, that's all they's be do," he spat.

Emma strained to hear what the men were saying as her shaking hands worked the knitting needles. Domko's stare brought in as much cold air as the open door. She tried to shake it off, dropping a few stitches, then had to pull the last row apart to correct the error.

"They are children, and you shouldn't treat them like workhorses," Gus said, trying to distract Domko from staring at his wife. "Now go home before I charge you with trespassing."

"Trespass?" Domko chuckled, then his laughter ignited into anger. "Vat? Me? I's be showink you some trespass!"

Knowing better than to turn his back on Domko, Gus took two steps back into the house then slammed the door. Sandy immediately began barking again.

Gus swore under his breath as he paced the floor.

"Is he gone?" Emma whispered.

"I sure hope so," he replied as he peered out the kitchen window, hand against the pane. "I don't see him, but I can see Sandy looking at the barn. Maybe that's where he went."

He could never remember meeting a more suspicious man. There was a word to describe his odd behavior, but Gus couldn't think of it at that moment.

"When should we bring Caroline and the kids up?" Emma asked.

"Not yet. We'll wait until Sandy stops barking. He just might come back to the house."

Gus still held the gun firmly in his hand, and the snow on his jacket melted into fat beads as he waited by the window.

Caroline's eyes adjusted quickly to the cellar's darkness. Looking around, she saw the room was similar to the crawl space under her house. Jars of preserves were stacked neatly in one corner, while bags of potatoes were in the other. There were two crocks of sauerkraut aging next to the potatoes and a few bags of carrots. The older children sat on top of the bags, while the twins played together on the dirt floor. Rosie was pressed against her mother while Kathy gurgled softly.

Caroline could see that Emma had worked hard to prepare for winter. The smell of sauerkraut filled the space, bringing back memories of the fall of 1942, just shortly after Walter was born. She and Bill had spent a full day chopping cabbage and preparing brine—a fall ritual for German people—and for them, it was a day filled with fun and laughter. Bill had loved sauerkraut, especially when served with boiled sausage. Those days seemed so very far away.

The only thing she and Bill had ever fought about was her religion. They had bickered about the same things that irritate all married couples but were always able to make peace, but religion was the exception. Caroline had tried to persuade him to join her as a Jehovah's Witness, but he refused. When his illness progressed, doctors recommended an operation that required a blood transfusion, and she tried to persuade him not to have the procedure, but he ignored her. Shortly afterward he died, and this reinforced her belief that taking blood from another person was evil and wrong. She concluded that by accepting the transfusion he wrote his death certificate, and she could never forgive him for that.

As usual, it was the children who interrupted her thoughts.

"I'm c-c-cold," Walter said.

"Me, too," Eunice added. "We shoulda brought our coats down here."

Dread filled Caroline's gut. They were still hanging in full view above the wood stove in the living room. Domko would see them if he looked in any window or door.

Shushing the children, she listened carefully as the floor creaked overhead. The dog was once again barking. She didn't dare push open the cellar door, in case Domko was standing in the kitchen.

The children were becoming restless in the tiny space. The twins examined the stone crocks, discussing what might be inside. Dennis watched as David lifted the glass plate that was pressing the shredded cabbage into the brine. Smiling, he reached in and pulled up a fistful of cabbage, showing it to Dennis who stepped forward and shoved his hands in the pot. They put some of the cold, fermenting cabbage into their mouths and then grimaced. David dropped the cabbage back into the crock, and Dennis rubbed his hands across the front of his shirt.

"Get out of there," Caroline scolded. "Eunice put the lid back on and make the boys sit with you."

Caroline smiled as she rocked Kathy in her arms.

Those two sure love to eat, she thought. The twins were hardy children who could take the cold and lack of food better than the others.

It was only a few minutes after Sandy stopped barking that Caroline heard footsteps move across the floor. Her heart raced a bit as the door to the cellar was slowly lifted. It was Emma who peered in.

"Is he gone?" Caroline asked, squinting as light from the oil lamps streamed in and hurt her eyes.

"I think so," Emma replied, reaching down to grasp Caroline's hand. "Come on out."

With Kathy in one arm, Caroline hoisted herself out of the hole. Gus stood behind his wife, watching as the children emerged from the darkness. The chatter that ensued once the entire family was in the kitchen prompted Marjorie to emerge from her bedroom.

"Can I come out now?" she asked.

"Yes, but only for a short while," Emma said. "It's getting late and already past your bedtime."

Walter herded the children into the living room while Caroline turned to Gus and Emma.

"What happened?" she asked.

Gus sat down at the table beside his wife, reverting to his quiet self, allowing Emma to tell the story. Caroline sat beside Gus who she'd considered a father figure these past few years.

Emma retold everything that had happened, ending the story by saying that Gus isn't a good liar. She poured them all a cup of tea from the pot that sat on a warming pad in the center of the table.

"Those devil eyes of his darted around so much I couldn't tell if he believed me or not," Gus said. "He may have seen the coats. We should have taken them down, but I didn't think of it." Gus didn't appreciate being caught in the middle of a lie, even if it was to Domko.

"It's not your fault," Emma said. "You scared the fool off, didn't you?"

Caroline flinched. Hearing them talk about Domko like that made her want to defend him. After all, he did have some good qualities. When he wasn't in a bad mood, Domko could be quite charming and good company. He had told her many times that she was beautiful and was quite an ardent lover. It was as if he had two personalities—one that was loving and cooperative, and the other was suspicious and violent. The children seemed to provoke his suspicion and Caroline was beginning to wonder if this wasn't her fault. After all, who else would want a woman with seven, rather, eight children? Tonight's incident probably wouldn't have happened if she could just teach the children to be quiet.

The sudden guilt she felt was overwhelming. She had involved the Harwarts in troubles of her own making. Her father and brothers had told her many times that the children were bad and needed discipline. None of this would happen if she taught them to be well-mannered and respectful. The twins were too noisy, always causing disruptions in the house. And that crazy chatter of theirs—no wonder Domko lost his temper with them. She decided she would try to make them behave.

"I think it will be best if I go home and talk to him," Caroline said. "Can I leave the kids here tonight?"

Emma didn't even try to hide her surprise. "Are you sure you want to go over there?" Of course, you're welcome to leave the kids here, but I'd rather you stayed, too."

"I'll be all right," she said. "He has probably cooled off by now."

Caroline got up from the table, and her reflection in the mirror by the door caused her to look twice. Her eyes were large, purple bruises.

He'll feel bad, she thought, mildly satisfied. *I'll try to be a better wife, and this won't happen again.*

"Take my coat and boots," Emma offered. "It's too cold to go out dressed like that. And make sure you come back here if he's acting crazy."

Caroline smiled in thanks, then without a word to the children, slipped out the door.

Finding enough quilts to cover eight youngsters was not easily done. There was a time when the house was full of beds and blankets, but now that six of their daughters were grown, all that she had left were old and worn, and neatly tucked in a box under the bed.

"These will just have to do, but I don't have enough pillows for you all," she said as she pulled out the box and shook out the quilts.

"That's okay Emma," Norman said. "We don't got no pillows at home anyways."

Eunice and Kathy would share the extra bed in Marjorie's room, while the twins shared the bottom bunk. The boys were happy about this as they chattered to themselves and climbed onto the bed, pulling a thick blanket behind them.

Walter was given a quilt and told to sleep on the chesterfield, while Norman and Steven shared the thick rug in front of the wood stove. Marjorie invited Rosie to share her bed.

Eunice took Rosie aside as they stripped off their dirty clothing.

"Now don't you go peein' in Marjie's bed," Eunice whispered.

"I won't," Rosie said, giving Marjorie a quick glance.

Marjorie's eyes widened.

"Don't worry, she only does it if she's scared," Eunice said.

"You're not scared now are you?" Marjorie asked.

Rosie smiled. "No Marjie, I like your high bed."

Steven and Norman began squabbling about who should sleep closest to the wood stove. Gus acted as referee, grabbing the rug and turning it so that both pairs of feet were close to the heat. Then he covered them with a thick, wool blanket.

As everyone settled in for the night, Emma dug an old baby bottle out of the cupboard and filled it with warm milk. Cradling Kathy in her arms, she pressed the nipple into her mouth. Kathy drank but seemed unusually quiet and passive. Emma stared into her eyes but couldn't make contact as the baby seemed unable to focus. She wondered if there might be something wrong her.

When Kathy was finished drinking, she tucked her in beside Eunice while Gus added extra wood to the stove. They put on their night clothes and climbed into bed.

Emma could hear the wind blowing outside, whistling through spaces in the thick sheets of plastic nailed around the outer edges of the bedroom window. She dreamed of owning a new home some day, but looking around, admitted to herself that she would miss this place. After all, she and Gus had shared a lot of memories in this old log home. She wished that Caroline could also find happiness.

"Life doesn't have to be easy to be good," Emma whispered, as Gus turned toward her and draped his arm across her. "I wonder if Caroline knows that."

Gus was quiet for a moment. "I don't think Caroline knows much of anything."

Emma nodded as she stared at the ceiling. She often discussed the day's events with her husband at night, lulling him to sleep with her soft chatter. She had a lot to say since this had been a particularly eventful evening.

"Did you see how the children didn't even notice when their mother left?" she whispered. "Did you see how satisfied they are to stay here? I wonder what goes on in that house. It must be pretty awful when kids don't want to go home."

Emma also wondered how Caroline could go back to Domko and what she'd have to do tonight to placate him. Emma couldn't understand letting a man like that into bed. Shuddering, she pushed the thought from her mind.

"Gus," she whispered.

"Hmm?"

"Did you notice anything peculiar about that baby? You know I think there is something wrong with her. Caroline seemed pretty careful with it, much more so than with the others. Did you notice? Her eyes roll around, and she can't control her head yet. Maybe she's retarded, what do you think?"

"Hmm," he replied.

"I just wish there was more we could do for those kids. Honestly, Bill would turn in his grave if he knew how Domko treats them. And that crazy religion of Caroline's doesn't help. I know that if Bill had been healthy, he wouldn't have allowed her to convert. She should be a Lutheran, like Bill and the rest of us around here."

"Now Emma, you know full well that he couldn't make Caroline do anything she didn't want to do," he whispered. "Bill was too soft for his own good. She took advantage of that all the time."

"I know," she rasped. "But I just can't stand this! Caroline is going down the wrong road, and I can see it plain as day, but I can't stop her."

"Well, we're her neighbors, not her parents," he said. "It isn't up to us to tell her what to do."

Emma sat in silence for a few moments. Gus was right. It was not her place to interfere in Caroline's life. If anyone was going to say something to Caroline, it should be her family.

Emma said a quick prayer, thanking God for her husband and her life. She drifted off to sleep only to be awakened a few hours later by Sandy's bark. A sound came from the living room, and her first thought was that Domko had come back for the children and it jolted her awake. She sat up and saw a figure standing in the living room. She immediately recognized it was Caroline whispering to the boys lying on the floor. Soon the whispering grew harsh, and the children began protesting that they didn't want to go home. Caroline's tone was firm as she roused the children from their makeshift beds. The twins and Rosie began to cry as their mother pulled them toward the door.

Gus reached over to stop his wife from getting out of bed. It was clear to him that Caroline didn't want them to interfere, so it was best they pretend to be asleep.

"But Gus," Emma whispered. "She's taking them back. I can't believe she's taking them back in the middle of the night."

"There's nothing we can do," he said. "They're not our children."

"Maybe so, but I love them like they are—"

Gus swallowed hard. He cared for the children, too, but was careful not to show it. "We can check on them tomorrow. Nothing more will happen tonight."

Emma laid back and listened to the children pulling on their jackets and shoes. Caroline continued to whisper as she told Walter to help her take the other children home. Within a few minutes, they were gone.

Emma turned to face the wall. The flurries had stopped, and the moon shone brightly through the window. A tear welled in her eye as she stared at the light and shadows the moon cast throughout the bedroom. She fell into a fitful sleep, marred by dreams of running from Domko with the twins crying in her arms.

TRYING TO FIND HELP

"I am going to find us a place to live," Caroline said as she pulled on her best dress. Two weeks earlier they had sought refuge at the Harwart house, and now she knew they needed to get away from the farm. Aside from occasional visits from Emma, Caroline hadn't seen another adult except for Domko for months.

He was berating her and the children constantly now, and she was not looking forward to another long, cold winter in virtual isolation with him. She should have kicked him off her farm a long time ago but was too frightened to follow through.

"No, Momma," Eunice begged. "Don't leave me. I wanna come, too."

"I can't take all you kids," she said, walking past her to the kitchen. Eunice followed quickly behind.

"He'll put me in the hole," she said, eyes welling with tears. "I'm too scared to go in there again."

Reaching into the cupboard, Caroline found a small piece of red crepe paper. Moistening it with her tongue, she dabbed it against her pale mouth. Then pursing her lips, she rubbed the ruby paper gently across both cheeks. The paper added just enough to brighten her face.

"Eunice, you take care of the twins," she said. "Domko is in a better mood today, so just stay out of his way, and I'll be back before dark. I'm taking Kathy and Rosie with me, but you and the boys have to stay here."

Tears streamed down her cheeks. "But Momma," she whined, "I should come with the girls, too."

Her objections were cut short as the twins came bursting into the kitchen from outside. Chattering to themselves, they stopped when they saw their mother. They knew that Caroline's best dress and shiny black shoes meant she would be going away for a while.

Caroline pulled a small piece of charred wood from the stove. Looking at herself in the mirror, she gently rubbed it across her brows accentuating her large eyes. The swelling on her face was gone now, although her nose was still sensitive to touch.

Dennis started to cry. David stood with his hands at his sides, his little shoulders drooping.

"Where are your brothers?" Caroline asked.

David told her they had gone to school.

"I wanna go," Eunice cried.

"You have to stay home and watch them," Caroline said kneeling in front of the twins, putting a hand on each of their shoulders. They stared at her solemnly, big blue eyes shining with tears. "You be good for Eunice. Things will be better when I find us a place to live."

Caroline knew that the twins would not tell Domko where she had gone. They never spoke to him, and even if they did, he couldn't understand their strange language.

"If Domko asks where I went, you tell him I've gone to town for groceries and that I'll be back this afternoon," she said to Eunice.

"What if he gets mad at me?"

"He won't. There's soup on the stove. Have it warm when he gets in."

Caroline disappeared into the bedroom, emerging with Kathy in her arms and Rosie tagging close behind. She wrapped the baby in a blanket and put a worn coat and boots on Rosie. She hoped to get away without having to explain. She estimated he would be outside for at least thirty minutes, almost enough time for her to get to the neighbor's house.

Stepping into the cool autumn air, she felt a chill run through her body. Her heart pounded as she glanced toward the barn.

"Come on Rosie," she whispered. "Hurry, so that Domko won't get us."

The three-year-old let out a squeal and began running down the driveway. Kathy grunted softly from somewhere beneath the blankets as Caroline's feet pounded along the dirt road. Once they were out of view, they slowed their pace. Caroline hoped that Emma and Gus wouldn't see her as she passed their farm. She didn't like the way Gus had furrowed his brow the other night. Gus wasn't her father, and she didn't appreciate his disapproving tone. Caroline decided to ask a different neighbor to help her this time.

There were only a few families she could go to, and they were the Harwarts, Deightons, and Galls. Everyone else in the district either sided with Domko, avoided her, or lived too far away to help.

They turned east on the Township Line Road, and she knew the three-mile walk to Ruby and Jim Deighton's house would be worth it. Ruby would welcome her with a smile and invite them inside.

The landscape was stark and quiet. The only sound came from Rosie's rubber boots, at least a size too big, clunking on the frozen road as they passed hay fields filled with large stacks and open fields of grain stubble. The sun shone brightly but a cool wind whipped leaves across the road in swirling gusts. A small flock of Canada geese flew overhead, honking as they migrated towards their winter home. Earlier flocks had eaten all the grain left in the fields, so the late travelers passed by without stopping.

Caroline tried hard to appreciate this autumn beauty, but the grim reality of her situation clouded any happiness she could muster. Winter would soon be upon them, a time that Caroline once loved, but the thought of being cooped up in that tiny house with the children and Domko was more than she could stand. Domko hated the winter and the beating he gave her two weeks before was just a prelude of what was to come.

As she approached the Deighton farm, Caroline wondered why some men could accept another man's child while others could not. Ruby had two sons from a previous marriage, and Jim seemed to like those boys just fine.

The Deighton's house stood amid a clump of trees on the north side of the road. She could see Jim in the yard splitting wood and piling it high along the fence near the back door. Some of it would be hauled into the house now, while the remainder was brought in as needed. When Jim saw Caroline approaching, he stopped to wave and then watched as she and the children turned into the yard.

Jim was born Canadian to British immigrants. He grew up in the Moosehorn area and had served in the Canadian army during the Second World War. He was a wiry man with high cheekbones and a chin that jutted straight out. He worked hard and had a reasonably successful farm because of it.

"Hello Carrie," he called out cheerfully as he quartered fallen poplar logs with an axe. Lifting one leg onto the block, he removed his cap and pulled a handkerchief from his pocket. Smiling, he wiped the sweat from his forehead. Jim was dressed in jeans, a checked shirt and a pair of coveralls. "What are you doing out walking with those children?"

Caroline forced a smile. "It's Domko again; he's been . . . you know." Looking at the ground, she kicked a small chunk of wood. "Is Ruby home?"

Jim swung the sharp end of the axe into the chopping block.

"She's making lunch, or at least I hope she is," he said, reaching down and grabbing Rosie under the arms, lifting her overhead. "I'm getting hungry. Come on in and have something to eat."

Rosie squealed as he swung her overhead.

Where Children Run

"How are you doing pipsqueak?" he asked, shaking her in fun. Rosie giggled, and her brown eyes sparkled.

The Deighton home was a two-storey, log-chinked house covered in white plaster. A red brick chimney protruded from the center of the wood-shingled roof. There were two windows at the front of the house, which Ruby had covered with thick dark curtains. A small lean-to made of tin protected the door against cold winds.

The house was reasonably well furnished, decorated and clean. The kitchen took up at least a quarter of the house. It had a large table, a cook stove, a two-piece wood cupboard and a pantry. The staircase leading to the upstairs bedroom was in one corner. A front room with a chesterfield and two chairs, a thick braided rug and the master bedroom ran along one side of the house while a guest room sat off the kitchen beside the back door.

Ruby was taking bread out of the oven when the door opened.

"I brought company," Jim called out. "And word has it they're mighty big eaters."

"Caroline, where have you been? I've missed you," Ruby said greeting her with outstretched arms. Caroline stood sheepishly in the doorway, knowing she'd soon have to explain her plans.

Ruby took the baby and encouraged them to remove their coats and take a seat at the table. Ruby was a curvaceous woman with curly brown hair, dramatic eyes and round, red lips. Her French-Canadian accent gave her an air of mystique, and she approached everything in life, whether it be cooking or entertaining, with passion and flair. Ruby was a divorcee from Winnipeg who didn't quite fit in here. The Deighton's marriage was turbulent because of it, but they were regarded as kind and honest.

"So what's this about Domko?" Jim asked, hanging his coat on a hook by the door. He slipped off his boots and put on a pair of thick moccasins. "Is he after the kids again?"

Ruby's eyes narrowed. She could tell by the look on Caroline's face that something was wrong. She also knew that Caroline didn't like being prodded for information. She invited her to join them for lunch. Caroline smiled, avoiding Jim's question, and the women began making small talk.

When Jim could stand it no longer, he interrupted. "So, what's Domko up to now?" he asked. Ruby sent him a disapproving look as she placed a bowl of hot soup in the middle of the table. Jim shot back an impatient look. She handed him a warm loaf of bread, the knife and whispered: "be quiet."

Caroline silently stared into her bowl. She blew on the soup and stirred. Ruby sensed she was getting ready to tell them why she was there.

"Domko's having one of his spells again," she finally said. "He's getting worse every day."

Jim let out a loud guffaw. "Spells my ass!" he said. "The only thing wrong with that bugger is that he's a miserable cuss, that's all. He shouldn't be picking on little kids and a fine wife like you."

Caroline hung her head while Ruby gave Jim a firm kick under the table. They were nearly finished eating before Caroline spoke again.

"I need to go see the welfare," she said. "I want to move to town."

A smile spread across Jim's face. "Well, that's about the smartest thing I've heard you say in a long time. You should've done this—"

"Does Domko know?" Ruby interrupted.

"Not yet," she said. "And I don't want anyone to tell him."

"Of course," she said, silently cheering to herself over the good news. She had never understood the relationship between Domko and Caroline. She was such an attractive, vibrant woman while he was foul tempered and unsociable. She and Jim had tried visiting them, but it seemed the men just grew to hate one another more and more with each visit.

"The health nurse is the woman you need to see," Jim said. "I'll drive you to see Margaret Burnett in Grahamdale if you like. She'll be able to give you all the help you need to get on welfare. And don't you be ashamed about that. I mean what's a woman like you with all them kids gonna do anyhow? It ain't your fault Domko's a crazy ass."

Ruby offered to keep Rosie and Kathy while she was gone. Caroline smiled with gratitude at the suggestion.

"And take as much time as you need," Ruby said.

"You are good friends," Caroline said, looking first at Ruby and then Jim. "I don't know what I'd do without you."

Eunice added a block of wood to the stove, then put the soup pot on top. As it warmed, she spooned a small amount for herself into an old ceramic bowl. She had eaten the soup before it was hot, knowing that there would be nothing left after Domko ate. Within a few minutes, she had finished and wiped the bowl clean. The kitchen door opened and he came inside. Her heart jumped.

"Vere be Carlorka?" he asked, hanging his old hide coat on a hook by the door. The sight of it reminded Eunice of a stinky, old buffalo, like the ones she'd seen in history books at school. She froze, feeling trapped with her back to the stove and Domko in the doorway.

"She went to Moosehorn to get groceries," she replied. Her hands shook as she lifted the hot soup from the stove and placed the pot on the table.

"But-a-some town?" he asked. "Ven?"

"About an hour ago."

"Huh," he grunted as he sat down at the table. He pulled the soup pot forward, filling his bowl. He kept his eyes on Eunice while he ate the potatoes, chicken, and carrots first then slurped the broth.

Eunice stood awkwardly in the middle of the floor. She would have to walk past him to get outside or into the living room, so she slowly backed up and began putting dishes away and tidied her small area of the kitchen. When Domko finished eating, he pulled a homemade cigarette from the plastic container in his shirt pocket. Eunice jumped when he stood and opened the firebox on the stove. He gingerly pushed the cigarette inside, lighting it on the burning wood. Then he poured himself a cup of tea. Eunice relaxed as he sat down, then watched as he shoveled two heaping teaspoons of sugar into the cup. He took an old piece of sliced lemon and squeezed it hard. He studied her carefully while the metal spoon clanged as he stirred.

Reaching down, he took a farm paper from the stack sitting on the floor near his chair, then sat back and began flipping through it. If he could read any of it, nobody knew. He lit another cigarette from the stub in his mouth and when he finished, folded the paper and threw it on the floor by the stove.

"Veres be some David ant Dennis?" he asked.

Eunice cleared the dishes from the table and began filling the washbasin with warm water. She didn't want to tell Domko where the twins were hiding but had no choice.

"They're in the bedroom," she whispered.

Turning on his heel, Domko stomped into the other room. Dropping her dish rag on the floor, Eunice ran as fast as she could out the kitchen door, letting it slam behind her. Stones and twigs poked the bottom of her dirty feet as she ran into the bush at the edge of the driveway and down the well-worn path. Tears of fear and relief streamed down her cheeks as she sped toward the schoolhouse.

The twins sat huddled under a blanket between the bed and the wall. The smell of warm soup made their stomachs ache with hunger, and they listened in silence as Domko ate his lunch. They had felt these pangs many times, especially since Domko arrived on the farm. Often he ate most of what was prepared, leaving just a little for everyone else to share. The twins, being only five years old, usually lost out to their older siblings when food was passed around. Walter frequently felt sorry for the twins and gave them part of what he was able to grab.

A mouse scurried under the bed toward them. It stopped for a moment to sniff Dennis' leg then raised its small head to listen. The pounding of Domko's feet sent the rodent scurrying back to its hole.

Their hiding place suddenly became bright as the blanket covering their heads whipped back. Too afraid to look up, the twins buried their heads under their arms. Domko reached down and grabbed each boy by the hair. They screeched in pain as he lifted them over the bed then dropped them on the floor at his feet. He kicked each once as they scrambled to their feet trying to escape.

"Fraa," Domko roared, pointing towards the front room. They ran to stand beside the heavy dining room table that sat in the middle of the floor. Wet stains appeared on their pants as Domko went to the porch then returned with a long piece of twine.

The boys flinched as he told them to take off their pants then grabbed their arms and shoved them onto the floor by the table.

"You's be peesink ant sheetink ant do nuthink all day," he said sarcastically, kicking their pants aside as they scrambled under the table.

They sat with their backs to the base, arms pressed tightly against their sides. Both started to cry as Domko took the twine and wrapped it around them. After tying a knot in the rope, he faced David. His gold tooth shone, and his eyes were flashing white.

"She's be beechin' around," he said.

David wanted to bring his hands up to cover his face but couldn't. Instinctively he lowered his eyes, hoping Domko would go away.

Satisfied that the twins couldn't escape, Domko stomped over to the wood stove and swung open the cast iron door. He tossed three oak logs in on top of what was already burning. Then he took his coat off the hook and slammed the door as he left. All was quiet except for the crackling in the stove.

"Is Satan gone?" Dennis asked.

"Yep, he's gone," David said. He started rocking back and forth to see if the twine would loosen. Dennis squirmed but couldn't pull an arm free.

"I'm stuck," David said. "How 'bout you?"

"Me, too."

They gave up struggling, hoping their mother would be home soon. They jabbered back and forth until they noticed it had become hot in the small house. Domko had put too much wood in the stove, so it was burning far too hot for this time of year.

"Daddy said not to put no more than two logs in," Dennis said.

"'Cause the house might catch fire," David said, finishing Dennis' sentence. "And Domko put in three."

As the stovepipe that ran across the ceiling into the kitchen grew hotter, they watched solemnly. Soon it was a blazing red overhead.

Dennis was starting to panic. "The h-house is gonna b-burn," he stammered. "Where's M-momma?"

"Momma went to find us some place to live," David said. He remembered months before when their mother had left, she had promised to move the family to town, but nothing happened. David believed that she wouldn't let them down again. "There was no places b-before, but they gots more houses in Moosehorn now."

"Do you think Momma gots us a house?" Dennis asked.

"Yep, she's gonna 'cause she promised," David answered, his voice confident. "Then Domko can't get us no more."

Dennis squirmed. The wet underwear was making his skin itch.

REMOVING BRICKS FROM THE FOUNDATION

"Well, we'd better get going," Jim said, glancing at his watch. "The health nurse won't be there much longer. Margaret's got a family at home, too."

Ruby waved from the front door as Caroline and Jim drove away in his 1949 Chevrolet. They rode quietly towards the gravel highway for a few minutes until Jim could no longer hold his curiosity.

"So what made you finally decide to leave Domko?" he asked softly.

Caroline hesitated before pouring out the events of the past six months. She explained that once Domko's bad moods started, he began working the children like slaves and began beating them for no reason. She said that Domko was now hitting her too—and even hurt the baby.

"The baby?" Jim asked. "He hit the baby?"

"Yeah," she said lowering her voice, holding back tears. "He really hurt her bad, Jim. I thought at first she was gonna die and I didn't know what to do. She came around, but you know, I'm pretty sure she's not right anymore."

Jim listened in silence as Caroline poured out her heart. He turned onto Highway No. 6, one of the province's main highways, and began driving north to the nursing station in Grahamdale.

"What do you mean she's not right?" he asked.

"She's not the same as before," she said. "I don't think she can see."

"She's blind?"

"I think so."

"Are you sure she could see before?"

"Yeah, she used to laugh at the kids and look at me when I came in the room. Now she looks the wrong way. You can put your hand by her face, but she doesn't even flinch."

"That's terrible," Jim said shaking his head in anger. How could he do that to one of the kids? His own kid, to boot!

It was like a giant weight had been lifted from Caroline's shoulders as she confided in Jim, describing the terror of the past eighteen months.

She relayed how just two days before, Domko had become so enraged with Steven that he hit him over the head with his rifle, knocking him unconscious. He then dumped him somewhere in the bush, returning home to tell Caroline that he "hoped the wolves would eat him." He wouldn't allow her to leave the house to go looking for Steven and forced the rest of the children to continue working so they couldn't go either. The following afternoon the ten-year-old staggered home. He was still in a daze and badly dehydrated.

"It's a miracle he didn't freeze to death," Jim said.

"That's what Domko wants," she replied. "If it hadn't been for the dog staying in the bush with him, he probably would have."

Jim and Caroline drove the rest of the way in silence. They arrived at the nursing station to find that the health nurse was not available. She had gone to a nearby farm for a postnatal visit and wouldn't be back until later. Caroline decided she would wait for her to return, rather than ask Jim to bring her back the following day. Besides, she didn't want to go home to Domko that night. Especially not after confessing to Jim.

"I can stay here by myself," she said as they stood in front of the brick building. "I'll be able to find a ride home later."

Jim hesitated. He didn't want to leave her there but had to get back to finish the chores. The days were getting shorter so he'd be finishing in the dark as it was.

"Only if you'll be all right," he said. "Ruby will have my hide if anything happens to you."

"I'm okay now," she said, motioning for him to get in the car and go home. "And by the way, thanks for listening. I feel a lot better now that I've told someone."

Jim smiled and waved as he backed onto the road. He drove back through the village, waving to the people he knew. As he pulled back onto the highway, he wondered if Caroline would tell Mrs. Burnett all that she had told him. With Caroline, he never knew what to expect. Sometimes she'd tell you the most intimate details of her life while other times she would clam up and say nothing at all.

Domko was the opposite. With him, you always knew what to expect.

He's no good. A curse, that's for sure, Jim thought. He knew why Caroline's family didn't help her. He'd heard rumors that the Kolodkas were much like Domko and that old Walter ruled with an iron fist.

There's a fine line between discipline and a beating, Jim thought. *Some of those old bastards can't tell the difference.*

Jim wondered how she could have chosen such different men as partners. Bill Pischke was kind and generous, but Domko was the opposite. At first, he seemed like a decent fellow, but soon he began taking advantage of his neighbors. Then people started to notice that his behavior was queer.

Support from Bill's family became almost non-existent after Domko moved to the farm. By then, Caroline was already pregnant with Domko's child and if she wouldn't kick him out, how could Bill's family help her or the children? What made matters worse was that Domko bristled at the mention of the Pischke name.

Jim remembered an incident just a few months ago that sent shock waves through the community. Bill's brother David went to Caroline's farm to claim the seeder that he had shared with his brother. David planned to make a few minor repairs to the equipment and the visit also gave him an excuse to check on Caroline and the children. He'd heard about Domko's odd behavior and wanted to see for himself if the rumors were true.

First, they had a disagreement about the seeder, and then Domko attacked David when he turned to leave—kicking him in the back. Domko was convicted of assault and ordered to pay a twelve dollar fine. After that, the Pischkes stayed away from the farm. Bill had ten brothers and sisters—all who had families of their own to support—and they likely didn't fully realize what was happening to Caroline and the children.

At that moment, Jim made up his mind that Domko wouldn't push him out of their lives.

"He'd better not try to kick my ass," Jim said out loud. "Or I'll give that sonofabitch exactly what's coming to him."

The Bayton School sat on the opposite side of the road, only a few hundred yards south of the Pischke farm. It was a typical one-room school in the area. The desks were arranged in rows and the teacher's desk was positioned at the front of the room. Slate blackboards hung on the wall behind the teacher, and a bank of large windows along the opposite wall let in ample sunshine.

The entrance was located at the back of the room through a small vestibule where children left their boots and hung their jackets. The building was heated by a large, round wood stove that stood along the back wall. The library was near the front of the room.

The interior walls were painted a light green while the outside was covered with gray, insulated brick siding. The school was administered by a board of local directors who were responsible for the upkeep of the building and the teacher's salary.

Attending class gave the Pischke children the opportunity to socialize with other children and escape Domko's watchful eye. Because each of them had failed at least once, they were not considered very intelligent. Had they attended regularly, they would have obtained better marks, but Caroline did not understand the value of an education. She had only completed grade six, and Domko was proud of the fact he only had a grade four education.

Eunice particularly loved school, and though she often missed the morning class, she usually arrived in time for a full afternoon of learning. She loved the smell of chalk and the squeaky sound of the hardwood floor as her teacher, Mrs. Nina Kiesman, walked slowly up and down the center of the room between the rows of desks. The youngest students sat at the front, the middle students in the center and the older students near the back. Eunice shared a desk with her best friend, Larry Meisner, near the front of the room. Larry was a quiet boy from one of the larger families in the district. People would say that in the Bayton area you couldn't swing a dead cat without hitting a Meisner. Most people were either born into the family or related by marriage.

Larry was a farm boy with a round face and timid disposition. He and Eunice shared jokes and helped each other complete assignments. In her opinion, he had the most important quality a friend could have—he treated everyone with kindness.

Norman was in grade three, so he sat in the middle row a few seats back from his sister while both Walter and Steven were in grade five so they sat together near the back of the room.

Each day the classroom broke into loud chatter as the teacher dismissed the students for the day. That afternoon Eunice dawdled, hoping Mrs. Kiesman would ask her to clean the blackboards or arrange the books neatly on the library shelves.

"Eunice, it's time to go home," Mrs. Kiesman said as she slipped on her coat. "Where is your jacket? And where are your shoes?"

"I was in such a hurry to get here that I forgot 'em," Eunice said.

"Well, you'd better hurry home then," Mrs. Kiesman said, "otherwise you'll catch a chill."

Mrs. Kiesman was a young, newly married woman who had been teaching at the school for a few years. She and her husband George lived just north of the Pischke farm. They were nice people who were helpful to Caroline after Bill died. Initially, George was friendly to Domko, but one day, after witnessing his brutality, George gave him a lecture.

"Those boys are going to grow up someday," he said, "and if you keep it up, the day will come that those boys are going to kick your ass all the way to Moosehorn."

To that, Domko promptly threw him off the farm.

Stepping out into the chilly afternoon air, Eunice could see her older brothers playfully teasing Marjorie and the other girls.

"Marjie!" Eunice called, running up to her friend, "Can I come home with you?"

"Sure," Marjorie said. "I've got some chores to do, but you can help."

The two girls walked across the field, while the Pischke brothers went in the opposite direction. As they neared home, they could see that Domko was not waiting for them in his usual spot at the edge of the driveway. The house looked too quiet, and there was no smoke coming from the chimney. Their spirits lifted immediately.

"He's gone," Walter cheered. "Let's go!"

Turning, they gave a few hoots as they began running down the road.

Steven, still a little dazed from the head smashing he'd received a few days earlier, struggled to keep up. "Let's go to Ruby's. She'll give us something to eat."

They ran through the ditch to the churchyard. Soon they were on a footpath that took them through the thick bush to the Deighton farm.

"Maybe we can stay at Jim's," Walter said. "I like them guys."

The twins weren't accustomed to sitting in one spot for hours, and they fell into a fitful, uncomfortable slumber. The afternoon wore on to evening, and the heat from the fire was long gone. Now, the cool wind was whistling through cracks in the floor as it swirled in the crawl space underneath the house. The floor was cold and sitting on it was becoming unbearable.

"Where's Momma?" Dennis cried. "You said she was comin' home."

"She will," David said. "She'll come home and untie us."

By now, the Twins had lost all track of time. Usually, the older boys came home right after school and went straight to the barn to do chores, but the sound of bawling cattle meant that the brothers hadn't fed, watered or milked the cows yet.

As if David could read Dennis' mind he answered his thoughts.

"They're at Deightons," he said, cut short by the sound of a tractor outside.

"Domko?" Dennis asked.

"Maybe it's Momma—"

The door swung open, and Domko came storming into the house.

"Valter! Steven! Norman! You bastards," he spat as he moved swiftly across the kitchen floor into the front room. They looked up to see him standing over them. The gold tooth flashed, and his eyes darted in anger. The scar across his forehead was beginning to turn white, and his arms were shaking.

The twins had seen the signs before. Domko was mad at the older boys, and it gave him an excuse to beat them. They began crying. By now, both had soiled their underwear, causing Domko to sneer as he pulled a folding knife from his breast pocket and lunged at them. They squeezed their eyes tight and recoiled as the blade sliced through the twine that bound them. Slamming the knife down on the tabletop, he slipped his belt off in one motion, and before they could crawl away, he began whipping them.

"Sheetink again," he screamed. "Steenkink soneebeech bastards, sheet-ink in but-a-some pant!"

The room whirled around David as he scrambled between the table base and the wall. Dennis tried to crawl into the kitchen, but the belt kept knocking him to the floor. They screamed until their senses were blunted and eventually felt no pain; as finally, their minds drifted to a far away place.

"Where are the rest of you?" Ruby asked when the three eldest Pischke boys showed up at her door. Rosie was sitting in the front room entertaining Kathy and called out a cheerful hello to her brothers.

"With our Momma?" Norman guessed, explaining that Domko was not home and that Eunice had gone to Marjorie's house after school.

Ruby's eyes narrowed. Everyone was accounted for except the twins. As she fed the boys, she boiled water on the stove and began filling the wash tub so that they could scrub off the filth before climbing into bed. As they took turns in the tub, Ruby gently quizzed them about what was going on at home. She gave each a pair of pajamas and sent them upstairs to bed.

Her teenaged sons came in with Jim after finishing the last of the chores around 9:00 p.m. After a bedtime snack, Jim sat relaxing at the kitchen table while the boys hurried upstairs to see their friends. Anxious to speak to Jim privately, Ruby put the girls to bed in the tiny bedroom off the kitchen.

"I think the twins are at home alone," she said in hushed tones as she pulled the door shut. "Should we check on them?"

Jim thought for a moment. "I saw a tractor go by about a half hour ago and I think it was Domko. Carrie hasn't come back yet?"

"Not yet," Ruby said. "I'm worried those boys might be outside by themselves or worse yet, in the house with him. Who knows when she'll be back."

Jim nodded, giving her a tired smile as he pushed himself up from the table and pulled on his boots. He closed the door quietly as he made his way to the garage. The car sputtered and coughed as he turned the ignition. Flipping on the lights, he backed slowly down the bumpy driveway. By road, it was less than four miles to the Pischke farm.

After slipping his belt back on, Domko pulled a cigarette from his shirt pocket. It looked as if he would have to do the evening chores himself since the older boys were not around, but he was in no hurry. He sat at the kitchen table leaning back against the wall with his legs crossed, chuckling to himself as he finished his cigarette. His musings were suddenly interrupted by a knock at the door.

He opened it to find Jim standing on the stoop. Jim stepped back, a little surprised by the pleasant look on Domko's face.

"I'm here to check on the twins," he said. "I thought they were at home alone."

Domko's brows knit together and his jaw clenched as his mood quickly shifted. "Vere's Valter?" he asked.

"The boys are at my place," Jim said. "They came because nobody was home and there was nothing to eat."

Domko shook his head. "Yit, yit," he said, waving his hand and spitting on the porch floor. "That's all they's be doink."

Jim stiffened. *It was no wonder the house was a mess, and the children stank so bad. How in heaven's name did Carrie tolerate this?*

"Where are the twins?" he asked.

"How's I be know?" he replied, lifting his shoulders innocently. "They's not be here when I come home."

Jim strained to listen for a sign the boys were there, but all he could hear was the rumble of his own car's engine. Domko pushed his way outside, pulling the door shut behind him.

"I's be doink chores," he said as he strode across the yard, tossing his cigarette butt onto the ground then patting himself on the chest. "Tell them lazy bastards that I's be doink it."

Jim watched as Domko opened the barn door and a stream of bawling cattle followed him inside. Jim waited until he was out of sight before cautiously opening the kitchen door.

"Dennis? David?" he called quietly, poking his head inside. "Are you boys here?" Stepping into the kitchen, he called out again. The house was unusually quiet.

They're probably hiding outside, he thought. *They could be anywhere.*

Backing out the door, he pulled it shut. It was unsettling that he hadn't found the boys and knew that Ruby wouldn't sleep much that night.

It was late, and he was anxious to get home. Scanning the yard and then looking out over the fields and into the surrounding bush, he knew there wasn't much more he could do.

Caroline found a ride from Grahamdale to the Deighton farm two days later. She arrived to pick up the girls to discover that her older sons had spent the entire time there. Ruby and Jim waved off her apology, saying that the boys were well-behaved, had helped with chores, and at the moment, were in school. Caroline avoided discussing where she had been but assured the Deightons that her life was about to take a turn for the better. She gathered up the girls and shushed Rosie who started to cry. Caroline waved a tired hand good-bye, and within a few minutes, Ruby's kitchen was quiet again.

She stood for a moment in the middle of the floor, trying to decide how she felt about events over the last few days.

"What do you think?" she asked Jim, suspicious about the length of Caroline's absence.

"It takes a few days to make that kind of arrangements," Jim said. "I just hope she gets out of there soon."

Ruby nodded in agreement. Her life now returned to its routine as she settled into finishing her mending—a job she'd set aside while the children were there. She made a mental note to pass on a box of used clothing to the Pischke boys the next time she saw them.

The school house door burst open, and the children flooded out. Eunice stopped at the top of the stairs and was overcome with disappointment at the sight of her mother standing on the road at the end of the lane. She was cradling Kathy in one arm and holding Rosie's hand.

"Momma's home," Steven said as he and Norman pushed past Eunice who sighed then reluctantly followed them. Walter ran by, waving excitedly at their mother. "D-d-did you find us s-someplace to l-live?" he asked. He hoped they could go immediately so that they wouldn't have to face Domko. "Eunice said you went to M-moosehorn to get us a h-house."

The children looked up at her.

Caroline's eyes rested on the horizon. "No," she said. "But I talked to some people who are gonna help us. Leaving just isn't the right thing to do."

The children grew quiet, absorbed in their worries as they shuffled down the road, the distance between them growing the closer they got to the farm.

"Hurry up," their mother called. "We've been gone long enough."

Caroline felt confident that Domko would greet her in a pleasant mood. He reminded her of a needy child who took advantage of her mercilessly but craved her at the same time. His need for affection was insatiable.

She had been right. Domko was happy to see her and the children because he worried she had left for good and dreaded the thought of having no one to help him do chores. The twins had disappeared after the beating and were still hiding somewhere.

"Carlorka," he said, meeting them in the yard. "Vere yous be goink for but-a-some time?" He tried to sound cheerful.

"I went to Moosehorn to get groceries," she said, reciting her planned answer. "But I couldn't get credit at the Co-op or the supply store, so I went to talk to some people about getting welfare."

Domko's eyes narrowed as he studied her. Standing about three feet apart, both looked unwilling to back down, but then Domko suddenly softened. He wasn't ready to pick a fight with her when she challenged him head on. Besides, he was too tired from all the work he'd done the past few days.

Turning to the children, Caroline told them to go inside.

Thankful that Domko wasn't going to hit them, the children dashed into the house. Walter put his finger to his lips and motioned for the others to follow, and they went to their mother's bedroom and opened the window slightly to overhear the conversation.

" . . . it was suggested by the health nurse," their mother said. "There are some city people who will take Rosie and the twins. They can go live there until we get back on our feet." She sounded confident that Domko would like the suggestion since he regarded the younger children as nothing but pests.

"It's being done privately so that there won't be social workers involved," she said.

"Vere did you sleep?" he asked.

"I stayed with friends from the church," she said. "They're coming to visit soon, so you can ask them yourself if you don't believe me."

The children dashed away from the window at the sound of the door opening and their mother's shoes on the floor, followed by Domko's heavy boots. They scooted under the bed and were surprised to find the twins huddled there, frightened and forlorn.

Where Children Run

In mid-November, a man came to the farm to discuss foster care with Caroline. It was early afternoon, so the older children were in school. Frightened of strangers, Rosie and the twins had hidden in the bush when the car pulled in the driveway.

Domko was sitting in his usual spot in the chair beside the cupboard with his back to the wall. He stirred his coffee continually while he sucked on the stub of a cigarette, a blue haze rising above him.

Caroline made small talk with the man for a few moments, then she went to the door and called Rosie and the twins inside.

"This is Rosie," Caroline said, brushing the front of the girl's shirt and straightening her pants. Then she pulled forward the twins. "This is David. And this is Dennis."

The disheveled children raised their eyes solemnly at the man.

"I know of a place for the twins," he said. "A couple in Winnipeg who can't have children want to take them. It might take a little longer to find a place for Rosie."

Caroline nodded while Rosie's hopeful expression faded and she looked at the floor. Caroline sighed and glanced at Domko who'd said nothing during the exchange. She invited the man to stay for coffee, but he declined.

"You can expect to see the couple here next Friday," he said, smiling at the boys. He stood up and turned to Domko. He hesitated. Good manners dictated that he shake the man's hand, but since Domko didn't extend his first, he nodded at Caroline and then quickly left.

The evening before the twins were to leave, visitors from the church stopped by the house for a visit. They sat at the kitchen table chatting and discussing Bible passages. Caroline and her friends were trying to coax Domko into switching faiths. The visitors had convinced Caroline that rather than leave Domko she should try to be a better wife; and that his mean-spirited ways would be tempered if he embraced their religion, so she'd been working on him when he was in a good mood but so far had had no luck.

Domko was unusually quiet and obliging this evening, trying to make a good impression. The children were told to sit and behave themselves and listen to what the visitors were saying.

"David and Dennis are goin' to live with city people tomorrow," Norman blurted out, catching Caroline off guard. The Witnesses turned to her when the comment was fully absorbed and they reacted with disbelief.

"What's this about?" the man asked. "Are you sending the twins away?"

Caroline swallowed hard. She knew by his tone that this was not considered appropriate. She had hoped to feign ignorance if confronted after the boys were gone.

"Yes," she said. "We're struggling, and it'll be best for the family."

The man thought for a moment. "No, Caroline I don't think you understand," he began. "By sending those children away, you will be removing bricks from your family's foundation."

She couldn't face him as he began lecturing, so she watched the twins playing together on the floor. They chattered quietly to themselves, oblivious the conversation was about their future.

"Are the family Witnesses?" he finally asked.

Caroline cringed. "I didn't think to ask."

The man shook his head. "Witness children cannot be sent to a non-believing family, otherwise; they will be raised without an understanding of the truth."

Now Caroline was confused. After seeing the health nurse, she was convinced the right thing to do was to take the children and leave Domko. But the friends she'd stayed with that night convinced her to stay, but make changes so that Domko wouldn't become so angry. The following day she met with the health nurse who suggested foster care—a solution that sometimes worked in situations where stepfathers and children didn't get along.

Caroline didn't like these people challenging her decision because she was having a hard time making up her mind as it was. When she was undecided, she was easily swayed, but once she made up her mind about something, she never changed it.

"Well there is still time to decide," she said, changing the subject and hiding the frustration she felt. The Witnesses stayed for another hour, focusing their discussion on the importance of the family unit. Everyone was exhausted by the time they left.

"I will never understand any of this," she whispered, as she fell into bed beside Domko. "I will never be the saint I must be to be accepted into Jehovah's Kingdom."

Domko nodded in agreement, saying that she was a terrible wife, mother, and Witness. She had heard this so many times from him that it didn't even bother her anymore.

She shook her head. In a moment of clarity while away from the farm, she'd decided that sending the children away would be the least selfish decision to make. Now she wasn't sure.

The following morning, she awoke to the realization that her beautiful twins

Where Children Run

would be leaving that day. While the older boys were outside doing chores, she made breakfast then filled the wash tub with warm water. She called David and Dennis and placed them together in the tub. As she gathered up the few things she could afford to send with them, the realization struck how very little they had. There were a few items of clothing, mostly dirty, and Domko had confiscated their only toy truck.

"David, Dennis, come dry off," she said, pulling an old towel from the cupboard. Within a few minutes, they were dressed in the cleanest hand-me-downs Caroline had in their size.

"The nice people from Winnipeg are coming today," she began. "You can go live with them for a while and then I'll come get you."

The twins stared at their mother. Their older brothers had talked about going to live in Winnipeg, but they had assumed that everyone was going except Domko.

"But Momma," David said. "you gots to come, too."

"No, David, I can't," she said. "They don't want me; they want you."

David looked at Dennis who was starting to cry.

"Momma, you gots to come," he begged. "We's gonna live in Winnipeg."

"Now stop your crying," she scolded, wiping the tears that had crept into the corners of her own eyes. "The people are gonna be here soon, and we don't want them to think you are crybabies."

The twins sat quietly in the kitchen. David thought about the situation, deciding that moving to Winnipeg was a good idea even without his mother. He didn't want to go without Dennis though, and his twin was resisting the idea.

"Satan's not comin'," David whispered in their secret language. "He won't get us there, and Norman says the nice people will give us toys and candy."

Dennis didn't want to leave his mother and his home, even though it wasn't a happy place. But he liked candy and missed all the toys that Domko had gradually thrown out over the past year. He was beginning to warm up to the idea since David was making it sound like an interesting adventure. Bored, the twins decided to go outside to play.

Opening the door, they stepped into the brisk November air, not bothering to put on their jackets. Instinctively, David glanced over his shoulder to see if Domko was nearby as they kicked a can back and forth.

A rumble caused him to look down the road, and he could see a car approaching with a cloud of dust behind it. Both boys stopped to watch as a large, white car slowed, then turned quietly in the driveway. It was about the biggest, most beautiful thing David had ever seen. He liked cars and hoped that these were the people who were going to take him and Dennis to Winnipeg. The people got out and smiled at them. They stood for a moment, waving at the twins, trying to coax them to come closer. David took the first step, with Dennis a few feet behind. Both knew it would be best to be quiet.

David liked the looks of them. They had crisp, bright clothes and pleasant smiles. The man was tall like Gus, but the woman looked different than anyone he'd ever seen before. David thought of the fairy princesses from the stories that Eunice told them at night.

They waited outside while the people went into the house. Glancing toward the barnyard, David could see Domko standing by the fence watching. The sight of him scared David so badly that he became anxious to get away.

"I'm goin'," David said quickly. He told Dennis to wait while he ran into the house to get the bag. Dennis cried softly but obeyed his brother who hurried past the people as they came out of the house. David ignored the sight of his sisters standing in the kitchen as he grabbed the bag from the table and then ran back out the door towards the big car. The beautiful woman was crying as she got in the passenger side. The man looked at him, then said a few angry words to Caroline who had followed him out the door.

David wanted to hug his mother goodbye, but the people seemed to be in a hurry. He grabbed Dennis' hand and pulled him towards the car that began backing away. David stopped and stared in disbelief as the people from Winnipeg gave him a half-hearted wave then continued backing out the driveway, onto the road and then drove away.

Their mother had changed her mind.

Now it was David's turn to cry.

A BRAVE ESCAPE

The months wore on, and soon the dreaded winter was upon them. January days were short and the temperature frigid. A storm early in the month dumped more than a foot of snow on the farm and that, combined with Domko's unsociable mood, kept neighbors away.

Caroline was feeling lonely and downtrodden and at her wits end trying to keep peace in the house as Domko continued to beat the children for no apparent reason. For them, there was nothing to look forward to except school—and often they were kept home to do chores—especially when the others ran away after being beaten.

Baby Kathy was growing, but it was apparent that something was seriously wrong with her. It appeared that she could hear and understand, but her physical development was slow, and her eyes did not focus. They all knew she was blind and within the confines of the house, Caroline used the fact to make Domko feel guilty. He'd started to accept the child as his own and was remorseful about what he'd done. He vowed never to hit her again and kept his word. Soon a close relationship developed between the two of them. Unfortunately for the rest of the children, no amount of chastising made him feel bad about how he treated them. He tolerated the older children, but hated the younger ones and wasn't afraid to make his feelings known. Caroline began planning once again to move herself and the children to town but now had to wait for a break in the weather.

Walter and Norman disappeared into a storm one afternoon after Domko became enraged and tried to hit them with a stick because they weren't milking the cows "right." That evening, the twins went to the bedroom the children shared to find Eunice laying quietly on the floor mattress and Rosie under a blanket crosswise on the bed.

"Hey Rosie, move over," David whispered as he tried to crawl in to warm up, but Rosie didn't move.

"Rosie?" he said, giving her a little shake. Lifting the heavy blanket, he was appalled by the steam that rose up as the cold air mixed with the warm dampness underneath. At first, he thought she'd peed the bed again, but this smelled different, and it was then he realized the blanket was oozing with blood. He tried to lift it higher, but the blood was beginning to dry and stuck to her motionless body.

Rosie was lying on her side facing him. Raw, bleeding, gashes covered her arms and legs, and she was covered in bruises. Her eyes were closed, and she wheezed softly.

"What's wrong with Rosie?" Dennis asked, peering over his brother's shoulder.

David swallowed hard. "He got her. I'm gonna tell Momma."

Silently he crept through the hallway and into his mother's bedroom. She was lying on the bed with Kathy beside her.

"Momma, come see Rosie, she don't look good," he whispered from the foot of the bed.

Caroline lifted her arm slowly and motioned for him to come around to the side of the bed then she took his arm and pulled his face close to hers.

"Shhh," she whispered through bloody lips. Her one eye was swollen shut. "Pretend everything's all right."

David nodded then crept back to the room. He motioned for Dennis to climb into bed, then slid in beside him. They were careful not to touch Rosie or the wet part of the blanket. David fell asleep to the sound of Eunice crying softly from the mattress on the floor.

Caroline awoke the next morning with a start as Domko roused everyone out of bed.

"They's be lazy ant goot for nuthink," he said, referring to the older boys who still hadn't returned. He blamed Caroline for their absence, saying that if she disciplined them, he wouldn't be forced to do it and they wouldn't dislike him so much. He called Walter and Norman "lazy like their father," a comment he had heard from Caroline's father and brother.

As she spooned porridge from a big pot into cereal bowls, she tried to pacify him by saying that she and Steven would milk the cows. Domko ate his breakfast and watched suspiciously as the two left the house. Once outside in the fresh, cold air, Caroline began planning their escape.

Inside, Domko drank a cup of coffee while the twins and Eunice sat at the table. Neither child dared look at him for fear he would interpret it

Where Children Run

as a challenge. He surveyed each child, looking carefully for a missing button or tear in their clothing. Satisfied that the children had done nothing to antagonize him deliberately, he got up and took off his belt. They froze and squeezed their eyes shut, each silently praying it wouldn't be them. Domko strode past them into their bedroom, and they began to weep tears of relief and remorse as Domko threw back the blanket and beat Rosie again.

"Lazy soneebeech bastard," he grunted. Unable to move, the little girl made no sound as the belt whipped against her blood-caked skin.

Once the milking was done, Caroline and Steven carried the pails and set them outside the kitchen door.

"Get the horses and sleigh ready, while I go into the house," she said. "But be careful he doesn't see you."

Unaware that Rosie had been beaten again, Caroline began putting the milk through the cream separator. She told Eunice to clear the dishes and sent the twins outside to bring in wood for the stove. Satisfied that everyone was busy, Domko went back to the bedroom for a nap.

Caroline motioned for Eunice to follow her outside. They met the twins at the doorway. Each boy was carrying an armful of wood.

"We're leaving so everyone, be quiet," she whispered, pointing toward the sleigh that sat along the barnyard fence. "Go wait."

The twin's eyes widened, and they dropped the wood then turned and ran to the sleigh with Eunice on their heels. They climbed quickly on top and began kicking off the snow. They could hear Steven getting the horses ready in the barn.

Caroline went back inside and quickly gathered a few belongings while Kathy and Rosie slept. She stacked the things she wanted to take outside, then slipped off her work clothes and put on her best dress, coat, and boots. Taking a warm cloth, she cleaned Rosie's face as best as she could. Rosie moaned softly as the cloth scraped across her skin.

"Shhh," Caroline whispered. "It's gonna be okay. I'm taking us away from here." Wrapping a fresh blanket around Rosie, she carried her to the kitchen door and laid her gently on the floor then went outside to get the sleigh. She decided to load everything then come back for the girls.

The horses, Queenie and Jack, were standing nervously along the fence as Steven labored to attach the traces to the double tree that fastened the team to the sleigh. These were uncooperative horses that often behaved wildly. Their ears pricked as they watched Caroline approach. She climbed into the driver's seat just as Steven finished fastening the team. The twins were so excited they began jabbering loudly.

"Be quiet; we're not gone yet," she said. She clucked gently as the horses jerked the sleigh forward. Pulling back on the reins, she stopped in front of the door. She told Eunice to hold the horses while she and Steven began loading the sleigh. Soon it was filled with dishes, blankets, and spare clothing.

"Whatever you do, don't spill it," she said as Steven lifted a can full of cream into the sleigh.

Steven packed the can solidly against the back rail then climbed on the sleigh and took the reins from Eunice. They waited in silence as their mother disappeared into the house. They whispered with relief when she emerged a few moments later carrying Rosie wrapped in a clean blanket. She laid the bundle across the twins' laps as they sat side-by-side on the floor of the sleigh and she told them to hold her tight.

"I'm going back for Kathy," she said hurrying to the house. She opened the door and then jumped back, letting out a startled scream. Domko was standing just inside the door.

He looked out and was surprised to see the children in the sleigh.

"Veres yous be goink?" he asked.

Caroline took a deep breath to steady her nerves. The horses raised their heads and snorted at the sight of him, so Steven pulled back gently on the reins.

"All the chores are done, so we're going visiting in town," she said.

Domko stared at her until she finally had to look away. She could hear the baby crying inside.

"I'm going to take Kathy," she said, trying to push past him.

"I's be keepink her," he said, blocking the doorway.

"I want to take her," she stammered. "She needs to see the doctor."

"She's be seek?" he asked. "Maybe yous not be comink back?"

"Of course I'll be back," Caroline replied casually. "We'll all be back. Tonight. I'll see if I can find Walter and Norman, too."

Convinced that Caroline wouldn't leave without the baby, Domko stood in the doorway with his arms across his chest while Caroline argued that Kathy needed to be seen by the doctor. The horses continued to shake their heads and stamp their feet, so she went back to the sleigh and began stroking their necks to calm them.

Sensing this might be their only chance, she jumped aboard and grabbed the reins from Steven, slapping them hard. The horses jumped forward, and the sleigh took off with a jolt. Everyone flew backward as the animals broke into a quick trot. Caroline pulled in the left rein and the horses quickly turned, then straightened as they found themselves on the familiar winter road that ran east behind the house toward the dense bush that led to the Deighton farm.

Surprised by Caroline's courage, Domko stood dumbfounded in the doorway. He began shaking his fist in the air and swearing in Polish.

She yelled loudly at the horses, encouraging them to go faster.

"I's be drownink her!" he yelled over and over again until they couldn't hear him anymore.

Once the children realized they had escaped, they let out a wild cheer. Caroline said a silent prayer of thanks and tried to push away frightening thoughts about what Domko might do to the baby. She didn't think he'd hurt Kathy, but he'd been so unpredictable lately that she couldn't be sure. It took nearly thirty minutes to reach the Deighton farm. Caroline hoped they could warm up there before continuing to town.

Ruby and Jim were sitting at the kitchen table listening to Walter and Norman plead that they should be allowed to stay there instead of going to school, fearing that Domko might see them on the road. The discussion was interrupted by a knock on the door.

"Come in," Ruby said, not at all surprised to see Caroline's battered face. "Are you all right?"

"We're fine," she replied. "I was wondering if me and the kids could warm up here for a bit. We're moving to town."

Jim raised his eyebrows. "You're going to town? What does Domko think about that?"

"He doesn't know," she said. "I'll tell him later when I go back with the Police."

"The police?"

"He kept Kathy."

"You left the baby?" Ruby asked, unable to hide her shock. "With him? He nearly killed her once, didn't he?"

Caroline explained by telling them what had happened, adding that she didn't think he'd hurt his own child.

Ruby didn't look convinced, and neither did Jim. He got up and put on his coat and boots.

"I'll go start the car," he said. "I'll take you and the kids to town. The sooner you get to the police station and come back for that baby the better."

Caroline smiled. She had hoped Jim would offer to help.

Ruby poured Caroline and herself a cup of coffee and began warming a pot of milk on the stove. "Would you kids like some hot cocoa?" she asked.

"Yes, Aunt Ruby," they chorused then waited patiently.

"Here you go," she said handing a cup to each child. "Now be careful—it's hot."

Eunice put the cup to her lips. She took a sip that scorched her tongue. It tasted incredibly good, especially since she loved chocolate, and so seldom had a taste of it.

"What about Rosie?" Ruby asked, holding a mug out to the little girl still bundled on Caroline's lap. "Is she sleeping?"

Caroline had her well covered. "She's not feeling well," she said.

Ruby nodded but said nothing more.

The family's belongings were transferred from the sleigh to Jim's car. The children piled in the back with the younger ones sitting on top of the older ones. Within an hour of arriving at the Deighton farm, they were once again on their way. The children waved to Ruby as the car backed out of the driveway. The snow was piled high in banks along the road. It was plowed just enough to let one car through at a time.

"Where do you want to go?" Jim asked.

"I hear that in Ashern the administrator will give welfare out without taking it to a meeting," she said. "And it will be harder for Domko to find us there."

Jim nodded. "I'll take you to the municipal office and see if we can find you a place to live, then we'll go to the police."

Caroline nodded. Already she was feeling better. There was still the matter of going back to get Kathy, but she believed the police would help her.

She asked Jim to stop at the creamery in Moosehorn so that she could sell the cream; then she asked him to take her to the Co-op store. While she met with the manager to discuss her account, the children scattered throughout the store. It was one of the few times the twins had ever been to town. They were amazed by the many delicious foods available to eat. Shoppers stopped to watch as the children ran wildly about and then begged their mother to buy them candy.

Caroline tried to hush them, explaining that all she had was eight dollars and that was needed to buy groceries. Jim disappeared and returned carrying seven boxes of Lucky Elephant popcorn. The children were so excited that they grabbed the popcorn and ripped open the boxes. Jim laughed as Caroline smiled at his generosity. She wished that someone as wonderful as him had come into her life instead of Domko.

It began lightly snowing as they pulled onto the snow-packed gravel road. As they traveled south, they met a northbound train. The children watched in amazement as the train chugged along, effortlessly plowing snow as it went. David and Dennis had never seen anything like it and listened, amazed, as Jim explained the train carried people and freight from the city all the way to the north. He told them that if they continued to follow the highway south past Ashern, it would eventually take them to Winnipeg.

Having grown up in virtual isolation northwest of Moosehorn, Caroline knew few people in Ashern. The only women she was acquainted with in this community were members of her church. She was anxious to see a familiar face but worried about what their reaction would be to the news that she'd left Domko. Peeking under the blanket at Rosie's battered face helped strengthen her resolve.

I'm doing the right thing, she thought.

It was Friday afternoon, so the business section on Ashern's Main Street was busy. Cars parked diagonally in front of the stores, cafés, and hotel. Jim stopped in front of the municipal office—a remodeled, two-storey frame house that was one of the first places you came to when turning off the highway onto the main street.

"I'll also check to see if they know of a place for rent," he said. "I'll try to get money for you, but you might have to come in."

Caroline nodded. She was thankful that he always knew what to do.

Jim opened the door and was greeted by the smell of official work: new paper, ink, dust and musty documents. Olive Porteous, the secretary-treasurer, was sitting behind a large desk. The hardwood floor softly creaked as she stood and with a pleasant smile, greeted Jim at the counter. He was relieved to see a woman in charge and hoped that she might be sympathetic to Caroline's plight.

"I'm looking for a house to rent for a friend of mine," he began.

Olive thought for a moment. "How big a place are you looking for?"

"She's got eight kids so I think she'd like to live somewhere close to the school."

Olive slid a piece of paper across the counter and picked up a pencil. "I do know of a place near the school, but it won't be available until the end of the month," she said as she wrote a few names then handed him the sheet. "There one is in the middle of town, but it's pretty small. Call this man."

Jim thanked her as he slowly folded the sheet, deciding how best to ask the next question. Glancing from side to side, he leaned forward so that the man waiting next to him wouldn't overhear.

"Do you know if she could get a bit of money? he asked.

Olive smiled softly then glanced at her watch.

"You get her settled and tell her to come back and see me Monday morning. We won't be able to give her much, but we can't have starving kids in town."

Jim smiled and nodded. "Thank you, ma'am," he said as he closed the heavy door behind him. He smiled to himself at the sight of Caroline watching him anxiously from the car, surrounded by six pairs of eyes, all wondering the same thing. He nodded and smiled that he'd been successful, then pointed down the street as he hurried along the wood plank sidewalk to the public telephone.

The operator placed Jim's call, and within a half hour, they were all standing in front of a small, frame house in the middle of the town's residential area. The landlord agreed they could stay there for a few weeks until they could find a larger place.

He unlocked the door and lit a lamp in the kitchen as the children flooded in behind him, carrying their belongings. Everything dropped on the kitchen floor as the children spread throughout the house, the noise level increasing as they moved from room to room. Caroline was pleased to see the place was clean and furnished. She made arrangements with the landlord to pay her weekly rent.

"It shouldn't take long for the money to come," she quietly said. "I . . . I've done this before."

The man's kindness was genuine as he handed her the keys. "Not that you have much need for these around here," he said. "But it's good to lock up if you're going to be away for a while."

Jim shook the man's hand and waited for him to leave. Then he began looking around himself. His first task was to warm up the place.

"You've got oil heat," he said as he emerged from the front room, slapping the dust off his hands. The heater hummed and clicked as it was turned up. "Good thing because it's a bad time of year to find wood."

Once they were settled, Jim offered to take her to the police station.

"It's getting late," he said. "You don't want to leave Kathy with him overnight."

Caroline agreed. Buttoning her coat and pulling her boots on, she put Walter in charge and told the rest of the children to behave.

"Lock the door, Momma," Eunice begged. "What if Domko comes when you're gone?"

"D-don't worry Beanie, h-he can't find us here," Walter said. "We's all the way in Ashern."

The RCMP office was located in the residential part of town. It was a hip-roofed, two-storey building that housed the administration office and jail cells in the main section, while the Sargeant and his family occupied the back part and the second floor.

Jim stood with his arms folded as Caroline explained to the two officers what had transpired over the past few days. She left out the excruciating details, preferring to say that Domko was "too hard" on her and the children. The officers listened but didn't seem overly concerned. They'd heard of Domko before and knew that he was backward, of below-average intelligence and could barely speak English. He was the last person they felt like visiting that night.

"Why did you leave her there?" the older officer asked.

Caroline looked at the floor. "He wouldn't let me take her."

"Wouldn't let you? You managed to get all the other children out of the house, why not her?"

"He blocked the door."

"Why didn't you take her out first? If he's that bad, why did you take a chance?"

"It was cold, and I didn't want her to start crying and wake him up."

"But you left her alone with him—weren't you afraid he'd hurt her?"

Caroline sighed. "No, he won't hurt her because she's his daughter. It's my kids he hates."

"Then what's the big hurry to go get her then?"

"Well, he said he'd drown her if I left."

"But I thought you said he wouldn't hurt her?"

Caroline didn't know what else to say. By this time Jim was hopping mad and fed up with the interrogation.

"Listen," he said, stepping forward and leaning close to the officers. "That Domko's off his rocker and about as predictable as a bull elk in rut. I've seen it for myself. He's nuts I tell you, and it's about time somebody did something about it. Now, if one of you don't take her back to the farm to get that baby, then I'll do it—but I'll take a loaded gun with me."

The Sergeant shook his head and scoffed. The younger officer lifted his hands in surrender and began apologizing.

"Now Jim, it's not that we don't want to go," he said. "We just want a full understanding of what we're walking into, that's all. We don't want to go barreling in there and run the risk of somebody getting hurt. You're right, the baby should be with its mother, and we can make him give her up on those grounds."

"Then why are we standing around gabbing?" Jim asked. "It's getting late, and I have chores to do."

The young officer pulled on his heavy RCMP issue coat and fur hat. "I'll go," he said to the Sergeant. "This shouldn't take long."

Jim said goodbye to Caroline and left the station. Within a few minutes, he was turning north on the highway, heading for home.

He'll see for himself, Jim thought. *Once he meets Domko, then he'll know what I'm talking about.*

As Caroline climbed into the cruiser beside the officer, she noticed he was carrying a gun. Although it was not something she'd ever admit, it was exciting to think that a shoot-out might take place on her behalf.

They soon caught up to Jim's car and passed it in a burst of speed. Caroline gave her friend a small wave as the police car whizzed by.

The officer understood why police hated handling domestic cases. Too often they were expected to side with one parent over the other without a full understanding of the circumstances. It was difficult to prove that a crime had been committed because children under twelve years of age were not considered credible witnesses so what they said didn't matter to the courts.

It wasn't the RCMP officer's job to take action against the husband—it was up to the wife. Police needed a woman to press charges, follow it through the court system then stay away from her husband. Unfortunately, few women did that. Often they went back to the situation within a few days or weeks. Charges, if laid, were dropped and then the pattern would start all over again. It was frustrating for police who couldn't help but ask: How bad can it be if she keeps going back?

For an officer to arrest the husband, he'd have to witness a crime in process or believe the family was in immediate danger. It was a judgment call and a tough one to make. Some officers did arrest husbands, but often the wife would show up at the station begging for his release. Sometimes it was just easier not to get involved—especially if the man was a well-respected member of the community. All a police visit did was create hard feelings between the officer and the husband.

"Tell me about Mr. Domko," the officer asked.

Caroline hesitated. She wasn't sure if she wanted this handsome young

Where Children Run

man to know the details of her sordid love affair with Domko and the birth of his illegitimate child. It was rather stupid on her part to have a child with a man and then show up on the doorstep to take it away from him.

"He's like the devil," she finally said, describing Domko without revealing the shame of the constant beatings. "This is all his fault. He starves the kids and works them in the fields and has spells that make him act crazy. He never bathes or cleans up after himself. I've had enough."

The officer listened carefully. This Domko person did sound like a monster, and he was curious to see the man face to face. He slowed as they pulled up to the farm and quietly as he could, got out of the car.

Caroline strode bravely up to the house with the officer close behind; his gun tucked neatly inside his overcoat. They went inside to find Domko sitting at the table with Kathy on his lap. He had made a supper of boiled potatoes and freshly killed chicken. He had bathed, was wearing clean clothes and his face was clean shaven. The baby cooed softly as he carefully guided the spoon into her mouth. He looked up at Caroline and the officer.

No one spoke for a moment. Caroline finally broke the silence.

"I came to get Kathy. Me and the kids are going to live in town."

A look of sadness passed over Domko's face. His shoulders slumped as he stood and handed the baby to Caroline. Kathy, who was still hungry, began to cry. She reached back for her father who took another step back, causing the baby to reach even further. "Ta-ta," she cooed.

"It's time to go," Caroline said, bouncing Kathy to stop her fussing.

"Go," Domko said sadly. "I's not be vantink lazy voman ant keets no more. I's be tryink to make farm goot ant vat you's be doink? Leavink me with Kathy ant goink to town vith all de mooney ant cream."

Caroline was shocked. She looked at the officer who appeared confused. Caroline noticed the glint in Domko's eye.

"Look," he said to the officer, waving his arm across the room. "She's not be cleanink or cookink, just sleepink all day."

"That's not true!" she replied, knowing the filth in the house was going to be hard to explain. "You're the dirty one who makes a mess."

"I's be vorkink all day!" he said. "Vat? I should vork in barn then smell like but-a-some flower? Ant de keets, vat they's be doink?"

The bickering continued until finally, the officer spoke up.

"Well, Mrs. Pischke, we have the child, it's time to leave," he said.

"I shouldn't have to go, this is my house," she suddenly said. "He is the one who should have to leave. He shouldn't even be in Canada. Ask to see his passport and papers." Caroline knew that Domko feared the threat of deportation more than anything.

"Maybe I's go," he said controlling his temper. "But vere the farm be then? Who's be payink but-a-some tax? Jim?"

Seeing that they were getting nowhere, the officer took Caroline by the arm and escorted her out of the house. During the ride back to Ashern she found it difficult to speak. She'd been outwitted and knew that the officer had sympathized with Domko more than she'd expected.

The officer wasn't sure what to think of the scene he had just witnessed. His training had taught him that domestic violence was never a clear-cut issue. No one was to blame, and yet everyone was to blame.

Who knows? he thought. *Maybe there is more between Mrs. Pischke and Jim than meets the eye. Everyone has a motive. What was hers?*

He decided that he'd met worse characters than Domko and that Caroline wasn't perfect either.

REGRETS

"She's be steelink but-a-some horses ant the cream," Domko said as he stood in Jim's doorway the following afternoon. His fists were clenched, and he looked ready for a fight.

"If I remember correctly she lives at the farm, too," Jim shot back. "You can't steal your own horses. You're just lucky she didn't sell them. And as for the cream, who milked the cows anyway? I know it wasn't you."

Domko grunted and then turned, storming towards Jim's barn. He emerged a short time later with the horses and hitched the team to the sleigh that sat at the edge of the yard. Climbing onto the seat, he took the reins and whipped the horses to get them moving. The animals reared slightly, then took off around the edge of the bush, pulling the sleigh out of sight.

Jim stood watching in full view from the doorway knowing how much it would irritate Domko.

"Is he gone?" Ruby asked after Jim came inside. She was sitting at the table visiting with Emma Harwart.

"Gone but not forgotten," Jim laughed.

"Honestly," Emma said shaking her head. "Leaving that man is the best thing Caroline has ever done."

Ruby nodded in agreement.

For the first time since she met Domko, Caroline felt free.

A month after moving to Ashern she and the children relocated to a larger house on the edge of town. Although the house was small, it had three bedrooms, a kitchen, and front room. The house was sparsely furnished with items scraped together from neighbors and the local secondhand store. The chemical toilet in the basement fascinated the children who had never used anything but the bush or an outhouse.

The school was located nearby, so it was easy for the children to walk to school. Steven, Norman, and Eunice seemed to enjoy their new teachers and classmates, but Walter was having a difficult time adjusting. He was accustomed to a one-room school where all the children knew one another. The school here was large with seven classrooms, and the students split according to grade level with a teacher in each room.

Walter complained to his mother that he was being teased and that the children at Bayton were much kinder than the kids here. He told her he wanted to go back to Bayton, but she brushed him off, hoping that soon he would make a few friends.

Caroline's social life was starting to improve. She became acquainted with neighbors Anna and Leon Koch who had a daughter and two young sons and lived a short distance away. The move to Ashern didn't seem to affect her friendship with the Deightons and Harwarts who stopped by shortly after they settled in and promised to see her whenever they came to town.

Caroline also received regular visits from members of her church even though some did not approve of her decision to leave Domko. They tried to convince her to return to the farm but with her confidence somewhat restored, she refused outright. She asked church members if she deserved to be punished for one mistake for the rest of her life, pointing out that since she hadn't married Domko, she was breaking no religious laws by leaving him. Her defiance put her in a precarious position with the church and on the path toward being shunned, so for a while, she found herself drifting away from her religion.

Periodic visits to the family were made by the social worker assigned to Caroline's case, a middle-aged woman named Martha Jeske. Martha was a tall, heavy-set woman with a rigid smile and no-nonsense attitude. She had curly graying hair and a booming voice. She seemed genuinely concerned about the children and how Caroline was managing on her own. She sat with her and worked out a monthly budget and explained that the mother's allowance payments were based on the needs of eight children. She also explained that because Caroline owned land, a lien would be put on it, payable to the provincial government as reimbursement if it ever sold.

Caroline had no choice but to agree. Although she was still quite poor, the monthly payment meant she could afford to feed the kids. As she sat visiting with Martha one afternoon, the children began filtering home from school.

"Well, who do we have here?" Martha asked the twins.

Where Children Run

David and Dennis looked up at her and smiled, recognizing her faint German accent.

"This is Dennis, and this is David," Caroline said.

"My, aren't they just the cutest little things," Martha said, her voice softening. "And look at those eyes—so blue!"

Caroline beamed. People often weren't that kind to them.

Late one spring afternoon, Caroline was reading in the front room when Walter came bursting in the house, startling her with his urgency.

"Momma, D-domko's coming!" he yelled.

Caroline jumped up and peered out the front window. The children had been playing tag outside but now were backing across the lawn as Domko ambled up the driveway. He was carrying a brown paper bag in each hand and greeting the children cheerfully.

Caroline hurried to the door, slipped on her shoes and stepped outside before he had the chance to come in.

"Carlorka, it be goot to seeink you," he smiled.

She crossed her arms defensively. "How are you?" she asked.

"Goot," he said thrusting the bags at her. "I's be brinkink for you ant the keets."

She hesitated, trying not to look at him.

"Vat?" he said, smiling wider. "You's be gettink too much food?"

Taking one bag from his outstretched hand, she looked inside. It contained a newly killed, plucked chicken. Setting it on the porch, she took the other bag and opened it. Inside there were eight bottles of soda pop.

Caroline softened. This was the Domko she remembered when he had first come to the farm. Where had he been these past two years? More importantly, was he back for good?

"I's be comink inside?" he asked gently.

She hadn't had enough time to decide what to do. Stalling, she called each child by name. As she handed each one a bottle of soda pop, they took it in disbelief.

"Domko brought it," she said. The children hadn't tasted pop since before their father's death. The twins and Rosie couldn't remember ever having it but knew they would like it by the way their older siblings raved about how good it was. Norman put the bottle in his mouth, trying to pry off the metal top with his teeth.

Caroline laughed. "That won't work," she said, pointing to a metal hinge on the shed door. "Walter, show them how to pry it off over there."

Walter widely smiled as he led the children away. He'd opened pop before and was confident he could do it again.

Domko kept his eyes transfixed on Caroline. "I's be comink in?" he asked again, this time gentler.

Caroline didn't want to be rude, especially after his generosity to the children. She picked up the chicken and motioned for him to come in and he sat at the kitchen table while she prepared supper. As they chatted, she was overwhelmed by feelings of normalcy.

This is what life should be like, she thought.

Handing him an ashtray, she smiled. He was clean and well-groomed. He looked like an average fellow, and nobody would have been able to convince her about his temper if she hadn't witnessed it firsthand. As they chatted and gossiped, she was amazed by the change in him.

"I's be better now," he said. "My head be but-a-some goot."

Domko apologized for his past treatment of her and the kids and asked if they would return to the farm. He told her that he needed her there and loved her very much.

Letting her defenses down, she smiled and invited him to stay for supper. The children were called in and told to sit at the table. Domko was friendly to them, and that made the older children wary, but the twins were eager to accept his kindness. Domko hid his suspicion as they spoke in their strange language.

Shortly after supper, he left, waving as he walked down the road toward the tractor he'd parked in the schoolyard. Caroline felt a little sad that he was leaving, but relieved that he didn't pressure her to make an immediate decision.

Domko continued to visit regularly, but he wasn't the only suitor trying to win Caroline's heart. Several men visited, and she enjoyed the attention immensely, openly flirting with them. In May, Domko began pressuring her to return to the farm, and she knew it was because he'd soon need help in the hay field.

"I's be keepink some farm goot," he said one afternoon in his kindest, most persuasive tone. "But I's can't be doink it alone."

Caroline thought for a few moments, then offered to take Walter and Steven out of school early and send them back for the summer. This satisfied Domko who arrived the following week in Caroline's brother's truck to get the boys who agreed to the arrangement.

Walter was optimistic that Domko had changed his ways and was anxious to get away from the town kids who teased him about his stuttering.

Steven was a quiet boy who demanded little attention and was proud of his mother's Polish heritage, so he always had gotten along better with Domko than the other children. They boys waved to their mother from the back of the truck as they drove away.

Norman stayed in school until the end of June, and then he began raking hay for one of the local farmers. This brought a little extra money into the household, and they were able to hide it from the social worker.

When summer came to an end, Steven returned to Ashern in time for the Labour Day long weekend. School started soon after that, giving him the perfect excuse to not go back to the farm. Walter decided to stay with Domko and attend school there. The arrangement suited Caroline just fine because Walter was happy and it kept Domko from pressuring her to return.

On their very first day of school, the Pischke twins found themselves in the middle of a busy, noisy classroom with thirty other children. They sat quietly near the front, watching the others chat and play. Eunice was also in that class, but because she was still in grade two, she sat on the other side of the room with the older children.

Their teacher was Margaret Sigfusson, a tall, attractive, 31-year-old dark-haired woman who was well liked by her students. She noticed how inseparable the twins were and that they couldn't speak English. She couldn't tell them apart, and both were too shy to say a word to her. She'd heard stories about these kids and wanted to help them fit in with the rest of her students.

"Eunice could you come here please," Margaret said at the end of the third day. "Give this note to your mother."

Eunice took the slip of paper. She ran home and watched her mother open the note and read it slowly. Caroline had received many notes before, usually about the older boys day dreaming or not completing their assignments, but this one asked for a meeting. She went to the school the next morning to discuss the twins.

"It is nice to meet you," Margaret said, extending her hand.

Caroline smiled and looked around the room. It had been years since she had been in a school. The smell of chalk dust brought back harsh childhood memories.

"I am having a hard time understanding the twins," she began. "What language do you speak at home?" Most children in the school spoke English, German and some were Icelandic.

Caroline felt her face flush. She didn't want to admit that she couldn't decipher everything the twins said either. She had hoped that the boys would outgrow the strange speech problem by the time they started school

"Eunice understands them," she said. "Can she help?"

"I suppose that's possible," she said. "They are so far behind the other students their age. They need to learn to speak and start communicating with the rest of us." Then Margaret stopped. She could tell by the look on Caroline's face that she was uncomfortable.

"I'll teach them English and see what happens. They may have to do some practicing at home, but we can discuss that later."

Caroline nodded. The air in the room was suffocating, and she tried to hide her panic. "Can I go now?" she asked.

"Certainly," Margaret said. She was genuinely concerned about the twins and had not intended to make their mother feel inferior. "We'll talk again."

Before classes began, Eunice's desk was moved to the front of the room beside her brothers. Sitting with them embarrassed her because she had already spent two years in grade one. It didn't take her classmates long to notice that she was interpreting for the twins.

"Retards," a few of the older children taunted during recess. "The twins are retards."

Eunice was embarrassed by the comments and pretended not to notice. The twins were oblivious to what was going on. They didn't care much about what other people said or thought of them. Most of the time they were in their own little world, and the only person who invaded that space was Domko, and as far as they knew, he was out of their lives for good.

"You's be tellink Carlorka," Domko said, as he scooped a spoonful of chicken and potato stew onto his plate.

Walter was being asked to relay how kindly Domko acted now, and that life had improved at the farm. He thought that life certainly was better since returning in mid-May. Domko hadn't lost his temper or threatened to kill him once. He was beginning to think that Domko might be able to fill the void that was left when his beloved father died.

"I'd l-like to go see Momma this Sunday," he said. "W-ill you take me?"

Domko smiled as he spooned food onto Walter's plate.

"I's be brinkink you, ant some potato ant carrot," he said.

Walter was also anxious to have the rest of the family return to the farm. He missed his brothers and needed help with the chores. They had put in long days to get the work done and now it was time for him to return to school. He didn't like attending class but was looking forward to socializing with his friends who he hadn't seen in a year.

"M-maybe you want to come back?" Walter asked his mother that Sunday afternoon as they stood together in the kitchen. "Domko's better, a lot better than he ever w-was."

Caroline thought for a moment. Domko was sitting in the living room looking at a farm paper. Kathy was playing with a small toy at his feet while the other children played loudly in the bedroom. The twins came running out, one behind the other, screaming with Eunice in pursuit.

"Gimme that!" she yelled, pulling a doll out of David's hand. "Get your own toys." Turning she flipped her nose into the air and marched back into the room she shared with her mother. Caroline glanced at Domko who seemed oblivious to the noise.

"I don't know," she said. "I like living in Ashern."

Walter worked on his mother for most of the day, and she began to waver. In quiet moments she mentally calculated the list of pros and cons of staying in town.

"I'll think about it," she said. Walter smiled and gave her a hug.

That night she allowed Domko to spend the night in her bed. Eunice and Rosie were sent to sleep with the boys, and they were all instructed not to disturb the adults once the bedroom door closed.

The following morning during breakfast, Caroline announced that they would be returning to the farm.

"No," Eunice whispered, in the hope that Domko wouldn't hear. "I want to stay here." The twins and Rosie started to cry.

"I won't go back," Norman yelled directly at Domko who was sitting at the table stirring his coffee. The eleven-year-old turned and ran out the door.

Ignoring the children's pleas, Caroline began packing. Domko was very pleased as he loaded their belongings into the borrowed pick-up truck parked in the driveway. Since Caroline had already paid the current month's rent, she had two weeks to remove the remaining furniture that couldn't be taken on this trip. Within a few hours, the children were sitting in the back of the truck, traveling north on the highway toward Moosehorn.

It wasn't so much Domko's actions the night before, but rather his words that convinced Caroline to give their relationship another try. He promised to be more supportive of her religion and also that he would become a Jehovah's Witness. His attitude change came after visits from a member of the church, Nick Skleparik—a well-respected Witness who many people admired. Domko said that Nick's words had helped change him and he quoted Bible passages while asking her forgiveness.

"I's be but-a-some goot father," he promised.

Karen Emilson

The children remained wary of Domko even though it appeared he was a changed man. They had been back at the farm for nearly a week, and they were looking forward to starting school the next morning. The twins were in the barnyard, chattering to themselves when suddenly they stopped.

"What's that?" Dennis asked, pointing at a hay stack.

On the ground at the foot of the stack was what appeared to be a large rag doll partially covered in hay. They took a few steps then stopped when they realized it was their little sister lying face down.

"It's Rosie," Dennis gasped.

David leaned forward for a better look. "I think she's dead. Go touch her and see."

"I ain't gonna touch her, you touch her," Dennis replied.

David shook his head and started backing away. "We gotta tell Momma."

They ran to the house and burst through the door to find their mother and Domko standing in the middle of the kitchen floor arguing.

"You's be beechin' around," he screamed. His back was to them so they could see their mother's face over his shoulder. She was crying and arguing that he was wrong. There was no one else in the house except for Kathy who was in the front room.

David and Dennis turned and ran back outside, not stopping until they found a safe place to hide in the bush. They stayed there for the rest of the afternoon, until just before dark, then crept into the yard. Cautiously opening the kitchen door, David listened and then peered in. He could see straight into the front room where Eunice and Walter sat solemnly on the chesterfield. Kathy babbled and walked around them, trying to persuade someone to play with her. Their mother walked from one bedroom to the next.

"He's gone," David said, sensing the serenity in the house.

They went inside to find Norman and Steven playing cards at the kitchen table. The twins went straight to their mother.

"Momma," David whispered. "Where's Rosie?"

Gathering their toys, Caroline walked past them to the other room. Her face was purple, and her arms were full of bruises.

"Me and Denny saw Rosie by the haystack," he said.

"Hush," Caroline scolded, running her hands through her hair. She was fighting the urge to cry. "Go get into bed."

"But Momma," Dennis protested. "We're hungry—"

"Never mind, just go to bed. You won't starve by morning."

The boys were surprised by their mother's indifference. They began to whine but stopped when she raised her hand up to her face and started to cry. "Go now," she rasped.

They scurried into the bedroom and jumped on the bed. Seeing their mother so unhappy again was unsettling. Life was so good in Ashern that they wished they were still there.

Domko drove the tractor in high gear all the way to Moosehorn. He had left the house in a jealous rage after discovering that Caroline had been seeing a few men during their separation. He'd naively believed that he was her only suitor.

Domko's anger rose as he envisioned Caroline being intimate with another man. Cursing, he drove into the residential section of town then stopped the tractor in front of a small house. Before jumping down, he reached back and grabbed his rifle. Striding up the front walk, he began banging loudly on the door with the butt of the gun. He shoved the door open with his shoulder, almost taking it off its hinges when nobody answered.

"Julius?!" he screamed into the house.

A man emerged from the front room where he'd been reading, shocked to see Domko standing just inside the door. His eyes darted from the angry face to the gun he carried.

"Vere be some Julius?" Domko roared.

"Julius doesn't live here," the man said quickly, raising his hands in the air. "You've got the wrong house."

He recognized the intruder as Bob Domko, Caroline Pischke's common-law husband. Domko eyed him suspiciously. He looked around for a moment then stormed outside. The man ran to the door and locked it. Then he went to the telephone to dial his neighbor

"Is Julius there?" he said. "You'd better tell him to get out of there. Bob Domko was just here, and the crazy ass is looking for him, and he's carrying a rifle." He slammed down the phone and ran to look out a side window, giving him a clear view of the neighbor's house. He'd heard that Domko was crazy and that he'd threatened to kill Jim Deighton many times. This was his first encounter with the man and hoped it would be his last.

The back door of the neighbor's house flew open, and Julius poked his head out. Glancing from side to side, he jumped off the porch and fled into the bush behind the house.

Rosie spent that night outside beside the haystack. The twins checked her in the morning to discover she was conscious and had covered herself with hay. Domko was back, so she stayed there alone all that day and night. Caroline didn't dare check on the girl, fearing it would send Domko into another rage.

The following morning, Walter snuck Rosie back into the house. When Domko went outside to check to see if the cows were milked properly, Caroline signaled the children, and in less than a minute they were all running down the road toward the Harwart house. Unfortunately, the neighbors were not home, so they were forced to continue to Ashern on foot. They made it to the Township Line then heard the rumbling of a vehicle approaching. Caroline's first thought was that Domko had come looking for them, but when she spun around, saw it was an unfamiliar truck. It slowed as it pulled up beside them.

"Do you want a ride?" the driver asked.

Caroline smiled with relief. The driver was a large Indian fellow with long thick hair, a few missing teeth, and warm, sincere eyes. His young son stood on the front seat beside him, while his wife smiled timidly.

"To Ashern?" Caroline asked.

"We're going to Fairford," he said. "We'll take you as far as Moosehorn."

As the children climbed into the back of the truck, Caroline thanked the friendly man whose last name was Woodhouse. The boy in the front watched the kids through the rear cab window. At first, he peered through the window, then turned and buried his face in his mother's hair. Gradually, he began warming to the strange faces smiling back at him.

Caroline could see the man and woman talking in front. The vehicle came to a stop at the highway intersection then turned south towards Moosehorn. Instead of slowing as they approached the town, the truck accelerated, and it became obvious that they planned to take them all the way to Ashern before making the thirty-five-mile trip north to the Reserve.

Once in town, Caroline leaned towards the driver's side window and gave the man directions to the little house which had sat unoccupied for the past week. As she and the children climbed out of the truck, Caroline offered to pay, secretly hoping he'd refuse, since she had nothing to offer.

Smiling, he shook his head.

"When somebody needs help, you help them," he said quietly. "That is payment enough." Waving, he backed out of the driveway and Caroline watched until they were out of sight.

Life fell into a comfortable routine as the children began attending school again. They'd fallen behind in their studies but would soon catch up. Walter got a job as a newspaper carrier for the Winnipeg Free Press and Tribune. Soon he'd earned enough money to buy a gun from Thorkelsson's store. He joked that if Domko came around, he'd shoot him, and secretly hoped for the opportunity to protect his mother and siblings.

But life in town wasn't without its difficulties. Caroline's aborted attempt to reconcile with Domko, and the fact he was threatening Julius' life, caused wild speculation about her in town. Their mother's reputation embarrassed the older children who were teased at school, and Caroline found it difficult to face people when she was out. Pressure from the Witnesses added to her problems as it was made clear they did not approve of her behavior. Once again she pulled away from her religion and remembering her neglected childhood, began to give in to pressure from the children to celebrate special occasions such as Christmas and birthdays. The twins turned seven years old February 8 and much to everyone's surprise, she baked a birthday cake for them.

One afternoon, a member of the church showed up at the door to guide her back on the right path. This man continued to visit regularly for the next few months. Soon Caroline was attending meetings again and reading the Bible. Sometimes the man would bring his briefcase, and they would discuss religion, but sometimes he wouldn't. The children usually had to stay outside for many hours while they had a private visit. They tried to avoid him because he wasn't very nice and criticized them whenever their mother wasn't around.

On a sunny Saturday afternoon, the children decided to go for a walk while they waited for the man to leave. They chatted to each other as they pulled Kathy on a small sleigh, west along the road toward the school. It had snowed the night before, so people were out shoveling.

"Hi kids," one neighbor called out as they shuffled along. "Where are you off to?"

"We're going for a walk," Norman said. "We gotta stay outside until the man from the church leaves."

The neighbor frowned as he looked at the children, then toward their house. He had heard rumors about their mother's promiscuity and wondered if they were true. The women in town were gossiping viciously about Caroline.

The children continued to the school grounds where they played until their hands and feet started to freeze. They arrived home to find the man was gone and their mother was in good spirits.

Heavy winter storms kept Domko isolated on the farm. As soon as the spring thaw arrived, so did he, bringing gifts and apologies again.

Suspecting that he only wanted them to return to work, Caroline vowed not to fall victim to his cajoling again. She refused to send Walter back to the farm because he was a good worker and could easily earn money by working for a farmer near town. But telling Domko this, was not easy. She just wasn't good at saying no to men. She was raised to believe that a husband was the head of the house and wives obeyed without question. She was expected to bear children, care for them and the house, and do half the farm work. She didn't mind the work but despised being beaten. As a way to placate Domko, she allowed him into her bed and gave him money from her mother's allowance check whenever he asked. As long as she stayed away from the farm, he treated her and the children well.

She had always longed for a better life, and now she had one. She was enjoying the attention of a few men and that added spice to her life and created the drama that she craved.

One evening while Domko was visiting, there was a knock at the door. Caroline answered to find a local drunkard who had been dared by a few men at the tavern to ask her out. Domko flew into a rage. Neighbors telephoned the police, but by the time they arrived, Domko had beaten the man unconscious. To the children's delight, Domko spent the night in jail.

Over the next year, he continued to visit and pester Caroline to go back to the farm. She dated him and a few others, refusing to give a firm answer. The children were settled nicely in Ashern, enjoying the freedom of town life. They made friends and even went to the Ashern theater a few times. Not one of them wanted to go back to the farm, including Walter, who was older now and had made some friends.

"I'm pregnant," Caroline said to her neighbor one afternoon that spring. Nobody dared ask who the father was. Caroline knew, but her options would be fewer if she told. She decided she would keep it a secret until the time was right.

This latest pregnancy did not please members of her church. To have a child out of wedlock was barely forgivable once, but twice? During the next few months, she received pressure from both the Hilbre and Ashern Witness groups to reveal the father's name. The older children listened as the Witnesses advised her to repent and ask forgiveness. She was also told to return to the farm and marry Domko. She refused. Once again she was alienated from the group that had been like family for the past ten years.

Soon afterward a social worker arrived from Winnipeg.

"Where's Martha?" Caroline asked after inviting the man inside.

"She married and moved to Selkirk," he said. "I'm her replacement."

He asked Caroline a few questions, recording her answers in a file. She sensed that something was wrong by the tone of his voice.

"Caroline," he began, "We have received an anonymous letter saying that you have had regular visits from your common-law husband. Could you please explain this?"

Caroline was shocked. She knew that the rules stipulated she could not have a man living in the house while she was receiving mother's allowance payments. Overnight visits were discouraged by welfare officials, but she could see no other way to stop Domko's harassment. She wondered who might hate her enough to report her to the authorities. A few names came to mind, including the father of her unborn child.

"He comes to visit his child," she said. "He doesn't come very often."

The man met her gaze and held it until she turned away.

"I'm afraid that we have a handwritten letter that says Mr. Domko has been staying overnight on a regular basis, showing that the two of you are behaving as husband and wife," he said. "Since it appears that you and he have worked out your differences, we have to cut you off."

Caroline was horrified and couldn't even argue. Recklessness had cost the family's freedom.

ANTICIPATION

Marjorie Harwart's favorite job was driving her father's team of horses. She loved the feel of reins in her hands and enjoyed putting in a full day's work with the beautiful, cooperative animals.

At thirteen years old, Marjorie was quite a tomboy. Her hair, cut short, was held off her face by a hat which also protected her from the sun. Her thin arms and legs were tanned brown, and a light sprinkling of freckles lined her nose. She liked haying season best since it gave her the opportunity to be with the horses. The days were long now, and she had spent that afternoon raking hay in the north quarter. Her father had left her alone while he cut hay in another field.

Marjorie sat on the seat as the hay rake tines clattered behind her while the horses trotted down the road. The sun threw a shadow in front of her as it set behind the tall trees lining her route.

It had been a wet spring, but June and July were warm and dry. Now, farmers in the area were concentrating on harvesting hay on the high ground. A few more weeks of sunny weather and they would be able to cut the low spots. If the weather held out, Marjorie would be raking the following day again, then helping her father stack the day after that. It was never a good idea to cut and rake too much before stacking since it would sometimes rain and spoil the hay.

The grumbling in Marjorie's stomach told her it was long past supper time. Mosquitoes swirled up from the grass as the horses trotted along, eager to get home. The cool evening breeze felt good on her sweaty skin.

Life for her had been different since Caroline moved the children to town. She had friends at school, but the Pischkes were her closest neighbors, and she missed their daily contact.

As she approached the Pischke farm, she saw more activity in the yard than usual. It looked as though Domko had visitors and she recognized Walter and Norman as she got closer. Then she saw Eunice pumping water from the outdoor well. The twins were at the edge of the yard.

"Hey you guys," she yelled, waving one hand high above her head. "It's me—Marjorie!"

Eunice looked up and waved excitedly. The children stopped what they were doing and ran to the road. Marjorie stopped the horses, jumped down and ran towards her friends. They were back.

The twins had grown quite a bit since she had seen them last. For a moment she couldn't tell them apart. Then the more aggressive one took a step forward, and she recognized David.

Eunice had also grown. She was ten years old now and just as talkative as ever. Walter was still skinny and awkward at fifteen. She glanced at Norman then looked away quickly. The thirteen-year-old caused her heart to flutter. He was still the most handsome boy she knew.

After a few awkward moments, the children were laughing and joking as always.

"What are you guys doing here?" Marjorie asked.

"Uncle John brought us back," Eunice said. "We're gonna live at the farm again."

"Yeah," Norman added. "Momma said Domko has changed, but he's makin' us work again already."

"Our Momma's gonna have another baby," Eunice said quickly. "Isn't that exciting?"

Marjorie nodded. She knew that Domko was mean to the kids but didn't know to what extent. Rather than thinking about him, she concentrated on how happy she was to have her friends home.

"She's back with Domko?" Emma asked.

"They came back today," Marjorie said, as she removed her shoes at the door. "Isn't that great?"

Emma didn't answer. She was glad to have her neighbor back for selfish reasons but knew it was not best for the children.

Gus shook his head. For the past two and a half years Domko had been crazy as ever. Following the botched reconciliation, Gus hoped that Caroline would have enough sense to stay away for good.

"I don't know what to think about this," Emma said. "Here's your supper."

"Oh yeah," Marjorie said, taking the plate from her mother. "Caroline's going to have another baby."

Gus and Emma looked at each other. Emma rolled her eyes, then slipped on her shoes. "I'm going over to talk with her myself," she said.

Gus nodded, then stared silently out the kitchen window.

Emma returned home to tell Gus that Domko seemed quite pleased with himself that Caroline was back. It validated his notion that he was the center of the universe, and that every decision or action was to his benefit or detriment. There were no gray areas as far as he was concerned, and she thought that his attitude was getting worse.

Caroline was noticeably pregnant again, but this didn't seem to bother Domko, as long as she continued cooking, milking the cows and doing all the jobs he detested. Emma noticed during the visit that he stayed in the kitchen so that the women wouldn't be alone. It was strange behavior for a man, listening in on women's gossip.

Walter had learned a lot the summer before while working for a farmer near Ashern. It made working for Domko again much more difficult. The day began when he rose with the sun and started barking commands. Everyone except Rosie and Kathy rushed outside to milk cows, feed and water the livestock, pigs, and chickens. By late morning they were cutting and sweeping hay. This was a long job that took most of the summer to finish, but because Domko's equipment was so antiquated, it was much more labor intensive than on land where farmers had tractors and modern haying equipment such as metal rakes and stackers. Walter casually mentioned this to Domko one day and was berated for even bringing up the subject—as far as Domko was concerned, the way he did things was best.

Walter could see that haying with horses and old-fashioned equipment was a dangerous job for children. A runaway team or miscalculation could cause a tremendous amount of damage or cost a young worker his life. He was both thankful and surprised that they'd managed to squeak through earlier years as farmhands virtually unharmed. While working near town, he'd heard stories about careless young farmhands who lost a limb after falling off the seat and landing in front of the mower. Another had become tangled in the rake tines and dragged across the ground and nearly killed.

Often in the afternoon, Domko would take a load of hay home and not return to the field until after taking a nap. This was a tremendous relief to the children who were able to stop working, have a drink of water and maybe play a bit. It was Walter's responsibility to keep his siblings on track. He'd let them have the occasional break but always made sure they got the work done. Sometimes they would come across a patch of ripe wild strawberries or Saskatoon berries. He always let them stop for a while and often it was all they had to eat the entire day.

After working for two solid weeks without a break, the children were hoping for rain. One evening while they were resting in their bedroom after a particularly long day, Domko called them to the kitchen. His voice was soft, almost kind. They looked at each other and then slowly went to see what he wanted.

Sitting in his usual spot, Domko had a row of eight chocolate bars on the table. "Kathy," he called in a soft voice. "I's be givink you some choklit bar."

Kathy toddled toward the sound of his voice. Domko had been giving her plenty of treats, so she came whenever he called. He took one bar from the table and pulled back the wrapper, placing it in her hand. Her eyes stared without focus, but she had no trouble getting the bar into her mouth. The other children were amazed.

"Who's I's be givink but-a-some choklit bar next?" he cooed. The children looked at one another and then finally all eyes turned to Walter for guidance. Walter was impressed. Here was the same man who had treated him kindly two summers before.

If only we could work harder and do a better job, he would treat us like this all the time, Walter thought. He looked at Dennis who was asking for guidance. Walter smiled at him.

Dennis loved sweets, and he missed his father so much. He believed what his mother said, that Domko would treat them better if they were good. He had tried especially hard these past few weeks and hadn't received a beating for a while. Maybe his mother was right. All he had to do was to be a good boy. Stepping forward, he gave Domko a wide, eager smile.

"Here Dennis," he coaxed, taking a bar from the table and holding it out. "I's be givink you some."

Dennis walked slowly forward and stopped. Just as he reached out to take it, Domko let out a roar.

"Fraa," he screamed, flinging his right arm into the air over his head.

Lunging forward, he grabbed Dennis by the arm. The other children scattered as Caroline hurried into the room in time to see Domko slip off his belt and begin strapping Dennis.

"Choklit bar?" he taunted, "I's be givink you some!"

Dennis screamed every time the belt snapped against his legs, and he could hear his mother yelling and felt Domko's arm jolt back as she tried to pull him away. He hadn't beaten the children for weeks and was particularly ferocious tonight. For a few moments, Domko turned away from Dennis and began beating Caroline, catching her across the chest, back and head until finally, she ran crying from the house.

Dennis lay in a heap on the floor, unable to move. Tired from the effort, Domko stood over him for a few moments, chest heaving. Then in one swoop, he gathered the chocolate bars and stormed past Dennis into his bedroom, hiding the bars in a dresser drawer that was off limits to the children. This time he sounded particularly satisfied with himself as he lit a cigarette and chuckled to himself as Dennis lay weeping on the floor.

It was a quiet, chilly night and the mosquitoes were thick. It was the time of year that the sky stayed softly lit, and during a full moon, it was barely dark at all. The children lay in a fresh haystack looking silently up at the stars. The only sound that interrupted the clear night was the chirping of crickets and David's soft, occasional moan. While the other children didn't understand it, they knew that when Dennis got a beating, David suffered as well. Tonight, his legs were sore, and he squirmed in the hay, moaning softly. It pained him to know that his twin was lying somewhere in the house without him.

Norman was the first to speak.

"You know there's a great place not too far away," he began, voice soft as a dream. "It's across the lake by the beaver dam. It's a place where there's lots to eat, and dads are good to kids."

The children liked it when Norman told stories. He had a great imagination and always knew what to say to make them feel better.

"I'm gonna build us a plane and fly us across the beaver dam," he said. "I got it started already."

They had noticed that Norman was sneaking away from work and even got a beating for it one night, but they had no idea he was putting his time to such productive use.

"Where is it?" Steven asked.

"It's hidden in the bush," he said.

"What color is it—" Eunice asked.

"You don't got a pilot license," Walter interrupted. "You can't fly without a license."

"Do we all gets to go? Me and Denny and Rosie, too?" David asked sitting up in the hay so he could see Norman's face.

"Shhh," Norman said, sitting up and crossing his legs. He looked first at Steven. He was hesitant to say where the plane was in case one of them told Domko in a weak or vengeful moment.

"It's in the bush, but that's all I'm sayin'," he said. Then he turned to Eunice. "It's just wood color since it don't got to be no color to fly." Then he looked at Walter. "I don't care 'bout no pilot's license. I been readin' how to do it and I'm gonna fly whether they like it or not. I'd like to see the police try and stop me."

The children listened intently as Norman's confidence grew.

"When I get the plane finished we'll all fly away," he said. "First me and Walter will go, then Steven, then I'll come back to get the twins."

David clapped his hands.

"What 'bout me an Rosie?" Eunice asked.

Norman smiled. "You can't come 'cause you talk too much."

"Hey," she giggled, throwing a clump of hay at him, some of it landing on his shoulder.

"Just kiddin'," he said, brushing it off. "I'll get you guys, too."

Norman talked for a while about the plane and how wonderful life would be for them once they got over the beaver dam.

"H-how long will it take to finish?" Walter asked.

Norman thought for a moment. "Well, I got the directions from a book I stole from school," he said. "I think it'll take about another week."

David looked at his older brother, and his heart swelled with admiration. He knew he could count on Norman to get them off the farm.

Morning came, and David could hardly wait to find Dennis to tell him the great news. He jumped up and brushed the hay off himself then trotted to the house and went inside. His brother was lying quietly on the bed. His forehead was beaded with sweat, and wide, purple blisters had swollen his legs. Flies buzzed around the dried blood where the belt buckle had cut through his skin.

"Dennis," he whispered. "Get up Dennis. I gots great news."

Dennis slowly opened his eyes. Their secret language was a welcome sound in contrast to Domko's ravings. Surprisingly, he didn't resent the fact he usually was the one caught by Domko. He'd felt sympathy pains, too, and honestly didn't know what he'd do without David.

"What?" he asked through parched lips.

"C'mon Dennis," he said, gingerly pulling his brother's arm. "Let's go 'fore he comes back."

David was right. They should get out of sight. He sat up on the bed then swung his legs over the side. Carefully he stood, leaning on David. Glancing around nervously, they hobbled to the door then opening it, could hear yelling from inside the barn. Hurrying in the opposite direction, they disappeared into the bush, following a trail for about ten minutes before deciding to rest. They decided this would be a good place to spend the day, rather than risk facing Domko again. Sometimes after a beating, he would challenge the child again as soon as he was on his feet. Walter and Steven were able to ignore the taunting, while Norman would talk back and then run away as fast as he could. The twins weren't that brave and usually started to cry—which was seen as a sign of weakness and he'd usually beat them again.

Except for the insects, being in the bush during the summertime was pleasant. The boys relaxed against a fallen tree and looked upwards, listening to the chirping birds and feeling bits of warm sun that shone through the leaves like confetti. This was an old bush full of oak and poplars, so the undergrowth was minimal and a perfect place for youngsters to hide.

"Norman's makin' a plane and he's gonna fly us outta here," David said, pleased that he had waited for the right moment to tell his brother the plan. "He says that over the beaver dam it's like Ashern and he's gonna fly us there."

Dennis was impressed with the idea. "Who gets to go?"

"Us all," David said. "But we can't tell Momma."

Dennis nodded. "Where we gonna live?"

David thought for a moment. "Maybe with some nice people like the ones with the big car," he said, remembering the time they were nearly put into a foster home.

"It don't matter," Dennis said. "Long as Domko ain't there."

Rain finally came in July. Domko rose early, looked out the window and grunted. He ate and shaved—a sure sign that he planned to spend the day in town. While the older boys helped their mother milk the cows, the younger ones played quietly in the bedroom, careful not to let their excitement show.

Caroline came in shortly after breakfast and spoke to Domko in Polish. Eunice listened in then nodded happily to her siblings that the adults were going to town and all the children would stay behind except Kathy.

The full cream can was pulled up from the well and loaded into the back of the truck that Domko had borrowed from Caroline's brother, John Kolodka. Caroline and Bill had owned a car, but there was a lien on it, so it was repossessed shortly after his death. Domko was embarrassed to travel to town by horse or tractor so he borrowed John's truck whenever he could and hoped to buy a vehicle of his own someday.

Domko was often pleasant when he returned from town as the trip gave him the chance to get away from the children, cash the cream check, and pick up a few supplies. He'd behave generously in front of others, buying treats for himself and Kathy while privately begrudging Caroline every cent she spent on her children. He'd show off and brag to anyone who'd listen about the number of cattle he had. Men at the creamery listened politely, but unbeknownst to him, they'd criticize and sometimes laugh the moment he left.

The children were left with a list of chores that had to be completed before sundown, but as soon as they were alone, they began cheering and playing in the rain. Then Norman told them to follow him into the bush.

They had been pestering him to show them the plane. The younger children struggled to keep up as the older ones ran along a well-worn path until they came to a small clearing at the edge of the bush. Behind a rock pile, was the makings of Norman's plane.

He had nailed together three wooden apple crates and was making a pair of wings from the box tops, nailed together end-to-end. He had painted a number eight with a circle around it on each side of the fuselage.

The children intently listened as Norman explained exactly how it would work. He held up a propeller to show how it would propel the plane through the sky.

"We gotta wait for a windy day," he said. "That way the prop will turn fastest."

Walter and Steven looked skeptical. They moved closer to take a better look. "It don't got no w-wheels," Walter said. "How's it gonna take off without wheels?"

"It don't need wheels, stupid," Norman replied. "It's a glider, but with a prop so it can go on wind power. We'll put it on the barn roof, and the wind will take us up." Picking up the book he was reading, he wiped a wet page across the back of his pants and pointed to the picture.

Walter and Steven looked at each other, shrugging their shoulders, and decided to go back to the house. The twins, Eunice and Rosie, stayed behind. They thought the plane was a good one and told him so.

"We'll go without 'em," Dennis said, trying to make Norman feel better. "We ain't got no room for them anyhow."

Norman started fiddling with what would soon be the tail of the plane. Even though he didn't show it, he appreciated his brother's faith. He could always count on Dennis to say a kind word.

By afternoon, the skies began to clear, and when the sun poked out from behind the retreating clouds, Marjorie came over to play.

The children finished the chores then followed Marjorie home, hoping

Emma would feed them, and as usual, there was always lots for everyone to eat. The children played outside until they saw the borrowed truck coming down the road.

Walter sent Steven home to see if Domko was in a good mood while the rest hid in the bush. Steven returned a few minutes later to say it was safe to go home. The first thing they noticed as they came up the driveway was a dog standing in the back of the truck.

The children gathered around the medium-sized, male dog that watched them from the truck box. He had wiry, blotchy brown fur and his ears perked, and tail wagged gently as the children patted him. He smelled their hands then his tongue lolled out of his mouth in what looked like a smile.

Norman began coaxing him to jump out of the truck.

"What are we gonna name him?" he said, just as his mother came out of the house. Nothing the children suggested seemed to fit the dog's appearance.

"When I was a girl, I had a dog like that, and I called him Bruno," she said, as Walter picked up a heavy bag of flour and carried it into the house.

"Bruno," Norman said, looking at the dog edging his way to the truck gate. When he finally jumped to the ground, the kids gathered around him. They rubbed his fur roughly and then began squabbling over who would be the first to hug him. Bruno enjoyed the attention, rolling onto the ground and sticking his feet in the air.

"C'mon Bruno," Norman called. "I got a stick for you."

The dog watched him carefully. Norman pointed the stick then threw it across the yard. Recognizing the game, Bruno ran for it, bringing it back and dropping it his feet.

"Hey, I trained him already," Norman said, then told everyone that Bruno was the smartest dog that ever lived.

That evening the children watched as Domko opened a package containing a cake. He cut a huge piece for himself, then called Kathy over. The other children sat on the floor watching as the two-year-old fumbled with the cake, their mouths watering as she stuffed the cake in her mouth, smearing icing all over her hands and face.

When he'd finished eating, Domko wrapped what was left of the cake and put it on top of the cupboard which sat against the wall. The cupboard was an old-fashioned, green, two-piece unit where Caroline kept towels, dishes, and jars.

Domko watched them with a grin as the children kept glancing up at the cake. Caroline noticed this and shook her head. Why did he enjoy taunting them so much? She had argued with him about this, and the fact that he didn't think money earned on the farm should support her children. Whenever she brought up the subject, it created a violent rift between them that lasted for days. She could never change his mind, so it hardly seemed worth the effort.

The next afternoon the children worked outside while Domko took a nap. Because the ground was still soft from the rain, Caroline and the twins went to the garden to pick weeds and vegetables.

The boys carried a five-gallon pail filled with new potatoes, carrots, and beets back to the yard. David used his weight to push down the handle of the outdoor water pump while Dennis held the vegetables underneath and scrubbed off the dirt. Walter had butchered a chicken that morning, so everyone was looking forward to a hardy meal.

As they carried the vegetables into the kitchen, David's eyes instinctively shot up at the cake on top of the cupboard. Trying to fool his stomach he took a bite from a carrot but soon realized this wasn't going to satisfy his desire for chocolate.

If I eat the cake he'll never know, he thought, mentally calculating how long it would take to grab the cake, eat it, and disappear into the bush. He looked at Dennis who was diligently dropping potatoes into their mother's large pot.

"Hey Denny," he whispered, pointing to the cake.

Dennis looked up then smiled mischievously. "Should we?"

David shrugged.

"Who's gonna get it?"

"You go watch," David said pointing towards the front room.

"No," Dennis protested, shaking his head. "If he sees me, I'm dead."

David rolled his eyes and motioned for him to go. "Hurry before he wakes up."

Dennis gave him another mischievous grin, then tiptoed towards the front room. Slowly he craned his neck around the corner, seeing that Domko was still asleep on the chesterfield. His arms were across his chest, and he snored quietly. Dennis looked back, signaling David to get the cake while he stood watch.

David slid a small stool in front of the cupboard, then quietly climbed on top. Gripping the side of the cupboard, he braced one foot on the edge of it then stretched to reach the cake but was too short. He glanced at Dennis who was motioning for him to hurry up, so he hoisted himself up onto

Karen Emilson

the edge. He stood on his toes then grabbed the cake with one hand. As he tried to step back down onto the stool, he slipped and grabbed the side of the cupboard causing it to rock forward. The doors swung open, and everything from inside began crashing to the floor. He lost his footing and fell backward then the cupboard came crashing down on him. He struggled to breathe as the heavy wooden box pinned him to the floor.

The commotion woke Domko who jumped from the couch, and Dennis froze on the spot. As he stormed by, he gave Dennis a backhand across the face, sending him tumbling across the kitchen floor. Dennis scrambled under the table and watched as Domko lifted up the cupboard.

"You soneebeech bastard," he said, the vein on his forehead protruding as he picked up a block of wood from beside the cook stove. "You's be breakink it. You's be some goot for nuthink!"

David covered his head with his arms as the wood crashed down on his arms and chest as Domko swung hard, the momentum lifting his feet off the floor. David screamed as pieces of bark flew in all directions. He turned on his side to try and escape Domko's heavy boots.

Caroline came running in to see David pinned against the cupboard and Domko kicking him.

"Boleslaw," she screamed, grabbing him by the arm and distracting him enough that David was able to scramble towards the door. "That's enough. You're gonna kill him!"

"Ruch a muchtork booken," David yelled in the secret language to Dennis as he disappeared outside.

Domko pushed her away and then lifting his leg up, kicked her karate-style directly in the abdomen, sending her flying across the kitchen into the milk pails piled near the door. She curled her arms protectively around her stomach as he kicked her twice in the back before storming outside after David.

Dennis waited for a few minutes then crawled out from under the table towards his mother. "Momma," he sobbed. "Get up before he comes back."

She sobbed and groaned then slowly pulled herself up and with Dennis' help, staggered to the bedroom. She slid onto the bed then turned towards the wall.

"Go hide Dennis," she cried. "Go find David."

Dennis stared at his mother's back, then glanced over his shoulder. He didn't want to leave but was too afraid to stay. He ran into the kitchen and before dashing out the door, grabbed the cake package that was sitting in the middle of the floor. He ran into the bush beside the house then turned east.

Within a few minutes, he caught up with David who was sitting alongside the path waiting for him. He was leaning against Bruno who looked as if he was standing guard.

"I gots the cake," Dennis said holding up the bag. "That ol' devil ain't gonna get none tonight!"

David laughed then coughed in pain as Dennis ripped open the bag and divided the cake. They ate slowly, knowing there wouldn't be much else in the days to come. When they finished, David got up and followed Dennis into the thick foliage with Bruno on his heels.

Caroline slept for the rest of the afternoon. When Domko came in, he stood by the bed solemnly as Caroline groaned and held her swollen belly. He softly apologized and begged her forgiveness, sitting beside the bed for an hour at a time.

He put the cupboard back in place then returned everything that wasn't broken to the shelves. As evening approached, he quietly told the boys to finish the chores while Eunice cooked supper and Steven kept Kathy from bothering their mother. Caroline rested on the bed all night. Domko slept in the children's bed, and they moved to the floor mattress. The older boys slept outside in the hay, but nobody knew where the twins were.

ALL HOPE IS LOST

"Do coyotes eat kids?" Dennis asked as they lay side by side at the edge of the bush, staring up at the night sky. In his dreams coyotes sometimes attacked him and their howling in the distance was frightening.

"No, they only eat mice and skunks," David said trying to sound brave. He felt better with one arm on Bruno whose ears occasionally perked at the eerie sounds in the bush. "We don't gots to worry 'cause we got Bruno here."

David was thinking about home and how helpless he felt.

"Do you 'spose that ol' Satan is ever gonna go away?" he asked as he patted Bruno's rough fur.

"I dunno," Dennis said. "But it don't matter no more 'cause Norman's gonna fly us over the beaver dam."

David was feeling bad that his mother had received a beating because of him, but he was too ashamed to admit this to Dennis. He silently vowed that she'd never receive a beating on his account again.

"Think we should tell Momma?" he asked.

"Norman said not to tell," Dennis said. "And it's his plane."

The following morning Caroline barely stirred. She trembled with fever and sweat poured from her body. Her groans caused the children to gather around, and they wondered if she might die. Domko ushered them out of the house, leaving only Kathy and Rosie in the front room where they played quietly, sensing that something was seriously wrong.

Caroline's water broke in the early afternoon. The contractions came fast and hard after that. Rosie didn't dare go into the room where her mother was crying in pain. Domko was in there, and she didn't know what he was doing to her. After a while, the moaning subsided then the room echoed with angry whispers.

Rosie followed the sound of her mother's footsteps into the kitchen.

She stood in the doorway watching as her mother padded around the kitchen, wrapped in a robe. She was angry with Domko, and he stood with his back to Rosie, stoop-shouldered, begging for forgiveness. Rosie slipped by, not sure what might happen next, wanting to get outside where it was safe. As she crept past the kitchen table, she glanced into a white washtub. The sight took her breath away. The basin was full of blood, fluid, and a large slippery mass. A bluish baby covered in a white film, its knees pulled up tightly to its chest lay on top. It was stiff, and dead-looking with eyes and mouth sealed shut.

Her gasp caused her mother and Domko to turn and see her staring into the washbasin. He grabbed a cast iron frying pan from the top of the stove and lunged at her.

"No, Boleslaw," Caroline screamed.

He immediately stopped. Rosie saw a look of anger and confusion in his eyes. His arm shook as he lowered the pan. He growled, and she knew that was her cue to run.

"She's too little—she'll never remember this," Rosie heard her mother say as she darted out the door.

"Norman, when are we gonna fly across the beaver dam?" Dennis asked two days later as he and David tagged behind. Their stomachs ached with hunger, but neither dared say anything as it was their first day back since stealing the cake.

"If it's windy, we can go tomorrow," Norman said, sticking one finger into his mouth then pointing it into the air. He gazed at the sky. "Yep, the wind's comin' from the right direction."

The twins looked at one another, clearly impressed.

"Domko's inside, so we'll work on the plane tonight," Norman said. "You guys gonna help me?"

The twins were eager to do whatever he asked. Flying over the beaver dam was all they could think about since he told them about the plane.

"C'mon let's go then," he said. "I need help getting it into the clearing."

Turning the plane on its side, they were able to carry it down the path, stopping for periodic rests before finally reaching the barn. Setting it down beside a haystack, they decided that it would be best to cover it with hay for the night.

Domko was sitting at the table reading when they went inside. They crept past, avoiding his gaze. Their mother was already asleep in the master bedroom, and the girls were whispering to each other on the bed in their room. The twins found a spot on the mattress and chattered quietly to one another in the secret language. They were famished but ignored the pangs, and even smiled. They weren't worried because, after tomorrow, they'd never be hungry again.

Morning came, and the twins jumped out of bed. They were thrilled to see the tree tops bending in the wind through the window. They smiled when their eyes met.

Walter, Steven, and Norman were already milking the cows, so the twins hurried out to the barn, avoiding Domko who stood watching until the milking was done. He assigned a chore to each child then went back into the house. It promised to be a good drying day, so he expected them to begin stacking hay by late afternoon. Wouldn't he be surprised when they flew past him overhead!

As soon as he was gone, the children ran to the back of the barn. Carrying her cat, Rosie tagged along, hoping that the big kids would finally explain why everyone had been whispering so much lately.

The boys had to figure out a way to hoist the plane onto the barn roof. Norman was growing impatient because the wind was blowing heavily from the West, exactly the direction he wanted, so he was anxious to get into the air. They decided to tie a rope around the plane just behind the wings. When he was satisfied that it was tight enough, Norman disappeared around the corner of the barn.

The twins chattered excitedly, and within a minute, Norman was on top of the shanty-style barn roof.

"Throw it up to me," he said, hanging over the edge. Walter grabbed the rope end and threw it up a few times until Norman caught it.

"Lift up the plane," he yelled, pulling the rope taut. Walter and the twins got underneath and lifted the plane as high as they could. Soon it was dangling six feet off the ground as Norman held it steady from the roof.

"C'mon up and help me," he called as he struggled to keep his balance. Walter climbed the loft ladder and hurried to the roof. His bare feet gripped the wooden shingles as he helped pull the plane higher. Eunice, Rosie, and the twins watched from below as it balanced precariously on the edge of the roof. Norman and Walter were able to pull it the rest of the way and then dragged it to the highest point facing north.

The wind was strong, and the children's spirits were high. The plane sat at the very edge of the roof with the front end hanging over. The Twins wanted to get a better view of the take-off, so they stood on the manure pile directly under the plane, watching as Norman and Walter climbed in. Since

Norman was the pilot, he sat at the front, and it was his responsibility to crank the prop while Walter pushed with his arms.

"What about Rosie and Bruno?" Walter asked pointing to his sister who stood a short distance away. Bruno was also watching.

"I'll come back for them later," Norman said. "We gotta go."

They tried to coax the plane closer to the edge by rocking their bodies back and forth, and once they got a bit of momentum, the plane began to inch its way forward.

Norman and Walter let out a yell, and the twins screamed as the plane suddenly tilted forward and plunged to the ground, crashing less than a foot from the twins on the manure pile.

On impact, Walter banged his face against the back of Norman's head then they rolled down the six-foot pile, laying stunned on the ground.

"What happened?" Dennis asked. "I thought you was gonna fly?"

Norman jumped up and kicked what remained of the fuselage. He knew deep in his heart that the plane wasn't going to fly but desperately wanted to leave the farm and take his brothers and sisters with him.

"Stupid thing," he said, kicking the box again. "One of these days I'm gonna get a real plane, and I'm gonna fly wherever I want."

The twins watched as he wiped his eyes with the back of his hand then ran into the bush.

"He almost flew," Dennis said, voice rising with optimism. "Maybe we can go next time."

After Domko had discovered the remnants of the plane, Norman received a whipping, which he took bravely, barely crying out as his siblings watched from the bush. Seeing Norman beaten was sobering for them, and they began to lose hope of ever escaping. Sadly, the younger children could not remember life before Domko came to the farm. His disposition was like a wildfire scorching prairie land—all consuming, rolling over whatever stood in his path, filling everyone around him with fear and desperation.

That summer, the twins spent as much time as they could in the bush not too far from the house. From here they could see what was going on in the yard, making it difficult for Domko to sneak up on them.

The twins slipped easily into their world of make-believe. They could play for hours with twigs, leaves, and stones. Each night brought hope that Domko would miraculously disappear, but when they awoke to find him still there the next morning, they would simply console one another in the hope that the next day would be better.

One afternoon David and Dennis dragged old pieces of wood to a hiding place in the bush and built themselves a crude fort. They made it comfortable with eating utensils, old dishes and the occasional tin of canned food they were able to sneak from the house. Nobody, including their mother, seemed to care that they spent most of their time outside.

One late August afternoon, the Twins were playing near their fort along the edge of the bush when David discovered an interesting hole near the base of a poplar tree, a hole they had never noticed before, one big enough for a rabbit or skunk.

"Hey, Denny," he said. "What you think lives in there?"

Dennis bent over to look inside. "I dunno."

"Stick your arm in and see."

Dennis shrugged and then kneeling beside the hole, stuck his arm inside. He got in up to his elbow then felt something. Quickly pulling his arm out, he jumped back, then edged forward again and peered in, but it was too dark to see anything. He reached in again and felt what appeared to be a box.

"Buried treasure," he exclaimed. He dug inside and grabbing hold of it, pulled, and a piece snapped off in his hand. It was part of an apple box, similar to what Norman had used to build his plane. Reaching in again, he tugged on something soft, ripping it as it pulled out, cotton filling from an old quilt. Now they were curious, and their imaginations began running wild—excited at the prospect of finding something valuable in the hole. David started digging beside him, and they became so engrossed in what they were doing, they didn't hear Domko's approach.

"Fraa," he yelled, causing the twins to scramble away.

"You's be gettink away from it," he roared. "If I's be seeink you here, I's be killink you soneebeech bastard."

They turned and ran into the bush until they were safely out of reach. They knelt down and watched as Domko fell to his knees and began stuffing the cotton back into the hole, then refilled it with dirt.

"What's he doin'?" Dennis asked.

"I dunno," David said, still curious about what was in the box. He told Dennis they should move their fort to this spot so that they could keep an eye on what was probably a treasure, and maybe start digging again. Dennis agreed. They moved their fort to the hiding place, but the following afternoon returned to discover it smashed apart.

Walter topped up his pail with a five-pound rock and then grabbing the handle with both hands, half dragged, half carried it to the wagon that sat a road's width away. Reaching into the pail, he tossed each rock up onto the wagon, and when the pail was empty, paused for a moment to squint at the sky. It was only late morning, but the sun was already hot. By noon, it would be ninety degrees, and if they were lucky, that same heat would bring a thunderstorm, breaking a week-long heat wave.

Steven and Norman each had pails to fill while the twins shared one. The land was freshly broken, and Domko hoped to seed it to oats next spring, but first all the rocks had to be picked off.

"Good l-luck," Walter said to himself, looking out over the rough field that was more rock than soil.

Domko hollered at him to get back to work, so he picked up his pail and went back to where he'd left off. The brothers worked in silence for a few more hours until Domko grew tired of barking orders from the horse's saddle, and decided to go home for a rest. He told them to keep working, and they did until he was out of sight.

The twins continued dropping rocks in their bucket until the older boys stood up, stretching their stiff backs.

"I shoulda done it," Norman said, squinting into the sun and then shaking his head. "I ain't no chicken like you."

Walter wiped the sweat from his forehead, and then he pounced on Norman, wrestling him to the ground. He was bigger and stronger, but Norman had a wild, mean streak that made him difficult to beat. The twins watched—not sure who to cheer for—until the boys agreed to a truce. They laughed and gasped for breath as they sat up and took turns to see who could fling mud chunks the furthest without standing up.

"Shoulda done what?" David asked.

Walter side-armed a chunk of mud that hit a tree at the edge of the bush. He raised his eyebrows at Norman, challenging him to do better. Then he looked thoughtfully at the twins. He almost didn't tell them what he was thinking for fear they might repeat what he was about to say. But their speech was nearly undecipherable, so his worry was short lived.

"Kill the bugger," he said.

Norman chuckled. "We were gonna kill him and burn his body so nobody'd ever find him," he said, flinging a rock but missing the tree. "If Walter hadn't chickened out, we wouldn't be pickin' no rocks today."

Walter shrugged. The twins begged him to tell them the story, so he did, explaining that the day before he'd hid near a rock pile with the gun he'd bought in town, but when Domko came by, he didn't have the courage to pull the trigger. The twins looked at one another in amazement. Killing

Domko was a better idea than trying to fly away in Norman's plane. The thought had never occurred to them, but now that it was planted in their minds, they could hardly think of anything else.

Domko returned a short while later, and everyone went back to work. If he noticed the lightness in the Twins' step and their smiling glances, he never let on. They slipped away later that afternoon and hid near the church. "Somebody's gotta kill him before he kills us," David said. "Do you think Norman will?"

Dennis thought for a moment. "If he don't, then I will," he said.

David was surprised. He'd always assumed Dennis was too timid to do such a thing, and the declaration forced him to look at his brother again, but this time, closer. Something had changed. He could see hatred in Dennis' eyes that he'd never noticed before.

"I'll help you," he said. While they lay under the stars that night, they planned how to kill Domko.

Early the next morning they snuck into the granary where the guns were kept. Since they had started hunting with their mother when they were only four years old, they were already experienced with low caliber rifles and shotguns. Even though they were only eight years old now, nobody worried that they'd kill themselves, so they didn't worry about it either.

They picked up their father's old .22 caliber rifle and two shells from a box on the shelf. They snuck into the bush carrying the gun, then hid it along the route they traveled morning and night to get the cows. Once the rifle was safely concealed, they went out to the pasture and returned with the bellowing cows in front of them. Domko was standing in the yard waiting. He smirked, knowing they were hungry but were too late for breakfast. They stayed out of reach, and when the older boys finished milking the cows, they chased them back through the fence.

Later that afternoon, they returned to the same pasture to fetch the cows, wading through knee deep water. Sometimes Domko allowed them to take a horse, but only when he was in a good mood, and today wasn't one of those days.

David stopped to listen to the sound of dogs barking in the distance. Following the sound, he could see the neighbor and his dogs chasing their cattle home. He watched as the large, golden-colored dogs nipped at the cows' heels as the man rode leisurely along on a horse.

"Look at that," David said. "They really do gots cattle-chasin' dogs." He had heard from the boys at school that they had special dogs to herd their cows. David thought they must be lying since any dog he ever owned had chased cattle for sport. He watched longingly as the dogs guided the herd out of sight.

"Did you see that Denny? We gotta get some cattle-chasin' dogs."

Dennis agreed that their lives would be much better if they had dogs to help do the work.

"Do you think they gots dogs that pick rocks?" Dennis asked. They burst into laughter. "And shovel shit?"

Their joking was cut short by a sudden, familiar odor. The wind was blowing from the direction of the farm, bringing Domko's smell with it.

"The devil's comin'," David whispered as they ran into the bush and crouched down. They waited a few minutes and then, sure enough, Domko emerged from a bluff of trees into the clearing where they had just been. He stopped and placed his hands on his hips, looked from side to side. Suspicious that the twins were playing instead of working, he continued along the edge of the bush looking for them.

"C'mon," David said. They cut through the bush and started doubling back toward home. He knew Domko would give up searching soon and start back along the same path.

The rifle was sitting where they had left it, leaning against a fallen oak, just a few feet off the trail. David grabbed the gun and fumbled with the bullets in his pocket. He loaded one in the chamber, then handed it to Dennis. They crouched behind a fallen tree just inside the bush.

"I dunno if I can do it," Dennis said, steadying the gun barrel on the tree trunk.

"Shhh," David whispered, leaning forward, straining to see and hear. He ducked his head once he saw Domko coming. He pointed frantically at Domko who was creeping along, hoping to catch the twins off guard. For a moment David was filled with a perverse pleasure in knowing that it was them lying in wait for him. That dissolved quickly, though, as the severity of what they were about to do struck him hard.

"Aim for his head 'cause you gotta kill him," he said, shaking off thoughts of what would happen if they missed.

Dennis took a deep breath, shut one eye and peered with the other through the sight. "Tell me when to shoot," he whispered. His heart was pounding so hard he was surprised that neither David nor Domko could hear it. He cocked the gun.

Domko continued to move closer, and when he was as near as he was going to get, David nudged his brother.

"Now," he rasped.

Dennis' finger shook as he took careful aim. He could see the side of Domko's head through the sight. With his finger vibrating on the trigger, he squeezed, closing his eyes at the last moment.

Click.

The gun jammed. The sound thundered in their ears, and they froze, expecting Domko heard it. He did hear something, turning to look in their direction.

"Try again, Denny," David whispered.

Dennis cocked the gun again. This time he aimed quickly and didn't hesitate to pull the trigger.

Another click. The gun jammed again.

Dennis slunk down beside his brother, and they looked at each other in disbelief. They sat still knowing that this time, Domko heard the noise and may have recognized it. The boys lay flat on their backs with the gun across Dennis' chest, listening for the sound of snapping twigs, but it didn't come. When all was quiet, they peeked up to see that Domko was gone. Jumping up, they ran in the opposite direction from home. Branches whipped their faces and legs as they veered off the trail through the thick bush. Tears of frustration streamed down their faces as they ran from the bush into a clearing and fell to their knees. Without a word, Dennis pointed the gun towards the sky and pulled the trigger again. This time the gun went off.

They looked at each other, but no words were needed to know what the other was thinking. Domko was the devil. In hopelessness, they fell back and lay in the grass crying, believing that no matter how hard they tried, they'd never escape his grasp.

A PLACE OF REFUGE

Just before the Labour Day long weekend, Mrs. Louise Collier settled into the teacher's cottage behind the school. Nearing retirement age, Louise had been a teacher most of her life and now that the summer break was finished, was pleased to be back at work, anxious to see her new school.

The warm, stuffy smell of an old building closed up for the summer greeted her as she opened the school's front door. She sighed with pleasure. This was the sort of school she liked.

Cobwebs lightly waved as she opened the windows to let in fresh air, brushing dead flies from the windowsills as she went. Using an old rag, she found in the cloakroom, she dusted off the desks then swept the floor. When the room was cleaned to her liking, she sat down to review last year's register.

Herbert Metner, secretary-treasurer of the local school board, told her to expect approximately twenty pupils that fall. She worked all afternoon preparing lesson plans for the first week. Taking a short break, she decided to go through the mail. There were numerous advertisements for teaching supplies plus books, contests and transfer slips for a family of six children named Pischke. She wondered out loud if Mr. Metner's estimate included these students.

The last piece of mail she opened was a white envelope addressed to the teacher at Bayton School. Tearing it open she pulled out a sympathy card. Puzzled, she opened it and read: "To the teacher at Bayton: Our sincerest condolences on the return of the Pischke children." It was signed by a few teachers at the Ashern school.

Just my luck, she thought as she tossed the card in the trash.

Louise stood at the front of the room as her students filed in that first morning. She was curious to meet the Pischke children and wondered if she'd be able to pick them out. Troublesome children were either overindulged or neglected, and it didn't take long to see the Pischkes fell into the latter group.

Even in poorer areas of the province, most children came to school clean and suitably dressed, but the Pischkes looked and smelled like they hadn't bathed in a long time. Their clothes were ill-fitting, and Walter was the only one wearing shoes—men's dress shoes that looked rather odd on a teenager.

Norman and Steven were unusually quiet for their ages, and she sensed that these two would give her the most trouble. They wanted to sit together, and that suited her since they were in the same grade and that way she'd be able to keep an eye on them.

Eunice was a cute little thing, but jumpy and nervous. She was hard to understand because she talked so fast. Every time she tried to speak, Louise had to tell her to slow down.

Then there were the twins who seemed to be in their own little world. They spoke a language that she had never heard before and thought this might partly explain why they had failed grade one twice. They were much too big to be in first grade, but she had no choice but to put them there with their younger sister, Rosie, who didn't utter a word.

Louise's first battle with the Pischke children came sooner than she expected. During opening exercises, they refused to stand and sing *God Save the Queen* or say the *Lord's Prayer*.

Louise slapped a ruler down on Norman's desk, but he refused to stand.

"Our Momma says we don't got to," he said.

Walter and Steven nodded in agreement. They'd been punished by their mother after she found out they had stood for the exercises at the Ashern school and weren't going to risk that again.

Louise was not amused. She smacked the ruler on the desk a few more times, then across the older boys' knuckles. The rest of the students sat silently watching, while the twins, fearing she'd hit them, slid underneath the double desk they shared.

At the end of the day, Mrs. Collier prepared a note that was sent home with Walter. The following morning, Caroline came to school with the children and asked to speak to Louise outside. Classes were delayed as the women had a heated discussion on the front steps as Caroline explained that her children did not have to take part in opening exercises because it was against the religious philosophy of the Jehovah's Witnesses.

Louise argued that she opposed treating one family different than the others, but when Caroline wouldn't budge, she finally conceded. Caroline marched victoriously down the steps and from that day forward her children had to stand in the cloakroom until classes began. This embarrassed the older children who didn't want to be treated differently from everybody else.

Watching the other children tease the Pischkes softened Louise toward the family of misfits, who weren't bad, just misguided. It was obvious that Caroline had fallen under the spell of a ridiculous cult and while Louise was too old to change her ways, she decided to make concessions as far as these children were concerned.

One afternoon the twins decided to ask their mother about the dogs they had seen chasing cattle. They described the animals to her, asking what breed of dog they were. She said they were purebred Collies.

"Can we gets a collie dog?" David asked.

"Those dogs cost too much money," she said.

"Maybe if them dogs have pups, we can get one," Dennis said. "Dogs are always havin' pups, and they get drowned."

Caroline smiled but said nothing. Later that evening, thinking Domko would find it amusing, she told him about the conversation. Instead, he became angry, and the next day he cornered the twins in the barn.

Grabbing Dennis by the shirt, he pulled him close. "Yous be vantink collie dogs, eh? I's be showink you collie dogs," he said, backhanding him across the face, sending him flying into the barn wall. David fell into a crouching position and covered his head with his arms.

"Dennis be some goot for sheet," he sputtered, kicking David in the hip as he strode out of the barn.

It took a few minutes for the twins to realize what had happened.

"Don't be saying no more about Collie dogs," Norman whispered from where he was milking. "You know the ol' bastard hates anything he ain't got."

Dennis and David nodded. They were going to have to be more careful about what they said to their mother.

One warm September morning there was a frantic knock at the Harwart's back door. Emma was standing at the stove canning tomatoes. Marjorie got up from the table where she was mending socks to answer it.

Eunice stood on the stoop panting. "Mrs. Harwart, you gotta come quick," she yelled. "Domko smashed Rosie, and she's lyin' on the floor."

Emma gasped and for a few flustered moments, wasn't sure what to do first. She pulled the pot off the stove then slipped on her shoes while Marjorie retrieved the first aid kit from the bedroom.

Eunice told them to hurry as she began running down the driveway. Marjorie easily caught up, but Emma hollered out for them to wait, not exactly sure what they were walking into.

Now, what has he done? she wondered, silently admonishing Caroline's decision to return. She'd heard that she'd miscarried what would have been her ninth child, a blessing really, if a person thought honestly about the situation.

A range of scenarios began running through her mind about what she might encounter at the farm. Her heart began to race as she hurried her weight up Caroline's driveway. She hesitated, but only for a moment, before pushing open the door and stepping inside.

The first thing she saw was Rosie lying on the floor beside the wood stove. A fresh blood stain stood out like new paint on the wall above her body. Caroline was kneeling beside Rosie, and it was obvious she'd been crying. The twins were wandering in an aimless daze around the kitchen, jabbering to themselves.

"She's dead," David said looking up at Emma. "R-r-rosie's dead."

"Yep, she's dead," Dennis added.

Emma was taken aback. The boys' indifference toward their sister was unsettling, and it made her wonder how much suffering they'd seen, what amount of trauma it takes to make children so nonchalant.

Forcing herself to stop thinking about them, she had to enter that mindset herself and set aside her fears to focus on Rosie.

"What happened?" she asked, kneeling beside Rosie and laying a hand on her neck with hopes of finding a pulse. Her heart was still beating, and it appeared that she was still breathing.

"I don't know," Caroline said weakly. "I was outside in the barn and when I came in found her like this . . ."

"Where's Domko?" Emma asked.

Caroline said that she didn't know. Then she began to pray.

Emma turned her attention back to the injured girl whose body was covered in bruises. Gently, she began feeling her limbs for broken bones, watching her face for signs of pain. She wiped away some of the blood on her cheeks, relieved that it appeared to come from a bleeding nose and not a more serious injury.

"Rosie," she whispered, stroking her hair back from her forehead. "Can you hear me?" But she didn't move. Dark bruises were starting to appear on her face and neck.

Emma's heart leaped at the sound of the kitchen door opening. Remembering Gus' advice to never turn her back on Domko, Emma spun quickly around, expecting him to be standing there. But it wasn't him. Norman and

Steven stopped in their tracks. They looked at Emma, at their sister, then their eyes went to the floor. They inched inside the door and watched without saying a word.

"We have to get her up off this cold floor," Emma said. Rosie flinched and moaned as Emma picked her up and carried her to the bedroom while Caroline and the rest of the children followed closely behind.

"I think we should get Doc Steenson to come see her," Emma said. "Being unconscious like this is a bad sign."

Domko would never approve of the doctor visiting the farm. Caroline shook her head and covered her face with her hands. Finally, without meeting Emma's gaze, she whispered, "Can we wait and see how she does first?"

Emma was disappointed by the question, but not entirely surprised. She turned her attention back to Rosie who began to stir.

"I'll stay with her then," Emma said, ushering everyone else out of the room. "Marjorie, you go home and tell your father where I am," she said. Their eyes locked for a moment and Marjorie nodded that she understood the hidden message before hurrying out the door.

"Caroline," she said, "get me a cool, damp cloth."

Gus was getting ready to check on his wife when the door opened, and Emma stepped inside. She looked exhausted and preoccupied. Gus took the first aid kit from her and motioned for her to sit at the table. Marjorie sat on the chair next to her mother, anxious to hear what had happened after she left.

"Well, it looks as if Rosie is going to be all right," Emma said, explaining that after Rosie had regained consciousness, she stayed to keep an eye on her, to watch for signs of a concussion.

"Did Domko come back?" Gus asked.

"Not while I was there," she said. "Did you all eat?"

"I made supper," Marjorie said, getting up from the table. "Are you hungry?"

Emma was so preoccupied that she didn't answer, so Marjorie just went ahead and made her mother a sandwich.

"I'm going to report this to the police," Emma said. "Will you take me to town tomorrow?"

Gus stared at his wife but didn't answer right away. He motioned for Emma to eat, but she waved it off, saying she wasn't hungry.

"You have to be careful," he said. "Caroline might be in trouble, too. If the social workers start coming around, she'll lose those children for sure."

Emma's frustration boiled to the surface. "Well, maybe that would be the best thing," she said. "Caroline must know this. You should have seen her. She was so scared that she wouldn't even call the doctor. A mother shouldn't have to put up with nonsense like that."

"Have you ever asked if he can be deported?" Gus asked.

Marjorie's eyebrows shot up. This idea was new to her and it sounded like a wonderful solution. It was obvious that her parents had discussed this before.

"I'd heard that after beating up that fellow in Ashern the police came down pretty hard on him," he continued. "He's not a Canadian citizen, you know."

Emma nodded. "All I know is that she refused to sign the paper to start the process. They asked her to do it while Domko was sitting right there. That would be just like the police, to expect her to stand up to him while they are there, but then fend for herself as soon as they leave."

Gus fully understood his wife's frustration. They continued to mull over the situation well into the night. Of course, they sided with Caroline but found it difficult to understand her way of thinking.

"The less we see Domko, the better," Emma sighed. She was tired and ready for bed. She'd finished the sandwich by now, and a cup of tea had helped settle her nerves.

"And you," she said pointing her finger at Marjorie, "you stay away from him. He has lost his mind and one of these days he's going to kill somebody."

Marjorie nodded solemnly. Staying away from Domko was foremost on her mind.

That autumn was unusually warm and dry. Walter spent one mid-October afternoon out by the granary, repairing and greasing the muskrat traps he'd inherited when his father died. He had more than a dozen traps to set that winter and daydreamed as he tested the traps, remembering everything his dad had taught him about trapping muskrats.

I'm gonna make enough money to buy myself a motor scooter, he thought. A friend from the church had one for sale, and he planned to buy it.

Domko stood in the kitchen peering out the window. He watched Walter working by the pump house, but he didn't have the energy to go find out what he was doing. His mood was turning dark again and when that happened all his energy seemed to disappear.

"Vat Valters be doink?" he asked Caroline.

"Getting his traps ready."

"Vat?"

"He's going to start trapping again," she explained, this time slowly. When Domko got like this, she always had to tell him things twice. "There's good money in fur."

Domko thought for a moment, then turned to look out the window again. "Mooney?" he asked.

Caroline nodded. "Lots of farmers around here trap."

Lighting another cigarette, Domko watched Walter. He decided to encourage the boy's hobby and maybe even get a few traps for himself.

The twins awoke the following week to the smell of cooking porridge. They waited patiently under the bed until they heard the outside door slam shut then they crawled out and ran to the kitchen. Their mother had cooked a big pot of rolled oats, but if they didn't eat some of it quick, there might not be any left after the older boys ate. They'd be in soon, once the cows were milked.

Each twin grabbed a bowl and peered hungrily into the pot that sat warming on the stove. They spooned giant globs of porridge into each bowl then went to stand by the window to watch for Domko as they ate.

"Hey Denny," David said as he took a spoonful of steaming porridge into his mouth, "want some cream?"

Dennis' eyes widened. Both boys looked at the cream can that sat on a shelf near the door. Domko only allowed them to drink skim milk since cream was saved, cooled, then taken to town and sold. Domko kept the cream can up high so that the children couldn't get at it.

"You watch at the window, and I'll get some," David said.

The thought of thick cream on his porridge was more than Dennis could resist. He ran to the window, looked out and signaled to David that nobody was coming.

Grabbing a cup from the counter, David pushed a stool under the shelf, then stood on it. Reaching up, he had to stand on his toes to get the cup into the can. Dipping it in, he filled the cup and was careful not to spill any of it as he hurried back to the table. He poured it over Dennis' porridge then ran back for some more.

Dennis grabbed his bowl and quickly stirring in the cream, started shoveling porridge into his mouth.

David climbed back onto the chair and reached into the cream can again, but this time felt resistance as he tried to dip the cup. Standing on his toes, he tilted the can slightly towards him and peered in. Floating on top of the cream was a large, black rat. Startled, he pushed the can back and jumped down from the stool. Wiping his hands feverishly on his shirt, he ran to his brother.

"Dennis," he choked. "There's a drowned rat in the cream!"

"Wha—?" Dennis said. Gagging, he spat the porridge onto the table then stuffed his shirt into his mouth to wipe it dry. The thought of the floating rat turned his stomach and he vomited on the floor.

David grabbed Dennis' bowl and scraped what was left into the slop pail. He knew how Domko would react if he saw the wasted porridge and cream, so he took a spoon and stirred the contents in the pail until it disappeared.

He scraped the porridge from his bowl back into the pot and returned the stool to the corner. Dennis had just finished cleaning up the vomit when the door opened. Their mother and brothers stepped into the kitchen, each carrying a pail of milk. Eunice sat down at the cream separator and began turning the handle as the milk was poured into the top funnel. The older boys grabbed a bowl of porridge and ate quickly before going back outside to finish the chores.

The twins sat solemnly at the kitchen table. Once the initial shock of what happened started to wear off, they began stealing glances at one another and smiled.

Domko came in and not bothering to remove his dirty boots, sat in his usual spot. He stirred sugar into a fresh cup of coffee. Seeing their mother add a bit of skim milk over Kathy's porridge gave them the giggles. Domko backhanded David across the head and called the twins 'goot for sheet.'

When he got up and went to the washbasin at the far end of the kitchen, and he and their mother began conversing in Polish, the twins looked at each other and smiled. Domko splashed fresh water on his face then covered it with shaving cream. He used a straight razor to shave off two weeks beard growth. He was going to town.

The twins waited in silence as Domko disappeared into the bedroom and returned a few minutes later wearing his town clothes. He didn't bother to bathe, just pulled clean clothes over his dirty long underwear.

Their mother got Kathy ready to go, then carried her outside. Domko went to the shelf and reached up for the cream can. Placing it on the floor, he grunted when he looked inside.

"Greedy bastard," he said. Reaching into the can with his dirty hand he grabbed the rat and threw it on the floor. Hoisting the can onto his shoulder, he carried it out to the waiting tractor, returning a few minutes later, kicking the rat aside.

He yelled at the twins to get into the crawl space under the house. They cowered as he pulled back the door cut into the living room floor. He grunted at them to climb inside. The draft on their feet made them instantly regret

Where Children Run

that they weren't wearing socks. They also wished they had run to school with Eunice and Rosie.

After they had lowered themselves into the crawl space, Domko slammed the door shut. It took a few minutes for their eyes to adjust to the cold, damp darkness. With only three feet of headroom, they had to crouch to move around. They avoided the far end because it smelled as if something had died in the corner underneath all the building material scraps and other bits of junk.

"Do rats live under houses?" Dennis asked nervously.

"I don't think so," David shuddered.

Once their nerves had settled, they sat on the ground beside a row of burlap bags filled with potatoes and began reminiscing about the enjoyable times they had while living in Ashern. As they talked, they listened for footsteps above, waiting patiently for one of their siblings to open the door.

"Dennis, you gots to run faster," David said remembering the first serious beating his twin received. "He gets you all the time, even when it ain't your fault."

"I know," he replied. "But I can't move when he yells."

David shook his head. They sat in silence. Then David asked a question he'd been meaning to ask for a long time.

"Dennis, how come you said you took the chocolate bar when everybody knew Rosie did it?"

Dennis shrugged. "I didn't want Satan to kill her."

Walter let the twins out of the hole in the late afternoon, but only after they promised to jump back in before Domko got home. Eunice kept watch, and when she heard the tractor coming, the twins scrambled back into the crawl space. The children sat quietly as Domko, their mother and Kathy came through the door. Domko was in a reasonable mood which was a tremendous relief to everyone. The older boys went out to unload and bring inside large bags of flour, sugar and rolled oats.

When Walter came inside, he was beaming.

"Domko b-bought me some traps," he said to Norman. "I'm gonna trap all winter and s-spring. Maybe I won't h-hafta go to school."

As Caroline put away a few groceries, she asked the twins' whereabouts. Eunice pointed to the front room. "In the hole."

Caroline sighed as she lifted the crawl space door. "What are you boys doing down there?"

"D-domko p-put us here," David stammered, squinting into the light.

Karen Emilson

"Well, come on out," she said, extending her hand. As she pulled each boy up, she considered confronting Domko but decided against it since he was in a good mood and she didn't want to anger him. Whatever they'd done was forgotten; so she encouraged them to mix with the rest of the children, be quiet, and not draw attention to themselves.

The following morning David finished feeding the chickens and pig then went looking for Dennis, who had disappeared before breakfast. As he skipped along the bush trail toward the school, he came to the spot where his toy, a front wheel from an old wheelbarrow, was hidden. The wheel was about eighteen inches in diameter and had a long shaft that stuck out of the center on both sides. It was fun to hold the shaft and run the wheel along the ground. Domko had seen him having fun with it once and threatened to destroy it, so he kept it hidden after that.

He called the toy his "wee-wee" and thought about how seldom he let Dennis play with it. His twin had been sad lately, so David decided that he'd let Dennis push the wee-wee home after school. As he hurried along he recalled how Domko had bought Walter traps the day before. He couldn't understand why nice things were never done for him and Dennis.

As he rounded a small bend in the path, he suddenly sensed that something was wrong in this usually safe spot. He came to a full halt, then threw his arms over his head and jumped off the path. Sensing there was something in the trees above, he looked up and screamed. Hanging overhead were three dogs. Each had a rope tied around its neck and strung over a pole suspended horizontally between two trees. The ends were tied to the tree trunk.

David stared at the swinging dogs in horror. Although he had never seen the neighbor's dogs up close, he knew these were the Collie dogs they had seen. They were the same golden color and looked to be about the right size. Their eyes bulged in death, and a black tongue lolled out of each mouth.

David turned and ran back towards home. He remembered hearing dogs barking the night before, but had thought nothing more about it. Domko must have caught the dogs and strangled them. That's what he meant when he said, "I's be showink you but-a-some Collie Dogs."

David ran through the yard into the house.

"Momma," he yelled as he ran into the kitchen. "You gots to come!"

Caroline was standing in the kitchen chastising the older boys who were also visibly upset. She was saying to keep quiet and not tell anyone what they'd found. She didn't want any more trouble with neighbors.

Domko sat chuckling at the table.

"That means you, too," Caroline said to David. "Now I don't want to hear another word about Collie dogs."

David started to cry as he ran out of the house. Instinctively he reached out with his right hand, but Dennis was not there. At that moment, he realized how much he depended on his brother.

Where is Dennis? he wondered as he looked frantically around the yard. He feared that Dennis had met the same fate as the dogs and the thought of Dennis hanging by his neck somewhere, sent David running down the road in a blind panic. He glanced nervously toward the bush, heart heavy in his chest as thoughts of trying to survive without his twin raced through his mind.

He ran up the school steps and burst through the door, interrupting the story Mrs. Collier was reading to the class. At first, the children were startled, but then they began to giggle as the teacher scolded him for being late and disrupting the class.

There sitting at his desk was Dennis. He'd come to school early, down the road, so he hadn't seen the dogs. A wave of relief passed over David at the sight of his twin smiled brightly from the front of the room.

THE SPIRIT OF CHRISTMAS

"I can't never understand what that stupid bastard is sayin'," Norman complained one day. "He beats the shit out of us, but I never know why."

Walter nodded. "We're not goddamned Pollacks . . . how we s-s'posed to understand him?"

It was a brisk, November day and the pair were in the field forking hay onto the hay rack. This would be the first of three trips from the field to the barn they'd have to make that afternoon. Old enough to understand that the living conditions at the farm were deplorable, they were beginning to rebel against Domko's tyranny.

"I'm gettin' outta here as soon as I can," Norman said. "I'm gonna move away and get a plane."

Walter nodded. He believed that Norman would achieve whatever he set out to do and wished he could be as tough-spirited.

"H-hey what did old Squeezer get you for yesterday anyway?" he asked. They nicknamed Domko 'Lemon Squeezer' or 'Squeezer' because he liked to squeeze lemons into his tea.

"He wanted me to get some eggs, but I thought he said axe," Norman replied. "So I walk over holding the axe and he gets so mad he almost shits himself. I shoulda smashed him over the head with it."

The boys laughed and began shoving each other into the hay. Walter pushed his cap back and sneered.

"Yous be goot for sheet!" he said, pretending to hit Norman who lay laughing in the hay. Their antics pleased Bruno who began running around barking excitedly. Norman reached out and grabbed the dog, pulling him into the hay. Bruno's big, wet tongue lapped his face.

"He sure is a good dog, eh?" Norman said stroking his head. "We don't need no Collie dog as long as we got Bruno."

Remembering the dead dogs abruptly took the fun out of their play. They sat and stroked Bruno somberly as he watched them with thoughtful eyes. Always in-tune with their feelings, Bruno would frisk and play when the children were happy and sit quietly beside them when they were sad. He was a devoted companion to Kathy, who grabbed him by the fur while he led her around the farm.

"Well, we'd better get finished before he comes back," Walter said, slapping his knees and standing up, brushing the hay off his clothing.

"Where's Momma?" Dennis asked his twin as they sat at the table in the dark, cold kitchen.

"Don't know," David said.

Their mother had disappeared early that morning, and nobody seemed to know where she went. The older boys were outside, and Domko had just left to check on them.

"The lamp don't got no fuel," Dennis said, nodding at the oil lamp sitting in the middle of the table. "Do you think we should fill it up?"

David thought about this for a moment then pulling off the top, stuck his finger inside as he'd seen Walter do many times, confirming it was empty. He picked up the lamp and carried it to the door where a large, metal kerosene can sat on the floor. He unscrewed the cap and peered in to see how much fuel was inside, but it was too dark to see.

"Lemme do it," Dennis said, grabbing a box of matches from beside the cook stove. Standing beside his brother, Dennis lit a match then stuck it inside the can. There was a bright flash and explosion that sent them flying across the room. Dennis screamed as flames seared his face and burned the front of his hair.

"You okay Dennis?" David asked as he crawled over to Dennis who was lying on his back with his hands covering his face.

"My face is burned," he moaned through his fingers, "is it gone?"

David pulled his brother's hands away. Dennis was covered in black soot except where the flesh on his forehead and nose was raw where the skin had peeled back. His hair was still smoldering.

"We gots to get the doctor," David said, looking closely at Dennis' nose. "So it don't fall off."

With the initial shock now over, Dennis' face was throbbing, and he started to cry. "Where's Momma?" he asked again.

A few moments later, the door opened, and Domko came inside. The matches had spilled beside the misshapen can, and the oil lamp had rolled to

113

the middle of the floor, and it was obvious what had happened. Whimpering, they braced themselves for the worst.

Domko threw back his head and roared with laughter. He looked back at Dennis' burned face, then laughed again.

"Dennnnis," he cooed. "Hows be but-a-some face? It's be oogly."

For the rest of the day, Domko sat in his usual spot, smoking and chuckling to himself. The older boys came in late that afternoon and their mother returned shortly afterward. The suggestion that Dennis be taken to the doctor was met with more laughter from Domko.

"I's not be spendink mooney on Dennis," he said.

By early December, everyone in the community and members of the church knew that Caroline was expecting another child in the spring. Little was said about the earlier pregnancy that she dismissed as a miscarriage, even though people closest to her knew what had happened.

By now, the Harwarts and Deightons were growing disillusioned with Caroline and others simply refused to get involved—everyone except church members who were pressuring her to marry Domko and live by the Bible. Weekly visits turned into pre-marital counseling sessions with the entire family present. The children were expected to sit for hours listening to Bible passages. Caroline was told to acknowledge and repeat the passages until memorized.

"The problem be her," Domko said one evening in his most innocent voice. He explained that he wanted to marry Caroline and raise the family together, but her reluctance to discipline the children bothered him. He said the children didn't listen and he was forced to be the disciplinarian. He went on to explain that the plate in his head caused him grievous headaches, made worse by the children's unruly behavior and this made it hard for him to work. Sucking on his cigarette, he pointed to Caroline. "She's not be lookink after but-a-some house ant keets."

The children listened solemnly, glancing at one another in amazement. The twins watched their mother, who listened without expression, as Domko criticized them all. The man from the church was also listening. It was obvious by his expression that he believed Domko and glowered at each child until one-by-one, they sank in their chairs.

When the visit finally came to an end, the man told Caroline that she should put more effort into pleasing Domko.

"You're lucky to have him," he said to her. "Nowhere else would you find someone to take on the responsibility of such a large, unruly family."

The following week, the children sat for nearly two hours listening to Bible recitations until they became bored and started horsing around. Tilting their chairs back, the older boys began a secret contest to see who could balance their chair back the farthest without falling over.

Dennis was sitting closest to the door and eager to be in the game, leaned back as far as he could. He started to teeter, and before he could regain his balance, Steven reached out with his foot and pushed the chair enough that Dennis lost his balance and crashed against the door. The children burst into laughter as Dennis rolled out the door.

Domko jumped up and confronted him in the doorway, out of the visitors' sight.

"You's be goot for nuthink!" he whispered, kicking Dennis in the side before storming back into the house.

David watched from where he sat and shook his head.

Poor Dennis, he thought. *He always gets it, no matter what.*

In spite of his erratic nature, Domko did make a few friends in the area. These were people who either did not realize how he treated Caroline and the children, or people who believed Domko's complaints that the children were incorrigible and needed disciplining.

That fall he went to Winnipeg with one of his friends and his two-day absence meant the children were able to relax and enjoy themselves. The children noticed that their mother was also far more carefree when he was gone which made them wonder why she didn't kick him out of the house for good.

When Domko returned, he carried a large cardboard box and called the children to see what he brought for them. They gathered around the box and peered inside to find it was full of secondhand clothing. They began scrambling for mitts, coats, and sweaters. While some of it was ugly or nearly worn out, they were happy to each find a matching pair of shoes or boots in their size, everyone except David, who ended up with one running shoe and a black rubber boot.

After that, the children were made to sit on the kitchen floor and watch while Domko called Kathy to his side. He pulled a brand new coat and warm, felt-lined boots from a bag. He helped her put them on then paraded her around the kitchen so everyone could admire how she looked.

"See," he cooed to Caroline. "I's be but-a-some goot father."

Preparations for the biggest event of the year began in late November. The annual school Christmas concert brought everyone in the community together and anticipated with excitement by children and adults alike.

During the last few weeks of school before the Christmas break, there was a tremendous amount of pressure on the students to prepare their costumes and memorize their lines. Concert preparations occupied most of the day and intensified as the date drew closer.

According to the Jehovah's Witness religion, Christ was not born in December and even if he had been, celebrating his birthday would not be considered appropriate. Christmas was considered a pagan ritual, so the Pischke children were not allowed to participate. Instead, they were segregated in the far corner of the room and given mathematics and spelling assignments, while the other students excitedly painted murals and sang Christmas carols.

Walter particularly longed to take part in the Christmas festivities because he remembered how they celebrated before his father died. He secretly discussed Christmas with his classmates then passed information on to his siblings. The Lutheran beliefs conflicted drastically with their mother's religion, and he desperately wanted the Lutheran beliefs to be the truth.

It bothered Walter that everyone would be at the Christmas concert except them, so the night of the pageant he snuck out of the house and ran toward the school. As he neared, he saw warm lights shining festively through the windows. The resonance of singing followed by laughing and clapping grew louder as he approached. He climbed the steps and opened the door, stepping silently into the cloakroom. A mixture of different scents greeted him from the many coats hung along the wall.

From the small vestibule, he watched quietly as his classmates acted out a scene in the pageant. A chorus of giggles erupted from the audience as a young shepherd adjusted the towel on his head, then waved and smiled a wide, toothless grin to his parents. Then Marjorie stepped out from behind a handmade tree dressed as an angel. She waited until the room grew quiet.

"Fear not," she called out, "I bring you tidings of great joy. For tonight born unto you in the town of Bethlehem is a child, and his name shall be Jesus Christ."

The choir, made up of mostly older girls, stood on a bench behind the scene. They began singing, their voices quiet at first but then grew stronger as parents gave approving nods.

"Hark the herald angels sing," they sang sweetly. "Glory to the newborn King! Peace on earth and mercy mild, God and sinners reconciled."

Where Children Run

A few of the mothers dabbed the corners of their eyes with handkerchiefs. A warm feeling came over Walter as he felt the love in the room. He stood there, taking it all in, letting his thoughts drift until they were interrupted by noise from behind. He turned to see a large man in a red suit come into the cloakroom carrying a bulging sack over his shoulder.

Santa Claus. He had come just as his classmates had predicted. Santa gave Walter a nod and a wink. Rubbing his beard, he burst into the concert, bellowing a chorus of "Ho, Ho, Ho!"

Walter was amazed to see the children all gather around Santa who handed out candy and small toys. It was then Marjorie noticed him standing in the doorway. She caught his eye then gave him a timid wave. She looked truly beautiful in her costume, just like the angel she was, and all he could do was smile meekly.

It would be best that his mother never knew he was there, so before too many people saw him, Walter slipped out the door. During the walk home, he decided to hang one of his socks by the wood stove on Christmas Eve. His mother would have a hard time denying the importance of Christmas when Santa Claus filled it with candy and toys.

The following day he told his siblings about his plan. Steven and Norman scoffed at the idea, but Eunice and the twins listened intently. They were too frightened to say anything to their mother who had disapproved of such ideas in the past.

Caroline and Domko were both in a pleasant mood on Christmas Eve. Although he was careful not to let the Jehovah's Witnesses know, Domko was born Catholic and had no intention of giving up his religion.

Remnants of Catholicism also remained deeply instilled in Caroline. While she never would admit it, the holiday season still made her feel warm inside. She cooked a nice supper, and the entire family ate well that night. The children quietly played while Walter worked diligently to make a hook to attach to one of his largest, cleanest socks. Steven and Norman chided him as he prepared to hang it by the wood stove.

"You guys will see," Walter said. "I'll be the only kid here who'll get candy and toys from Santa Claus."

The boys laughed. Domko overheard the conversation but said nothing. Caroline did not discourage him either, and this surprised the twins. They had all been warned against outside beliefs. They'd been taught that other religions were evil and that people who believed them were lesser than the Jehovah's Witnesses. Because of this, they were discouraged from associating with people outside of the religion. Walter was behaving as they had been told not to.

The next morning Walter jumped from the bed and ran to the front room. His sock was still hanging by the stove, and he stood there for a moment, eyes wide with wonder. The long, black sock was bulging and straining on the hook.

"See," he said to his siblings, who were gathering around. "I told you."

Grabbing the sock from the hook he excitedly stretched open the top and stuck his hand inside. The shock caused him to pause for a moment, and then he pulled out a fistful of potato peelings. At first, he couldn't believe it and then when the realization struck, his face grew red and hot. Turning the sock upside down, he shook out the rest of the peelings and three rocks.

Steven and Norman couldn't help themselves and began laughing while Eunice, Rosie, and the twins watched with disappointment. Walter looked from his siblings to his mother then at Domko. Tears stung his eyes as he ran past them, grabbing his coat as he went out the door.

Domko sat chuckling quietly at the kitchen table while Caroline stood cooking oatmeal. She knew that she should follow Walter and comfort him but thinking back to her childhood woes kept her in front of the stove. Believing in the Catholic God had never done her any good.

Life is miserable, and the sooner Walter realizes it, the better off he'll be, she thought.

Walter didn't return to school that January. Determined to make money on his trap line, he spent most days in the bush and every evening stretching and curing the skins of the animals he caught. Because Caroline and Domko approved of his scheme to make money, he no longer had to do chores, so Steven and Norman now had to do his share of the work. Since Christmas, Walter had withdrawn somewhat from his siblings, preferring to be alone. He kept it a secret that as soon as he had enough money saved, he planned to leave home.

They gotta get used to me not being here, he thought. *I won't be around no more to make fun of. They won't be laughing at me when I got my own place.*

After a particularly terrifying week, the twins fled late one evening and ended up on the Harwart's doorstep. Emma answered the vigorous knock to find them shivering without coats or mitts. Dennis was wearing a short sleeve shirt, pants and a pair of dress shoes that looked too big. David had on a sweater, light pants, and a rubber boot on one foot, running shoe on the other. Their hair was matted and their faces covered with grime.

"C-an we come in?" David asked.

Emma hurried them inside. The days had been unseasonably warm for January, rising to five degrees during the day, but Emma knew this would be short-lived. These children wouldn't survive long if Domko chased them out on a regular winter night.

Emma told them to sit at the table beside Marjorie who looked up from her homework. They smiled at her, and each took a seat, glancing back at Emma to see if she was making them something to eat.

Marjorie was glad to see the twins who she hadn't seen at school much the last week. In fact, all of the Pischke kids missed a lot of school, and she knew it was because they were laboring on the farm.

"W-what did ya l-learn at school today?" David asked.

Marjorie smiled. It was so much easier talking to the twins now that they spoke better English. They had learned a lot at school, and Mrs. Collier was surprisingly patient with them, even putting them in grade two for the second term.

Emma put a plate of sandwiches in front of them and watched as they gobbled them down. By now they were relaxed and chatted until they were finished eating. When they were done, Emma herded them into the front room where their chattering wouldn't distract Marjorie.

The boys sat on the chesterfield and looked around. To them, the Harwart's modest home felt like a palace. The sight of Gus sitting contentedly in a recliner made each of them long for a real father figure.

"Hey Dennis, look," David said, pointing to a pair of stereo speakers mounted on the wall.

Dennis looked up at the small brown boxes and shrugged his shoulders. David began explaining in the secret language what he thought the boxes contained. They got up off the chesterfield and went for a closer look.

Gus peered over his glasses at them. He listened as David pointed to the radio and speakers and tried to see how they were mounted on the wall. Their eyes were wide in amazement. They spoke to each other as if nobody else was in the room.

Gus got up and turned on the radio. They jumped back and then smiled at one another as the sound came through the speakers.

"Big shots," David said. "They gots radio all over the place."

Dennis was very impressed. This was the best house they'd ever been in, but he was too young before to fully notice and appreciate the surroundings. They sat and listened to the radio program as Emma sat on the chair knitting. She glanced at the clock a few times and then announced it was time for them to go to bed.

"You all have school tomorrow, and I don't want Marjorie failing her test," she said. The twins obediently followed her into the kitchen where she cleaned them up with a damp rag and then sent them to Marjorie's room. They went willingly, anxious to sleep in the bunk beds. Emma followed soon afterward and tucked Dennis into the top bed while David crawled into the bottom bunk. Marjorie came in a short time later, crawling into her bed along the opposite wall. The three talked for a while until Marjorie drifted off to sleep.

Dennis brought the sheets and quilt up to his nose and took a deep breath. The blankets smelled so clean and warm a feeling of joy passed over him. This bed was comfortable, and he loved being in it all by himself. In the silence, he could hear David breathing quietly below him.

Dennis knew that when morning came, he and his brother would have to go home, and thought desperately for an excuse to stay.

How he wished he had been born to Gus and Emma.

"I don't want to send the twins home tomorrow," Emma said as she climbed into bed. "I'll never forgive myself if anything happens to them."

Gus thought for a moment. "We've fought enough with Domko. If we try to keep those boys here just imagine what will happen."

Emma agreed. She had meant to report Domko to the police earlier that fall but had lost her nerve. Now she had another idea.

"If we involve a social worker, maybe they can step in and do something," she said. "If they lived here with us, they could visit their mother whenever they want but still be away from Domko."

Gus sympathized with his wife. Neither wanted hard feelings with the neighbors but felt they should do more to help the children. Once again they discussed Caroline's plight and her children's future well into the night. They reached the same conclusion as always—it was Caroline's responsibility to kick Domko out of the house. How much could they do when the children's mother seemed indifferent about their care?

"Besides," Gus sighed, as he rolled on his side. "I'm getting too old to start raising two young boys. It's almost time for us to retire."

Emma reluctantly agreed. "If only Bill were still alive this wouldn't be happening," she sighed. "If he knew what was going on in that house, it would break his heart."

A NIGHT IN THE BUSH

Caroline arrived at the Harwart house the following afternoon to persuade the twins to go home. Emma overheard her telling the boys that things were going to be better from now on. The twins were apprehensive but wanted desperately to please their mother. Caroline gave Emma a timid wave then left.

A few nights later, Domko stormed into the bedroom where Caroline slept with the children and began attacking her. They had argued earlier that day about the Harwarts and he'd warned the children that if they ever went to their house again, he would kill Gus. For that reason, Caroline refused to sleep in their bed. The older boys ran out the kitchen door towards the barn with Eunice and Rosie close behind, but the twins were wedged between their mother and the wall.

Domko yelled at the twins to get out of the room and began punching them. He was angrier than they'd ever seen and he seemed fueled by passion as he threw himself on top of their mother. As the twins ran out the door, they worried that he would smother her.

"Get your coat Denny," David said as he pulled on his boot and shoe. Reaching up, he grabbed a jacket from the hook and ran out into the cold night with Dennis on his heels.

"Should we go to Harwart's house?" Dennis called out.

"No," David said, worried for Gus' safety. "We'll go to Deightons."

They started out on the long walk across the field and through the bush to Jim's farm. Dennis labored to keep up since his leg was still stiff from a bad beating he'd received earlier that week.

The snow banks were three feet high in some places, but the recent warm weather had melted the top layer and followed by a cold snap, froze a thick crust on top of the snow. They were able to walk on top, but occasionally one of their feet would break through a soft spot, and their leg would plunge deep into the snow. David had to stop to empty his rubber boot many times, and Dennis' ankles were rubbed raw.

Fortunately, Dennis had grabbed Walter's coat, and it was too big, so the arms hung down past his wrists keeping the wind off his hands. David's was too small, so he tucked his arms high up in the sleeves.

After more than an hour in the frigid temperature, both boys lost all feeling in their frozen toes, and their fingers were numb and stiff. They had no idea how much further it was to the neighbor's farm.

"Denny, we gotta stop," David said as they trudged through the bush.

"We gots to keep going," Dennis replied, "I don't want to sleep in the bush—it's too cold out."

"But I'm mixed up. I don't know if we're going the right way no more. I think we should be there already."

Dennis groaned at the thought of sleeping outside again.

"It'll be okay," David said quickly. "I got matches."

After spending a few cold nights in the bush earlier that fall, David snuck a box of matches from the kitchen drawer to keep in his coat pocket. Domko was at his worst in the dead of winter, so learning to survive in the bush had become a matter of life and death for them. Domko had noticed the matches were missing but didn't know who to blame since everyone was stealing supplies.

The twins marched about one hundred yards into the bush until they came to a trail that ran east to west. It looked like a reasonable spot to spend the night, so they gathered some deadfall and piled the branches and logs against two trees that were growing close together. Using their feet, they cleared snow from the ground to make a modified fire pit. They peeled the damp bark from the fallen branches to expose the dry, seasoned wood. Using sticks, they scraped the ground close to the pit until most of the snow was pushed aside. It had taken nearly a dozen matches before their kindling sparked the beginnings of a fire. They sat on the ground, slowly adding wood to the flames until it was burning hot, warming their hands and feet. They pressed close together and tried to sleep. The crackling fire was the only sound to interrupt the cold, clear darkness of night.

They barely slept, fidgeting on the frozen ground while diligently adding wood to the fire to keep it going. The coldest part of the morning came right before dawn.

"Davey, I'm hungry," Dennis said. Not able to sit still, he began pacing in front of the fire. "What are we gonna do?"

"I'm hungry, too," David replied. "We'll wait here 'til almost lunchtime then go to Deightons."

"Why don't we go now?"

"If we go, they will make us go to school, and Domko might see us."

Dennis agreed that it would be best to wait.

Jim shivered as his bare feet touched the cold floor. The fire in the house had gone out hours ago. Making a fire in the big wood stove in the living room and the cook stove in the kitchen was the first thing he did each winter morning. Soon the house would be warm and cheery. Ruby would make coffee and breakfast while he milked the cows. He would then eat before finishing the rest of the morning chores. This morning ritual he shared with most farmers in the district.

Jim opened the outside door, and the brisk air struck his face like a slap. The thermometer nailed to the side of the house read twenty-four degrees below zero. It was a typical January morning—cold and clear. As he walked toward the barn, he could see the sun rising in the east. He stopped and squinted at a thin cloud of smoke rose up from the middle of the bush about a mile away.

"What could be burning in the bush?" he wondered out loud as he patted the dog who was stretching himself awake.

Maybe a plane crashed in the night, he thought. There was a lot of activity in the air since the Canadian Forces Base was established in Gypsumville, about thirty-five miles north of Moosehorn. He often saw planes flying low overhead, sometimes three a day. He could think of no other explanation.

He trotted to the barn to harness the horses, preparing himself to have to rescue someone. He hitched the horses to the sleigh, and soon the team was pulling him along the familiar path he used weekly to bring hay in from the field. The animals lowered their heads as they plowed a fresh trail through the deep snow. Jim hoped that whatever was on fire was close to the trail. Otherwise, he'd never be able to find it in the thick undergrowth.

Less than a half a mile into the bush, Jim saw something up ahead blocking the trail and as he got closer, recognized the Pischke twins huddled around a fire.

His first thought was that they were up to some mischief. Rumors were rampant in the community that the children were causing trouble and the twins were incorrigible. While Jim had no respect for Domko's opinion, so many people in the community were saying how bad the kids were, that he started to wonder if he was the one who'd been wrong all along.

"What are you kids doing?" he asked as he halted the horses and jumped down from the sleigh. "Trying to burn down my bush?"

The children cowered.

"N-n-no Jim," David stammered. "We had to make a fire to stay warm."

"How come you're not at home?" Jim asked.

"Satan kicked us out."

"How long have you been here?"

"All night."

Jim could hardly believe what he was hearing. There was a pile of wood stacked neatly by the trees, and the snow had been pushed away and packed down. There was a thick pile of ashes in the fire, and it looked as though they were telling the truth.

"He b-b-beat us up, and we got lost," Dennis said. "We was comin' to your house."

"C'mon," Jim said, kicking snow in the fire, thinking what a miracle it was they hadn't frozen to death. "You kids are coming with me."

Stiffly, the twins got up. Their young voices were suddenly full of enthusiasm. Since Jim wasn't afraid of Domko, they couldn't have wished for a better person to come along.

They unhitched the horses and turned the sleigh around. Within a few minutes, it was gliding briskly to Jim's home. The boys took turns telling Jim what happened the night before. David started a sentence, Dennis would add to it before David would finish. It was the way they always told a story, and those who knew them had grown accustomed to it. Their stuttering and odd pronunciation made them difficult to understand, so they tried to speak slowly.

Jim shook his head in wonder, feeling ashamed he'd assumed the worst.

"He doesn't know his arse from a hole in the ground," Jim said shaking his head.

The twins looked surprised.

"A farmer I was talking to said you boys are the bad ones, always giving Domko a hard time," he said.

They were astonished. "No Jim," David said, fearing their friend would turn against them. "It's not us; we is not the bad ones. Ol' Satan just tells everyone we is."

When they arrived at the house, the smell of breakfast cooking and Ruby's warm smile greeted them. Jim explained to Ruby what had happened while the twins took off their coats. They immediately went to stand in the heat of the wood stove while Jim explained to Ruby what had happened. They spoke in hushed tones then Ruby went to the twins and asked them to lift up their shirts and pull off their pants. Some of the bruises that covered their bodies were old; the rest were new.

Seeing that Ruby was sympathetic to their plight, Dennis showed her where his leg was sore. David interrupted to describe the beating he received a week ago that made it hard to raise his right arm higher than his shoulder. Jim poured himself a cup of coffee while he watched—and listened.

"We don't gots to go to school do we?" David asked.

"No, not today," Jim said. "We're going o to Ashern. There's somebody else who should see those bruises."

After eating breakfast, Jim finished the morning chores then took the car battery from the house to start the car. By early afternoon he and the twins were on their way to town.

Glancing over his shoulder, Jim's heart softened at the sight of them sitting solemnly in the back seat.

Why Caroline had returned to the farm that past summer he didn't understand. He knew that she'd been cut off welfare because Domko was spending the night. That was something else he couldn't quite understand.

Why would such an attractive woman have a relationship with such a crackpot? he wondered.

Now she was associating mostly with the Witnesses, and that made her non-Witness friends and family uncomfortable, but it suited the Witnesses just fine. It was hard to help when they wouldn't let you in.

The twins became excited as the car approached Ashern. Jim followed the highway through town, and they pointed excitedly at the house where they had lived.

Jim stopped in front of the RCMP office and led them into the building. An officer, who Jim didn't recognize, was sitting at a desk drinking coffee. Jim introduced himself and explained why he was there.

The officer quietly listened as Jim told the children's story from the night before and then described Domko's erratic behavior. The twins said nothing as the officer studied them.

Finally, he spoke. "Leave the boys with me. I'll talk to my superiors to see what we can do."

Satisfied with the arrangement, Jim extended his hand to the man in friendship. He was confident that this officer would see to it that Domko went to jail. Turning to the twins, he assured them that they were in good hands.

Jim drove back to Moosehorn, stopping at the supply store. He loaded the car with groceries then went to the café where he sat and had coffee with a few men who intently listened as he relayed the shocking story. They were anxious to hear gossip about Caroline since her relationship with Domko was a hot conversation topic.

"I swear if something isn't done about him, he's gonna kill one of those kids," Jim said, shaking his head.

By late afternoon he started for home. Shortly after turning onto the Township Line, he glanced in the rearview mirror and saw a police car approaching. Slowing down, he pulled far to the right. Snow swirled up as the cruiser passed. Once it settled, Jim could see the outline of the officer and two little heads in the back seat.

The officer glanced in his rear view mirror at the boys sitting behind him. There were some families in the area that weren't considered "normal," and the Pischke family was one of them.

The boys talked hurriedly among themselves, pronouncing words that he couldn't understand. He couldn't help but like these strange little characters and had been warned before he left that their stepfather was quite odd.

The police couldn't take Jim Deighton's word that the children were being beaten because everyone knew that Deighton and Domko hated each other and fought over land all the time. He'd have to get a complaint registered by the mother to file charges, and he'd been cautioned by the other officers that she likely wouldn't cooperate. Domestic cases were often a waste of time. Seldom was the father ever charged because usually, the mother would end up defending him. It seemed that women like Caroline did nothing to help themselves.

Removing the children was an option, but not something the police were authorized to do unless the situation was life threatening. If children weren't in immediate danger but noticeably neglected, the provincial child welfare department was called. The officer decided he'd check out the situation and if warranted, file a report with the Winnipeg agency, but realistically, how could he trust the word of two little boys?

The twins sank in the seat as the cruiser turned north toward the farm. Domko was going to be livid that the police were summoned to the house. They hoped that Jim's story had been convincing enough, and their bruises had made an impression on the officer. They were confident that he would arrest Domko and take him away just like the time in Ashern after he beat up the drunk man.

"Is this your house?" the officer asked, slowing and pointing. The twins nodded that it was. The car turned into the driveway, and the officer got out. The twins waited in the car until they were told to follow him into the house. A scowling Domko answered the brisk knock at the door. He invited the policeman in, while the twins followed close behind. They didn't look at Domko but kept their eyes glued to the floor.

The officer asked Domko a few questions, then asked where Caroline was. Domko said that she was visiting her father and brother near the town of Faulkner. He said that Eunice and the older boys were at school and that he was left to look after Kathy and Rosie, who played quietly on the floor.

The officer asked why the neighbor had brought the twins to the police station. It was obvious to him as he looked around the house that the family was very poor.

"They's be runnink away," Domko said. "I's not be knowink vat else to do."

Domko explained the boys' bruises by saying that they were always playing and fighting with their older brothers.

Because the officer couldn't question Caroline and felt uncomfortable waiting for her to return, he soon left the house.

The sight of Domko glaring at them in anger caused each boy to wet his pants. He waited until the car had pulled out of the driveway before turning on the twins who stood frozen on the spot as he slid off his belt. They screamed as he whipped them until they couldn't scream anymore.

THE YELLOW DRESS

It took nearly a week for the twins to recover from the beating. Their mother knew that Domko had injured them but was too afraid to say anything. The boys lost all confidence in the police's ability to help them and decided that when they went to the neighbors again, they would ask that the police not be called.

Caroline and Domko married secretly on January 26. Domko had pushed for marriage after hearing the people he'd harassed suggest that he be deported. But now that he was married to a Canadian citizen, he could stay in Canada.

Caroline's father and members of the church seemed satisfied with the union. Her father was from the old school and believed that the man was the head of the household. He hoped that now that Caroline was married she might start obeying her husband. Church members hoped that marriage would smooth out their relationship and the pair wouldn't be an embarrassment to the congregation any longer.

Old Walter understood Domko's complaints about the children. He agreed with his new son-in-law—supporting Bill's children isn't something he wanted to do either. So shortly after the wedding when Caroline and Domko approached him for a loan, he agreed. They desperately needed to renovate the house and update the farm equipment. He gave them a substantial loan with an open repayment date, hoping that this would finally get the couple headed in the right direction. He kept careful records so that if the money weren't repaid, the amount would be subtracted from any inheritance left for his three children. Caroline had already used up a good portion of her share.

Fifteen-year-old Walter accumulated a healthy pile of pelts that winter, but by mid-March found it impossible to check the lines after a four-day storm dropped more than seven inches of snow. By the end of the month, he brought the majority of his traps home. He had been trapping muskrats since February and by the beginning of spring thaw, had more than enough furs to pay for the motor scooter he'd been dreaming of all winter.

Once the last of the muskrat skins were stretched and cured, Walter asked Domko to take him to Sidney I. Robinson, a fur buying company in Winnipeg. Domko agreed they would go later that week and he'd sell his cream at the same time.

Walter bounded out of bed Friday morning to discover that Domko had changed his mind. Instead of taking Walter to Winnipeg, Domko was going to take his friend, Hugo Russell. Walter protested but was told he'd have to stay home and do chores. He joined his brothers in the barn as Domko drove out of the driveway with the furs piled high in the back of Hugo's truck.

"I thought you were going to Winnipeg," Norman said as Walter picked up a milking pail.

"No, the old bastard changed his mind," he said, but his spirits gradually lifted as he talked about the furs and how much money he'd receive for them.

"I'm gonna buy the motor scooter," he beamed. The bike would make him the envy of the neighborhood boys. "And then I'll get Momma whatever she wants. I think she'd like a new dress."

They worked quietly for a few minutes then Walter asked Norman what he would do if he was rich.

"Whatta ya mean IF I turned rich?" Norman laughed. "I'm gonna be rich someday, and I'm gonna buy a plane. I've been reading about them, and I'd buy one I could give people rides in." Norman cheerily discussed his plans for the future as Walter's mind wandered back to what he would do if he had a lot of money. He decided that he would build a brand new house then kick Domko off the farm. He'd buy up land from the neighbors and have at least two hundred cows. He figured he'd continue to trap even if he was wealthy.

"Yeah, and I'd buy a car so we wouldn't hafta go to town with the horses no more," he said interrupting Norman's description of plane engines. "Yep, if I was rich I'd buy you all whatever you wanted."

Domko was excited when he arrived home early that evening. He bounded through the house as the children scavenged through the box of used clothes he brought full of pants, shoes, and shirts.

"Punks, Punks," he said. "I's be givink but-a-some punks sheet!"

"What are you talking about?" Caroline asked. She had never seen him so animated before. His eyes flashed as he acted out the scene that took place that afternoon.

When Domko was carrying the clothes through downtown Winnipeg, he'd been accosted by two young men. The punks wanted the box and threatened him with pocketknives. They told him to hand it over and wanted the wad of cash in his pocket.

Pretending to oblige, Domko put the box on the ground then reached into the breast pocket of his coat. Instead of giving them his money, he pulled out a hunting knife and let out a roar. He chased the would-be muggers down the sidewalk, slashing the air behind them as the teenagers ran for their lives.

Domko's chest puffed out as he told the story, and predicted that he would be the last person those punks ever tried to rob. Caroline and the older boys laughed, but the twins and girls sat in silence because they were terrified of the knife.

Domko must have sensed David's anxiety because he smiled and reached into the pocket and pulled it out again. David gasped at the sight of the razor-sharp edge shining in the dim kitchen.

"Punks," he said as their eyes locked. "I's be givink them some."

David fidgeted where he sat and was thankful when Walter changed the subject. "So how much did I get for my furs?" he asked.

"Fur?" Domko innocently asked as he began filling his plate with stew. "Vat fur?"

"The furs you took in for me today," he replied.

"You?" Domko asked innocently. "They's not be yours."

Walter was stunned. He stood there for a moment trying to comprehend what Domko was saying.

"B-ut I spent all winter trapping them," he said, following him to the table. "T-those were my furs."

Domko sat down and began spooning food into his mouth while Walter waited for an explanation.

"Who's trap they's be? Marjie?" Domko said as he chewed. "They's be my trap."

Walter's face began to flush. "Y-you gave me those traps," he stammered. "The f-furs were mine, and the m-money is mine."

Domko looked up from his plate. His eyes flashed, and the area near the scar on his temple turned white.

"Who's food yous be yit?" he demanded, standing up to face him. "I's be buyink you pant and coat, and yous be trowink it in the bush." Domko called him ungrateful, stupid and useless. Suddenly in the midst of it all, the picture became clear. Domko had planned to keep the money right from the start. Walter stared back and shook his head.

As soon as Domko sat down, Walter went to the door and slowly put on his shoes and coat. He glanced over his shoulder once more, before opening the door and stepping out into the cool evening wind. He'd had enough. He walked away from the farm and vowed never to return.

As the snow melted and the water in Lake Manitoba and its tributaries began to rise, the farm became an island. Caroline warned the children about the dangers of deep water, especially Pischke Lake, the body of water bordering the east side of the farm, which the twins called "the beaver dam." She told them that the bottom of the lake was soft and said that she'd seen adults wading across suddenly disappear when the lake bottom would cave in. She told them never to try to swim the lake alone.

The twins looked at each other. They had discovered the deep water just days before while playing on the softening ice. Norman had pushed a six-foot-long pole through a hole, and rushing water underneath had caught the stick and wrenched it from his hands.

Caroline heard through the grapevine that Walter was living with George and Nina Kiesman just a few miles away. Domko told her to go and pick him up and bring him back to the farm, but Caroline refused. She had also heard that the Kiesmans were moving to Winnipeg and that there was a job waiting for him as soon as he turned sixteen—an opportunity she didn't want her son to miss.

In the battle of wills that followed, Domko insisted that the twins start doing morning and evening chores. Caroline eventually gave in, so the nine-year-olds were expected to work each day beside their older siblings.

One afternoon in mid-April, the children returned home from school to discover their mother was gone. Apparently, Gus and Emma had taken her to the hospital. When they asked when their mother would be coming home, Domko didn't reply. He just stared out the window.

The following day it started raining early, and by the end of the day, the already full ditches were overflowing. Frustrated that nothing could be done outdoors, Domko flew into a rage, and the children raced to the barn to escape him. The floor in the loft creaked and groaned as they scurried to the far corner, one of the few spots where the roof didn't leak. The tin sheeting that Domko had bought with Walter's fur money still sat piled in the barnyard.

The youngsters slept in a stack of old hay as rain pounded the roof. They awoke the next morning to find it still drizzling. They did the morning chores and tried to stay away from Domko who was pacing the floor and muttering about the hay crop, as another five inches of rain fell that day.

Just before nightfall, Domko sent Eunice to the henhouse to gather eggs. She returned with a half dozen, but before she was allowed to cook them, Domko took the eggs from her and cracked one on the edge of the table, threw back his head and slid the raw egg into his mouth. The children watched with disgust as he ate all of the eggs then wiped his face with the back of his hand before belching.

The following morning the children went willingly to the barn to do chores. They were hungry and knew that Domko's strict routine meant he'd go back to the house once they started working, and that would give them some time alone. As soon as he left, Eunice ran to the far end of the barn and got a tin cup out from under a stack of hay. Norman watched from the door as Eunice dipped the cup into the milk pail. She drank the warm milk, then dipped it again and handed it to Rosie. Then it was the twins' turn, and finally Steven and Norman. They took turns drinking until their stomachs were full. The milk helped ease their hunger and lifted their spirits. When Domko returned, he didn't suspect a thing, and since they did it most days, he never missed the milk.

That morning, Rosie's cat paced and meowed by the barn door. The cat had almost starved over the winter but had since grown fat eating mice that were easy to catch as they searched for dry ground. She found a comfortable spot on the floor between the two rows of cows and watched thoughtfully as the children worked.

The cat turned her head to listen to the sound of milk squirting into the small tin pails. She knew that if she waited long enough, Rosie would sneak her some milk. She meowed and purred softly each time she passed. Rosie's job was to hold each cow's tail and then take the filled pail and carry it carefully to the door. She'd pour the milk into the larger cans, then return the pails to the older children. She'd stop to pat the cat each time she went by, and the cat arched her back in appreciation.

Domko never approved of having a cat in the barn and would kick it every time he saw it. Since pets were of no value to him, he thought the children shouldn't have them either. Caroline had saved this cat's life more than once by removing it from his sight, and it had become less cautious in his presence.

When Domko returned to the barn, he stood in the alleyway leaning against a shovel. He watched Rosie's exchanges with the cat and then without warning, lunged forward. The cat screeched in pain as he pinned it to the barn floor with the cutting edge of the shovel. Startled, the children turned in time to see the cat struggle out from under the sharp edge, its back end almost severed from its body, intestines spilling out onto the floor. The cat looked around helplessly as it dragged itself past the cows into a feeding stall. A crying Rosie crawled into the manger and cradled the cat in her lap until it died.

The other children didn't dare stop milking because they knew that Domko was watching them. Then apparently pleased with himself, he grunted softly and carried the milk can to the house.

Caroline arrived home a week later to find the house and children in an awful mess. Manure had been tracked across the floors, and the dishes hadn't been properly washed since the day she left. The house stunk badly, and the children were dirty and hungry. Complications at the end of her pregnancy meant she had spent a few weeks in the hospital before giving birth prematurely. Both she and the baby were fine now—but she was weak and tired, and her first inclination upon seeing the mess was to return to the hospital. But instead, she went to the bedroom and called the children to look at their new baby brother. Domko beamed at the sight of his first son, a boy who looked much like himself. They named him Raymond.

A month later, the public health nurse came for a routine visit. Margaret Burnett was surprised to see that although the farm seemed better managed, the children were as neglected as ever.

"How come you aren't in school?" she boomed at the twins. She was a staunch British immigrant who spoke with a distinct accent.

David hesitated. He'd never met such an assertive woman before and was frightened by her height and her strange voice.

"W-we had to do ch-chores," he stammered, looking at the ground. "We're g-goin' n-now."

The nurse watched as they walked past her car, then into the bush towards the school. They carried no books or lunch, and their feet were bare.

She shook her head. She had heard that Caroline had returned to the farm from Ashern after her mother's allowance payments had been cut off. She had also heard stories about Caroline's infidelities and Domko's violence. Apparently, the children were thieves who couldn't be trusted, and she wondered how much of this was true. Margaret knew all about small towns and how the rumor mill turned. She would decide for herself once she got to know the family better.

Her first impression of Domko was not good. He sat at the table holding a dirty coffee cup in one hand and a cigarette in the other. He smoked during the entire visit, eyeing Margaret suspiciously as she examined the baby.

Raymond was a stocky, contented child who nursed well and had put on just the right amount of weight. It was obvious that Caroline loved babies and was proud of her new son. She was delighted when Margaret rated his health as excellent.

Margaret asked to speak with Caroline privately, glancing over her shoulder at Domko who was listening carefully to everything she said. Caroline nodded and motioned for Margaret to follow her into the bedroom where they quietly discussed birth control. Caroline smiled sheepishly and nodded as Margaret repeated Dr. Steenson's advice that she shouldn't have any more children since this ninth pregnancy had hurt her health. But when she finished the long explanation, Margaret wasn't sure how much good it did.

What troubled Margaret most about this visit was the fact that Rosie and Kathy were nearly the same size despite their age difference. She didn't expect the blind girl to be so robust and that Rosie, almost three years older, would be so timid and gaunt. Caroline told her that Kathy was blind since birth, but Margaret had already heard the rumor that Domko had blinded her during one of his rages. If that was true, she certainly didn't seem to be neglected or abused now.

She also noted that the twins looked awfully thin. Without seeing the older children, she was unable to make a full assessment. She thought the differences between the Pischke and Domko children could be attributed to the fact their fathers were very different. She remembered Bill Pischke as tall, thin and in failing health—markedly different from Domko.

Once she finished, she was glad to be out of the cramped, dirty house and into the fresh air. She decided to return that fall, late in the day, so that she would see the older children, too—convinced that if something bad were going on in the house, they would tell her.

Farmers were just beginning to nourish the hope of getting into the fields when it started to rain again. By the end of May, more than fourteen inches had fallen. Domko was inconsolable, pacing the house all day long, his mood darkening. He had just bought more cattle and was worried he'd have no hay to feed them that winter.

To take his mind off of the cattle and make use of the time, Caroline began pushing him to build an addition onto the house. This was a promise he'd made before they were married and they still had the money borrowed from her father earlier that year. Convincing him was not hard since he also wanted more space and a bedroom for himself, Caroline and his two children.

Crude plans were drawn, and the project began with the help of local carpenter Henry Herzog. Henry arrived one morning with his tools and started measuring and discussing the renovations with Domko. Lumber was purchased, and soon the kitchen area was removed from the east end of the house and dragged over the well and outdoor pump. They built a lean-to style addition on the north side, and this became the new kitchen. The attic was opened up as part of a plan to create an upstairs bedroom for all the children except Kathy and Raymond.

One evening when the job was half finished, Henry met Gus on the road while on his way home. They exchanged pleasantries then Henry described the work he was doing on the house.

"Why would you want to help that miserable old son-of-a-gun?" Gus asked. He was surprised that the quiet, kindly man appeared to like Domko.

"Why not?" Henry asked. "He seems all right to me."

"Well, what I know of him I don't like," Gus shot back. "And the way he treats those kids is a disgrace."

Henry thought for a moment. "I think he's doing a good job with the kids. He's straightening them out, that's all. Domko told me all about those kids and how they run away every time he tries to make them work."

Gus was stunned. He shook his head in disgust. Henry's ignorance explained why so many people disagreed when he complained about how Domko treated the children. Domko had the community convinced they deserved the beatings. He was poisoning everyone against the Pischkes by saying they behaved like little animals.

Arguing with Henry wasn't worth the effort. It was obvious the man had made up his mind, and nothing Gus could say would change it. All he could hope for was that Domko would eventually show the side of himself he kept carefully hidden.

"They are all freshly washed and pressed, so you don't have to worry about them smelling like they've been in storage," Marjorie said as she pulled back the lid of the cardboard box. She had just finished going through her closet and brought what no longer fit over for Eunice. Her mother always insisted that when she give clothes away that they be clean and in good shape so that the girls wouldn't feel bad while accepting charity.

"Thanks, Marjie," Eunice giggled as they began pulling shorts, t-shirts, a pair of cotton pants and a sweater out of the box. Eunice let out a delighted gasp when she discovered a dress at the bottom. Her eyes glowed as she pulled out a shin length, yellow crepe dress. It had puffy short sleeves and a low neckline. Small bows adorned the front and the sleeves. It was the most beautiful piece of clothing she'd ever seen.

"I love it," Eunice exclaimed, pulling it close. She instinctively glanced over her shoulder at Domko who was sitting in the kitchen, watching their exchange.

"You're welcome," Marjorie said, glad her favorite dress would be appreciated. "It's going to look real good on you."

Eunice was anxious to try on the dress, but the idea of undressing near him made her feel uneasy since he'd been looking at her in a strange way lately. Blocking his view of the dress, she quickly placed it back in the box and covered it with the rest of the clothes. She didn't want Domko to find it, just in case he thought it was too frilly for the farm and destroyed it. She would show it to her mother, though, since she could appreciate the desire to own a beautiful dress.

The following afternoon, Caroline and Domko went to Moosehorn to pick up more building materials for the house. As soon as they were gone, Eunice ran to the bedroom and dug through the box of clothes. She pulled out the yellow dress and marveled at how lovely it was. Stripping off her dirty slacks and t-shirt, she pulled the dress over her head. Looking at herself in the full-length mirror on her mother's bedroom wall, she could see the dress was a little big, but it was still the most beautiful thing she'd ever owned. Cinching it in at the waist, she stood on her toes. Tossing her chin into the air, she tried very hard to look grown up.

Pretending that she was Cinderella, Eunice twirled in the dress. Closing her eyes, she visualized a handsome prince riding up the driveway to take her away to his castle. Then suddenly, Domko appeared in her fantasy, causing her to frown. Domko would never let her leave the farm. He began yelling at the prince who jumped down from his horse. The prince showed no fear as he pulled a long sword from a sheath and swung it at Domko who stood in stunned silence. The sharp blade sliced easily through his neck, and Domko's head dropped to the ground.

The prince then took two steps forward and kicked Domko's head into the bush. Eunice giggled out loud at the thought. Then she visualized the prince turning to her, saying that she was the most beautiful girl he'd ever seen. He helped her onto the back of his big, white horse where she would sit side-saddle like the fancy ladies in books. She wrapped her arms around his waist as they galloped down the road to a big castle. She sighed as she played the scene over again in her mind. Flopping on the bed, she closed her eyes and dreamed of the day she would be able to leave the farm. How truly wonderful it would be to live in Moosehorn with a handsome husband.

The sound of Henry pounding nails on the roof brought her back to reality. The noise reminded her that Domko would be home in a few hours and the cows needed milking soon, and it was her job to bring them from the pasture. She decided to leave the dress on a little longer.

The image of herself in the dress, combined with her earlier fantasy, helped lighten her step as she skipped outside. It was a sunny, warm day, and for the first time in a long time, she felt glad to be alive. She skipped past the barn onto the well-worn path to the pasture, her bare feet squishing on the cool, wet grass. She picked up a piece of twine and wrapped it around her waist.

Her brothers were supposed to help her, but to her relief, they were nowhere around. Alone, she could be whoever she wanted to be. At first, she hummed a tune silently; then she began to sing out loud as her confidence soared. Twirling, she looked down to see the dress flowing and twisting as she changed directions. She was giddy from the dress as she rounded the bush dancing and singing.

The cows were relaxing in the shade of the trees a short distance away. The sight of Eunice skipping and singing in the flowing dress startled a handful of the younger animals and they took off in the opposite direction. The cows, skittish from Domko's harsh and erratic behavior, also caught sight of Eunice and began bawling. It wasn't long, and the entire herd was up and running full speed away from her. Eunice watched in dismay as the cows disappeared down the path into the next bush. She began chasing after them, slipping on wet grass and manure as she ran. It had taken more than an hour before the cows were calm enough to chase home.

As the barn came into view, the cows began to bawl and trot towards the familiar building. Eunice's daydreaming was spoiled by the ruckus with the cows, but she had been very careful that no harm had come to the beautiful, yellow dress.

TRYING TO HELP

When school finished at the end of June, Steven went to live at Elmer Ruchotzke's farm near Ashern. Now, with the two older boys gone, it put a lot of pressure on Norman and Eunice to get the work done. They never complained, but no matter how hard they worked, Domko berated and criticized them endlessly. Their only break was walking the seven miles to Moosehorn to pick up the mail, and since Norman was now the oldest child at home, this privilege was reserved for him.

Renovations to the house were finished by mid-summer. The addition to the east end of the house plus the opening of the attic made their home more than twice its original size. Domko arranged his belongings in the large room at the far corner of the house. He bought himself a double bed and chest of drawers. Nobody was allowed to go inside except Caroline and his two children. The twins were happy about this, planning to stay as far away from him as possible.

The children moved their few belongings and the double bed from downstairs to the attic. The room ran the full length of the original house and was partially finished, with sheeting covering the rafters of the A-shaped ceiling. A four-foot wall was built the length of the room on each side, creating a three-foot crawl space between the walls and where the ceiling joined the floor.

A small window at the top of the stairs let in fresh air and afternoon sunshine. The children dragged the bed to the far end and bumped it up against the wall.

One evening after a full day of mending fences, the children were awakened by Domko's ravings as he stormed up the stairs in the middle of the night.

"I's be lookink at but-a-some feet," he bellowed as he lifted up the blanket and stuck the lantern underneath.

The children quivered with discomfort as he examined their feet. David and Dennis' were caked in blood since they had outgrown their shoes and were working in bare feet. Normally they were lined with a tough callous, but because it had been such a wet spring, their feet had become soft.

As soon as Domko finished, he dropped the blanket then went back downstairs. The children whispered about his possible motives but could think of no reason for him to do this. The next day they reported his bizarre behavior to their mother, but she offered no explanation.

"He's been doing a lot of strange things lately," she said. "Just keep out of his way."

The feet-checking continued nightly for almost two weeks.

The added space in the house meant the children were not underfoot and this seemed to settle Domko, although it didn't stop the beatings altogether. While in bed one night the children listened intently to the sound of a cow bellowing somewhere outside. The calf, who was separated from its mother, was answering somewhere in the distance. The bawling was enough to send Domko flying up the stairs, removing his belt as he went. He accused the children of leaving a gate open then tearing back the blanket, began strapping them. As they struggled to escape, no parts of their bodies were spared as he viciously whipped them. Soon, all but one had scrambled off the bed and ran downstairs. It was David this time who found himself trapped in the corner between the bed and wall. David was older now and starting to realize that Domko's rampages were more than just a reaction to a throbbing head. Each time his heavy boot connected with David's back or leg, he grunted with satisfaction. David knew that to stay alive, he was going to have to understand him better and learn to outsmart him. At that moment he decided that Domko would never trap him like this again.

"You's be chasink into some Deighton," Domko ordered as he pointed to the fence that separated their pasture land from Jim's oat field. It was late summer, and Jim's oats were heading out nicely and on the verge of ripening.

Dennis and David looked at each other. Usually, it was their job to keep the cows off of the neighbor's land. Now they were being told to allow the cattle to graze Jim's field on purpose. Sixty-five cattle could do a lot of damage in a short time.

They protested until Domko picked up a stick causing David to run in one direction while Dennis took off the opposite way, a trick they'd learned after they got caught running together. Domko could run incredibly fast for a short distance as long as he kept to a straight line. They knew if they split up and zigzagged, he could never catch either of them. This time, though, he flung the stick and hit Dennis in the back of the head, knocking him to the ground.

"What if Jim comes?" David hollered taking a few steps back toward Domko, distracting him.

"Vat? Yous be scared of your daddy?" Domko spat.

David shrugged and made a few excuses, buying Dennis some time.

As soon as Dennis wobbled to his feet, Domko demanded that they get the cows and chase them into Jim's field.

As the twins strolled behind an old, lame cow, Domko snuck up on them and smacked each on the head. It was a familiar warning that if they didn't do as they were told, they were in line for a beating. The boys shrunk under his glare.

"You's be bringink some out later," he said before marching back to the house. David and Dennis stood and watched as the cows greedily chewed and trampled Jim's oats.

Before long, they saw a tractor appear from the south. It accelerated when the driver saw the cattle spreading far and wide in the field. They knew it was Jim when he stood up and began waving his hat in anger. The twins had mixed feelings about their neighbor's timing. While they were glad that Jim's field wasn't entirely destroyed, they were embarrassed to have to explain this to him.

Their faces flushed as he jumped off the tractor.

"What the hell is this?" he yelled. "Get your goddamned cattle off my field!"

"Domko m-made us do it," David said.

Jim looked at the youngsters who stood trembling in front of him. Each had huge bruises, and Dennis had the telltale signs of a black eye.

Jim shook his head and sighed. "Well at least help me get them off here," he said. "Then I'll go talk to that stupid ass."

The twins ran in opposite directions in a wide circle to gather the cattle and chase them out of the field. It was a difficult job because the cows were enjoying the fresh oats, but finally, once they got the lead cows going in the right direction, the others followed.

As the boys chased the cows back to their pasture, Jim followed on the tractor. Then he turned and accelerated towards the farm as they ran behind. Even though they were afraid to be near Domko when he was mad, they couldn't resist watching the confrontation. Jim was one of the few people in the community who had enough guts to stand up to Domko.

Jim cursed as he drove along the edge of the pasture.

We didn't need fences in this part of the country until that fool arrived, he thought. *Most of the farmers around here are too proud to steal from one another.*

But everyone knew that Domko didn't have enough land to support the number of cattle he owned. He wanted to fatten the animals on neighboring crops in case he was short of hay that coming winter. Jim wasn't surprised, in fact, he expected it. That's why he'd gone to check the field that day because late one night a few weeks earlier, he'd seen Domko chase his cows into Herman Gall's field. As a precaution, he'd been checking his fields regularly since then.

That Domko is a curse, he thought. *Thinks he owns the entire countryside.*

Jim drove his tractor from the field and up onto the grass in Caroline's yard. He jumped off in front of Domko who was standing by the chicken coop. They argued for a few moments, then Domko pointed to the twins who had stopped a safe distance away.

"I's not be doink it, they's be," he said.

"That's bullshit, and you know it," Jim replied. "If those boys chased the cattle into my field, it's because you told them to."

"They's be vatchink but-a-some cow," Domko explained. "They's be goot for sheet!"

"You can't fool me with that innocent act," Jim replied. "I can see right through you so don't waste your breath lying to me."

Domko threw his arms up in the air. He screamed at Jim to leave the property, threatening to kill him if he didn't.

"I's be killink lots of men. I's be shootink but-a-some Deighton!"

"You're gonna shoot me?" Jim asked sarcastically. "I'm not afraid of you, you stupid sonofabitch. I've got a gun, and I'm not afraid to use it either."

Domko stepped back and stared at his neighbor. Usually, his threats were met with fear.

"I've shot lots of men, too," Jim lied. "You keep your cattle off my land, or I'll shoot you." With that, Jim turned and climbed back on the tractor. He roared through the yard, past the house and accelerated down the road.

Impressed with Jim's spunk, the twins laughed and ran into the bush towards the beaver dam. Glancing over their shoulders as they went, they saw Domko punching the air in frustration as he swore that he was going to kill them and Jim.

Dennis and David stayed in the bush near the lake for a few days. By the end of the second day, they were tired of foraging for berries and decided to try to catch a rabbit. Walter had taught them to set snares, and luckily, Dennis had a piece of string in his pocket. David took it and made a snare. Examining the ground closely, he found a rabbit run and tied the snare to a branch. The twins crept out of sight and watched for a while, expecting a rabbit to appear immediately. "We got to catch one soon," Dennis said, his stomach growling. "I'm hungry."

David was also hungry. He'd lost track of time and couldn't remember the last time they had eaten. Bored with sitting and waiting in the bush, they decided to go for a walk along the lake.

"Do you think old Squeezer's gonna kill us?" David asked.

"I dunno," Dennis replied, kicking a stone. "He sure hates me. He hates me the most."

"Nope he hates Rosie most," David laughed, picking up a stick and flinging it ahead. Domko hated Dennis with a passion, but David didn't want to make his brother feel any worse.

"What 'bout Norman?" Dennis added. "He don't like Norman at all."

"Yeah, poor Norman," David said, shaking his head as he remembered the beating his brother got after forgetting to close a gate behind the cows. "He hates Norman almost as much as taking a bath."

The twins laughed and pushed each other in fun. They climbed the bank of the lake and stood under the oak trees, looking out over the expanse of dark water stretching more than a mile wide before them. Tall reeds growing close to the shore blew softly in the wind. The sun reflected brightly off the shimmering water, causing them to squint.

"Have you seen how funny he looks at us?" David asked, picking up a stone and skimming it out over the water. "Like we're evil."

"Yeah, and he never talks, just yells," Dennis added. "He thinks we're like them negro slaves I read about at school. There ain't no such thing as havin' slaves no more, is there?"

David shook his head. "Nope."

"Hey Davey," Dennis asked softly, "what do you 'spose people is like over the beaver dam?"

"I dunno," David replied, picking up another stone. He ran his thumb across the smooth surface then flung it across the water. "Maybe they're good like in Ashern."

"Too bad Norman's plane didn't fly us there, eh?" Dennis said, looking up into the tree overhead. Jumping up, he grabbed a lower limb and let himself dangle there. "When I'm big, I'm gonna make us a boat so we can float across."

David smiled at the idea. He looked at his brother and shuddered at the thought of his life without Dennis.

"C'mon," he said, smacking him playfully on the stomach. "Let's go swimmin."

The boys fell asleep that night under the stars without having anything more to eat. In the morning they woke early to find a fat rabbit caught in the snare.

"I knew this was a good spot," David said. "See Denny? I told you."

Dennis eyed the furry animal. At first, he felt sorry for it, but once the shock wore off of seeing its limp body, his stomach began growling.

David skinned and gutted the animal as Walter had taught him, while Dennis made a fire, then poked two sticks in the ground to make a spit. David speared a sharp stick lengthwise through the carcass then hung it over the fire. Within a few minutes, the smell of roasting meat permeated the air. The fire sputtered as juice from the meat dripped into the flames.

"Is it ready?" Dennis asked.

"Almost," David said. He could hardly wait to taste it.

"We'll split it half, right Davey?"

"Yep, I'll take the big half, and you can have the little one."

They grinned at each other while sitting on the ground waiting for the meat to cook. Caught completely off guard, a rustling in the bush caused them to turn to see Domko emerge on the path. He must have seen the smoke and followed the smell.

"Vat?" he asked. "You's be yitting ant peesing ant sheeting and doink nothing all day long."

Domko was too close for them to both get away. David gave Dennis a sideways glance, and they silently agreed it would be better to go back to work than risk a beating. They jumped up as Domko kicked dirt into the fire. He grabbed the skewer and pointed towards home.

"Fraa," he yelled.

They started down the path with Domko close behind. Fearing he'd kick them from behind, they glanced nervously over their shoulders, wanting to stay more than a leg length ahead of him.

Chuckling, Domko slipped the rabbit off of the stick and began ripping it apart.

"Hey," Dennis muttered. "That's ours."

Domko smiled as he took a bite and then with a whining voice, mocked Dennis. He lunged forward and kicked him.

"Denny," David cautioned in their secret language as he pulled him ahead, "shut up, it's not worth it and be careful you don't turn your back."

The twins spent the rest of the day pitching hay alongside Norman and Eunice. In the evening they had to get the cows from the pasture and chase them in for milking. When those chores were done they were allowed to eat whatever supper was left over after Domko, Caroline and Kathy had eaten. They fought over bits of boiled pork and potatoes.

That night the boys wearily climbed to the attic bedroom and fell onto the bed. They could hear Domko chastising Caroline downstairs for something she had forgotten to do that day.

"Hey, Denny I don't think we should sleep here," David whispered. He sensed something ominous in Domko's tone.

"I'm tired," Dennis said, closing his eyes.

David lay on the bed but was unable to fall asleep. Quietly he got up and looked for a place to hide. He noticed a six-inch space along the far wall where the builder had run out of Buffalo board. Examining it closely he could see that if he pulled the piece of the wall back, he'd be able to squeeze in behind it. He began searching for something to pry the nails out of the wall. Norman noticed what he was doing and joined in.

"Never mind," he said, gripping the edge of the board. With the two of them pulling hard, they were able to snap the board off, giving them enough space to slip in if they turned sideways.

Eunice and Rosie followed the boys into the hiding spot. The space was just over three feet wide and the roof angled sharply to the floor, so everyone except Rosie had to bend over to keep from bumping their heads. They giggled at the genius of it, and each found a spot to lie down. David went back to the opening and called to Dennis.

"Come hide in here," he said as loud as he dared. Dennis was enjoying having the bed all to himself and muttered that he wanted to be left alone.

"Denny, c'mon," David said.

Rolling over, Dennis turned his back to his brother. Finally, David gave up and found himself a spot to sleep. It wasn't long, and the children were startled awake by the sound of Domko's feet pounding up the stairs.

David was disoriented from sleep, so his first instinct was to run, forgetting he was already behind the wall. He relaxed slightly, hoping that Domko couldn't figure out where they were. He tensed as he heard Domko approach the bed.

"Huh?" Domko grunted, surprised that everyone but Dennis was gone. Incoherent from sleep, Dennis looked around, not knowing where his siblings were either. Domko began taunting and slapping Dennis until the slaps turned to punches. The boy wailed each time Domko's fist crashed into his

Where Children Run

face. David cringed at the sound of his twin choking back tears and blood.

Dennis whimpered as Domko lifted him up and threw him against the wall. David knew everyone was listening, but nobody dared say a word.

Feeling good about himself again, Domko stomped across the floor and down the stairs. The children could hear their brother sobbing softly on the other side of the wall, but not even David went to comfort him. They had to keep this hiding place a secret.

Summer wore on, and the children continued to work long hours in the hay field. They looked forward to the bit of time they would be left alone while Domko went in for meals or coffee breaks.

Bruno, the dog, tagged along wherever the children went, barking and running in circles. Late one afternoon, the twins climbed onto a horse, a black mare named Dolly, and told her that they needed to bring home the cows. She whinnied and carried them toward the pasture. The children loved this horse who they rode bareback, and she seemed to love them, too. If one of them slid off her back, she would stop and patiently wait for the child to climb back on. Sometimes, when the children slept in the barn at night, they nestled against her for warmth.

Domko disliked Dolly because after being beaten a few times the horse became wary of him and he could seldom catch her. The horse was too valuable to dispose of so he reluctantly kept her, relegating her to the worst corner of the barn, behind his horses, Queenie, Jack, and Darby. He fed her the bare minimum and used her for the most miserable chores such as cleaning out the barn or working in the rain. The one time she allowed him to trim her hooves, he impatiently cut too far into the pulp of her foot, and she walked with a limp for months afterward. Once she recovered, she'd flatten her ears and whinny whenever he came near, and if he got too close, she'd try to kick him.

Now that the twins were old enough, riding the horse to bring home the cows made the job much easier. In the summertime, the cows didn't like leaving the lush pasture, and the horse helped coax them along. Once they located the lead cow and got her going in the right direction, the rest of the cattle would follow.

"I bet ol' Satan made her the lead just to bug us," Dennis said, pointing at the stubborn old cow with the bell around her neck. This time she was off in the far corner of the pasture, and when they tried to chase her, she went the opposite way. The rest of the cows were spread over a wide distance, and they knew that bringing them in that afternoon was going to be difficult.

Karen Emilson

They worked for a long time and finally got all the cows headed for home. They groaned at the sight of Domko coming toward them on the path. He was riding his horse, Darby, a miserable animal that bit the children whenever it got the chance. Dolly's ears pricked and she sniffed the air. She whinnied and stopped but remained alerted.

"Yous lazy soneebeech bastards," he said as he rode up beside them. "I's be waitink ant you's be playink some." Pulling a twelve-inch two-by-two out of his back pocket, he cracked it over their heads. Dolly whinnied and snorted at Domko as he smashed her over the head as well. The horse reared and then took off running with David holding her mane tightly, and Dennis holding onto him. The commotion frightened the cows, and they scattered throughout the field. Eventually, they were able to turn her back and get the cows home, but they stayed away from Domko for the rest of the night.

One afternoon the twins were sitting in the granary straightening used nails that Domko had bought at an auction sale. It was a boring way to spend the last day of the summer holidays, sitting for hours, banging nails into shape. Hearing a car pull into the driveway, they stepped out of the granary to see the health nurse, Mrs. Burnett looking around the yard.

"Come here boys," she called out with her thick, English accent as she walked across the grass towards them. "I want to talk to you."

The twins looked at each other and for a moment considered running into the bush. What would Domko do if he saw them talking to her?

They waited shyly, staring at the ground.

"Bays Bickt?" Dennis whispered in their language.

David didn't know if she was a bad person or not. He remembered the whipping they received when the police brought them home and didn't want another beating like that. He looked the woman over carefully then told his brother to be quiet.

"What were you boys doing?" the nurse asked.

"Straightnin' nails," David said shyly. He stared up at the tall woman and thought she might be a dark-haired angel.

"Where's Bob Domko?" she asked.

David shrugged. He liked her unusual voice and hoped she would talk to them more.

Mrs. Burnett looked at the twins carefully. They were dressed in ragged clothing and covered with dirt. Both had matted hair and snotty noses from summer colds. They eyed the woman shyly as she knelt to their level.

"The police were called about you children," she said. "The neighbors say that Domko hits you. Is that true?"

The twins said nothing. It was so seldom that anyone outside the family spoke to them that they weren't sure how to answer. They knew they were difficult to understand and most outsiders didn't like them very much. They were also afraid that if they told this woman about their stepfather's rages, the police would come and Domko would beat them again.

"It's okay. I won't tell him what you say," she said. "I can only help you if you tell me the truth."

The twins stood for a long moment until Dennis decided this woman could be trusted.

"S-satan smashes us all the t-time," he stammered.

"Who?" she asked.

Dennis looked towards the house.

Margaret glanced over her shoulder to be sure nobody was watching, then asked the twins to lift their shirts. They looked at one another then slowly complied. The nurse shook her head. The boys were obviously malnourished, and large bruises covered their backs and arms. David had open sores on his legs from a serious poison ivy infection that was never treated. Dennis had patches on his head where his hair had been pulled out. Margaret suspected that the repeated beatings were even beginning to alter their once identical appearance.

It's high time that somebody did something about this, she thought.

THREE CENTS

Mrs. Burnett filed a report recommending that a social worker from the Manitoba Child Welfare Department investigate a case of child neglect at the farm. While the health nurse was welcomed by families, social workers caused embarrassment since their visits usually meant there was serious trouble in the home.

Because most workers had a full case load of clients, they didn't have a lot of time to spend with the families they visited. Over time, workers sometimes lost track of their cases and didn't know if a file was closed because they'd helped resolve the conflict or if the parents and children had simply learned to keep things quiet. This was a difficult, sometimes thankless job and staff changed regularly. Workers seemed to stay in one area for a few years then transferred to another region.

It took a few weeks for the social worker to arrive at the farm, unannounced, for a visit.

Caroline was relieved to see that the social worker who'd canceled her mother's allowance payment was not the same one visiting that day. The man pulled a new, clean file out of his briefcase.

Glancing around the house, he did a quick assessment and made a few notes in his file. Caroline and Bob didn't appear to be a loving couple, but most impoverished families he saw weren't very happy. It was evident that their lives centered on making a living and it wasn't an easy life. Caroline was a textbook case of a poorly educated, isolated woman with no life experience other than becoming a mother at a very young age.

Bob Domko was harder to assess. His grasp of the English language was so poor that the social worker could not carry on a conversation with him. One thing was obvious - he loved Kathy and Raymond.

Domko played the model father, holding Kathy and lovingly glancing at Raymond. The social worker could see that the affection was sincere. The

Where Children Run

two children appeared to be well-cared for, and neither feared their father. Kathy climbed happily onto his lap while Raymond giggled and cooed when he came near.

"Would you mind taking the children into the other room?" he asked. "I'd like to speak to your wife alone, please."

Domko eyed him suspiciously but then gave a gracious smile. He picked up Raymond and held Kathy's hand as he led her to the front room. The worker watched until he was gone then turned to Caroline.

He asked her a few questions about her husband and their relationship before stating the reason why he was there.

"Does Bob mistreat the children from your first marriage?" he asked.

Frightened by the prospect of having her children taken away, Caroline said he did not. "The boys are having a hard time believing their father is gone," she said. "I've been too easy on them, and now they don't want to work or listen to Bob. It's not his fault that they run away, they just do, and the neighbors take them in. The neighbors don't like Bob and listen to the lies that the kids tell. They're just kids telling stories, that's all."

"What about reports that the Twins have bruises all over their bodies?"

"They are always fighting with their older brothers who are too rough," she lied.

"They also appear awfully thin," he asked. "Why is that?"

"Bill was thin like that, and besides they don't eat for days when they run away. There's nothing I can do if I can't find them to feed them."

"What about their school attendance? I've been told that the boys are forced to work instead of going to school?"

"The kids have chores before and after school, just like all the kids around here," she explained. "They'll never learn to work if we don't make them. They miss school only when they run away."

The social worker knew Caroline's answers were not entirely accurate. Unfortunately, since this was his first visit, he didn't have enough family history to make an informed assessment. By acceptable standards, these children were neglected, but because they weren't in immediate danger, there was nothing more he could do.

No judge in the country would support an order to apprehend the children after only one visit. The social worker would be reminded that his job was to help families resolve their problems not pluck children from a familiar environment and place them in another home. It would be best for everyone if the situation could be settled here, at home. Apprehending the children should be the last option as it would create a lot of paperwork and red tape.

The social worker decided that scaring Domko would be the children's best chance. So, he had a lengthy discussion with him saying he was putting the family on probation. He said that if there were more complaints from the neighbors, there would be a further investigation.

The social worker's threats seemed to work for a little while. Domko was deathly afraid of anyone employed by the government, and he was easier on the children for the next month.

The twins were sitting at the top of the stairs one evening, and overheard their mother and Domko talking about the social worker.

"Hey, Denny," David said, "that man's gonna help us."

"Yeah, and Domko's scared of him," Dennis said. "When do you think he's gonna come back?"

"I dunno. He gots to come all the way from Winnipeg."

"Yeah," Dennis said. "I wanna be home next time he comes."

The following afternoon Caroline was sitting alone in the kitchen. She called the twins to sit with her because she had something to discuss. They were eager to talk with her since it wasn't often that she paid attention to them.

"I have an idea that I think will be good for both you boys and Domko," she said.

The twins listened intently.

"I think that maybe we should change your last name to Domko," she said, "and that you boys should start calling him dad. He might consider you his children and not be so hard on you."

David and Dennis' hearts sank. They were hoping that she had another foster home in mind. When the realization of what she had asked sank in, both boys shook their heads.

"No," David said. "We can't do that—we don't wanna be Domkos."

"Yeah," Dennis added. "I'd rather be dead than call him dad."

Exasperated, Caroline shook her head. "What's wrong with that?"

"He ain't our dad," Dennis exclaimed. "He's nothin' like dad, nothin' at all. I hate him and wish our real dad was still alive."

"Well he's not, so just quit talking about him," Caroline scolded. "Because you miss your real dad you don't want to give Domko a chance."

"No, Momma that's not why," David argued. "He's mean to us, that's why we don't like him. We can't call him dad."

"I'd rather be dead," Dennis said again.

The twins sat with their arms folded tightly across their chests. Their expressions were identical, and Caroline knew there was no way she'd be able to convince them this was the sensible thing to do.

"Fine then," she said. "But I don't want to hear you mentioning your father ever again then, do you hear?"

The boys stared at her—but neither would agree.

Domko was going to be short of hay that winter, so he wanted to fatten his animals on the neighbor's feed before the snow fell. On the first of October, following afternoon chores, he told David to take the horses and let them into the hay field where Gus had four large stacks of hay waiting to be hauled home.

Reluctantly, David took the four horses by the reins and led them north of the barn to the section of Crown land that Gus leased. David opened the gate and watched helplessly as the horses trotted in, knowing that Domko was somewhere in the bush watching him. He sat on the fence as the horses ate Gus' hay. They had been on thin pasture all summer long and were hungry.

The horses fed for about ten minutes until Gus and Marjorie arrived pulling the hay mover behind the tractor. Gus became angry when he saw the horses and surprised to see David sitting on the fence.

"I'm s-sorry Gus," he apologized in hushed tones, glancing over his shoulder. "Domko m-made me chase them in h-here." David hated obeying Domko, knowing that he was trying to create bad feelings between the neighbors. He couldn't explain this to Gus, though, so he just grabbed the horses' reins and led them out of the field.

"Well, I'm sure glad we came today to haul this hay home," Gus said. "Otherwise, Domko would have you in here with his animals every day until the snow flies."

David heard the exasperation in the older man's voice. Gus tried hard not to show it, but David knew that his sympathy was wearing thin. Domko already controlled every aspect of their lives and was now trying to ruin the only decent relationships they had.

Marjorie stood by the tractor frowning. Her dad's livelihood depended on having enough hay to feed his cows, but she also didn't like seeing her friend in trouble. There was no doubt in her mind that this was not David's fault.

David led the horses home and then reluctantly told the story to Domko who laughed and spat on the ground at the mention of Gus' name. Later that afternoon, Marjorie and Gus hauled most of one, four-ton stack home in three trips. They usually left the hay in the field and went for it as needed, but could no longer trust their neighbor. So far, it had been warm and dry all month, so they hoped to haul the rest of the hay home by the end of the week.

The twins spent the next two days picking rocks in a field that Domko had cultivated earlier that spring. He wanted to seed it to oats the following May, but the rocks needed picking first. He pulled the stone wagon behind the tractor while the boys loaded rocks until they were too weak to continue.

Still insulted that their mother would suggest they take Domko's name, they dragged themselves upstairs without speaking to her that night. They had little to eat and were dehydrated from being in the sun all day. Both boys fell into bed without a word. Neither enjoyed going to school, but they were looking forward to it the next morning. Anything was better than the manual labor they were forced to do at home.

The next morning, they finished their chores then ducked off to school before Domko noticed they were gone. Mrs. Collier was their teacher again this term. Although they were still in grade two, she had promised that if they worked hard, she would move them to grade three for the second term which began in January.

Gus stuck his head through the door just as Marjorie was almost finished washing the supper dishes.

"Fire!" he yelled. "The hay is on fire!"

She dropped a plate on the floor then ran out the door after her father. Emma came bounding out of the bedroom, pausing for a moment by the door to slip on her shoes. She ran as fast as she could down the driveway behind Marjorie. Gus signaled them to hurry as he climbed on the tractor waiting by the road. Pails and shovels were thrown on the hay mover that, luckily, was still hooked to the tractor. Gus frowned as he looked to the north.

Emma and Marjorie jumped onto the hay mover then motioned for Gus to go. They held on tightly to the edge of the wagon as he accelerated past the Pischke farm. The wind, blowing briskly from the south, was beginning to pick up speed. The Harwarts could see thick, billowing smoke rising a short distance away. The smell of it permeated the air, and they wondered why they hadn't noticed it sooner.

As Gus sped past the bush to the edge of Caroline's quarter section, he came to a clearing. Flames from a grassfire at Pischke's had spread to their land. The fire was engulfing the base of one of the haystacks that Domko's horses had been eating two days before. The flames crackled as the fire spread quickly up the sides of the dry hay.

Gus halted the tractor on the road, then the three of them jumped off and began running towards the fire. Using shovels, Gus and Emma began beating the flames, while Marjorie filled two pails with water from the ditch. She had a difficult time running without spilling water, but she was a strong, capable girl who never lost her cool.

She threw water on the stack then ran back for more. After nearly a dozen trips it became apparent that they would be unable to save the stack. The flames grew overhead, and Gus and Emma were forced back away from the heat.

"We'll keep it from spreading to the other stacks," Gus said, pointing to the remaining hay in the field.

They ran ahead and beat out the fire as it crept forward. Flames licked the dry ground, fueling themselves on small clumps of hay that were left behind when the stacks were built. Marjorie continued to carry pails of water and dumped it on the ground around the stacks. Her dad didn't have to tell her how important it was to save this hay. She had worked beside him long enough to know.

"That son-of-a-gun," Gus yelled. Looking at her father, she could see he was pointing south. On the other side of the fence, not more than one hundred yards away, stood Domko. He was watching and laughing as the Harwarts struggled to save the hay.

"He did this," Emma yelled, choking from the smoke. "He can't have it, so he doesn't want us to have it either."

They beat the ground even harder. The sight of Domko laughing at them caused a knot to swell in Marjorie's stomach. She hated Bob Domko for what he was doing to them and for causing harm to her friends. His presence made her work even harder to prove that he couldn't beat them. Tears of frustration welled in her eyes, ironically helping to relieve the sting of the smoke.

The blaze was almost under control when neighbors arrived. Domko disappeared into the bush when the men from a neighboring family joined in to help. In the end, they lost only one stack which continued to smolder as the men stood back to assess the situation. Gus was thankful that he had placed the stacks far enough apart that he didn't lose them all.

Fed up with Domko, Gus went to the neighbor's house to borrow their telephone. He wasn't going to let him get away with it this time.

That following morning there was a knock at the school room door. The students all turned and began to chatter when they realized there was a visitor. They gasped, then grew quiet as two RCMP officers stepped from the vestibule into the back of the room. For some of the younger children, it was the first time they had ever seen a police officer.

Mrs. Collier talked to the uniformed men for a moment, then called for David and Dennis. The children let out another gasp, as they walked slowly to the back of the room.

"You're going to jail," an older boy taunted.

"Shut up," Norman said, poking the boy in the arm with his pencil.

The teacher followed as the twins were taken outside. The moment she was gone, the older children jumped up and ran to look out the windows. They watched as the twins were taken to the police car and put in the back seat. Mrs. Collier came back inside and ushered everyone back to their seats.

"See what happens when you're bad," she said.

Norman shot her an icy look but said nothing. Rosie, who was in grade one, was frightened because her brothers had been taken away by the police. Eunice hunkered down in her seat, hoping that nobody remembered that she also was a Pischke.

Dennis and David sat quietly in the back of the cruiser. Out of the corner of his eye, Dennis could see some of his classmates staring and pointing from the school windows. The officers sat in the front seat.

"Did you boys light a grass fire yesterday afternoon north of your house?" one of the officers asked. David recognized he was the same officer who had brought them back to the farm last winter.

"No, sir," he stammered.

"Are you sure?"

"Hey, Denny, we didn't light no fire did we?"

"No, sir," Dennis said.

"Your stepfather said that you boys lit a fire in the bush then went to school. It spread to Gus Harwart's hay. Do you know anything about that?"

Their eyes met. Domko had blamed them again.

"No sir," David said. "Ol' Squeezer just says we does stuff like that."

The officers turned and began talking quietly among themselves. David strained to hear what they were saying. Then as the policeman put the car in gear, they thought for sure they were going to jail, but then the car turned towards the farm.

"Oh no," Dennis moaned.

Both boys began to cry as the officers turned in the driveway. Glancing in his rearview mirror, the officer at the wheel could see the boys hugging each other. Reluctantly, the twins followed the officers out of the car but refused to go in the house. Domko came outside and frowned when he saw them standing quietly behind the police officers.

"Mr. Domko I'm afraid that we're going to have to charge you under section 9 (a) of the Fire Prevention Act for letting a fire get out of your control and damaging another person's property."

"I's not be doink it," he said pointing at the boys. "They's be—"

"I'm sorry, sir, but since these are your children and this is your farm, you are responsible for what goes on here," he said.

Domko glared at the twins who looked silently at the ground. The officers discussed the charge with Domko then got back in their car. Before the cruiser had backed all the way out the driveway, the officers caught a glimpse of the twins running frantically into the bush.

"They probably lit the fire and are now in trouble with the old man," one said, but the younger officer wasn't convinced.

"It was no accident," Gus said to the officers sitting at his kitchen table. "Domko set that fire on purpose to burn my hay."

They looked at the thin, old man and smiled. They had seen plenty of feuding neighbors before.

"I'm sure he didn't mean to burn your hay, Mr. Harwart," the older officer said. "He's blaming those twin boys, and they are blaming him. There is certainly no proof that he set fire to your hay with intent, not unless you saw him do it."

Gus frowned. "Of course I didn't see him do it, but I know he did. And you're only charging him with letting a fire get out of control? What about arson or willful damage to my property?"

"We'll admit he's a strange guy," said the younger officer, "but you can't prove he did it on purpose."

Gus laughed. "I understand now," he said standing up, folding his arms across his chest. "You're afraid of him, aren't you?"

The officers looked at each other and shook their heads.

"That's why nobody ever does anything about those kids," Gus continued. "He works them like they are in a concentration camp. The wife and I can see it, so can Jim Deighton. Can't anybody else see how Domko manipulates everyone?"

Emma stood silently with her hands on her hips until the officers left the house. Gus didn't speak up often, but when he did, he was usually right.

Caroline and the children stayed far away from Domko for the next few days. He was so angry about being charged with burning the Harwart hay that he threatened to shoot them all. He paced back and forth, glancing out the window while sucking on his cigarette. He dropped the ashes on the floor and ground them into the linoleum as he murmured to himself.

By now, Caroline knew that there was something seriously wrong with her husband. His behavior had become increasingly irrational as he lamented that Gus was trying to destroy their farm. She suspected that Domko had set the hay on fire and wondered if he'd forgotten all about it. She sat at the kitchen table and listened, but dared not say a word as he paced back and forth.

She had hoped that their marriage and the addition to the house would give them a fresh start. For a while, his temperament had improved, but soon he had fallen into his old pattern. His constant outbursts and belittlement of the children were depressing, and she now found it hard to stay optimistic for the children's sake. She began looking for answers in the Bible, and immersed herself deeper in the church, the place she had always been told was a pillar of comfort and advice. She hoped that her friends could give her support during this troubling time. Now that the busy summer months were over, they would begin visiting again, bringing Watchtower magazines and news from the annual Jehovah's Witness gatherings. She hoped to go to a Winnipeg meeting the following spring. They'd told her what an enlightening experience it was, and she needed one of those right about now.

"I's be goink to town," Domko said, grabbing his coat before strutting outside. Opening the door quietly behind him, Caroline could see her husband marching towards the lean-to against the side of the granary. He backed the tractor out a few minutes later and drove it to the house. She lifted the cream can down from the shelf and met him at the door. Smiling weakly, she held the can out. His eyes were cold and unfeeling as he roughly took it from her. Within a few moments, he was gone.

That's another cream check I'll never see, she thought.

That afternoon the twins played happily in the ditch near the front of the house. The mud was thick and sticky, perfect for molding small figurines. Rolling the clay in their hands, they made cars, tractors, farm animals, and buildings. Marjorie watched in amazement as Dennis took two small pieces of wire and poked them through the bottom of a tractor he was making. Rolling four balls into perfectly even wheels, he poked the wheels onto the wire, then added a small piece of clay on the ends to keep each from falling off. Few people recognized the twins' capabilities, but Marjorie knew they had artistic talent and that they were meticulous in their work. As they finished making each figurine, they were carefully set on a piece of wood to dry in the sun.

Dennis and David spent most of the afternoon dreamily making toys until the sound of the tractor jolted them back to reality. Marjorie had left a few hours earlier while Eunice and Norman were bringing in the cows for the evening milking. The twins could hear the lead cow's bell as she made her way into the barn. Bruno jumped and barked as Norman threw a stick for him to retrieve. The twins lay flat in the ditch, hoping that Domko wouldn't see them.

Domko stopped by the house to unload a few groceries then drove the tractor to the lean-to and parked it. He strode across the yard and then disappeared into the barn. There was yelling, and a loud commotion and then Norman burst through the barn door and began running with Domko on his heels. He slipped under the fence and scrambling up, ran through the yard. Domko caught him on the other side of the house, just out of the twins' view.

"C'mon," David said, crawling out of the ditch. Hunched over, they crept to the corner of the house. Their brother was screaming in pain around the corner from them. Peering around, they saw Domko towering over Norman.

"Vas it goot?" Domko yelled as he beat him with a stick. "You punk!"

"No," Norman lied, "I didn't do it."

"Vat?" Domko roared. "Who's be doink it? Marjie be doink it?"

Eunice stood by the barn, her hands drawn up to her face. She flinched every time the stick smashed down. The twins watched sadly from a safe distance as Domko beat Norman, his feet lifting off the ground as he put the entire weight of his body into it.

A warning growl began in Bruno's throat as he lowered his head and tail and walked slowly toward Domko. The growl deepened, and he bared his teeth. His warning grew louder every time Norman cried out. Domko didn't notice the dog as it crept closer, the hair on his back now standing straight on end. The twins gasped in disbelief as Bruno lunged at Domko, digging his teeth deep into his forearm. Domko let out a scream as he knocked the snarling dog to the ground.

"Fraa," he swore as the dog stepped between him and Norman. Bruno's eyes remained lowered as he continued to growl deep in his throat.

"I's be showink it some!" Domko roared as he strode through the yard towards the granary. He emerged seconds later carrying a .308 caliber rifle, snapping the clip in place.

Disoriented, Norman lay on the ground while Bruno stood protectively over him. Then he saw Domko's gun.

"Bruno, get outta here," Norman yelled. "Run, Bruno, run!"

The dog turned to him, and his tail began to wag softly. He pressed his wet nose on Norman's face then his thick, soft tongue lapped the boy's cheek.

"Go away," Norman said as he struggled to sit up. Once he realized the dog wasn't going to run, he turned to his stepfather.

"Please don't," Norman begged. "It's not his fault."

Without a word, Domko cocked the hammer. He smirked as he took careful aim, then pulled the trigger. Norman jumped in surprise.

Bruno yelped and fell to the ground, shaking violently as the bullet pierced his abdomen, rendering his back legs useless, his soft brown eyes were wild with fear and shock. Norman watched as the dog began pulling himself along the ground with his front paws toward the bush where he'd run behind the children so many times. Norman pulled his hands up to his face and began crying as his stepfather sauntered behind the dog who struggled valiantly to escape. Domko took his time, enjoying the dog's fear and desperation, chuckling at the dog's whimpering, and stepping carelessly in the smear of blood on the hard ground. He made sure that everyone was watching as he placed the gun just a few inches from the dog's head. By now, Bruno had given up and was lying still and softly panting. Then he slowly pulled the trigger.

Caroline was bagging carrots in the far garden when the first gunshot rang out. Turning, she could see Eunice in the barnyard and the twins at the corner of the house. Domko was standing near Norman who was lying on the ground. Caroline saw her husband raise the gun again.

"No," she screamed, running through the pasture towards the house. Her heart thumped hard as she waved her arms. "Norman!"

Another shot rang out, and Caroline screamed in anguish. She could see the twins running around the side of the house and Eunice turn quickly into the barn. Norman was struggling to stand up, supporting himself by leaning against the house. Domko turned and walked slowly back to the granary.

As she continued running through the field, it took a few moments for her to realize that Domko hadn't shot her son after all.

"What's going on?" she breathlessly demanded as she met Domko at the granary door.

"I's be shootink that soneebeech," he replied, pointing towards the brown lump of fur lying on the driveway. The look of pleasure on his face made Caroline both uneasy and angry. She had liked the dog and was tired of Domko killing the children's pets.

Domko explained that he was punishing Norman for stealing when the dog attacked him. Caroline eyed him suspiciously but said nothing. She was so relieved that it wasn't Norman that he'd shot, she decided it was best to forget the incident.

"Take into some bush," Domko said pointing at the dead dog. Norman stared at him but said nothing. The Twins waited until Domko and their mother went inside before they reappeared.

Norman's body was bleeding and swollen from the beating, and his face streamed with tears. He turned away from the twins and hobbled down the driveway.

"Me and Davey will do it," Dennis called out as they watched him walk into the bush across the road.

The twins picked up the dog and carried it into the bush by the church. They chose a spot near where they had buried Rosie's cat, and using a shovel from the barn; they began to dig a shallow grave. Kneeling beside the hole, they put Bruno's body in and then shoveled dirt on top.

"What did Norman do?" Dennis asked.

David pushed a wooden marker into the dirt.

"He went for the mail and put an apple on the bill at the Co-op," David said, wiping his hands on his shirt. "It costed three cents."

NECESSARY KINDNESS

Domko considered Norman's love for Bruno a weakness. He had enjoyed killing the dog and snickered each time he thought of it.

"Norrrrman," he taunted. "Where's be Bruno?"

Norman continued working without answering, and for the next week, he was called a liar and thief. Norman listened silently to Domko's ravings, not once making eye contact. He knew Domko was baiting him, looking for an excuse to beat him again. He also knew that his misery wouldn't end until one of the other children did something wrong.

One Friday night after chores were done, the twins saw Norman sneak out of the house. They knew better than to follow the fourteen-year-old who was likely going to meet friends. He didn't come home that night, and when they chased the cows into the barn the next morning, Norman came down from the loft. His skin was gray, and he smelled awful.

"What's wrong?" Eunice asked.

Norman shielded his eyes from the sunlight streaming through the open barn door. "Nothing," he said. "Where's the old black bastard?"

"In the house," she said turning her attention back to the cow she was milking.

Norman groaned as he staggered outside. He fell to his knees then vomited beside the barn door. He came back in holding his head in his hands.

"Do you want some milk?" Eunice asked.

"No—" Norman winced.

The children worked quietly, listening to the rhythmic squirt of milk into the tin pails. Norman picked up a stool and joined them.

A few minutes passed, and then he spoke again.

"Guess what I did last night?" he asked.

"What?" Eunice replied, peering at him under her cow.

"I got drunk," he boasted. "Me and the Meisner boys drank a whole pile

Where Children Run

of homebrew."

Eunice giggled, and the twins gasped.

"Don't tell anybody, not even Ma, I don't want the old bastard to know." Norman groaned, as he slipped off the stool and fell to hands and knees. He crawled outside and vomited again.

"I can't do no more," he said when he staggered back in toward the loft ladder. "I'm going up to sleep for a while."

It wasn't long before Domko came to the barn to check on them.

"Where's be some Norman?" he asked.

The twins kept their foreheads pressed against the cow's belly, pretending they didn't hear him.

"I don't know, he didn't sleep upstairs last night," Eunice answered, heart pounding. She never knew if Domko was asking a sincere question or if he was trying to trick her.

"Huh," he grunted, clearly disappointed, as he turned and went back to the house.

Later that morning the twins ran from the yard into the bush when they saw Domko come out of the barn, pushing Norman toward the garden. He handed him a potato fork. A quarter acre of potatoes had to be dug before the snow fell. The twins watched as Norman shoveled into the hills, bending to brush the dirt off the potatoes. As his pace slowed, Domko chuckled.

"Seek?" Domko teased. "Vat, yous be some seek?"

Norman didn't say anything as he bent over and vomited again. He wiped his mouth on his sleeve then leaned against the fork for a moment. Domko told him to keep digging. Norman finished half a row but then finally staggered and fell to the ground.

"Lazy," Domko roared as he strode across the potato hills. Swinging his leg back, he kicked Norman in the stomach.

"Now you's be seek," he said.

When Norman didn't move, he kicked him again. Then he took the potato fork and smashed the handle across Norman's back. When he strode back to the house, he yelled into the bush for the Twins to finish digging the potatoes. If the work wasn't done by the time he came back outside, he said he'd kill Norman.

Once the porch door slammed shut, the boys ran to the field. They checked to see if Norman was dead, but once they knew he was still breathing, they started working. Within an hour, Norman groaned and began moving and then stood up.

He rubbed his face with his hands and then looked at the twins.

161

"I ain't coming back," he said.

They watched as Norman turned and walked out of the garden, stepping over the rows of potatoes drying in the sun. Knowing what this meant for them, a weight settled in David's gut as he watched Norman walk silently past the house then stagger north along the road until he was out of sight.

Norman ended up at Bert and Hilda Nachtigall's home in Steep Rock. Caroline had once told him that if things got too bad on the farm, he could go there and the Nachtigalls would take him in.

When Domko heard about this, he went wild, demanding that she get him and bring him home. Caroline tried, but Norman refused. Fearing a ruckus would alert the social worker, she returned home without Norman explaining to Domko that if they weren't careful, all the children might be taken away.

She consoled him by saying that Eunice and the twins were old enough to work and that although Rosie was only seven years old, she was a capable girl who would be big enough by next summer to help with the haying.

It took all of her courage and resourcefulness to reassure Domko that the neighbors and members of her church were not trying to thwart his plan to build a successful farm.

Life for the twins and Eunice became almost unbearable. They were forced to work long hours before and after school to get the chores done, and with Norman gone, there was one less sibling to share the beatings.

By early November, there was no meat left in the house. When Domko tired of potato soup and holopchi, he decided to butcher one of the pigs.

"Yous be come," he said to the twins as they brought armfuls of wood into the house. Dreading the job ahead, they followed him outside.

Domko stopped at the pump house for his gun while they continued walking to the pigpen beside the chicken house. The pig, thinking it was time to be fed, snorted and looked at the twins expectantly. Dennis felt bad for the animal they had fed since it was a weanling while David turned away so that he wouldn't have to look at its face.

"I's be shootink ant yous be catchink it some," Domko said.

The twins waited at the edge of the pen as the pig began rooting the ground near their feet. Domko walked to the opposite side of the pen and taking careful aim, shot the pig behind the front right leg. The pig let out a terrified squeal and began running around the pen, its short legs giving way to the weakness on one side.

"Fraa," Domko swore, pointing at the pig.

Where Children Run

The twins jumped into the pen and slid around in the manure until they were able to corner the pig, which by then had lost a lot of blood, and wrestled it to the ground. Domko jumped into the pen and reaching into the breast pocket of his coat, pulled out his hunting knife. Grinning, he grabbed the squealing pig's head with his left hand and wrenching it back, sliced through its neck in one swoop.

The animal's cries became fainter as it began choking on blood. Domko continued to hack away, severing the dying animal's head. As the pig convulsed, blood squirted all over the boys. Seeing their disgust, he reached out and grabbed David by the shirt, pulling him close.

"I's be cuttink Peeschke neck," he spat.

David didn't dare move. His eyes darted from the knife to Domko, then back to the knife again. It wasn't until Domko relaxed his grip and slipped the bloodstained knife back into his pocket that David could breathe normally again.

Domko ordered them to drag the carcass to the barn. There, the animal was placed on a board, and it was their job to scrape the hair off the carcass before it was gutted. Then it was hoisted overhead using a rope and pulley, where it hung for a while before being cut into large chunks that were stored in the granary.

Classes were done for the holiday season less than a week before Christmas. This meant that the children had no place to go during the day to escape Domko, who now had an obsessive dislike for Dennis. This put a tremendous strain on David as well, since he wanted to protect his twin. And while they could speak English, they deliberately used their many strange words when Domko was around, to squirrel away food or establish hiding places in the bush. The language irritated Domko who complained to Caroline that he wanted the boys to learn Polish but the twins flatly refused.

One evening they sat on the bed upstairs listening to the door slam as Domko went outside to do his evening check. They knew if anything was out of place, then one of them would be in trouble. Getting up from the bed, the boys went to the top of the stairs.

Having spent enough nights out in the cold, they now slept in their outdoor clothes, just in case. Looking at Dennis' bruised face, David didn't think he could take another beating. Quietly, he opened the bedroom window and looked out.

There was only a light sprinkling of snow on the ground, so travel wouldn't be difficult. The stars were bright so finding their way through the bush would be easy. It was the twelve-foot drop that made him uneasy, and he wasn't sure if he'd be able to convince Dennis to jump.

It didn't take long before Domko was back in the house.

"Tramps, they's be some goot for nuthink," he yelled. "They's be playink, not workink."

David knew that Domko had found the mud toys they had made the afternoon Bruno was shot. They'd hidden them in the barn and were playing that afternoon but must have forgotten to hide them again. He knew that Domko's rage would have started by smashing their little farm scene.

"C'mon," he whispered. "We gotta jump."

Downstairs Domko was yelling, and their sisters were scrambling to hide. David swung one leg out the window and straddled the sill while he summoned enough courage to lift the other leg out. He sat there for a moment until he heard the pounding of Domko's boots across the floor. Closing his eyes, he jumped, his stomach lurching into his chest as he fell helplessly to the earth. He landed feet first, and the impact sent him rolling backward across the frozen ground. A moment later, Dennis tumbled to earth beside him. There was no time to waste.

"Are you okay?" David asked as he shook his hand and stood up.

"Yeah, how 'bout you?"

David nodded. "C'mon, let's go," he said, sprinting into the bush. When they were a safe distance away, they stopped to decide where to spend the night.

"Let's go to Deightons," Dennis suggested.

David agreed, so they followed the trail through the churchyard then across the field to the neighbor's house.

"What's he barking at now?" Jim said as he got up to look out the living room window. The dog was barking at the edge of the yard. Jim could see two figures coming across the field, and when the dog recognized the boys, it ran out to greet them.

"The Pischke twins are here again," he said to Ruby who was sitting on the chesterfield knitting. Looking up from her work, she set it aside and told him to let them in.

Jim opened the door just as David lifted his hand to knock, startling him. David's eyes were wide.

"C-can we come in?" he asked. "The Devil's after us again."

Once they were warmed up, Jim demanded a detailed explanation. They sat at the kitchen table as the twins described Domko's month-long rampage, including how he killed Bruno and butchered the pig.

"He said he'd cut my throat," David said.

Ruby gasped and shook her head.

Not wanting to be outdone, Dennis lifted his shirt and turned around. His back was covered in huge, purple bruises.

"I gots those when Domko got mad 'cause I didn't 'member which horses bridle I hung up. I mixed 'em up, and it took me too long to get the horses ready in the morning," he said.

Jim slammed his fist on the table and shook his head.

"Yeah, and he says we're good for nothin'," David added, looking for sympathy. "He calls us tramps and hobos and soneebeech-bastards."

Ruby and Jim looked at one another.

"What happened the last time I took you to the police?" Jim asked.

"They took us back," Dennis began. "Satan told 'em a big story about us bein' bad—"

"Yeah, and he got us again," David added. "Denny peed his pan—"

"You peed, too," Dennis interrupted.

David smiled and gave his twin a little shove. They settled down once their stories were finished, and sat quietly listening as Jim and Ruby discussed what to do. A twinkling in the front room caught David's attention, and he gasped.

"Denny," he whispered. "They gots a Christmas tree."

Jim and Ruby watched as the twins got up from the table and followed them into the front room. They began whispering in their language as they stopped in front of the tree, pointing at the glass ornaments and homemade decorations. They stood for a long time, soaking in every detail.

Jim quietly opened a box of matches then lit the tall white candles standing in holders on the ends of the branches. The twins watched in fascination, examining every inch of the tree as the flames flickered.

Ruby prepared sandwiches that they ate greedily, only glancing away from the tree to take another sandwich from the plate. Each drank a glass of milk and belched loudly. Ruby tsked and Jim laughed. The boys were unaware that their wonder was being enjoyed so much.

"Well it's getting late," Ruby finally said.

Jim blew out the candles as the twins followed Ruby to the kitchen. Using a wash cloth, she scrubbed their hands and faces.

"I'm going to get you some fresh clothes," she said, disappearing upstairs. She returned with clean underwear and pajamas.

The boys left their clothes, which stank of pig manure and blood, in a heap on the floor. Ruby picked them up, depositing them in the porch.

"I'll burn those in the morning," she laughed to herself.

Her son was home visiting for the holidays and occupying the upstairs bedroom, so Ruby led the twins to the bedroom off the kitchen. David and Dennis climbed into the bed as she tucked the covers up under their chins.

"Good night," she whispered.

"Good night, Aunt Ruby," they said, watching as she turned and left the room, pulling the door almost closed. They stared at the ceiling, listening to the quiet warmth of the house.

"Someday I'm gonna get me a Christmas tree," Dennis whispered.

David was also thinking about Christmas, hoping that they would be able to stay here until the holiday was over. The baleful howls of coyotes began, making him thankful they weren't in the bush.

Soon, Dennis was breathing heavily. David lay awake, listening to Jim and Ruby talking quietly in the kitchen. He wondered if the Deightons were always this nice or if they just pretended to be that way when he was there.

He'd seen Domko behave that way. Most people in the area thought he was providing well for the family. 'A good man,' his grandfather and uncles had said. David wondered if Jim treated his family poorly when nobody was around to see. He pushed the thought from his mind and chastised himself for betraying one of their few friends.

It must be late now, David thought. He could hear Jim and Ruby getting ready to go to bed. Footsteps came quietly towards the room, so he closed his eyes and pretended to be asleep. Ruby padded softly across the floor. She stopped beside the bed and kissed Dennis' forehead. David hoped Ruby wouldn't realize he was still awake as she pushed back his hair, then leaned down and kissed him softly on the cheek.

"You're good boys," she whispered, "always remember that."

Then she left the room. David's heart swelled as his cheek burned from the warmth of the kiss. He didn't dare open his eyes or touch his face for fear the sensation would disappear. He played it over many times in his mind, vowing to remember the kiss forever.

No effort was made to send the twins home in the days that followed. The children happily played with Ruby's teenage son Charles, skating on an outdoor rink and building forts in the snow. They helped with the farm chores, embarrassing Jim with their eagerness.

One afternoon after they had finished shoveling out the barn, David pointed to the farmhouse across the road.

Where Children Run

"Hey Jim, who lives over there?" he asked.

Jim frowned. "That's Newman's place," he said.

"Are they nice?"

"The mother and girls are friendly, but don't ever go there in the middle of the night," he said. "That old bugger Henry loses his mind when he drinks. Almost as bad as Domko."

The twins found this hard to believe.

"People are funny," Jim continued. "You never can tell what they'll be like when they take a drink."

"Domko never drinks," David said. "Do you 'spose he'd be worse if he did?"

"What do you think? Can he get any worse?" Jim smirked.

David laughed out loud. "I hope not. That black bastard is mean like the Devil already." He looked back toward the Newman house. It seemed hard to believe that there was another person like Domko living so close. David was thankful that they'd been warned and would be more careful in the future.

The next day Jim told Ruby he was worried that people might think the only reason they allowed the twins to stay there was so they would help with chores.

"You don't have to worry about that. Everybody understands."

Just then the door opened, and the boys came in for lunch. After the meal, Dennis offered to help Ruby with the dishes. He was waiting for the right time to ask a delicate question.

"Aunt Ruby, are you gonna get us anything for Christmas?"

She handed him a dish to dry then put her hands back into the washtub.

"You won't be here for Christmas will you?" she asked. "Don't you want to go home?"

Dennis shook his head. "No, ma'am. We're gonna stay here. We don't got no Christmas tree."

Ruby smiled as she watched him stack the dishes in a neat pile. He'd become much more outgoing the past few days. She felt bad that she'd taken his question so lightly.

"What do you want for Christmas?" she asked.

"Don't matter," he smiled. "We like everything."

Ruby's eyes stung. "You'll find out tomorrow," she said.

The children bounded out of bed early the next morning. There were nearly as many presents under the tree for Dennis and David as there were for Ruby's son. After the discussion over the dishes with Dennis, Ruby insisted that Jim make a quick trip to town to buy them each a toy. Fortunately, Ruby had a surplus of knitted mitts and socks. She had one homemade sweater on hand, so she had quickly made another to match, working late Christmas Eve to finish it. She smiled as she watched the twins open their stockings, both filled with fruit, chocolate and hard candy.

That day they sang Christmas carols, ate a turkey dinner and spent the day playing games. The twins were in a state of bliss, barely able to comprehend that life could be so good.

Word soon spread through the community that the twins were at Deighton's farm. A few days later, Caroline arrived to take them home. Fearing the social worker, she hoped that the latest incident hadn't been reported to police.

Jim stood in the kitchen and watched with his arms crossed as Caroline stood in the doorway persuading the boys to go home.

Ruby noticed an immediate change in their posture. Dennis began to withdraw while David's shoulders slumped as they listened to their mother tell them that Domko was sorry he had chased them out of the house.

"You don't live here," she whispered emphatically. "You don't want Ruby and Jim to get sick of us, now do you?"

The twins started to cry as they gathered up their gifts. Caroline shot Ruby a disapproving look when she saw the wooden cars each boy grasped tightly. Ruby guessed what she was thinking. She didn't like contradicting Caroline's religious beliefs, even if they were odd.

"Well, I couldn't very well give to my son and not the twins," she said. "Besides, the mitts and sweaters will come in handy."

Caroline nodded. At one time she also knitted for her children, but Domko criticized her and even stuffed a pile of hats and mitts in the stove.

"Thank you, but it wasn't necessary," Caroline said.

"Yes, it was," Ruby said.

Caroline said nothing as she turned and left, pushing the crying boys ahead of her.

ALL GOD'S CREATURES

A WEEK-LONG COLD SNAP IN THE MIDDLE OF FEBRUARY KEPT THE family close to home. One afternoon while the twins were sitting on the floor drawing, David caught his pants on a nail as he stood up, tearing them. David's gasp caused everyone to look. He trembled as he tried to hide the rip.

"Fraa," Domko said as he dropped a log in the wood stove. "See, I's be buyink some pant ant he's be breakink it."

Caroline scolded David and told him to fetch her mending kit from the bedroom. David skittered past Domko, returning with the box tucked under his arm. His mother whispered a warning to go quickly to the far corner and keep quiet. David nodded as he skittered away. Within a few minutes, he had the needle threaded and still wearing the ripped pants, began sewing as he'd seen his mother do many times before. He worked for nearly an hour in a contorted position, sewing small, precise stitches while Domko watched from across the room. David hoped he'd become distracted by someone else, but the other children had the good sense to keep quiet.

When he finished, David stuck the needle in the spool of thread then hurried to show his mother, but before she had the chance to look, his stepfather's voice boomed across the room.

"I's be lookink at some pant," he said.

David felt his siblings silently assessing the situation. He let his mind numb as he inched toward Domko. Keeping his body as far away as possible, he held out his leg and turned so Domko could see the mending job. The only sound was his heart pounding in his ears as Domko leaned forward.

"Vat? You's be playink," he shouted.

David squirmed out of reach and ran toward the door as his sisters scattered and Dennis pushed him from behind on their way out.

Domko ran after them screaming obscenities but didn't see Kathy who stepped in front of him, tangling in his legs. Trying not to hurt her, he lost his balance and went down.

The twins ran along the snowy path to the chicken coop, darting inside. David pulled the outer door shut, but knowing there was no time to find a hiding spot, grabbed the knob of the inside door. Pushing Dennis behind first, he slipped in beside him and pulled the door tight against their chests.

They stood with their eyes squeezed shut, listening as the snow crunched outside and then the outer door swung open, and Domko's heavy boots stepped inside. With the door just inches from their faces, they didn't move as Domko searched the hen house, knocking over chop pails and pushing the squawking birds aside as he checked the roost.

"Daaaavid," he called, " Dennnnis, I's be givink you pie."

The twins held their breath as his footsteps neared, and then stopped at the door. Domko stood there for a moment, muttering to himself, perplexed. A few steps towards the door, then it opened and slammed shut. His boots crunched in the direction of the barn, and he began calling their names again.

The boys exhaled in relief. They stepped out from behind the door and hurried to the small window that faced into the yard. Peeking out, David could see Domko sneaking along the barnyard fence.

"We gotta get our coats and boots," he said.

They waited until he disappeared into the barn, then flinging open the door, ran to the house where their coats were hanging just inside the door. Their mother was standing at the window.

"Run," she shouted, "he's coming back."

They nearly fell over one another as they pulled on their boots and scrambled out the door. David took the lead as they disappeared into the bush onto a path that led to the church, with the sound of Domko's heavy boots pounding behind them. He hated being tricked.

As the bush began to thin, they found themselves nearing the churchyard fence where snow had drifted up over the top wire. On hands and knees, they scrambled up the drift then rolled down the other side. Back on their feet, they continued, now in knee-deep snow, through the cemetery.

David glanced back over his shoulder to see Domko pacing on the other side of the fence, swearing, shaking his fist in the air. David slowed, before stopping to watch in disbelief. Domko would not step onto the church grounds.

Buoyed by the discovery, David cheered. "C'mon," he said, leading Dennis to the far side of the church and out of sight.

Where Children Run

Panting, they fell into the snow. They laid on their backs staring up at the dusky sky. Domko's cursing seemed out of place in such peaceful surroundings.

"Ah, shuddup you ol' flatfoot," Dennis said under his breath.

David chuckled. They had escaped.

The twins stayed on their backs until they caught their breath, then stood up and brushed the snow from their clothes. They stayed out of sight until they were sure Domko was gone. As the sun lowered, their thoughts turned to where they would sleep that night.

Rounding the corner of the church, they climbed the wooden steps to find the front door padlocked.

"How do you s'pose Norman got in?" Dennis asked.

"It never used to be locked," David said, glancing around. "Not 'til he went and crapped on the floor. Then the church people had a meeting and locked the door."

"Oh," Dennis said, pulling at that lock. "He wrecked it for us."

David thought for a moment. "Gimme your wire."

Dennis opened his coat and slid the wire he used as a belt from the pant loops and handed it to his brother. He stood there holding up his loose pants, watching as David stuck one end of the wire into the key slot.

"This is called pickin' the lock," David said. "I read about it in a comic book. You watch that nobody's comin'."

Impressed, Dennis looked up and down the road. He asked David if he had "got it yet?" so many times that David finally kicked him in the shins. Tired of waiting, Dennis suggested that they climb in a window.

David pulled on the lock one last time. He tucked the wire in his pocket and motioned for Dennis to follow as he jumped down into the snow. They looked up at the windows as they circled the building.

"They're so high," Dennis said as he trudged behind, one hand bunching his pants, the other wavering as he kept his balance through the snow. They stopped at the back of the church and looked from one window to the other.

"We gots to get somethin' to stand on," Dennis said, looking around.

David chuckled as he pushed his twin into the snow. "I got somethin' to stand on—you."

Dennis crouched on hands and knees and grunted as David placed a boot on his lower back and hoisted himself up. There were no handles on the window, but David was able to coax it open by pinching the wood dividing the panes then pushing up.

"My back's gettin' sore and my hands are cold," Dennis grunted, feeling the tread of David's boots on his shoulder blades and lower back. He tried to tuck his hands into his jacket sleeves.

"I think I got it," David said as the window rattled high enough he was able to slip his fingers underneath. He pushed it open as high as he could reach. "Now you gotta stand up."

Dennis wobbled slowly up until David was balancing on his shoulders. He pushed the window up the rest of the way then reached inside with his arms. He gained a toehold on the wood siding and wiggled his way inside, landing head first on the floor in a closet-sized storage room. He picked up a wooden box then pushed it out the window.

"Here stand on this," he said dropping it into the snow.

Dennis stood on top of the box while David leaned out the window and grasped his forearms and with David's help, was able to shimmy inside. They stood for a moment in the stillness, noticing a few boxes on the floor and a broom. Dennis opened the storage room door, and they peeked out, half expecting someone to be standing there. It was the first time they remember ever being in the church, a strange sensation since it was so close to home. Stepping out, they found themselves right up at the front near the Minister's vestibule. Two rows of empty pews faced them, and a thick Bible sat open on the podium. A large wood stove sat at the back of the room by the double front doors.

"We'll get in trouble if we get caught," Dennis said, his voice echoing as it bounced off the high ceiling.

"It don't matter as long as we don't crap on nothin'," David replied.

Fearing that the neighbors would see smoke and investigate, they decided against making a fire in the wood stove. Instead, they lifted two candle holders from the table and placed them on the carpeted floor. David found a box of matches, lit the candles then instinctively jammed the box in his coat pocket.

Dennis sat cross-legged in front of the candles and stared into the light while David disappeared into the Minister's vestibule. He called out to Dennis a few minutes later from the podium.

Dennis gasped at the sight of his brother wearing the Minister's cloak.

"Take that off," he exclaimed. "What if Momma sees you?"

David smiled. "She ain't gonna see us here." His expression turned serious as if he were about to address the congregation. He flipped through the Bible, read a bit out loud, in a strange booming voice, then holding up the end of the robe so he wouldn't trip, plopped down beside Dennis in front of the candles.

"It's real warm, feel it," he said. Dennis took one end of the robe and pulled it over his shoulders. David knocked one of the candles with his foot but was able to catch it before it burned the rug.

Dennis snuggled close. "Momma would be mad if she saw us."

"Yeah," David agreed, "wouldn't Satan be glad if we just froze to death. We gotta take care of ourselves Denny 'cause nobody else is gonna."

They sat in silence listening to the wind whistle softly through the bell tower. Overhead, the rafters creaked and groaned.

"What if one of us turns blind like Kathy?" David asked.

"We won't. She was a baby when he made her blind, and we're big already."

"Yeah, but Denny he can make you blind, too," David said. "You gots to cover your head when he hits you."

"I do," Dennis replied.

"No, you gots to do it like this," David said, wrapping his arms in front of his face and his wrists over the top of his head. "If he smashes you and you turn blind you won't be able to work no more. You know what will happen then."

Dennis thought for a moment. "Shoot me like the dogs?"

David nodded. He'd lost count of the many dogs Domko stole from the neighbors then shot when they misbehaved.

Then he wondered out loud what it would be like to be dead. He didn't pay much attention to the weekly lessons but knew that Dennis held onto the hope that someday they would be saved.

"Momma says that when we die, we'll be in the new order and things will be better," he replied.

"What about the ol' Devil?" David asked.

"He ain't good enough to make it to the new order."

"Are we?"

"Ruby says we're good," Dennis said. "Momma used to say we was good until Satan started telling her we're not. The people from the church don't think we're good, but they don't decide who goes to the new order."

The brothers laid down as close to the candles as they dared and stared up at the ceiling. It was completely dark outside now, and all they could do was hope that the glow couldn't be seen from the road.

"Maybe we're wastin' our time," Dennis said, surprising his twin. "Maybe it would be better if we just died and went some other place."

David shook his head. "All I know is I can't just stand there like you and let Satan kill me. I got to run, and you got to run, too," he said. His tone had an urgency neither of them expected.

"I know, but I freeze up," Dennis said, then he yawned, and David mimicked him. Their thoughts went back to that afternoon.

"How come he got so mad 'bout your pants?" Dennis asked.

"'Cause I stitched 'em to my long underwear."

Dennis elbowed his brother and felt the sharp poke of wire, reminding him that David hadn't given him his belt back. He gave him another shove and reached into the pocket and pulled it out.

"Why didn't you use your wire instead of mine?" he asked, sitting straight so he could re-thread it through the loops.

David smiled. "'Cause I didn't want my pants to fall down."

Morning came, and gnawing hunger jolted them awake. They rolled up and stretched their cold, stiff limbs. It was freezing in the church but not nearly as cold as outside.

The candles had burned out, so David plucked the stubs from the holders and tossed them in the corner. He returned the holders to the table while Dennis hung the robe on its hook in the vestibule. They kicked the creases out of the carpet before pushing open the storage room window and lowering themselves to the ground.

David hid the box they used as a stepping stool behind a small bush then suggested they go to Harwart's house for something to eat.

The air was crisp and quiet, the sun just beginning to rise so the sky was golden-pink. The only sound was their rubber boots crunching in the snow. Before leaving the church grounds, they looked to see if Domko was by the road. Seeing no sign of him, they hurried past the school toward the log house, its warmth shining brightly in the window. Smoke from the chimney lifted gently into the sky, freezing mid-air in the stillness.

"It's c-cold," David shivered. "Prob'ly the coldest day yet."

"Uh-huh," Dennis replied, tucking his chin into the top of his coat. It was too cold to breathe through his nose, so he took short breaths through his mouth and watched as the steam froze on the metal zipper, forming little frost buds that grew with every breath.

They hurried up the driveway to the house, glancing toward the open barn door and saw the glow of a lamp hanging at the entrance. David rapped on the old wooden door, and Marjorie opened it a sliver, then wider when she saw it was them.

"C-can we stay for a bit? Satan k-kicked us out again," David asked.

Marjorie hurried them inside then closed the door quickly.

Emma bustled into the kitchen. "It's too cold for children to be outside," she said, pulling out two chairs and motioning for them to sit down. "Now, what's this about Domko kicking you out again?"

Before they could answer, she told Marjorie to get them slippers so that their feet wouldn't be cold.

"This floor is good an' warm, not like the church," Dennis said without thinking, then his face flushed as he glanced at David.

Emma tilted her head slightly. "What do you mean?"

David sighed, kicking Dennis' foot under the table. "We ran out yesterday and crawled into the church and stayed overnight," he said.

"You slept in the church?" Emma asked, eyes narrowing.

"We didn't break nothin'," David said quickly, "and we shut the window when we left."

Emma frowned. "Children shouldn't have to sleep outside in the dead of winter. You boys could have frozen to death. Did you make a fire?"

"No, ma'am, we was too scared," Dennis said.

Just then the door opened, and Gus came inside. He was bundled in a thick coat, felt hat and heavy mitts. He pulled off his boots and unwrapped the scarf covering his face.

"Forty-two degrees below zero—the coldest morning yet this year," he said. Then he noticed the twins sitting at the table. "By jimminy, what are you two doing out in weather like this?"

"They slept in the church last night," Emma said in German. "Can you believe it?"

Gus shook his head. He sat down and waited for Emma to pour him a cup of coffee then pulling a handkerchief from his pocket, wiped his dripping nose.

"Hope you boys didn't make a mess," he said.

"No sir," David said.

"People will be arriving for services soon, and I don't want you boys getting into trouble," he added.

Emma served a breakfast of eggs and toast. They hungrily ate while trying their best to be polite.

When breakfast was finished, Marjorie disappeared outside to do chores while Emma got ready for church. Winter was always so long and lonely that she was looking forward to an afternoon of visiting with neighbors and friends. The twins took this as their cue to leave and thanked them for breakfast.

Once they were halfway down the driveway, they noticed a car parked in front of the church. Someone had arrived early to light a fire so the building would be warm when the service began. The Twins waited until the man drove away before they trudged into the bush and found a fallen tree to sit on. Hidden from sight, they watched as cars filled with families arrived, and people hurried to the church door. Soon, the congregation began singing, and while they couldn't understand the words, they knew that the hymns were being sung in German.

"We-wa, we-wa," Dennis sang quietly. David joined in, and they swayed back and forth. It was a long time before either boy spoke.

"Gus and Emma are Lutherans, you know," David said. "And they're not bad. How come Momma's church says that all other religions are wrong?"

"I dunno," Dennis said. "Momma says Witnesses never lie."

"Jim Deighton never lies, and he's not a Witness," David said.

"He's good, but he ain't going to the new order like us."

"What's gonna happen to him when he dies?"

"He'll just turn to dust," Dennis said.

More than an hour later, the church door opened and the men hurried out to start their cars. The women and children followed soon afterward. The Minister stood for a few moments on the stoop padlocking the door. The twins were anxious to feel the warmth inside so as soon as his car was gone, they hurried to the back of the church. Getting in was easier now that they had done it before.

David tossed another log in the wood stove thinking that if anyone saw the smoke, they would believe the fire was still smoldering from the afternoon. When it started to get dark, they put another log in the stove then lit the candles and once again sat cross-legged on the floor with the robe draped over their shoulders.

"It ain't so bad in here," David said, feeling his heart swell a bit. "And I don't care what no Witnesses say, the Lutherans ain't bad people."

Dennis' eyes fixed once again on the candles.

"Do you think God cares Witness kids are in his Lutheran church?"

David mulled this over but said nothing. It wasn't until they were lying pressed against each other and he could feel his sleeping brother's heartbeat that he whispered, "There ain't no God, Denny."

Hunger drove them home the following afternoon. They crept into the house when Domko was outside. Since there was nothing else to eat, they each stuffed a fistful of rolled oats in their pocket before running upstairs to hide.

The following morning, they quietly came down in time to help with the milking. Domko watched as each picked up a pail by the door. The twins were beginning to realize that he didn't beat them when they came home. He would taunt them, ask where they'd been and call them lazy, but he never beat them unless they were brought home by the police.

That morning when chores were finished, the twins walked to school with Eunice and Rosie.

"Thanks a lot for leavin' me with Domko and all the chores," Eunice said. "Next time take me. Where did you guys go?"

David knew he could trust her. "We hid in the church and had breakfast at Emma's," David said. "But don't tell Momma."

"I think she knows anyway," Eunice said. "You shoulda seen how mad Domko was yesterday. He came in the house complainin' about havin' to listen to all them Germans singing at the church."

The boys laughed and started chanting, "We-wa, We-wa!"

After school that day, Domko was waiting on the road to catch the children before they tried to run away.

"Hitchink a some horse," he said to the twins as they followed him to the barnyard. "Bringink but-a-some hay."

They hated going for hay in the middle of winter. It was a tiresome job because Domko's horses were so miserable that they would rear up and upset the hay rack on the sleigh. When this happened, the boys would first have to get the horses under control and then fork the hay on again.

Domko stood in the doorway watching as they led Darby and Jack through the barnyard. Darby reared and as Dennis tried to bring him under control, the horse bit him hard on the forearm. Domko thought this hilarious, but the sound of his laughter startled the horses, and they took off running, dragging the twins behind. They were able to hold on for a while but lost their grip when the horses galloped through the yard. The twins jumped up and ran down the road after them.

"Fraa," Domko yelled, shaking his fist in the air.

The twins knew not to bother returning home until they had the horses under control. They followed until, a half a mile down the road, the team veered into a field. The boys tromped through the heavy snow toward them, but already spooked, they took off again, this time toward Harwart's yard.

Marjorie was in the barn and saw the horses trotting up the lane with the twins running behind. When the horses stopped, she positioned herself between the sweating animals and the barn. The horses' eyes rolled back and then suddenly, they bolted into the field.

"Satan's gonna kill us," Dennis fretted as they struggled behind while the horses ran easily through the deep snow. "We can't go back without them."

With Marjorie's help, they continued chasing the horses until all three fell exhausted into the snow. They lay on their backs panting, looking up at the sky.

"We got to get the hay before dark," David said, turning to face Marjorie. Her hat was pushed back, and her bangs were plastered to her forehead.

"Maybe once they settle down, they'll go into the barn," she said. Sitting up, they waited quietly watching as the team worked its way slowly toward the open barn door. Inspired, Marjorie jumped up and ran to the house where she found a small pail. She went to the granary and filled it with oats. Gradually they were able to coax the horses close enough with the oats to grab their reins then lead them home.

As soon as the twins were back, Domko barked at them to fetch the hay. Eunice followed and together they hitched the horses to the sleigh and rode to the hay field. By the time they finished loading, hauling and unloading at the barn, it was well past dark. They snuck into the house and hurried upstairs to hide in the crawl space behind the wall.

"I hate them horses," Dennis said, gently rubbing the bite mark on his arm. The wide, purple bruise was tender and swollen. "How come he makes us use Darby and Jack when Dolly is so good?"

David shook his head. "Whaddya think? His horses hate us like he does. He likes watchin' us fight with them."

Carrying a book, Eunice crawled in beside them. She loved to read but had to do it without Domko knowing.

"Be quiet," she said as she made herself comfortable. She had waited weeks for this novel from the school library and didn't want to be disturbed. Her eyes adjusted quickly to the dark as she leaned close to the edge of the eaves. By scraping away the sawdust insulation, she was able to see into the kitchen, and this gave her enough light to read.

This was the most comfortable spot in their hiding place, and because she was the oldest, she took it for herself. The others had to sleep along the outside walls. They often complained they couldn't sleep because of the cold and sometimes when they awoke; their hair had stuck to the frost accumulated on the wall.

The following morning, Rosie was allowed to go to school, but Eunice and the twins had to stay home. They would have rather gone to school than clean out the barn, but were thankful for the breakfast of porridge and skim milk that awaited them. They ate as much as Domko allowed, knowing a long day of manual labor was ahead.

Where Children Run

Hauling manure from the barn was a job nobody enjoyed, including the horses, so the children weren't surprised when Domko told them to harness Dolly. They went around to the back of the barn where she stood most of the winter. She whinnied as the children approached and let them lead her to the front of the barn where she patiently stood while they hitched her to the stone boat—a platform of boards on heavy wooden runners. Then they lead her inside to the far end of the barn where the odor was overwhelming. They began shoveling onto the stone boat, and when it was piled high, they led Dolly out to a nearby field. Climbing on top of the pile, they forked the manure onto the ground then led the horse back to the barn to begin again. It would take many trips before they would finish.

Domko checked on them a few times that morning. In the late afternoon, he came out to check again. Thinking they were on the last load, the children piled the manure a little too high, making it a heavy pull. Seeing this, Domko called them lazy and wrenched the horse's reins from David's hands then tried to lead Dolly out of the barn. She became stubborn at the sight of him and locked her knees, refusing to move. Furious with her defiance, he picked up a shovel and hit her over the head. Dolly reared slightly, and that forced him to back away.

Dropping the reins, Domko smashed her over the head again, but Dolly still wouldn't move. Cursing, he pushed his way past her into the barn to find a pitchfork, barking commands at the children to get the horse out of the barn. The twins grabbed the reins and began coaxing Dolly, who took a step, jolted the stone boat forward, but then slipped on the icy, wet cement. The boys realized they had filled the wagon too full and began apologizing for the horse who was struggling to get back on her feet. Her back end banged into the stone boat, causing her to stumble again.

"Lazy beech," Domko said. With all the force of his weight behind him, he rammed the pitchfork prongs into Dolly's rump. Pulling the pitchfork out, he jabbed it in again, this time pushing it as far as it would go. The horse whinnied in pain as she struggled to stand.

Grunting and swearing, he jabbed her again, this time enjoying perverse pleasure as he penetrated the delicate area beneath her tail.

"Dolly, get up," the children begged, pulling the reins, tears streaming down their faces. The horse's back legs were trapped underneath the stone boat, and her front legs slipped on the cement.

"Lazy, beech bastard," he swore as he strode to the doorway and pounded the shovel down on the horse's head again.

The children backed away as he continued to beat her and they could do nothing but cry. He smashed her over the head one final time, then threw down the shovel and stormed towards the house.

As soon as he was gone, the children gathered around Dolly and unhitched her from the stone boat. Blood streamed down her back end, and she whimpered as the twins coaxed her up and then lead her to a straw bed behind the barn.

Dolly wobbled and then laid down on her uninjured side. Eunice and Dennis stroked her sweaty neck while David snuck to the granary to fetch a can of oats. He poured the grain onto the ground by her head then rubbed her nose gently. He had to turn quickly away from the sickening sight of blood congealing in long streams down her legs.

"Oh, Dolly," he sobbed, "We're so sorry."

The horse neighed softly as the children nestled in close. Too afraid to go inside, they slept huddled beside the horse that night. David could see Dolly's eyes wet and shiny in the moonlight. As she whimpered, he could tell that Dolly was crying, too.

NIGHTMARES

AFTER DOMKO HAD BOUGHT TWO QUARTERS OF LAND AND A CAR, HE began complaining that there was little money for groceries and bought even less. Fortunately, fish spawned in nearby creeks each spring, and the Twins became experts at fishing with a spear. One morning they carried home a half dozen mullet and walleye strung on a stick with the idea of giving them to their mother to cook for supper. Domko took the fish and sent them back for more. Once they had filled a washtub, he said it would make good feed for the pigs and chickens.

They took the fish into the kitchen and began cutting them into small pieces with Eunice's help.

"I don't wanna feed this to no pig," Dennis said under his breath.

"Me neither," David said as he chopped off the head and tail of a big mullet. It had been two days since he and Dennis snuck a tin of food and shared it while sitting in the hiding place upstairs.

Their conversation stopped as the door opened and Domko came in carrying a full can of skim milk. He poured it into a large pot before he went back outside, and told the twins to put the cut fish, including the entrails, into the pot.

They were scooping up handfuls of fish when Domko returned carrying a sack. He poured in a quarter bag of crushed grain then started a fire in the cook stove and placed the pot on top. He told Eunice to stir it occasionally while he was outside. Soon it smelled incredibly good to the starving children.

Pushing a chair in front of the wood stove, Eunice stood on the seat and peered inside. The twins climbed beside her. David handed her a large spoon.

"Yuk," she said as she poked a fish bladder with her finger. The sausage-shaped white bags ballooned to the top and bounced as the mixture cooked.

Cocking their heads slightly, they became completely silent, listening for their stepfather. Using the spoon, Eunice scooped some of the chop into her mouth, making a face and exhaling as it scalded her tongue, then took another spoonful.

Dennis reached in and pinched a piece of fish, blowing hard before placing it in his mouth. He chewed carefully, pulling the bones from his mouth, dropping them back into the pot.

David joined in. They ate as long as they dared then jumped off the chair, returning to sneak spoonfuls at every opportunity while Eunice stood guard at the window.

"He's coming!"

David jumped down and went to stand at the table with Dennis, and they all practiced looking innocent. Domko eyed them suspiciously but said nothing as he went to the stove, picked up the spoon and began stirring. The children were pleased that they hadn't been caught and helped themselves to more as soon as he went back outside.

"I wonder what it's like to eat good like this all the time," David dreamily said as he spat fish scales into his hand then rubbed them into his pants pocket. He smiled at Eunice as they watched Dennis put a handful of fish in his mouth.

As the fire in the stove went out, and the contents of the pot began to settle, the children stood solemnly at the far end of the kitchen. Domko came in, peered into the pot and grunted. He glanced at them and smirked. Placing a thumb on one nostril, he blew out the other side of his nose into the pot. He wiped the back of his hand across his face then strode out the door.

They stood there stunned.

"Blech," Eunice convulsed.

David held back the urge to throw up.

Dennis exhaled slowly. "Well, I guess we won't be eatin' that no more."

Domko openly bragged about his new car, a 1949 Ford, to anyone who'd listen. To the children's knowledge, it was the first vehicle he'd owned since coming to Canada. The cream-colored car helped elevate his status in the area, which pleased him greatly. He always bragged what a good farmer he was and how more productive the farm was since his arrival.

"Momma says he's a lousy driver," Dennis said one evening as they climbed into bed. "She says that he's gonna kill himself or somebody else."

David smiled. "Maybe he will, and we don't have to think about shootin' him no more."

Where Children Run

The twins giggled and then paused to overhear Domko talking peacefully with their mother downstairs. She had been disappearing a lot lately, leaving the house early and not coming back until after supper. It sounded like Domko was trying to make amends so that she wouldn't leave him for good.

The following morning the twins tackled their early morning chores. On their way in from the barn, they realized that Domko was not watching them as usual. They went into the kitchen to find him in front of the mirror shaving. They sat at the table and watched as he slowly removed a month's worth of beard growth using a straight razor. David shuddered at the sight of the blade sliding across his neck.

Domko turned to face them, and the contrast between his clean cheeks and dirty forehead caused them to look away, softly giggling as he grunted in satisfaction at himself in the mirror.

"I's be takink some cream," he announced as he lifted the cream can off the shelf. The children relaxed once he was out the door and they heard the car running.

"I ain't never going anywhere with him," Eunice said to Rosie. "You can't run away if you're trapped in the car."

The twins agreed, and Rosie listened solemnly. Eunice had become quite adept at avoiding Domko, so they paid attention to her advice.

Outside there was a roar that sounded like Domko speeding away, followed by a crashing sound. They ran to the front room window and saw that he had smashed into a tree at the edge of the driveway. He was leaning in the front seat deathly still, his chest against the steering wheel.

They gasped in shock and then began to cheer.

"He's dead! He's dead!" Dennis said jumping high. "Satan's dead!"

They laughed and danced but then looked out the window again and saw that he was starting to move.

"Oh no," David cried. "He's not dead; he's just pretending."

Dennis didn't want to believe it. He blinked his eyes and stared, willing Domko to fall down as he opened the door and stepped out of the car. The huge gash on his forehead gave Dennis hope.

"Maybe he's hurt bad," he said to Rosie who was staring hopefully at her siblings. "Sometimes people don't die right away. They die later when you take 'em to the hospital."

The children watched as Domko, seeming dazed and confused, walked to the front of the car to inspect the damage.

"The ol' bastard isn't gonna die," David sighed. "We better go."

"Yeah," Eunice agreed. "He's gonna be real mad now."

The children scurried out and stood on the driveway, watching him curse his bad luck.

"Bring but-a-some pail," he yelled at nobody in particular.

Eunice ran to the barn and returned with a small can. She approached him cautiously, stretched the pail out to him, then hurried away. Domko muttered to himself as he placed the can under the front end of the car to catch the liquid that was flowing to the ground.

"Bring but-a-some horse," he said to David.

A few minutes later David returned leading Darby. Domko took the reins and attached a chain between the horse's harness and the car's back axle then coaxed the horse to pull. Darby struggled forward, pulling the car slowly away from the tree. Domko motioned for David to take the horse back to the barn. Then without a word, he strode to the shed and returned driving the tractor. He loaded the cream and held it between his knees as he set out for town.

Once he was gone, the children examined the car.

"Do you think it's wrecked?" Eunice asked.

"It looks like it to me," David said.

Domko returned that afternoon with a tow truck following close behind. The children stood watching as a man stepped out of the truck and walked around the car. They knew his name was Kurt because it was written right on his shirt. Kurt looked at the tree and the broken branches lying on the ground. Small twigs and leaves were scattered across the hood and roof of the car.

"So, what happened here?" he asked.

Domko shook his head and sighed. "The horse be kickink it some."

Kurt deciphered Domko's words then raised his eyebrows. He looked at the car and then at Domko again. "Eh?" he asked.

"The horse, she be kickink it some," he said impatiently, pointing to the front of the car.

Kurt looked taken aback but said nothing. He began chewing absent-mindedly on a toothpick which appeared from somewhere inside his mouth.

"Whatever you say," he muttered as he got back in his truck and backed towards the rear of the car.

The twins tried to stifle their laughter.

"The horse?" David whispered.

"Be kickink it some?" Dennis added.

Domko glared at them as Kurt hopped down and crawled under the car, fastening the tow hook to the undercarriage. They spoke for a few moments, then Kurt waved as he climbed back in the truck. Domko watched sadly as his car was towed down the road.

The children took that as their cue to get the cows for the evening milking. They hurried towards the wintering area just north of the barn.

"Did you see that's guy's face when ol' Squeezer said the horse did it?" David asked.

"Yeah, where'd that horse go, you know, the one that's got branches for legs," Dennis laughed.

"Yeah, that's one funny lookin' horse."

Always looking for ways to expand the farm, Domko had bought a truckload of bred beef cows the fall before, and they calved in February. Instead of removing the calves from their mothers as he did with milk cows, he decided the calves would be raised by the cows all summer and then sold as feeders in the fall. This was an easier way to make money than expanding the milking herd, and he was able to keep pace with other farmers in the district.

The twins were kept home from school one day to help castrate the bull calves before the cows and calves were turned out to pasture.

To do this, the cows had to be separated from the calves. This resulted in a huge commotion as the cows were chased to one side of the fence while the calves were confined to a large holding pen. Once that was done, Dennis was given the job of chasing the calves from the holding pen into the long chute where Domko stood waiting at the end. David waited part way down the chute and was supposed to let only one calf through at a time.

Controlling the smaller calves was easy, but some of the early born calves weighed more than two hundred pounds. David sent the first calf forward, holding another back, as he tried not to watch.

"Yous be holdink it some," Domko yelled as he wrestled with the first calf, grabbed its testicles and using his knife, cut them off. The calf's bawling turned David's stomach, and he almost fainted. He released the second calf when the first one wobbled out the end of the chute.

When there were only five calves left in the pen, they decided they all wanted to go down the chute at the same time. One calf kicked Dennis hard in the leg, knocking him down. He writhed in pain and called out to David who tried to stop the charging animals. Domko was just reaching under a calf's tail when two barreled forward, knocking into Domko and startling the calf he held. The bawling animals pushed their way past and forced the gate open, kicking as they ran away.

Furious, Domko turned on David.

"You's lazy goot for nuthink bastard," he said as he strode toward him. Pointing the bloody knife at David's groin, he sneered.

"You's be watchink, or I's be cuttink it some," he said.

David cringed, promising he'd be more careful. They chased the calves back into the holding pen as Dennis limped to catch up.

David shut his eyes each time Domko sliced off a calf's testicles while carefully guarding the chute. Something in the way Domko sneered at him made David feel sick. By the time they were done, he was weak with fear. Domko wiped the knife on his pants then put it back in his breast pocket. He told the boys to chase the calves through the fence to where the cows were waiting.

"What did he say to you?" Dennis asked.

"He said he's gonna cut it off," David whispered.

"Cut what off?"

"You know," he said lowering his eyes. "It."

"What?"

"My putz," he whispered.

Dennis gasped. "What are you gonna do?"

"I don't know," he said looking toward the house. They decided to stay in the barn for the rest of the afternoon, hoping Domko would calm down. They knew that he would be primed to beat one of them and David was the most likely target.

They climbed into the loft and sat on a pile of soft hay. Tiny streams of sunlight shone through thin spaces between the barn walls.

"It's almost like he's gotta beat us," Dennis said.

"Yeah, the same way he's gotta eat and sleep and smoke," David added.

"Then he's happy again until he gets worse and smashes us again."

They talked about Domko's hatred toward them.

"Do you think he wants to kill us?" Dennis finally asked.

"Prob'ly. He hates us 'cause we're German. And we're not his. I heard him talkin' to Momma, and he thinks we're gonna take the farm."

"Then how come he doesn't just do it?"

"Doesn't wanna go to jail," David said. "He's tryin' to make it look like we kill ourselves."

Dennis thought about the theory. "Do you think he's nuts?"

"He's smart enough to make himself look good. He tricks everyone and knows how long he can smash us before killing us," David said. "Does that sound nuts to you?"

That night David awoke screaming. The nightmares began soon after he saw the dogs hanging from the tree and now were made worse by the fear of castration. Most of his bad dreams started as small, frightening scenes that woke him almost immediately, but some continued, torturing him as he slept. Now, Domko was haunting David both day and night.

Social worker, Martha Jeske-Patterson, made another surprise visit to the farm. She had been transferred to another district but was filling in until the department found a replacement for the area. Martha brought along a male colleague from the child welfare department. As their car pulled into the driveway, the twins ran into the bush.

"Did you see that?" she said to her co-worker as they stepped out of the car. Walking towards the trees, Martha was surprised that the twins would run. She remembered them as being very friendly and outgoing when they were living in Ashern.

"Come out of there boys," she said. "I want to talk to you."

At first, there was no movement, but then slowly the boys edged their way out of the trees.

"How come you aren't in school?" she asked.

Neither one said a word. Martha looked carefully at their poorly-fitted, torn clothing and dirty faces. They were terribly thin and sorrowful. She remembered the look of sadness in the health nurse's eyes when she said she suspected these children were neglected.

"Where did you boys sleep last night?" she asked.

They looked at her solemnly.

"Do you understand English?"

David nodded that they did.

"I asked where did you sleep last night?"

"In the barn," David quietly said.

"How come you're not in school?"

David shrugged his shoulders. "We don't gotta go."

"All kids have to go to school," she replied. "How old are you?"

David looked at Dennis who began counting on his fingers.

"We's ten," Dennis answered.

"How come you run away when visitors come?" she asked.

David kicked the ground with a bare toe.

"Are you afraid?" she asked.

He refused to look at her. He wasn't sure what she'd say to Domko, who was likely standing at the window watching.

"That's all right. You don't have to tell me everything right away," she said. "I'm here to help you, not make things worse."

David nodded and looked up into Martha's eyes. They looked vaguely familiar, like eyes he could trust.

The kitchen door opened. Caroline came out with Domko right behind her. Caroline tried to sound polite and steady as she invited the social workers inside. She told the twins to stay out, which they happily agreed to do. They wanted to look at the social worker's car and after they did, disappeared back into the bush.

"There's nothing we can do," Caroline said. "They run away."

"But why do they run away?" Martha asked.

Caroline glanced at the man who was busy taking notes.

"Because they don't want to do chores or go to school," she replied.

"The neighbors say the boys are afraid of Mr. Domko," she asked. "Is that correct?"

Domko scoffed while Caroline tried hard to sound composed.

"They miss their father and treat their stepfather badly because of it," she said. "We can't control them anymore."

Martha explained that when parents lost control and children ran away from home, the children were deemed incorrigible. If an investigation proved this, the department obtained a court order, and the children were placed in foster care.

Caroline looked at Domko who was visibly upset by the explanation. His reaction confused her because she knew in her heart that he hated the boys, and might like having them live elsewhere.

"We only remove children as a last resort," Martha explained. "We have to think of what's best for the boys. Something will have to be done if you can't control them—"

"We'll start now," Caroline said. "They're good boys, just full of mischief that's all. And we'll make sure they go to school—"

"You've said that before," Martha interrupted. "The files show school attendance was a problem even before your first husband died. I have copies of their school records which show they missed eight days in the first term and have already missed ten this term."

Caroline bit her bottom lip and sat back in her chair. Her arms crossed over her chest. "Well, David was sick, and Dennis doesn't like to go anywhere without him."

"We need to understand why these boys keep running away," Martha persisted, looking at Domko who lit a cigarette. He seemed to enjoy watching his wife scramble through her lies. There was no doubt that something was wrong with this man. Based on the assessment by the health nurse and Dr. Steenson, Martha was certain Domko had a mental problem.

"Have you thought about seeing a doctor?" she said to him. "I can arrange it if you like."

"He's been to see Dr. Steenson, and there's nothing they can do about the headaches," Caroline said.

"I'm not talking about the headaches," she said. "I'm talking about his temper. There are doctors who specialize in problems of the mind."

Domko's initial reaction was to chuckle, but then after a few moments, he began to understand what she implied.

"Vat?" he spat, standing up. "I's be crazy in but-a-some head? I's not be, she's be. Ant they's be," he said pointing in the general direction of the Harwart and Deighton farms. He began pacing around the kitchen, ranting that the Harwarts and Deightons were jealous and conspired to ruin his farm.

Caroline tried to persuade him to sit down, but finally just stared at the table, knowing he was making matters worse by showing this side of himself.

Martha and her co-worker carefully watched as Domko worked himself into an angry state. Then he stopped as quickly as he had started. He eyed Martha suspiciously, quietly putting an end to the meeting by opening the door and suggesting it was a long drive back to Winnipeg.

Reluctantly, the social workers got up and left the dark, dirty house. Caroline followed them outside, but Domko stayed in, slamming the door behind them. As the social workers climbed into the car, Caroline apologized for Domko's behavior saying that he had a headache.

Since the children were in no immediate danger, there was nothing more they could do. Martha made notations in the file as Caroline backed away from the car. Where this would take her, she wasn't sure, but Martha had a gut feeling there would be a confrontation soon.

"How can children survive under those circumstances?" her co-worker asked as he backed the car out of the driveway.

"You'd be surprised. There are a few families around here who do."

After the social workers left, Caroline looked around her house in disarray and then at herself in the mirror. Why had her life turned out like this? Why didn't she have a nice job, like Margaret Burnett? She had wanted to be a nurse, too, and often thought what a satisfying job it would be—traveling around visiting new mothers with babies, giving shots and helping those in need.

Caroline hated her life and had tried running away, but there was no choice except to return home when she ran out of money. She always believed that if she was successful in finding a new life somewhere, she could send for the children later. But now she was losing hope and the realization that things weren't going to change anytime soon, sent her into a deep depression. She spent the next week in bed.

Caroline listened as Domko berated the children, but felt helpless to do anything about it. Sometimes he would come into the bedroom and force himself on her, but she accepted this the same way she allowed him to beat her with his fists. She was too frightened to stop him—afraid of what he'd do, scared of how strong she would have to be to change her life. Instead, she just looked at the ceiling and daydreamed.

Sometimes he would come into the room to argue and be suspicious about why she refused to leave the bed. She did no housework or chores, and nothing he said could force her to listen. He called her lazy and good for nothing, but she just turned her back. If he hit her, she simply covered her head in silence until he stopped.

All of this terrified the children. They hated seeing their mother like this and thought it was as if their real mother was gone and a stranger had entered her body.

One evening, the twins stood alongside her bed.

"Don't worry, boys," she quietly said. "Justice is right around the corner. It looks as if we'll be dying on this farm, likely by Domko's hand. But death isn't something you need to be afraid of. It is something to welcome. I've done all I can here, and I'm ready to go to heaven."

"But Momma," Dennis cried, "we don't want you to die. We don't want to die. We want to live in Moosehorn some day."

"Maybe that will happen, but maybe it's not meant to be," she said.

"But I don't want to go to heaven yet," David said.

"Don't worry, son. It's a wonderful place. You children won't have to worry about Domko. It is a place where everybody loves everybody, and only the best people are chosen. You are such sweet boys, you'll be there with me, and it will be wonderful because there are beautiful animals and there's lots of food for everybody."

They listened to their mother, and by the end of the evening, Dennis wanted to die, too.

Caroline came to her senses within a few weeks, and while she was still depressed, she moved around and was able to carry on a normal conversation. This wasn't the first time she'd suffered such an episode, but she emerged this time a slightly different person. Now she seemed to accept her life. She told the boys she was no longer going to fight.

Domko arranged to have a local electrician, Mr. Milner, come to the farm to wire the house and barn. Knowing she'd soon have hydro brightened Caroline's spirits, especially when he said he'd buy her some electrical appliances.

When Mr. Milner arrived, he brought along his son, Walter, who was a few years older than the twins and big for his age. David and Walter became instant friends, and soon they were roughhousing together. Dennis watched from the sidelines as Walter wrestled David to the ground. Domko also watched, and one day after David had once again conceded defeat, Domko called him to the house.

"Vat, you's be losink again?" he said.

David was shocked. "We're just playin', nobody's gettin' hurt."

"You's be hittink some bastard like this," Domko said, making a quick kicking motion towards David's groin. He then showed David how to punch with the palm of his hand, a karate move he'd learned in the army.

Embarrassed, David looked around hoping that the Milners couldn't hear what Domko was saying. "I don't wanna hurt him - we're just playin'."

"You's not be playink no more," Domko said, adding that if he saw Walter win the wrestling again, he'd beat David until he couldn't walk.

David went back outside, and when Walter came near, he made an excuse that he had to do chores. He stayed away until Walter and his father left. The following afternoon when he could avoid Walter no longer, he told him to go home.

"I don't want you comin' around no more," David said. "Me and Denny don't like you."

Walter was shocked. His face reddened as he struggled to gain his composure. "Don't worry," he said, voice quivering. "I won't."

Disappointed that the fight between Walter and David had failed to materialize, Domko taunted David for weeks. He called him a coward and tried to goad him into doing something foolish so that he could beat him. David ignored him and eventually Dennis did something wrong, so Domko beat him instead.

One morning Domko told the boys that they would be going to an auction sale. Except for hiding at the neighbors, it was almost a year since they had left the farm and had never been to an auction sale before.

They climbed into the back seat of Domko's car and rode the five miles to the sale. At first, seeing so many strangers, they became frightened and refused to get out of the car. Domko scowled in warning, so they got out and followed him around for a while as he looked at old equipment, household items, lumber and some junk.

Soon the twins felt relaxed enough to venture off on their own. People watched as they examined things and talked animatedly among themselves. Many people in the district believed that the Pischke children were thieves, and while David and Dennis didn't know it at the time, they were being watched for that reason.

Dennis noticed two men pointing and talking about them. Feeling self-conscious, he persuaded David to move with him to the center of the crowd. The sale had just begun, and they wanted to see what would happen.

The auctioneer spoke very fast as he worked to get bids from the audience. At first, the buyers were quiet and careful, but as the sale progressed, they began bidding aggressively. Domko bid on a bundle of lumber and got it, but there were three more stacks of approximately the same grade and size that he bid on but didn't get. The crowd gradually moved down the field, coming to an assortment of guns.

Domko moved over to where the boys stood and told Dennis to bid on the next gun. Dennis shook his head no. He'd never be able to stand to have everyone looking at him, and fast bidding would be too difficult. Plus, his stuttering worsened when he was nervous.

Dennis looked at David who shrugged, glad that Domko didn't ask him to do it.

Domko glared at them. He didn't want to buy the gun himself because he believed Gus and Jim were circulating rumors about him. He demanded that Dennis bid and waited with his arms crossed.

The auctioneer's assistant held the gun up, and the bidding began. Dennis' heart beat fast in his chest as he stared at the ground. He couldn't bring himself to bid even once on the gun. It sold for approximately eight dollars to a young man from Ashern named Gilbert Geisler. Gilbert took the gun proudly as Domko glared.

"You's be tellink him I's be givink him one dollar more," Domko said. Domko made a hitting motion signaling that if Dennis didn't approach Gilbert, he'd get a beating.

Slowly Dennis made his way over to Gilbert and tried to offer him one dollar more for the gun. He stammered so bad that the man became uncomfortable as Dennis tried to spit out the offer. Finally, he was able to make himself understood, but Gilbert got the gun for a good price, so he wasn't willing to part with it.

Dennis turned and slowly walked back to Domko, who called him "useless" under his breath. He told the twins to go home and get the tractor and wagon so they could load the lumber.

Thankful to be out of there, Dennis ran as fast as he could away from the crowd, with David on his heels. A few men snickered at the sight of them and wanted the men to know he also thought the boys were strange, Domko shook his head in disgust.

"Strange little buggers," one man said.

"That's for sure," the other agreed.

The twins arrived back at the sale a few hours later. The crowd had moved around a bluff into another field, so nobody was around except Domko. Nervously, he told them to load the wood. Within a short time they had it on the wagon and thinking it was time to go, David tried to climb back on the tractor.

"You's be takink some pile," Domko said pulling him down and pointing to another stack.

"But that's not ours—"

Domko glared at him before punching him in the head. He motioned for them to hurry while he turned and walked back toward the crowd that was steadily moving in the opposite direction.

"Should we?" Dennis whispered, looking around.

"We gotta," David said. "Or he'll kill us for sure."

Dennis climbed onto the wagon, and David drove close to the other pile. He jumped down and then as fast as he could, handed the planks up to Dennis who stacked them neatly on top of their pile. Soon the wagon was overloaded.

"Hurry up," Dennis whispered. "We gotta go before they come back."

David hoisted himself onto the tractor seat and drove quickly through the field. He passed by the farm house and accelerated, driving in high gear all the way home. His stomach turned over a few times at the thought of what they had just done.

Domko arrived home later that afternoon in an incredibly good mood. He went out to the back of the barn to inspect the huge pile of wood. He strutted through the kitchen, bragging about how smart he'd been and how the other fellow hadn't had the good sense to stand guard over his wood.

The twins listened in disgust then went out to do evening chores, just as a truck pulled in the driveway. It was the man who had bought the wood and someone had suggested he look for it at the Pischke farm.

Domko looked convincingly innocent.

"They's be takink it?" he said pointing at the twins. Motioning for the man to follow, he walked to the barn and then acted surprised to see such a big stack.

"I's be tellink, but they's be stupid soneebeech don't be doink some," he explained. "I's say one pile; they's be takink two."

Domko told the man to bring the truck into the barnyard, then instructed the twins to load half the amount into the man's truck.

The man watched silently as the boys once again loaded the wood—this time for the rightful owner.

NOT MUCH OF A FATHER

Within a few days, everybody in the district had heard about the stolen wood. The twins were branded as thieves, and they and their stepfather were watched carefully from that day forward.

Domko arrived home from town one afternoon a few weeks later, ranting and raving that he'd been discounted at the creamery for having too much milk in the bottom of the cream can. It was a trick he pulled most of the time, pouring in milk to top up the can, but this time he'd been caught during a random check.

Employees at the Co-op were also watching Domko. He'd been caught stealing goods by stuffing them inside a stovepipe. He also lined his coat pockets with chocolate bars and small tools. Sometimes they caught him; sometimes they didn't.

One evening while the children sat quietly studying, Domko tried to coax them into taking a chocolate bar. It was an old trick that they all knew, so they all ignored him. Domko watched them, huffing, then zeroed in on Dennis who was so involved in sketching an elaborate farm scene that he absentmindedly began banging his foot against the wall. Domko listened to the sound for a while and then flew into a rage.

Marjorie had gone for a walk down the road that evening. A teenage girl sometimes needed to be alone with her thoughts. Her parents didn't mind so long as she finished her chores first, and returned home before dark. The sun was setting behind the bush to the west, and the mosquitoes were buzzing in the damp grass. Sandy ran ahead, doubling back, sniffing the ground and when she picked up the fresh scent of a rabbit, ran excitedly into the bush.

Marjorie was a little upset as she thought about her life. A few children in school tried to embarrass her by reminding everyone that her parents were poor. Her mother always told her to be thankful for the things she had and to remember that money did not guarantee a happy life.

As Marjorie walked down the road, she could see Caroline's newly renovated house. Things certainly appeared to have improved since Domko's arrival at the farm. The house was larger now; they had hydro, a car, and more land. The barn was being fixed with tin siding, and Domko had bought more cattle.

Marjorie remembered overhearing a discussion about Caroline by a handful of women in the community. They had said she should be thankful for a husband like Domko, especially since she had seven children when they met. The women also complained that the twins were spending too much time in the church and were making a mess. One woman said that a box of candles, which should have lasted two years, needed to be replaced at the end of the winter because the children were breaking into the church and lighting the candles. They also took things from inside the church and left them outside. The women decided not to say anything to Caroline fearing the church would be vandalized out of spite.

Marjorie remembered looking at her mother during the conversation. Emma bit her lip as she listened and scoffed a few times. She had told Marjorie many times that it was pointless to argue with a group of stubborn, old German women. Then she'd laugh, saying that she knew this first hand because she was one herself!

When Emma could listen no longer, she stood up and said, "The good Lord put that church beside the Pischkes for a reason." She then strode out of the room. The women sat silently, not knowing what to say. Marjorie's heart was bursting with pride as she ran to catch up with her mother.

"Let that be a lesson to you, Marjorie Harwart," her mother had said. "Just because a person has money in his pocket it doesn't mean he has kindness in his heart."

Marjorie continued walking down the road and as she neared the Pischke house, could hear a commotion coming from inside. Domko was yelling and smashing things. Her friends were screaming and crying. Horrified, Marjorie stopped. She had never before heard anything so heart-wrenching. Just then, Sandy came out of the bush and stopped beside her, ears perking at the sound of Domko's voice. She barked a few times sharply. Marjorie couldn't listen any longer and began running toward home. As the screaming began to fade, it was replaced by the sound of chirping of birds and crickets. Tears stung her cheeks as she tried not to imagine what her friends were facing. She ran up the driveway and burst into her house. Out of breath, she wept as she told her mother what she'd heard.

The children screamed as Domko cornered them in the kitchen. He began strapping whomever he could reach and soon all but Dennis had escaped. He received a vicious beating as he lay on the kitchen floor. When Domko was finished, he sat grunting at the table. Dennis crawled up the attic stairs, and David helped him climb into bed. Too stiff to move, Dennis fell on the bed while David took a thin blanket and covered them both.

The following night the entire family was awakened by David's screams. Sitting up straight in bed, he screamed as loud as he could. When Eunice was unable to wake him, they all became frightened and moved to the other side of the room. Caroline dashed up the stairs and grabbed him. David continued to thrash around, his wide, unseeing eyes witnessing something terrible somewhere in his mind. Eventually, he stopped screaming but continued trembling as he fell back to sleep.

David's nightmares continued all week. Caroline began sleeping upstairs in the children's bed to wake David before the screaming started, but Domko soon tired of this. He was jealous that Caroline was paying so much attention to David. One night as the children were going to bed, he decided to go upstairs and have a talk with him about the nightmares.

As he began making his way up the stairs, the children panicked and ran to hide. Dennis went to the window, but Domko had nailed two spikes through the base of the window into the sill. Dennis' struggles drew a wide grin from Domko, who forgot why he'd come upstairs and began beating Dennis.

"We-wa!" David yelled as he ran down the stairs in bare feet and out the kitchen door, straight into the bush and onto the path that led to the church. Out of breath but certain that he was safe, he sat down at the back of the building to wait for Dennis who would know where he was hiding since "We-wa" was their secret word for church. His body ached in sympathy as he watched the bush for over an hour. He kept pushing the thought from his mind that one of these times Dennis might not come.

Soon he began to doze. The sound of someone approaching woke him with a start. He could see Dennis hobbling toward him. He cringed at the sight of Dennis' swollen eyes and bleeding lip. There was blood all over his chest and arms, likely from a bloodied nose. Dennis reached into his mouth and winced as he checked a loose front tooth. He wiped a bloody hand on his pants.

"You strong enough to climb in?" David asked pointing up at the church window.

"No," Dennis slurred.

"Okay, we'll sleep here then."

David rested on the grass for a few moments. "Hey Denny,"
"What?"
"You look awful."
"I know," he said, then cried himself to sleep.

"It's a miracle he made it this far," Ruby said as she wrung a cool cloth in the wash basin. "This boy is half dead."

Jim watched as his wife wiped the blood from Dennis' face.

"Well, this time the cops are going to have to listen," Jim said. "One look at that boy and they'll realize what a crazy fool Domko really is."

Within an hour, Jim and the boys were on their way to Ashern. The twins sat quietly in the back seat while Jim watched them carefully in the rear view mirror.

"Hey Jim," David softly said. "What if the police take us back to the farm?"

"That's not going to happen this time; I promise you that."

"Why not?"

"'Cause it's pretty obvious how beat up your brother is. The police can't ignore it this time. They will have to do something."

The boys trusted Jim, believing if he made a promise he'd keep it When they arrived at the police station, the cautiously followed Jim inside. They waited in the vestibule while he went to speak to the officers. A few minutes later he poked his head around the corner and called them in.

Timidly, they went to his side. An older officer towered over them in the middle of the floor. They were relieved to see that he wasn't the same officer who had taken them back to the farm a few years earlier. And he wasn't the same one who'd charged Domko after he set fire to Gus' hay. He was a big, rather ugly looking man who showed no emotion at all. Another younger officer sat a short distance away.

"That ain't so bad," the ugly officer said, looking at the twins then Jim. "My dad used to beat me like that all the time."

The room fell silent. The twins watched as Jim's neck began to flush and the color spread across his thin face.

"Well then," Jim said, poking his chin toward the officer, "I don't think you had much of a father."

Turning, he grabbed each boy's arm and stormed out the door.

"I'm not leaving you here with an asshole like that."

"Where we goin'?" David asked as they climbed into the car.

"I'm taking you home," he said. "To my place."

Where Children Run

As Jim drove out of town, the young officer made a discreet call to the child welfare department in Winnipeg.

That evening, Ruby and Jim invited the Harwarts over to discuss Caroline's family and the children's plight. All agreed that something had to be done about Domko. They would have to convince Caroline to either leave Domko or make him leave. The difficult part was deciding who should talk to her.

"Well, I know I can't," Ruby said. "We were good friends, but she won't have much to do with me now. Since she became involved with that church, she changed, and was mad when I gave toys and clothes to the boys at Christmas."

Everyone agreed.

"I can talk to her," Jim said. "I can make Carrie listen."

Ruby tsked. "You're far too easy on her, and you know it. She's not going to listen to you anymore now than she ever has."

Sheepishly, Jim agreed. Most of what he'd said to her went in one ear and out the other.

The group looked at Emma who shrugged her shoulders.

"I suppose I could talk to her," she offered. "Gus and I will do it."

"It's not going to be easy," Ruby warned.

"I know, but if she has a mind to, she can get rid of him," Emma said. "That's her house and her quarter of land, and I say she has a right to it."

"Yes, but Domko paid for all the renovations and owns all the cattle. He's not going to want to go . . ."

"I'll kick him out of there," Jim said. "Hell, I'd kill the bastard myself except I've never killed anybody before . . . and besides, I don't want to get thrown in the hoosegow for the rest of my life."

Gus laughed. "If Domko turned up dead, everybody would know who did it. How would you plead anyway?"

"Guilty, and I'd be damned proud of it, too. I'd say that I was doing a community service," Jim laughed, banging his hand on the table for emphasis. "I'd be doing everybody a big favor."

The four adults chuckled, and then the mood turned serious again, and they discussed the issue long into the night. The Harwarts promised they would talk to Caroline given the first opportunity.

The following morning, while Jim was out mending fences a half a mile away, Domko arrived to pick up the boys. The twins hadn't seen him approaching and turned around to see him standing in the yard. Reluctantly, they climbed into the back of his car. By the time Ruby saw them leaving, it was too late.

"That coward," Jim scoffed later. "Just like him to turn up and take them when I'm not home. Did he say anything to you?"

"Nothing. He just waved politely and left."

"Polite my ass. That Domko can sure be a charmer when he wants to be."

Late that afternoon, Emma invited Caroline to the house for coffee. The women had chatted for a while before Emma was able to work her way around to the real reason for the invitation.

"It must be hard for you," Emma said, "raising the children without Bill. How are you doing?"

Caroline eyed her friend suspiciously. "What do you mean?"

"Well you know, kids never like a stepfather as much as their real father," she said. "How's Domko managing?"

Just then Gus came into the house. He'd been in the yard pretending he was doing something important while he waited for the women to get through the idle chit chat. He sat down at the table as Emma got up and poured him a cup of coffee.

Enough beating around the bush, he thought.

"So, how's he doing?" Emma asked again.

"All right, I guess," Caroline quietly said. "He's a little hard on the kids, but they need disciplining."

"How come the boys have been sleeping in the church?" Gus asked.

Caroline was stunned. She stammered and looked at the table as she searched for an excuse. "They run away. We've tried to keep them at home, but there's nothing we can do."

"How come they run away?" Gus asked.

"I don't know," Caroline replied, thinking how familiar this conversation sounded.

"Are you sure? I remember how badly Domko was treating you and the kids before. That might be enough to make them run away," Gus suggested.

"Well he's the head of the house, and the boys just can't accept that," Caroline said.

"What about the girls?" Emma interrupted, then in a hushed voice, "Are you sure he's not, you know, bothering them?"

"No," Caroline insisted. "He wouldn't do that."

Gus shook his head. "I wouldn't be so sure. The longer he stays, the harder it's going to be to make him leave. We've talked to Jim and Ruby about this, and we all agree that if you need help, we're here to give it to you. Heck, Jim even offered to help kick him out if you like."

Caroline's back stiffened when she realized what was happening. She hadn't been invited over for coffee; this was a plot to get rid of her husband. She couldn't believe that Emma, Gus, Ruby and Jim had been conspiring behind her back. The people from her church were right—she couldn't trust outsiders.

"I have no plans to kick my husband off the farm," she said emphatically. "And I don't want to hear any more about it."

"What about the kids?" Gus asked.

"What about them?"

"Well, they are turning up hungry and beat up on everybody's doorstep. Doesn't that matter to you?"

"Of course it matters, but there is nothing more I can do."

Exasperated, Gus stood up and paced across the floor.

"Caroline, we've heard that the social worker has been coming to your place and we both know that's not good news," he said. "If you're not careful, she'll take those kids away from you and put them in a foster home. Do you want that?"

"Of course not."

"Well then? You're going to have to make a choice," he said. "Either Domko or the kids, otherwise I can see that you just might lose Bill's kids."

"The kids can look after themselves," Caroline said.

Stunned, Gus and Emma stared at her. "What?" Gus asked.

"The boys can look after themselves, but Domko needs me. He loves me and can't manage on his own. If they behaved, he wouldn't get after them so much. The kids will be grown soon, and then things will be better for us."

"So you're saying that if given a choice, you'd pick that old coot over your own children?" Emma asked.

"Yes, but it won't come to that."

"It will," Emma said.

"No, it won't, because I won't let it."

"Well, what are we supposed to do?" Gus asked. "Mind our own business?"

Caroline looked at the ground as she stood to leave.

"When the boys come here, you could send them home," she said.

"To what? More beatings?"

"I can take care of the children myself," she said.

With that Caroline turned and walked out the door.

Emma and Gus sat in utter disbelief for a moment. Was this the same Caroline they'd always known? They concluded that she'd been beaten and harassed so much by Domko that she was beginning to side with him.

"She'd better not show up on my doorstep again," Gus said.

The twins sat upstairs and listened to their mother and Domko discussing all that Gus and Emma had said that day. They overheard their parents fuming about the neighbors' interference and talking about ways to even the score. They listened with fear as their mother began to sound almost as unraveled as Domko.

The following morning, the twins had just finished feeding the chickens when they noticed a familiar car pull into the driveway. Frightened, they ran into the bush.

Martha Patterson stepped out of the car.

"Come on over here boys," she yelled. "Come out of the bush."

The boys cautiously edged their way into the yard. It was the social worker coming to visit them again.

"You don't need to be afraid of me," she said in a forceful voice. "I just want to talk to you."

Just then Domko came outside to see what the commotion was. He took one look at the social worker and began to pace back and forth.

"Vat?" he seethed. "I's not be vantink you here. I's be callink the police."

"I came to check on these boys, and it's a good thing I did," she said. "I'm here in response to a call from the police. They told me the neighbors brought the boys into the station again."

Domko flew into a rage at the mention of his neighbors. "They's be not tellink the truth," he yelled.

Martha let him complain for a while then interrupted his ravings. "Why does this boy have bruises all over his face?"

"He's be fallink down," Domko said innocently.

"With a little help from you?"

"Vat?"

"Why do you beat these boys?" The question came out a little blunter than Martha had intended. She regretted it immediately but didn't waver.

Suddenly, it appeared that something in Domko's brain snapped. He began growling viciously and screaming at her.

"They's be lazy German bastards," he yelled.

His eyes darted in anger, and the scar on his forehead began to turn white as the blood drained from his face. The gold tooth shone menacingly as he approached her. Martha refused to step back as the boys cowered behind her.

"If anything ever happens to one of these kids," she threatened, pointing her finger aggressively at him. "I'm going to know who did it and the police will haul you away for good."

Domko hated being challenged by this woman and began punching the air in front of her. He inched his way closer, screaming that he wasn't afraid of a fat, German bitch and that given a chance, he would show her who the real boss was.

Martha didn't back down. She almost wished he would hit her. At least then she could charge him with assault, and he'd end up in jail. Her arms shook with anger as she faced him. There was no way she could leave the boys alone with him, knowing the pattern of his potentially violent rages.

"If you kill one of these kids, so help me God," she seethed, "I'll string you up myself."

Martha held her ground until Domko's pent up energy eventually got the best of him. Soon he became exhausted and surprisingly calm. Martha sent one of the twins into the house to get Caroline who appeared a few minutes later.

Unfortunately, Martha was not prepared to take the twins that day. She had no court papers and hadn't made arrangements for a foster home. She knew it would be horrible to split up the twins, especially since they were so ignorant about life off the farm. It would be better to return when prepared, but in the meantime, she would try an old trick that often worked.

"Your husband is out of control and should not be left alone with these children," she said to Caroline. "You have a choice. Either he finds somewhere else to stay, or I take them with me."

Caroline looked at Domko, then yelled at him to take his things, get in the car and leave. Much to the surprise of the twins, he went into the house quietly and emerged a few minutes later carrying his duffel bag. He threw it in the back seat of his car and sped past Martha's car before turning north.

Caroline and Martha talked for a while, and then it was time for her to go. She waved to the children and said goodbye as she left to visit a family near Grahamdale. Wanting to be sure that Domko wasn't hiding somewhere along the road so he could return, she also turned north. She drove along the road for a few miles then satisfied that he was gone, turned west at the next intersection.

The children were surprised at how easy it had been to get rid of him. As they played and competed for their mother's attention, they noticed how preoccupied she seemed.

They finished the evening chores, had supper and went to bed. The twins discussed the day's events until they fell asleep. They awoke a few hours later to the sound of laughter.

Creeping along the floor, they went to the top of the stairs to listen. They could hear their mother talking to someone in the bedroom. Then they heard it—Domko's voice. He was back. He'd come in the middle of the night, and their mother sounded glad. They were laughing about the trick they'd played on the social worker.

Where Children Run

David and Dennis at 18 months.

Karen Emilson

Caroline as a teenager

Bob Domko's passport photo

Bill Pischke

The farm view from the south bush where the children would hide

Where Children Run

Caroline and the twins

the St. Thomas Lutheran Church

Marjorie Harwart

Emma and Gus Harwart

Karen Emilson

Ruby and Jim Deighton

Mrs. Louise Collier

Jim and Ruby Deighton's house

Where Children Run

Miss Leah D'Hoore and the class from Bayton. Dennis and David are in the back row wearing white toques.

The inside of the Pischke barn. Taken in 1996.

Karen Emilson

Gus and Emma Harwart's house. Taken in 1996.

Mrs. Marion Gering

Margaret Burnett

Where Children Run

A view of Pischke (Reed) Lake from the bank where David and Dennis walked in the middle of the night.

Anna and Leon Koch

Kenny and Alvin Koch

Karen Emilson

Dennis, David, Eunice, Caroline, Rosie, Kathy and Raymond in front of Domko's car

Jim Deighton

Ruby Deighton

Frederick's old barn

Dennis and David in front of school

A PUPPY NAMED BO

Caroline was able to convince Domko that if the social workers took the boys, he would have a difficult time managing on the farm.

Reluctantly, he agreed to watch his temper if she would discipline the twins. The children noticed the positive effect Martha had on Domko and wished she'd visit more often.

Domko then transferred his anger from the boys to the neighbors. He now had an obsessive dislike for the Harwarts and Deightons and maligned them to other neighbors and friends whenever he had the chance. Word got back to Emma and Gus that Domko had been making threats in town. He said that if Gus didn't start minding his own business, he'd "show him what he could do to a young girl like Marjorie."

The threat again alerted the Harwarts to the grim reality of the type of person they were dealing with. They sat Marjorie down at the table and talked to her about the threat and explained that while they would continue to help Caroline's children, they would be subtle in their tactics.

"We'll be telling the police every time we see something out of place," Emma said. "Sooner or later, they'll have to do something, especially if we keep pestering them. I'm sure the social worker is pretty close to doing something, and I just might call her. But you have to remember that Domko's crazy and that he just might hurt you if he gets the chance."

Marjorie nodded in understanding. She was frightened by the thought of Domko anywhere near her.

"If he ever tries to catch you, run away as fast as you can," Emma warned. "Don't be afraid to scream or yell."

"Okay Mom," Marjorie said. "I know what to do."

The rest of the summer was filled with more hard work. The boys and Eunice spent long hours doing chores and haying. Their farm had been very wet that year, so the boys were kept home from school in early September to help clean up the fields. Many families in the area considered it socially acceptable to keep children home from school to assist with farm work. At ten years of age, though, the twins were considered a little young to be held out of school.

The boys were still in grade three and had a difficult time. While they disliked staying home with Domko, they didn't enjoy sitting in the classroom either. Because they were absent so many days, they were trapped in a never ending cycle. They would miss school, try to catch up, work late at night and then return to school tired and hungry the following day.

The return of fall sent Domko on his semi-annual trip to Winnipeg. He hired the local transfer owner, a man named Hugo Russell, to haul his cattle to the Winnipeg Stockyards. Domko was never confident enough to drive that distance himself, so he accompanied Hugo. He came back late that afternoon from his one-day trip with a box of used clothing and a puppy.

"I's be gettink some goot Collie dog," he announced proudly.

The children were surprised and pleased to see the puppy. It was a big pup, but they could tell it was young. It whined and cowered as the children gathered around. It was white with brown and beige markings on its head and back. Domko explained to their mother that he'd seen it playing in somebody's backyard in Winnipeg, so he'd called it over and taken it.

Caroline smirked but said nothing. The children didn't seem to care that the pup was stolen, they were just glad to have a dog that Domko liked.

He won't shoot a valuable dog like this, Dennis thought. The poor little pup had been sick most of the way home, so David hurried to get it something to eat. They decided to name him Bo.

The puppy took an instant liking to the twins, which disgusted Domko. Annoyed, he watched as Bo followed closely on the boys' heels wherever they went. The pup would run after them, hiding behind their legs when they tried to teach him to herd the cattle and to be brave.

"He's just too little," Dennis said. "When he's big, he's gonna help us."

"Yeah," his brother agreed. "But we better not let Domko know it makes us happy 'cause then he'll kill Bo for sure."

One late fall afternoon the twins took the shotgun to the beaver dam to hunt ducks. The old single barrel 10 gauge gun was a relic that would blow apart after each shot. The 'blunderbuss's' clips were worn out and had to be snapped together again before the gun would re-fire. This was a fun game for the pup who would bark at the loud bang of the shot and get in the way

Where Children Run

as the twins scrambled to pick up the pieces. To them, shooting ducks was a matter of survival. If they didn't hit a bird, they went hungry.

"Okay, you hold me while I shoot," David said.

Dennis nodded and braced himself against his David's back while he took aim. They waited along the lake until a small flock of ducks, which they could hear coming, flew overhead. David closed his eyes and squeezed the trigger. The impact from the gun flung them backward.

"You got some," Dennis yelled as the water splashed. He pointed toward the reeds. "Over there."

"Do you think Bo will be able to get the ducks outta the water next year?" David asked.

"Hope so," Dennis said as they waded up to their chests among the tall reeds to fetch the downed birds. They shivered as they swam to shore. Within a few weeks, the beaver dam would freeze over.

When they ran out of shot and had a decent number of birds, they looked toward the sky. The sun was beginning to set, and it was time to round up the cows for the evening milking. They chatted as they walked through the field to the spot where the cows were resting. The animals were accustomed to the daily routine, so they stood and began lumbering along the tree-lined path to the barn.

"Give him one to carry," David said pointing to the pup.

Dennis gave one of the ducks to Bo. The dog looked at it for a few moments then took it in his wide jaw and proudly carried it.

"Look, he thinks he got it himself," Dennis said.

The twins laughed at the sight of the puppy struggling to carry the big mallard. Bo watched the twins out of the corner of his eye.

It was then Dennis noticed a yearling calf among the herd.

"That ain't ours," he said. "Where do you think he came from?"

"I dunno," David said. "We better leave him here in case someone comes lookin' for him." They tried separating it from the cows, but the eight hundred pound animal kept returning to the herd.

"We better just go," David said, "Satan's gonna be here any minute lookin' for us."

Domko was waiting at the barn. They gave the ducks to their mother for cleaning, including Bo's, which Dennis had to carry after all when the pup became bored and dropped it.

The cows moved into their familiar stalls leaving the stray calf to wander in the barnyard.

"Who she's be?" Domko asked, pointing to the dark brown calf.

"Don't know," David said, lowering his eyes. "We tried chasin' him out, but he kept comin'."

Domko cornered the calf long enough to lasso it. The calf bawled as he led it into the barn and tied it to a back stall.

Later, the boys listened as their mother and stepfather discussed the stray calf. They said they would put a word out to the neighbors over the next few days, hoping someone would claim it.

During the week that followed, Domko fed the calf hay and oats twice a day. The boys thought the treatment was odd since he never paid that much attention to the pail-fed calves.

Nobody claimed the calf, but it was gone one day when the boys returned home from school. They asked their mother who had taken it, but she didn't answer. They shrugged it off, then forgot about it.

A few days later, they came in late from doing chores to find a beef roast cooking on the stove. The smell was unbelievable. Their stomachs growled as they sat beside Eunice and Rosie on the chesterfield while waiting to be called to supper. Caroline softly hummed as she poured a generous helping of boiled potatoes and carrots into a bowl and then carried the meat and gravy to the table. Caroline and Domko were in exceptionally good moods that evening as he served himself a generous portion first, and then Caroline filled Kathy's plate. When they had finished eating, the other children were allowed to sit down.

David and Dennis gave each other a suspicious look as they took their slabs of meat. They had eaten beef many times at the Deightons and Harwarts but never ate anything but chicken or pork at home until now. They expected Domko might reach across the table and take away their plates, but he didn't. Later that night in bed they discussed the unusual, but tasty meal.

"Whaddya think?" David asked.

"I dunno. Whaddya think?"

"I think we just ate that calf."

"Do you think Momma knows?"

"'Course she knows. She cooked it."

"I mean 'bout it bein' stolen."

David thought for a minute. "If she don't know, then she's pretty stupid 'cause we ain't never eaten beef before. We're 'sposed to think he's gonna start feedin' us good now?"

Dennis stared up at the ceiling. "It was good, wasn't it?"

"Yep, it sure was."

One blustery November evening members from the church came to visit. Caroline was still trying to prove that she was worthy to the congregation, so she was nervous when they came inside. They looked around the house for a few moments then sat at the kitchen table. The children were forced to sit still and listen to the small talk until the lecturing began.

"Caroline, you know that you must get your house in order before you can begin spreading God's word," the man said. "The way you are living is not worthy of His approval."

Domko snickered, and she shot him a disapproving glance. While the two were getting along better, he still enjoyed watching her squirm.

They discussed how important it was for members of Jehovah's Kingdom, to be honest, kind, upstanding citizens. They said church members must treat everyone with respect and never lie. Jehovah's children must be clean, respectful and well-mannered. Caroline knew that her family was falling short on all counts and was ashamed. She was going to have to change and so were the children so that they might start representing Jehovah door to door.

Domko reached across the table and picked up the Bible. He began reading thoughtfully and nodded in agreement. In a soft voice, he apologized to the church members, saying that his wife would try harder in the future and that he would also like to begin studying. To this, the Witnesses nodded in approval. Having both Caroline and Domko practicing the faith would be the key to straightening out this family.

David and Dennis looked at each other and made a face. They knew Domko well enough to know when he was lying, but the visitors couldn't see it. They giggled softly, much to the chagrin of their parents.

"And you must not spare the rod," the visitor said as he looked at the boys. "Spare the rod and spoil the child."

The twins shrank in their seats. Domko had been tolerable since the social worker had been there, now his chest was puffing up as he listened to the visitors and eyed the children. As soon as the Witnesses prepared to leave, the twins slipped upstairs. Hiding behind the wall, they didn't want to be around if Domko decided tonight would be a good night to "not spare the rod."

"Whaddya think it means?" Dennis asked.

"I think it means you gotta smash kids to make them good," David said.

The following day the boys received a beating because the bull escaped through the fence and was found roaming among the neighbor's cows. This neighbor had heard that Domko allowed his animals to roam free on the land of other farmers. He'd had enough firsthand experience with Domko to know the man had no respect for the property of others. The police showed up at the door and Domko was fined again, this time for $55, under the Animal Husbandry Act after admitting it was his bull.

The boys ran to Harwart house. Nobody was home, so they continued walking until they came to an old barn owned by the Frederick family. It had been used for many years but was now abandoned. They went inside the clean building, and David climbed halfway up the ladder to peer into the loft. The huge hip roof made the area very spacious and piles of soft hay covered the floor.

David suddenly felt a familiar feeling as he looked around. He sensed he'd been there before. A brief, fuzzy memory came to him and he remembered that he and his siblings had accompanied their mother and father to a community barn dance there once. David remembered planks of wood sitting on top of bales along the sides of the barn, and he recalled the sound of adult feet stomping across the floor, to laughter and fiddle music. Children ran and played, darting between the dancing adults.

David smiled. This looked like a warm, safe place to spend the night.

"Gimme Bo," he said to his brother, who waited below.

Dennis picked up the puppy and struggled to lift the growing dog over his head. David carried Bo and Dennis followed. They decided to make themselves a bed in the hay.

They stayed in the barn all day. Just as it was beginning to get dark, they peered out the window facing their farm. There was no sign of Domko, so they decided to walk back to Emma's house. They were relieved to see a light in the kitchen.

"Can we have somethin' to eat?" David asked when Emma answered the door.

Looking at them, she shook her head in disbelief, then disappeared. She returned a few moments later with a loaf of bread and a plastic container filled with jam. The boys nodded in thanks and gave her a timid smile then turned and walked back toward the old barn.

"Those boys are sleeping in Frederick's barn tonight, I just know it," Emma said to her husband.

"Well, at least they are nowhere near Domko," Gus said. "And by jimminy, you heard what Caroline said—they can take care of themselves."

"Well, I don't care what she says or how much Domko threatens. I'll never turn those boys away," she said. "If they don't feel comfortable coming here to sleep no more, then so be it, but I won't allow them to starve."

The following morning Emma asked a neighbor to phone the police. Since the phones were party lines, many people in the district listened in on conversations, so the whole community soon knew what was going on. Luckily, Caroline didn't have a phone.

Not wanting to stay in the barn another night, the twins walked through the bush to Deighton's house. Ruby and Jim welcomed them, so they stayed overnight while Bo was allowed to sleep in the indoor porch.

During breakfast, Ruby and Jim watched as the boys slid down the wooden banister that went to the attic bedroom. This was great fun for the boys who had never done anything like this before. Out of breath from racing up and down the stairs, they plopped down at the table. They happily ate a big bowl of porridge with toast. When they were finished, they fed their pup and went outside to help Jim with chores.

They stayed another night and enjoyed the time away from home.

A police cruiser drove slowly up Caroline's driveway. The officer glanced at Martha who sat beside him in the front seat. She gave him a weak smile as she rehearsed what she planned to say.

"How do you think this will go?" he asked.

"Hard to tell," she said. "No matter how badly kids are beat up, they seldom want to leave home. It's all they know. In this case, these kids are so bushed it could be difficult persuading them to leave. They might kick and scream and Mr. Domko isn't going to want to let them go. His kind never does."

The officer nodded in understanding. They got out of the car and slowly approached the house. Martha carried an apprehension order from a judge. It transferred the care of the children from their parents to the province. She had a foster home ready to take both boys.

"I gave their parents plenty of warning," she said defensively. Then her tone softened as she turned to the officer. "I hate doing this you know."

"I understand," he said.

The officer rapped quickly on the door while Martha prepared herself for the worst. Caroline answered and the moment she saw the social worker she knew why she was there. Caroline backed away from the doorway, allowing the pair inside. Martha wasn't surprised to see Domko sitting at the kitchen table. She knew that when she'd banished him from the house a few weeks earlier that he would come back. Maybe even the same night, but at least his short absence would have given him the chance to cool down before taking his frustrations out on the children.

"I know how much this is going to upset you, but I'm here to pick up the twins," she said handing Caroline the court order. "I really think that it will be in the boys' best interest."

Domko looked at Martha and grunted. "They's not be here."

"What do you mean?" Martha asked, her heart beating heavy in her chest. "Where are they?"

"We don't know," Caroline said. "They ran away again."

Martha thought for a moment. These people were not going to tell her where the children had gone. She felt slightly embarrassed that she was unprepared for this. She watched Kathy and Raymond playing happily on the floor with their father's tools. She wondered why it had to be this way. Why couldn't this man treat the twins with the same love and affection as his children?

"Do you know where they are?" she asked.

"No, try the neighbors."

"Do you mind if I look around?" the officer asked.

Caroline agreed, wiping her hands absentmindedly on a dish towel.

The officer went into the front room, poked his head in the downstairs bedroom then went upstairs. He looked under the children's bed and whispered for them to come out if they were hiding. He returned to the kitchen and shook his head.

"All right," Martha said. "We'll look elsewhere but before we go, we'll bring the boys back here. You do understand, though, that we will be taking them with us tonight?"

"Yes."

They turned and left the house. "Now what?" the officer asked as they stepped into a cool north breeze. The sky was overcast and it felt like it was going to snow.

"Do you think they're in the bush?" she asked.

"Not a chance. If they'd slept outside last night, they would have frozen to death for sure."

Martha looked at the bush. "That's what I'm worried about."

They got in the car and drove slowly down the road. They checked the schoolhouse but the teacher and the boys' siblings hadn't seen them in days.

"This is where the call originated," the officer said as he turned into the driveway. "Mrs. Harwart might know something."

Emma invited them into the house and told them all she knew. She said she suspected that the twins had spent the night in an old barn near the township line. Martha and the officer thanked Emma and drove until they came to the abandoned building. The big wide doors easily slid open and they stepped inside.

"Dennis, David," Martha called. "You boys can come out now."

Everything was quiet. The officer climbed the loft ladder and returned a few minutes later carrying the plastic container.

"Well, here's the jam she told us about, so I guess they were here for at least one night. Where do you suppose they went after that?"

"Who else has been calling the police about these kids?"

"Well, I have a few names, but the main one who comes to mind is Jim Deighton. He and his wife live just a few miles from here. They might have gone there."

If you boys are going to stay here much longer, I'm going to have to put you in school," Ruby said as the three of them sat together talking in the front room.

"We don't like school," Dennis said.

"Like most boys your age," she laughed. "But you won't get anywhere in life if you miss school. You have to learn to read and do arithmetic."

"I don't wanna read and add stuff," said David. "I just like drawin'."

"Maybe so, but you can't make a living drawing. What will you do?"

"I dunno," he said.

"Are you going to farm?"

"No," he said. "Me and Denny just wanna get away from the farm."

She chuckled. "I know how you feel."

"Walter's got a good job in the city, so we wanna go live with him," Dennis said.

Just then Ruby noticed a police car pulling slowly into the driveway.

"Run upstairs and hide," she said. "Don't come down until I tell you to."

Without looking out the window, the twins ran upstairs. Ruby remembered the twins telling her how the police always took them home. After the officers left, they always got a horrible beating. Ruby looked out the window and saw a police officer and a woman get out of the car. She tried to look casual as she opened the door.

"Hello," she said smoothly. "What can I help you with?"

Bo jumped up and down, scratching the officer's pants and forcing Martha to protect her skirted legs from his sharp claws.

The pair introduced themselves.

"Come in," Ruby said, pushing the growing pup back. "Don't mind him, he won't bite, he's just very friendly."

"We're looking for Dennis and David Pischke. Do you know where they are?" the officer asked.

"Uh, no I don't," Ruby lied. "Why? Are they missing?"

"Yes," he said. "Miss Patterson needs to ask them a few questions."

"Is this about their stepfather?"

"We can't discuss the situation with anyone except family, Mrs. Deighton," Martha said.

Insulted, Ruby bristled. "I am like family."

"Well, we seem to have a few people in the area who feel that way," she said. "They're laying claim to these boys, but all it does is get them in trouble at home." Martha was becoming frustrated because it was getting late and she hadn't found them.

"Are you saying that I should just turn them away when they show up here in the middle of the night?" Ruby asked. She didn't appreciate being scolded by strangers who didn't understand the situation, especially in her own home. She frowned at the officer.

"It's just that people sometimes mean well but say and do the wrong things. I'm sure you're thinking of what's best for the boys."

"That's right. I worry a lot about those boys," Ruby said her chin wavering. "Me and my husband think about those boys more than you'll ever understand."

"Do you mind if I look around?" the officer said.

Ruby hesitated. Her heart skipped lightly in her chest as she tried to look relaxed. She hoped that Jim wouldn't come in and spoil everything. "No, I don't mind at all."

The officer checked the spare bedroom off the kitchen then went into the front room. Martha continued to talk to Ruby, who was having a hard time concentrating while the officer edged his way through the kitchen to the stairs. His legs disappeared and she could hear his heavy footsteps above her as he looked around the attic bedroom. It was then she noticed the boys' coats hanging by the doorway. She was thankful that they were much too big for the twins and could pass as Jim's.

Ruby nodded when Martha said that she needed to take the boys back to the farm. Ruby's mind whirled and the thought occurred to her that if the officer did find them, they might arrest her for obstructing justice.

Justice, she thought to herself. *There is no justice for these boys. These people aren't going to help them now any more than last time. The poor little beggars will probably get another beating as soon as they get home.*

The officer returned and Ruby breathed a sigh of relief.

"If they come, will you contact me please?" Martha asked handing Ruby her phone number.

Ruby nodded and within a few minutes the pair were gone. She watched them drive away, before hurrying upstairs.

"Boys," she whispered, "you can come out now."

There was no movement for a few moments, and slowly two little heads poked out from under the bed.

Ruby was astonished. "How come he didn't find you?" she asked.

"'Cause we're good hiders," David grinned.

Martha and the police officer continued to look for the boys but found that people in the community were very uncooperative. Martha stayed in an Ashern hotel that night then returned to the farm the following day. Caroline met her at the door offering no suggestions on their whereabouts.

"You're welcome to go through the bush if you like," she said. "And you can bring the cows home while you're at it."

Martha was angry and frustrated when she returned to Winnipeg that night. She'd spent two days looking and still hadn't found the twins. She suspected somebody was hiding the boys but wasn't sure which of the neighbors were the culprits. To find out she'd need a search warrant for every house.

Her case load was piling up and she knew she wouldn't get an opportunity to go to Moosehorn for a few weeks. The police promised to phone her as soon as they were found.

Caroline arrived at Deightons the following morning to pick up the twins. Ruby was not pleased but felt very uncomfortable about keeping the boys from their mother.

"We need the boys at home to do chores," Caroline said coolly. "Why should they be here helping Jim instead of us?"

Tired of fighting with everyone, Ruby agreed to let them go. She knew she couldn't stop Caroline from taking her boys and felt foolish thinking she could keep them. Besides, she had other things on her mind. Things that the boys, Caroline and Jim, just wouldn't understand.

About a month later, David received a bad beating and the boys ran to the Deighton house again.

"Where's Aunt Ruby?" David asked when Jim opened the door wide to let them in.

"She's gone," he said.

"Gone in town?"

"No, gone for good. Ruby's not coming back to the farm," he said, his eyes filling with tears. "She just couldn't take livin' here anymore I guess."

The twins were shocked. "When did she go?" David asked.

"About three weeks ago."

David thought back to the day the social worker had come to the house and confronted Ruby. "Did she hafta go to jail?"

"Jail?" Jim asked, distracted. "No, she didn't go to jail, she's living in Winnipeg."

The twins stayed overnight but found things weren't the same there without Ruby. Jim was very depressed and would cry a little bit, then become angry. Even though he only seemed angry at himself, this frightened the boys. They felt very uncomfortable and left the next day.

"Thanks, Jim," Dennis said as they began walking through the snowy fields toward home.

They walked in silence for a while then David spoke. "Why do you 'spose she left?"

"I dunno. Whaddya think?"

David hesitated. He'd given this a lot of thought.

"'Cause of us," he said sadly. "Ruby left 'cause of us. Mrs. Patterson and the police yelled at her and got her in trouble. She didn't wanna have to hide us no more so she left."

"Do you think so?"

"I know so."

Dennis started to cry. "She got scared and ran to Winnipeg so they wouldn't put her in jail."

"Yeah, I know. I'm glad she ran away 'cause I don't want Ruby to go to jail neither."

The boys decided not to go to Jim's anymore since they'd already caused him enough trouble. They spent that night in the bush. They found a sheltered spot just off the trail and built a small fire so Domko wouldn't see it. They huddled close to the flames as the temperature dipped to about twenty degrees below zero. Bo had grown quite a bit in the last few months and slept beside them, blocking the cold north wind. The twins fell asleep that night nestled in the dog's warm fur.

THE ACCIDENT

In the weeks that followed, no obvious effort was made by the police or the social worker to find the twins. A quick call by Martha to the Ashern detachment confirmed that the boys were at home and that there had been no additional reports of violence. The police assured her that things seemed to have settled down. They said they would call her immediately if anything else happened.

Martha was relieved to hear this because December was one of the busiest months of the year. Her replacement was hired and she was in the process of training the young woman. She would brief the new social worker on the family and leave implicit instructions that if the boys were brought to the Ashern detachment again, they should be apprehended.

Satisfied with the arrangements, Martha hung up the phone and opened another file.

Winter had set in. Domko's behavior was worsening as it had in the past. He was most violent during the cold weather, ranting and raving that the neighbors were trying to ruin his farm and that the children were conspiring against him. He seemed obsessed with Gus and Marjorie, bringing them up in conversations for no reason. As he demanded more affection and attention from Caroline, she faded in and out of her own depressed state.

Their relationship had become very one-sided, and Caroline's desire for affection, love, and understanding was ignored by him. While caught up in their personal wants and needs, neither thought of the children whose lives were dismal. The children craved a life of normalcy that by now had become nothing but a faded memory.

Marjorie enjoyed being left at home alone. At fifteen years old, she was quite capable of doing the chores while her parents went to town.

She softly hummed as she opened the barn door. The horses stood patiently in their stalls. Marjorie approached one and softly patted the animal on the rump.

"C'mon boy," she said. Pulling a halter off the hook, she put her knitted mitts on the horse's back then slipped the halter over the horse's head. It was time to lead him to the water trough outside.

Something caught Sandy's attention, and the dog ran barking toward the house. While this was happening, Marjorie hummed as she fastened the reins to her favorite horse. He whinnied softly, pawing the earthen floor and nudging his nose near the pocket of her work jacket.

"Nothing tonight," she said as she patted him gently. "I don't have any sugar cubes. Mom said she would bring some from town."

Slipping her mitts back on, she led the horse toward the door. She stepped into the barnyard and turned toward the trough. Looking up, she stopped. Standing just a few feet in front of her was Domko. He wore a thick, buffalo hide coat and felt rubbers on his feet—high felt insoles with a rubber shoe that covered the toe. He held a rifle stiffly at his side. Sandy was circling him angrily.

Marjorie took a step back. She tried to hide her surprise as well as her fear. Sandy growled deep in her throat as she stood in front of him.

"Vere's be Gus?" he asked.

Marjorie hesitated. Her parents had gone to Winnipeg and weren't expected back until late.

"They're in Moosehorn," she lied. "They should be home soon."

Domko's eyes narrowed. He stared intently at the girl then at the horse she was leading.

"I's be vantink to go huntink," he said. "Yous be tellink him."

Marjorie nodded and swallowed hard. It struck her as odd that he would want to go hunting with her father since they despised each other.

Domko took a step closer, and she let out a tiny gasp. She remembered what her mother had said. Run.

The horse pricked its ears back, sensing her fear. With nostrils flaring, it began pawing the ground. It also reared slightly signaling Domko to stay away. Sandy continued to bark while baring her teeth aggressively.

Domko sneered as he looked at both animals. Marjorie fought to control the horse that seemed to sense the dubious intent of the unwelcome visitor.

"Yous be tellink Gus," Domko said as he looked into the barn.

By this time, the animals had become so unruly that Marjorie didn't think she could control them much longer. They created a welcome diversion, and it was the first time she'd ever been pleased to have a horse rear while under her control.

Domko glared at her then slowly began to back away. Marjorie loosened her grip on the horse as Domko turned and slowly walked toward the house. He looked over his shoulder at her then strode down the driveway.

By now Marjorie's legs had turned to rubber. Her mind whirled as she led the horse to the trough, then quickly back to the barn. In a panic, she ran to the house. Bursting through the door, she kicked off her boots and threw her jacket and mitts on the floor. Running to her parent's bedroom, she pulled her dad's .22 caliber rifle from its rack on the wall. Opening his bureau drawer, she took a handful of shells and with a shaking hand pressed one into the empty chamber. She took the remaining bullets and put them in her pocket then paced through the house, jumping at every sound. Gradually as the evening wore on, a steely resolve replaced her initial fear.

If he shows his face here again, I'll shoot him, she thought as she sat at the kitchen table in dim light. *He's not gonna hurt me.*

She went to her bedroom and opened the window. Sandy was sitting watchfully which made her feel better. The dog's tail began to wag as Marjorie dropped some food into her bowl in the snow. She told the dog to watch for Domko and Sandy, who seemed to understand what she was saying, looked toward the Pischke farm.

Marjorie climbed into bed that night wearing her clothes. She placed the rifle on the floor beside the bed then eventually fell into a fitful sleep. She awoke each time Sandy barked, or she heard a strange creak in the house. It was well past midnight before Gus and Emma arrived home.

Marjorie emerged from her bedroom to tell her parents what had happened. Trying to make light of the situation, Emma sent her back to bed, but not before Marjorie saw her mother shoot an anxious glance at her father. There was fear in Gus' eyes, but he tried not to show it.

Domko rejoiced when he heard that Ruby had left the farm. He ridiculed the twins about her sudden departure saying they were responsible. He could sense the boys were embarrassed and knew that if they didn't go to Jim's, there would be less interference by the police.

Caroline used this opportunity to tell Domko that the boys should be attending school regularly. Doing so would keep the teacher and school board from reporting their absences to the social worker. Domko agreed, not wanting to face Martha again.

For the first time since they started school at Bayton, the twins were being encouraged to attend regularly. They'd missed so much already that year that Mrs. Collier could not promote them to grade four as promised. In January, they were still in grade three.

As their language skills improved, David and Dennis began enjoying school. While they mostly kept to themselves, they did make a few friends.

During recess and noon hour, their classmates would skate on a patch of ice in the schoolyard. The boys would use half the ice to play hockey while the girls twirled and jumped at the other end as they pretended to be world-class figure skaters. The twins, and a few other students whose parents could not afford skates watched from the sidelines.

Mrs. Collier saw this and encouraged students with extra skates at home to bring them to school. Odd pairs were matched, and the leftovers were kept at the school.

One day the twins were in the cloakroom.

"Hey, Denny look, a pair of skates!"

Lying on the floor were two skates. Dennis picked one up and examined it. It was a men's skate about size 10, and the other was a woman's figure skate about size six. Both were for the right foot. These were strays that had been too good to throw away, and the teacher still hoped to find a match, but this hadn't happened yet.

The boys watched the mismatched pair sit unclaimed for a few days. They discussed taking turns wearing them during the noon hour so they could skate with their classmates.

"No, we better not," Dennis said. "We don't know how and we'll fall down. They'll make fun of us."

David agreed. That Friday afternoon when school was over, the twins each tucked a skate inside their jackets and ran home. They darted up to their bedroom.

"Here, lemme put 'em on," David said, taking the girl's skate from Dennis. He jammed his right foot inside.

"Can you get it on?"

"Yep. Hand me the other one."

Dennis gave him the man's skate which was much too big.

"I'll get somethin' you can use," Dennis said, running down stairs. He returned a minute later carrying a newspaper. He scrunched up a page and stuffed it into the toe of the boot. David slid his foot in and wiggled it around. "It's good," he said, tying it before walking across the floor. "Here you try."

Dennis put on the skates and smiled.

The next morning, they finished their chores then snuck along their

Where Children Run

path to the beaver dam with Bo on their heels. They were happy to discover enough clear spots on the ice so they wouldn't have to scrape it, which was fortunate since neither one of them had a shovel.

They decided that Dennis would try skating first. David walked along the ice in his rubber boots while Dennis clung to the back of his coat. They had fun sharing the skates, slipping and falling as the pick on the figure skate dug deep into the ice. It sent them reeling forward while the smooth men's skate caused them to fall over backward.

"Hey Davey, if we get to be good skaters, we can go across the beaver dam and never come back."

"Yeah. The ol' Devil won't never catch us on these!"

The boys played and laughed. David was pretending to be Domko on skates when a strange noise coming from across the beaver dam caught their attention.

"What's that?" Dennis asked, pointing to the east. Their eyes squinted against the bright snow as they watched as an unusual-looking vehicle crept along the snow. It turned and began coming across the ice in their direction.

David quickly untied the laces of the skates and pulled on his boots.

"C'mon, Dennis, " he said, whistling for Bo. "Let's get outta here."

The boys ran up the bank and paused on top to watch as the noisy vehicle crawled along. They ran as fast as they could along the trail as the noise grew louder behind them. They stayed on the twisting path, hoping whatever was coming wouldn't catch them.

"Do you think it's Martians?" Dennis asked fearfully.

"I dunno but it's gotta be some kinda spaceship," David gasped. "I ain't never seen nothin' like it before."

Their hearts pounded loudly in their chests as they ran. For the first time, Dennis was happy to see the farm as they emerged from the bush. As they ran into the yard, they yelled to Domko that something was coming. They hid behind the chicken coop as Domko strolled to the edge of the yard. They crouched on the ground and waited. Curious, David peeked around the corner of the barn. He could see two men standing beside a strange-looking tractor that had skis instead of wheels. Domko was friendly to them, extending his hand. It was now obvious that these were men and not Martians, but the twins were still too shy to leave their hiding spot.

David looked carefully at the impressive machine. Blue and silver, it had a seat, a bicycle steering wheel, and skis in the front. Domko was asking the men questions as they lifted up the hood.

"It's some kinda snow crawler," David said.

"Lemme see," Dennis said, pushing his brother out of the way. "It goes pretty fast, eh Davey?"

"Yeah, but I don't know why it don't get bogged down in the snow."

"Me neither."

"Do you think they got more of 'em or it's the only one?"

"I dunno but it looks fun to go over the snow like that."

They watched as the men climbed back on the snow machine and turned in a wide circle. They waved goodbye to Domko then drove back through the bush. As soon as Domko went back into the house, the boys ran from the chicken barn over to the tracks which were the strangest they'd ever seen.

"So how do they make it go?" David asked.

"I dunno. It looks like a big, bumpy snake trail," Dennis said.

They looked at the tracks for an hour trying to figure out how the machine was driven. As it began to get dark, they decided to preserve the tracks by covering them with armfuls of hay.

That evening they overheard their mother and Domko discussing the men and their snow machine. They were from the Helm family who lived across the lake. They had been asking about a yearling calf of theirs that went missing that fall. They thought it must be dead but found a break in the fence so decided to ask all their neighbors who had land bordering their pasture.

The twins heard Domko and Caroline laugh. Dennis looked at David who had an "I told you so" look, and it made him scowl at their mother.

It was a few days before the twins' birthday in early February. It had been a warm, overcast day and evening was quickly approaching. Domko and Caroline decided to drive to Moosehorn to buy flour and pick up the mail. Domko told the twins they had to go along while the rest of the children stayed home with Eunice.

The twins weren't pleased that they had to go, knowing that Domko couldn't drive on slippery roads, and the only reason he took them along was so that they could shovel and push the car out when he hit the ditch.

A three-day storm near the end of January had dumped quite a bit of snow in the area, making the roads impassable until the plow came through and created a narrow passageway.

As the car crept along slowly, the Twins avoided looking at the shotgun and steel whip on the floor beneath their feet in the back seat. It was already dark when they passed Deighton's house, and a set of lights appeared in the distance.

Knowing he was going to meet a car, Domko became increasingly nervous, but rather than slow down; he started driving faster. The boys were sitting on their knees watching over their mother's shoulder as the other car pulled over to the side of the road and came to a halt.

"Boleslaw, slow down," she yelled in Polish. "Slow down!"

Panicking, he slammed his foot on the gas pedal and made matters worse by turning toward the other car instead of away from it. Domko roared, and Caroline screamed as he drove head-on into the front of the parked car.

Domko smashed his face on the steering wheel upon impact, and his door flew wide open. Caroline lunged against the dashboard then banged her head on the windshield. Dennis hit the back of the seat with his chest, while David smashed his face against the top of the seat. The car came to an abrupt halt, and everyone sat in silence for a moment as they gathered their senses and all began groaning at once. The impact re-opened the wide gash on Domko's forehead from his accident earlier that fall. He wiped the blood away as Caroline massaged her ribs.

"Are you boys okay?" she asked.

Dennis said he was, but David cried hard since his teeth were smashed in. Blood was dripping from his mouth, causing him to panic.

"I think David is hurt," Caroline said.

Domko grunted as he stepped onto the road. The other driver got out and walked to the front of the cars to assess the damage. Domko recognized the man as Henry Kort.

Caroline got out of the car and walked down the road in a state of shock. The twins watched from inside as Domko began yelling at Henry. He accused him of being a poor driver and claimed that he would have seen the car if both of Henry's lights had been working. Henry ignored Domko since he was mostly concerned about his wife who appeared to be injured.

Another car came along soon afterward, and Henry hitched a ride to phone the police and tow truck. He returned about fifteen minutes later, and the twins watched as Mrs. Kort hobbled to the waiting vehicle, favoring a broken ankle.

"He really did it this time," Dennis whispered. "Maybe they'll take him to jail now."

David nodded. His mouth throbbed as he gingerly touched his front teeth. They'd been pushed all the way back and were still bleeding.

Soon afterward a passing car stopped, and the driver offered to take Caroline and David to the hospital. She refused, asking to be taken home instead. The driver nodded, and before long they were back at the farm.

The following morning, Caroline was in so much pain that she sent

Eunice to the neighbor's house to ask for help. The girl returned with Herman Gall who offered to take Caroline to see Dr. Steenson in Grahamdale. Domko would not allow David to go.

Caroline arrived at the doctor's office, and he was not surprised to see her. He'd treated Mrs. Kort's ankle the night before.

Dr. Steenson was of medium height and built stoutly. He had a chubby round face, and his head was topped with a thin layer of black hair, and he sported a thin mustache. Underneath the extra weight was a fine-boned man with a soft, almost feminine voice, and skilled hands. He was very confident and moved at basically the same speed whether it was a routine check-up or an emergency. He read extensively and was aware of all the new medical theories and treatments worldwide—some said he was brilliant and others swore he read minds.

Dr. Steenson had a somewhat gruff bedside manner and finished most of his statements by asking a question. He also wasn't overly concerned about sterilization of the equipment, a chore he left up to the nurse. He thought nothing of appearing in the clinic waiting room in a bloodstained smock after removing an abscessed tooth from a patient's mouth. He'd call in the next patient then disappear.

Dr. Steenson was much too rough when he gave needles, but the sickest of babies would find comfort in his gentle embrace. How he found the time to raise a family with such a large practice nobody knew, but the communities he served had great respect for his wife, Edith. She was a trained nurse who assisted him on many occasions.

In spite of Dr. Steenson's eccentricities, he was a trusted and respected physician. He examined Caroline then bandaged her rib cage to protect the three ribs she'd cracked in the accident. He prescribed bed rest and reached into his pocket for a bottle of painkillers. He placed a dozen in a small envelope then handed them to her.

"How are things with you and Bob?" he asked.

Caroline looked at the floor. "Fine," she answered.

"I've heard rumors and think that he should come in for another check-up," he said. "He probably should see a specialist, do you know what I'm saying?"

Caroline stammered. She hadn't expected to discuss her husband.

"Because if it is a mental problem, it isn't going to get better without treatment," he said. "He has two personalities, doesn't he? One that he shows you and his friends then one that erupts when he's angry, am I right?"

She didn't answer.

"Medical treatment has come a long way, do you know what I mean? There is a medication that can help and it can be done quite discreetly at this stage. If things go too far, well then the whole community finds out."

Caroline nodded gently.

"It's not my place to make a diagnosis on the few times I've seen Bob, but he's displaying the symptoms of a disorder that will only get worse if left untreated. Let me know if things get out of hand and we can force him into treatment if we have to. Do you know what I mean?"

Caroline nodded.

"Good," he said opening the examining room door.

The police came to the house later that afternoon. They needed to file an accident report and wanted to hear Domko's side of the story. As the officer got out of the car, Domko called the twins and told them to sit at the table.

"Yous be sayink he's only be havink one light," he whispered as Caroline answered the door. "It be his fault."

The twins sat quietly and watched as the officer came into the kitchen. After they had exchanged pleasantries, the officer asked Domko what had happened the night before.

Domko explained that it had been dark and the snow was piled very high along the sides of the road. The wind was blowing snow from the tops of the banks, making it difficult to see. He said that when the cars met, he noticed the other vehicle had only one light, and it was on the far side. By the time he realized where the car was on the road, it was too late, and he couldn't stop. He hit Kort head-on. He said it was Mr. Kort's fault.

The children sat quietly listening to the story. Domko looked at the family and nodded at them for approval. The officer watched as Caroline and the boys agreed that this is what had happened.

The officer made a few notes in his notebook, then tucked it in his pocket. He said that since the two drivers had given different accounts, determining who was negligent would be difficult. Domko insisted that he was not at fault, but was careful not to push the officer too far.

David's teeth were so sore that he was unable to eat. A week after the accident he walked to Herman Gall's and asked that he take him to see the doctor. Herman agreed and drove David to Grahamdale. Dr. Steenson was surprised to see him.

"Why didn't you come in sooner?" he asked.

David shrugged.

"He wouldn't let your mother bring you, is that right?"

David looked at the floor then nodded. He stood in front of the chubby doctor who wore a stethoscope like a necklace. The doctor then instructed him to open his mouth wide. His small, warm hands prodded inside David's mouth.

"If you were a man, we'd never be able to adjust your teeth like this," Steenson said as he pulled the jammed teeth forward. "But young gums are soft, and the roots of baby teeth dissolve once a tooth comes out, do you know what I mean?"

David nodded.

"I get a lot of people in here needing dental work," he said as he started an elaborate story. He pulled roughly on the boy's teeth, and David's eyes began to water. He let out a small groan but tried very hard not to offend the doctor.

"I had a boy in here once who fell out of a tree, and I had to pull all his teeth out," Steenson continued. "Lucky for you we don't have to do that, isn't that right?"

David nodded again.

When Dr. Steenson finished, he reached into his pocket and pulled out a small bottle of painkillers. He gave a few to David then patted him on the back and sent him on his way.

The twins decided that they needed a reliable place to hide from Domko with Ruby gone. They didn't feel comfortable at Jim's, and their mother forbade them to go to Harwart's house. They stayed in Frederick's barn many times, but Domko discovered this hiding spot and brought them home. They still spent many nights in the church but knew the congregation was becoming angry.

"They're gonna lock the window, and then we won't have no place to go," David said one day. "We got to make our own place to live."

Dennis agreed.

"Wouldn't it be great if we had a place that Satan couldn't find?" he asked.

"Yeah, we could do whatever we want," Dennis added.

They discussed the idea of building themselves a hut in the bush.

"Where would we build it?" Dennis asked.

"Along the trail to Jim's," David said. "You know, where we slept with Bo. That's a good spot that ol' Flatfoot has never found."

Dennis agreed. "We can take some nails and get wood from the barn."

The more they talked about building a hut, the more excited they became. It was spring, so the days were beginning to lengthen. The warm sun had melted the snow from their bush paths and along the road.

One afternoon when Domko wasn't home, the boys started gathering materials for the hut. Bo tagged along as they dragged old planks from Frederick's barn through the field into the bush. They chose a spot just inside the trees along the trail to Jim's. Domko never came this way so they felt they would be safe.

The twins made countless trips that day and the next. They filled their pockets with nails and took one of Domko's hammers. Carrying a piece of an old tire and some tin, they trudged into the bush to begin building.

"How big should we make it?" Dennis asked.

"Big enough for me, you, Bo and maybe Beanie and Rosie."

"That's pretty big. Are you sure we got enough nails?"

"Yeah, and if not we can always get more. Flatfoot will never notice."

Dennis nodded as he trudged along beside his brother. He could always count on David to come up with good ideas.

"I got it all thought out," David explained. "We'll make it with a leaning roof, so the snow doesn't pile on top in winter. We'll make a door, that's why I brought this rubber, so it'll bend. You can do the hammering 'cause you do that good, while I hold on to the wood."

They discussed how the hut should look finished, just to be sure they had the same building in mind.

The boys hammered boards together until dark. They crept to their bedroom that night, did chores in the morning and went to school. That afternoon they finished chores then went to work in the bush for a few hours. They returned home hungry and exhausted. The following day they called Bo as they ran into the bush and the dog came bounding down the path.

"We're almost done," Dennis said as they ran along. "Should we tell Eunice and Rosie?"

"Not 'til we're done," David answered. "Today we can put the door on, and it'll be ready for sleepin'."

The boys reached the familiar spot, but couldn't see their hut at first. Because of its color, it blended well with the bush.

"Once the leaves come out, he'll never find us," Dennis said. "We can live here forever, and he'll never know."

Picking up the last of the boards, they laid three of them on the ground horizontally then placed the fourth board crosswise. They pounded nails with determination. The building gave them hope that Domko wouldn't always have a hold over them. Flipping the door over, David cut the rubber

Karen Emilson

into three big pieces and placed them along the edge of the door. Dennis nailed on the rubber hinges, and together they put the door in place.

They stepped back to admire their work.

The hut was about five feet tall and six feet wide. The boards ran horizontally between four well-placed oak trees. The front was higher than the back, and they had planned it that way to allow rain to drain off the roof.

"Next we'll put on the tin," David said. "That way it won't leak."

"What if Domko sees it? He'll say we're stealin' again."

"Stealin' what? The tin? Walter's fur money bought that tin and so really it belongs to him. Walter wouldn't mind if we used it."

Dennis laughed. His brother was right.

Pulling back the door, they stepped inside. The ground was still damp from the melting snow.

"We gotta make a stove," David said. "There's gotta be some old scrap around that we can use."

Dennis laughed. "How 'bout parts off ol' Satan's car? It's not good for nothin' now."

Bo poked his head inside, and they called him in.

"Tomorrow we'll bring some wood and hay and make beds," David said.

The next day Domko was waiting on the road for them after school. Disappointed, they followed him home to do chores. He knew they had some fun planned, so he kept them working until dark. He watched them suspiciously as they chatted to themselves in their secret language. They each ate a bowl of potato soup for dinner then went to bed. It had been a few days since anyone in the house had received a beating, which was a warning to the boys. They knew to stay far away from Domko since he'd be looking for an excuse.

They slept behind the walls of their room that night as a precaution. David was still plagued by nightmares about having his neck, or private parts slashed. He was too frightened to sleep. There was always a chance that Domko would beat him because of the nightmares.

After tonight I don't have to worry about that no more, he thought.

The boys tried to hide their excitement as they finished milking the cows the following morning. The girls sensed something exciting was happening and pressed for details.

"You'll find out," David teased. "When we're ready to tell."

"Yeah," Dennis added. "when we're ready."

As the boys carried the milk, Domko intercepted them between the barn and the house.

"Yous be cuttink wood," he said handing David the old Swede saw.

Reluctantly, David traded the milk pail for the wobbly saw.

"Yous not be runnink away or I's be killink you bastards," Domko warned.

"We won't," David said as he stood waiting in the yard with his brother. Eunice came outside to help.

"Boy, I hate cuttin' wood," Dennis whispered.

"Yeah, me, too."

Domko came out a few minutes later, and they all went to the woodpile at the edge of the bush. The trees had been hauled in to dry the fall before. Now they had to be cut into one-foot lengths so they would fit in the stove firebox. The children knew this was an all-day project.

It would be Eunice's responsibility to hold the long end of the log across the sawhorse while the boys sawed chunks off the other end. Draping her body over the log, she held it in place as David pulled one end of the saw and Dennis the other. They seesawed back and forth until a one-foot piece dropped to the ground, then they started again. It was a long, boring job that the children hated. He always made them cut wood in cold weather, which froze their hands.

The morning was sunny, but by early afternoon, a strong north wind brought wet snow. Out of breath, they listened as Eunice filled them in on what had been happening at the house when they weren't there. They continued working, punctuated by tense intervals when Domko came to inspect the job they were doing. He often stayed for a long time, and the children had to quickly work while he stood and watched. When he was satisfied the job was progressing, he went back to the house. This gave the children a break.

"I'm cold," Eunice complained as she pulled her sleeves over her hands.

"Me, too," Dennis said. "How long is he gonna make us work?"

"I dunno," she said. "He's mad at you guys for runnin' away."

Bo was scrounging food by the chicken coop and lifted his head to listen to the children.

"Here's how I stay warm," David said. "Come here, Bo. Here, boy!"

Hearing David's voice, Bo lumbered over to where the children worked. The dog, still at the clumsy puppy stage, almost knocked them over. David grabbed him and buried his hands deep in the dog's fur.

"Yuk, he stinks," Eunice said turning up her nose.

"He don't stink," David said defensively. "All dogs smell like that. Besides he don't smell as bad as ol' Satan."

Eunice agreed and laughed. "Yeah, and I don't go near him either."

The dog enjoyed the children's laughter and barked a loud, deep bark. His mouth hung open loosely and drool dripped from his heavy jowls. He was mostly a dirty white color, with big dark and light brown patches on his eyes, ears and across his back. He was growing to be a huge dog in spite of seldom being fed. By now it had become apparent to everyone that Domko had mistaken his breed.

"That ain't no damned Collie dog," David said as he grabbed his end of the saw. "Ol' Squeezer was so proud of himself for stealin' a Collie."

Dennis laughed. "Yeah, do you think he noticed yet?"

"I dunno, but Marjie says Bo's some kinda Saint Brenard."

"That's BER-nard," Eunice corrected.

"That's what I said," David said. "Brenard."

Domko came back ten minutes later, and the children began sawing quickly. The saw wobbled a few times then suddenly, the thin blade broke.

"You's be breakink it some!" Domko yelled lunging at them. Eunice darted into the bush as he grabbed David by the hair then knocked him to the ground. Dennis did not move fast enough, and Domko grabbed him by the arm. He backhanded the boy hard, sending him toppling over the sawhorse. He began punching and kicking the twins as they covered their heads with their arms. They held their breath against the blows, hoping it would hurt less.

They noticed he was alternating between boys so that neither of them could get away. They also knew that this beating was for more than being there when the saw blade broke—it was because they had a secret from Domko.

I don't care, David thought as he tried to ignore the heavy boots kicking his back. *We won't come back no more. We're gonna live in our hut in the bush, and he'll never find us.*

Domko grunted each time his boot connected. He didn't care where he kicked them and lately had been trying even harder to injure them. The boys were twelve years old now, and beating them was hard work. Though Domko never admitted it out loud, the twins were tough and had a stubbornness that made them hard to beat.

He kicked them until they stopped moving. Then he grabbed the broken saw and threw it in the grass. He picked up enough wood for the night and breathlessly labored to the house. The twins lay on the wet ground for a while until they knew he wouldn't be coming back.

"He's gone," David groaned in the secret language. "You okay?"

"Yeah."

"C'mon, let's go to our place. We can stay there from now on."

The boys struggled to their feet and slowly walked along the bush path toward the church. They came out near Harwart's house, then cut through the field to the old barn. David gathered an armful of hay while Dennis pulled two boards across the wet ground through the field to their hut. Bo followed closely behind as wet snow whipped against their faces. To get to the hut, they had to wade through ankle-deep water and mud.

Dennis was disheartened from the beating and beginning to tire. David did his best to keep his brother's spirits up.

"I got matches," he said. "Just think about how nice and warm it'll be in there tonight. We don't got to worry about Squeezer no more. We even got Bo to sleep beside, and you know how warm he is. If we feel better, later on, we can go to Emma's and ask for bread. It'll be good from now on, Denny, I promise."

They waded through the last slough to the edge of the bush. They felt the wind subside as they walked into the bush, and felt happier. They'd made it. Looking around in the dark forest, they were having a hard time finding their hut. David looked back for a moment and realized they had come too far south.

"It's this way," he said.

Walking north, they came to a small clearing where the hut was. Dennis gasped and dropped the wood he'd dragged all the way from the barn. The twins stood in agonized silence staring at the charred remains of their hut.

DEFIANCE

That night the boys slept around a campfire. They returned home two days later, and nothing more was said about the hut. Domko chuckled about what he'd done, but the boys refused to acknowledge that anything was wrong. The twins continued to go to school and work hard during evenings and weekends. If Domko beat them, they would run to where the hut had been since it was still an excellent hiding spot. They considered re-building but had used all the scrap lumber they could find the first time around. Besides, he'd just burn it down again.

Domko's cattle were escaping and grazing the neighbor's pastures because his fences were in desperate need of repair. Domko feigned ignorance when the neighbors came to complain. He blamed the children, saying they'd left a gate open. The boys wanted to yell that they weren't responsible, but preferred the scowls of neighbors to Domko's fists. They continued peeling fence posts as he blamed them and their mother for everything that went wrong on the farm.

One afternoon David returned from school upset because Bo was not waiting in his usual place by the fence across from the school. David had a horrible feeling that something wasn't right. His mother was standing in the kitchen.

"Ma, have you seen Bo anywhere?" he asked.

Caroline didn't answer right away.

David's stomach started to churn. "Ma?"

"Domko shot him about an hour ago," she finally said.

"What?" David yelled. "Why'd he do that?"

"I don't know. But he's not dead. He ran that way," she said, pointing east.

Dennis stayed behind to milk while David took off running into the bush. Tears streamed down his face as he called the dog. He stopped to listen each time he thought he heard whimpering, but the sounds turned out to be splashing water or chirping birds.

David ran first through the bush to the beaver dam. Then he cut back through the east meadow toward home, he went to the church then to Harwart's house. He checked the abandoned barn and then went to Jim's house along the bush trail. He hoped that Bo had remembered going there as a pup, but Jim shook his head that he hadn't seen him.

David looked in the barn and around the buildings. He went home on a different path, calling Bo as he went. It was late and dark by the time he got home.

Domko was chuckling in his usual spot when David walked in the door. He avoided eye contact and went immediately upstairs to find Dennis who was crying on the bed.

"You okay?" he asked.

Dennis nodded, his body tender and throbbing. "Did you find him?"

"No. I'm gonna look again tomorrow."

He sat down beside his brother.

"Do you think the coyotes will get him?" David cried.

"No," Dennis said bravely. "He's stronger than a coyote."

"But he's hurt."

"He'll be okay David, don't worry."

The next morning David left fifteen minutes early so he could search for Bo. He met Dennis on his way home with the cows.

"Did you find him?" Dennis asked.

David shook his head.

That night he looked again and then again the next morning but still couldn't find the dog.

The following day the twins fled into the bush to avoid a beating. They ran to the spot where their hut had been. As they approached, a sickening smell permeated the air. The twins looked at each other.

Cautiously, they came around the edge of the bush and peered into the clearing where their hut had been. There, lying on the ground beside the campfire was a giant mound of fur.

"Oh no," David groaned, covering his eyes. "He went here 'cause I told him it was a safe spot. I walked right by and didn't see him."

David was heartbroken that Bo had chosen to die in their hiding spot. He remembered the night when Bo had sheltered them from the wind as they slept cuddling his fur by the campfire.

"We woulda died if it hadn't been for him," he whispered. "He was there for us, and I shoulda been here for him."

Dennis didn't know what to say. He was accustomed to David having all the answers and being strong. He'd also loved Bo, but not as much as David. It hurt him deeply to see his brother in so much pain. Physical pain was one thing, they'd felt plenty of that, but the feeling that someone was ripping out your heart was altogether different.

"C'mon," he said. "We'll go someplace else."

The school year finished in mid-April that year because of tremendous flooding. This pleased Domko since he needed full-time workers. One early May afternoon, he returned home from town with a load of poplar rails and the boys knew they were in for a long, hard job turning the logs into posts. They'd seen their older brothers do it a few years before and groaned as Domko called them over to unload the wagon.

While they worked, they noticed Gus walking down the road toward the farm. He hadn't been over in more than a year, so they were surprised to see him. They stopped unloading the rails and gave him a faint wave. His angry expression slightly softened as he looked at the twins.

"Where's Domko?" he asked.

"Over there," Dennis said, pointing at the lean-to where the tractor was kept. "He'll be back in a minute."

Gus watched them working as he waited. He hadn't seen the two up close for quite awhile and was surprised by how much they'd grown. They were still awfully thin, but big boned and strong. He'd seen them many times trudging through the fields east of his house and wondered where they were going.

Domko's not going to be able to push these kids around much longer, he thought. *Hopefully, he won't kill one of them first.*

Gus made small talk with them as he watched Domko approach.

"Domko, your cattle are in my field again," he said. "I want them out of there right now."

"Vat?" he asked surprised.

"Don't give me that innocent look. You know what I'm talking about. It's the third time this week they've got in, and I'm sick of it."

Domko laughed.

"Then yous be keepink them out," he taunted.

"Me? They are your cattle. It's your responsibility to keep them in."

Domko laughed and shook his head.

"You won't be laughing if somebody loads them up and ships them to Winnipeg," Gus warned. "You can start taking better care of them, and while you're at it, you can take better care of these kids, too."

The twins smirked at the comment. They had never heard Gus yell at Domko before and stopped to admire his nerve.

Having said all he came to say, Gus turned to walk out of the yard.

"Fraa!" Domko yelled as he lunged, kicking Gus in the back, knocking him forward. Shocked, Gus turned. A look of understanding came over his face. Now he understood the fear the twins lived with every day.

Domko continued to swear and chase Gus, who at sixty-seven years of age, was no match for the 45-year-old. Ashamed that they had witnessed such a disrespectful display, the boys hung their heads as Domko pushed and kicked Gus down the road.

"We can't get Gus in trouble no more," Dennis said. "He's too old to fight Satan."

There were more than one hundred poplar rails that needed to be peeled, sharpened and soaked in bluestone before they could be used for fence posts. The boys worked on this for more than two weeks.

"Why do you 'spose he never gives us nothin' to eat?" Dennis asked. He and David had snuck away from work and stood in the granary flicking mouse droppings out of the handfuls of chop they ate.

"He don't want us to get strong," David said. "As long as we're skinny and hungry, we can't fight back."

Dennis nodded in understanding.

"Wait here," David said. "I gotta go outside."

Dennis nodded and continued eating the chop.

David walked calmly into the bush and off the usual trail. He needed to go to the bathroom, and since Domko had never bothered to build an outhouse, there was a spot in the bush where everyone went.

As David came quietly around the edge of the bush, he saw Eunice crouching down. She finished and stood up, but didn't notice him standing there. She turned and went in the other direction.

David gasped. He forgot why he had come and turned, running as fast as he could back to the granary. Out of breath, he burst through the door.

"Denny," he yelled. "You should see what happened to Eunice!"

"What?"

His eyes were wide with fear. "He did it."

"He did what?"

"He cut it off. Eunice don't got one no more."

Dennis couldn't believe his ears. "No, It can't be."

"Remember hearing her scream?" he gasped. "And notice how she's been arguin' back? And sometimes she cries at night, and we don't know why."

The twins ran to hide upstairs to finish discussing poor Eunice.

"Are you gonna look?" David asked as they sat on the bed.

Dennis nodded that he would spy on her the next time she went into the bush. The pair decided that if Domko ever had the other one trapped and brought out the knife, the other would have to do something to distract him.

"Are you ever gonna fight back?" Dennis asked.

"I dunno," David said. "I'm too scared."

"Me, too."

"I'm scared he'll just kill us and throw us in the beaver dam, and nobody would even know."

"Yeah, like that time when he took us fencing," Dennis said. "He woulda killed us 'cept old Gus was sittin' there."

The twins remembered the afternoon Domko told them they had to fix a fence near the beaver dam. They had sat on the wagon as Domko sped through the field toward the lake. They sensed something was odd about this because they had no fences there. They recognized the bags and hammer between Domko's knees as the same equipment he carried when he went to drown litters of puppies. Believing they were in danger, they planned to jump off the wagon and run into the bush the moment it stopped. When they arrived at the lake bank, Domko was surprised to see old Gus Gall sitting on a rock fishing. This unnerved Domko who turned the tractor around and took them home.

"There was no fence to fix was there?" Dennis asked.

"If there was," David said, "we never fixed it."

Caroline had been gone for over a week, so they weren't able to tell her about Eunice. Domko sent them out to mend fences and while they were working, looked up to see Norman coming across the field.

"Hey, Norman," David called. "Whaddya doin' here?"

"I'm back for awhile," he said. "I'm sick of living with those people, and Ma came and asked me to come back. She said you guys can't get all the work done. They're gonna pay me a dollar a day, and I'm gonna get my grade eight at Bayton."

The twins smiled, happy to have him home. Not only because he'd help with the work, but because Norman was a lot of fun.

In the time he'd been gone, Norman had grown about three inches and filled out nicely. The twins suddenly felt a little safer.

Where Children Run

"So," Norman said as he grabbed the heavy hammer, "how's the old bastard been treating you?"

The twins groaned.

"Like shit," David said.

"So you haven't killed him yet?"

"Not yet," David said trying to sound grown up. "We tried, but Dennis couldn't make the gun work."

"It wasn't my fault. You were just lyin' there shakin' behind the tree. I didn't see you doin' no killin'."

The three of them laughed as they caught up on each other's lives.

"Where is he anyway?" Norman asked.

"Dunno," David said.

"Who cares?" Dennis laughed.

They walked home, and as they came into the yard, the twins noticed a shiny black motorcycle sitting near the house.

"Wow, is that yours?"

Trying to act nonchalant, Norman strode over to the bike. "Yeah, I got it last month. Do you like it?"

"Like it? It's great," David said.

Dennis reached out to touch the seat.

"Don't touch it!" Norman said.

He pulled his hand back. "Why not?"

"Because I said so. I don't want you to ever touch it without asking first, you understand?"

David walked around the bike, looking it over carefully. "Wow, this is great Norman, are you ever lucky. When I grow up, I'm gonna get me a great bike just like this one."

One morning shortly after Norman's move back to the farm, the children were doing chores when a family from the church stopped by for a visit. They were on their way to the Jehovah Witness annual gathering in Winnipeg. The man and woman were dressed in their best clothes, and their little girls wore dresses and had ribbons in their hair. The older girls were pretty and turned up their noses as Caroline insisted Eunice and Rosie say hello.

The boys watched from a distance as their mother invited the family in for coffee. They declined, saying they had a long drive ahead of them. David listened to them chatting to his mother, and felt embarrassed for Eunice and Rosie who were dressed in their barn clothes.

"Hey Denny," he whispered. "See the rouge and lipstick on them girls?"

All Beanie's got for rouge is cow shit."

Both boys giggled half-heartedly, feeling ashamed that their family was so poor. They thought making light of the situation might make them feel better, but it didn't. They knew Eunice didn't want to be standing there while the visitors compared her to their well-dressed daughters.

"Next year we will go," Caroline said. "We just can't get away this time."

The families exchanged pleasantries until the visitors left.

"Phoney bastards," Norman said under his breath. "It makes them feel good to come here because you guys are poor, and they look rich."

"Are they?" David asked.

"'Course not, but they can say, 'see you girls are lucky, not like that Eunice and Rosie.' And don't worry, they don't like old Squeezer either. I know because I've heard people talking about you guys."

"People are talkin' 'bout us?"

"Yeah, since you stole that wood," he said.

"We didn't mean to do it," David said. "He made us."

"They say you guys are stealing all the time. Some think you're driving poor old Domko nuts. Poor Domko my ass! He was nuts long before he came here. Anyways, that's why I came back 'cause you guys need my help. I ain't afraid of the old bastard anymore."

The twins were stunned. "You're not?"

"Nope. I'm bigger than him, and I'm fast and strong. I'm not scared of him."

David and Dennis stared at him in disbelief.

"Don't let him hear you sayin' that or he'll kill you," David warned.

Norman laughed. "Christ, you're bushed, don't you ever go to town?"

David felt his face flush.

Summer came, and soon haying began. Having Norman back was a relief to Eunice and the twins since it lightened their workload. They hayed the high spots early and worked their way into the low spots as the ground dried. There was a lot to do that year since the land Domko bought the year before was also producing.

"Listen, I'm taking off early so don't tell him where I went," Norman said one afternoon. "Just pretend like I didn't say anything."

The twins nodded. They watched as Norman led the horses pulling the mower through the field toward home. There was only a little bit of stacking left to do that day, and Domko was gone, so they sat in the grass under a tree and took a break.

Where Children Run

They sat chatting for a while then suddenly saw Eunice in the distance running through the field. Domko was right behind her.

"Look," Dennis laughed. "His pants fell off!"

David also laughed. "He shoulda waited before he pulled off his belt."

Dennis stood up and watched as she disappeared into the bush. "Beanie will be okay; she's a pretty fast runner."

The boys finished stacking then drove the team home. It had been a long day, and they were tired and hungry as they unhitched the pair.

"Don't mix up the straps," David warned.

Dennis fumbled with one pair but was careful to hang them in the right place. "Yeah, I remember what happened last time."

They strolled into the house where their mother was making supper. Raymond was crying because Kathy had taken something away from him. He let out a screeching noise that caused the twins to cover their ears.

"Let's get outta here," Dennis said. David nodded, and they went back outside. They sat in the bush and talked for a while then decided to get a drink of water. David ran to get a sealer jar he had hidden nearby.

The boys walked cautiously into the yard, looking over their shoulders. Domko wouldn't like it if he saw them taking a break and having a drink of water. They had to get to the pump house quietly without him noticing. They came around the corner of the house, and stopped short. Domko was leaning over the water trough. They could see Eunice also; her arms and legs were flailing, and it was then they realized he was holding her head under water.

Dennis turned and ran toward the bush while David ran to the house.

"Ma! Come quick," he yelled. "He's drowning Eunice in the trough!"

Caroline dashed out of the house then screamed. She ran over to her husband and pulled on his arm.

"Boleslaw," she screamed. "Let her go! You're drowning her!"

Shocked by the intensity of his wife's voice, he let go of Eunice.

"She's be some moonkey," he spitted.

Caroline grabbed her and pulled her out of the trough. Eunice fell to the ground unconscious, her face already blue.

David watched as his mother slapped Eunice's face and massaged her chest. She shook her, screaming for Eunice to wake up. Within a few seconds, Eunice began to sputter and cough. She opened her eyes and turned over, vomiting in the grass.

"What were you doing?" Caroline screamed. "You could have killed her!"

Eunice stayed limp on the grass for a few minutes as Caroline fussed over her. Domko stood ominously close as Caroline helped Eunice to her feet. The teenager wiped her face with her hands then shot her stepfather a glaring look.

Neither said a word as Eunice went into the house and upstairs. After supper, Caroline followed and much to Domko's displeasure, stayed in the children's bedroom that night. She had started doing that a few months earlier when she wanted to punish him. It worked well since he hated sleeping alone.

"What happened?" David asked Eunice that night when he climbed into bed. "What did you do to make him so mad?"

Eunice's face flushed and she was glad it was too dark for him to see. She turned on her side, away from the brother who had saved her life.

"Nothin'," she said.

The boys fell asleep, but Eunice was still awake well past midnight. She could hear Domko snoring loudly downstairs. The sound disgusted her, and she shook as she played back in her mind what had happened earlier that day.

Domko had approached her in an odd way that afternoon when she was outside working. He'd been looking at her differently since she started maturing and knew enough about male-female relations to keep away from men with that hungry look, but this time he'd caught her unaware. He pulled off his pants and tried to push her down. She'd squirmed free then ran into the bush. He chased her and caught her, and that's when she'd lashed out at him.

"Don't you come near me," she'd screamed. "You touch me, and I'll tell Ma and the police." At that point, he'd backed off but watched her suspiciously from a distance for the rest of the day. She'd been walking from the barn to the house when he jumped out from behind the water trough and grabbed her. He must have been afraid that she was going to tell her mother what had happened.

Lucky for me David came along. Otherwise, I'd be dead, she thought as she cried herself to sleep.

"You don't believe me, do you?" Norman said to the twins as they sat in the bedroom. "Not everybody's afraid of him like you."

"Well, he's crazier now," David said. "He tried to drown Eunice a couple days ago, and you should see how he smashed Denny last week."

Standing up, Norman put his hands on his hips. "You guys look like you need a good laugh," he said. "Guess what I'm gonna do?"

"What?" Dennis asked.

"I'm gonna moon him."

"What?"

"I'm gonna moon him."

The twins jumped up. They had heard about mooning in school.

"No Norman," David begged. "Please don't. He'll kill you."

"I'm gonna," he said as he strode toward the top of the stairs.

"Don't, or he'll cut it off," Dennis warned.

Norman looked at him and smirked. "What the hell are you talking about?"

Dennis said nothing as he glanced over his shoulder at Eunice who was sitting on the bed reading. "Ask Eunice."

She looked up from her book. "Shhh, I don't want Domko to know I'm up here."

Norman smiled then walked confidently down the stairs. When the twins realized he was serious, they followed him into the kitchen.

Domko was sitting at the table stirring his coffee. He looked up suspiciously at the twins who went to stand by the door. Norman came around from behind, startling him.

"Hey, Domko," he said.

"Vat?"

"I'm gonna moon you."

"Vat be moonink?"

"I'm gonna show you my ass!" Norman yelled as he turned and pulled his pants down. He stuck his bare rear at Domko and gave a little wiggle.

"Fraa," Domko yelled as he jumped off the chair.

The twins ran out the door and split in different directions. Seconds later Norman followed, scrambling with his pants down around his knees. Domko caught him three strides into the yard, and the pair tumbled into the grass.

The twins grimaced as Domko beat Norman as he struggled to get his pants up. Instead of cowering as the boys always had, Norman stuck out his arms and legs to block a few of the blows. Domko beat him with a ferocity that they had never seen before. Soon, Domko's energy was spent and satisfied, he grunted and went back into the house. When he slammed the door, the twins ran over to where Norman was lying flat on his back, panting.

"Oh, Norman we told you," David said, stomach turning over at the sight of blood streaming from his nose.

Norman raised a hand and wiped face.

"Yeah," he smiled. "But it was worth it."

TIME TO GO

THE TWINS SAT AT THE KITCHEN TABLE THAT EVENING WHILE THEIR mother and Domko discussed Norman. Domko complained angrily about the boy's belligerence and disrespect.

With eyebrows furrowed, he paced the floor, telling his wife what had happened that afternoon. Caroline glanced quickly at the twins to gauge their reaction to this outburst. The boys showed no emotion as Domko ranted and raved. He said nobody would be able to control Norman if he wasn't stopped soon.

"Ant then they's be doink it, too," he said, pointing at the twins.

David and Dennis shook their heads. They were too afraid of Domko to do such a disrespectful thing. They did admire their brother, though, but kept that fact to themselves.

Caroline listened to her husband and agreed. Her support heartened him, and he became even angrier. His eyes darted back and forth, and he slammed his fist on the table. Their mother was beginning to think like Domko, and this frightened the twins. Caroline began discussing ways to keep Norman, and the twins under control and Domko's solution was to work them harder.

"Then he's not be moonink no more," Domko yelled, thrusting his arm into the air as the boys quietly slipped away from the table.

They looked at one another in astonishment.

"More work?" Dennis whispered. "We can't work harder than this."

"I know. How come ol' Flatfoot always finds ways to make us pay, no matter what?"

"I dunno. It ain't our fault Norman mooned him."

"Yeah. And Norman's lucky he's got that motorbike so he can go whenever he wants."

Where Children Run

Norman returned late that night, humming to himself as he climbed into the bed. It was obvious he'd had a good time wherever he'd been that night. He chuckled to himself remembering the reactions of his friends when he told them he'd mooned Domko. Norman was an excellent storyteller who always had an audience that thought his stories were hilarious. Norman fell asleep quite pleased with himself.

The next morning Domko glanced out the kitchen window and saw Norman's bike parked in the yard. With a roar, he woke the children and herded them outside to do chores. Instead of going back to the house as he normally did, he remained scowling in the center of the barn.

The children worked quickly and silently. Even Norman didn't have much to say. Then instead of allowing them into the house for breakfast, Domko made them hitch the horses and go directly to the field to haul hay.

The children sat on the hay rack as it bumped across the field. Norman softly whistled as he held the reins.

"Thanks a lot, Norman," Eunice said. "Now 'cause of you, we gotta work even harder."

"What are you talking about?" he asked.

"Domko's mad 'cause you mooned him, now we gotta work harder."

Norman laughed. "That's bullshit. It's just an excuse. He's trying to turn Ma against us."

"Yeah, well it's working," she said. "He's worried we're all gonna start moonin' him."

"He's full of shit and so are you guys if you're mad at me because of that," he said. "The old bastard deserves more than being mooned."

Dennis started apologizing. "We're not mad at you, we just don't wanna have to work harder, that's all."

Norman laughed. "Well, I'm not worried. He's paying me, and that's all I care about."

Domko kept his promise. During the next few weeks, he worked the children hard from early morning until late evening. He watched them closely and used a short stick to beat all of them except Norman whenever they made a mistake. Soon the children were behaving like robots, methodically cutting, raking and stacking hay. They weren't allowed to talk, eat, or take a break from the exhausting work as long as he was watching. Occasionally he would go to the house, which gave them a short reprieve.

One afternoon Domko returned from lunch with Caroline, Kathy, and Raymond tagging along. There was a thick patch of Saskatoon bushes nearby.

251

Sometimes the blossoms failed to survive spring frosts, but this year the wild berry bushes were hanging with ripe fruit that needed to be picked before it fell to the ground.

The children each took a pail from him and followed their mother along the wooded trail. Stepping from the hot sun into the shade soothed their sunburned skin and raised their spirits. Raymond toddled ahead of them with Rosie. Kathy marched to avoid tripping over roots and stones.

David looked around in wonder as if seeing the bush for the very first time. Everyone instinctively spread out, each finding a picking spot. A feeling of normalcy swept over him. *This is how family life should be.*

The children chatted quietly among themselves, pulling the branches down near their pails. They ran their hands along the small branches, gently stripping them of the luscious fruit. The first fat, dark blue berries made popping noises as they dropped into the pails.

As David and Dennis picked, they scooped small handfuls of berries into their mouths when Domko wasn't looking, careful not to stain their lips. David wet the back of his hand with spit then rubbed it across his mouth.

"Hey, Denny," he whispered. "Any on my face?"

Dennis looked carefully. "Nope. How 'bout me?"

"No, you're okay."

They were the last to fill their pails, except for Kathy and Raymond who were eating heartily from the trees. Domko eyed the twins suspiciously as they tried to get Eunice, Norman and their mother to help them top up their pails.

"Vat?" he spat. "They's be lazy hobos. See? I's be tellink you they's be goot for nuthink."

He walked toward the boys and forced them to look up at him.

"You's be eatink some?"

The twins shook their heads. Confident that their mouths were clean, they faced their stepfather as he looked them over carefully.

"Open but-a-some mouth," Domko commanded.

The twins hesitated then began to shake as they slowly parted their lips. Domko's eyes bulged in anger at the sight of dark purple stains on their teeth and tongues.

"Fraa," he screamed. Reaching out, he punched David in the face, sending him sprawling backward and his berries flew through the air. Dennis fell to the ground anticipating a punch but was kicked instead.

Domko stood over them and screamed for Dennis and David to pick up their berries. Caroline led the rest of the children down the path toward home while the boys scrambled on the ground, scooping what they could back into their pails.

"Yous be some goot for sheet," Domko fumed.

David could hear his twin crying. He wanted to explain to Domko why they had eaten berries, but knew his pleading would fall on deaf ears.

We're starving, he thought. *I'm so hungry my stomach feels like somebody is cutting it out with a knife.*

"Fraa," he screamed again, this time thrusting his arm into the air toward home. The boys grabbed their pails and hurried down the path. Domko grunted as he followed close behind.

David sobbed as he trudged along. A knot of frustration welled in his stomach. He wondered if he would ever grow strong enough to escape Domko. The thought of how many years it would take sent a wave of despair through him.

The following morning Caroline and Eunice worked in the kitchen cleaning and preserving the saskatoons. They chatted and gossiped as a breeze blew softly through an open window.

Eunice wanted to talk about Domko and how uncomfortable he made her feel, but Caroline was in such a pleasant mood that she didn't want to spoil their time together. She tried to push her unhappiness aside as together they boiled the berries on the stove. When it was thick, it would be poured into hot, sterilized jars that sat on the table.

The kitchen was sweltering, so any excuse to stand by the window was welcome. Eunice paused as she listened to Rosie playing outside. It made her wonder if life was as bad as it seemed.

Maybe this is just what it is like, she thought. *Maybe this is what being a kid is about. When I grow up, I can be or do whatever I want, and that's not long off. I'm thirteen now, and in a year or two, I can leave here for good.*

When Eunice's mother sent her to collect eggs from the hen house her spirits brightened. She grabbed the basket by the door and went outside. Not surprisingly, it was cooler outdoors than in the kitchen.

Rosie had found herself a piece of rope and was skipping on the worn grass along the driveway. She hummed skipping songs softly to herself, counting how many times she could jump before catching the rope on her foot. She loved to skip and lost herself completely in the activity.

Eunice sauntered to the hen house then stepped inside the dank building. The birds clucked noisily as the door shut behind her.

"Okay chickens," she said. "I'm here to take your eggs."

Karen Emilson

The hens flapped their wings and tried to peck her hand, but Eunice reached deftly underneath the bossy birds.

"Blech," she said as she avoided touching the little pellets of manure surrounding the nests. "I hate chickens."

She finished gathering the eggs and started back to the house. She stared into the basket and wondered how the contents of these little vessels turned into chicks. Looking up, she could see Domko walking from the barn to the house. He slowed almost to a full stop when he noticed Rosie skipping happily in the driveway. A familiar look crossed his face, and Eunice knew what would happen next. She set her basket of eggs on the ground and ran to her sister. She intercepted her stepfather just as he reached out to grab her.

"No," Eunice screamed. "Leave her alone - don't hit her anymore!"

Rosie clung to Eunice and buried her face in her shirt as Eunice squarely faced Domko.

"Huh?" he said, taking a surprised step back.

It was the second time that Eunice had stood up to him. She could sense his confusion and continued to scream until her mother looked out the window. To her amazement, Domko backed away. He went into the house and berated Caroline about the children's behavior. He complained that they were conspiring against him and that Eunice had attacked him for no reason. Caroline listened as he complained that the children were always snickering and pointing at him.

The girls were shocked by what they overheard. They hoped their mother didn't believe his lies and decided to stay outside for the rest of the day.

Late that afternoon, Marjorie chased the Harwart cows down the road past the house, so Eunice and Rosie joined her. It was a twice-daily ritual that gave the girls an excuse to visit.

Domko watched the children carefully over the next few days. He tried desperately to listen to their conversations in hopes of learning how they were plotting against him. His solution was to divide the children into work crews, believing that if he kept them apart, they would be less likely to turn against him. Whenever he was able to corner a child alone, he gave him or her a sound beating.

One evening after a particularly long, hot, day, the children were relaxing in the kitchen before bed, when Domko singled out Dennis who had become his favorite target since he was too frightened to run away.

"Dennis," Domko said firmly. "Vy's yous be valkink like dat?"

Dennis stopped and looked at him then lowered his eyes. "I dunno."

"Vy's you's be doink it?" he said, swinging his shoulders from side to side.

"I don't."

"Yous be doink it," he roared. Domko stood up and in an exaggerated fashion, strode across the floor imitating Dennis' walk. He made the other children watch as he wiggled his back end and swung his shoulders. This looked hilarious, but none of them dared laugh since Domko was deadly serious. He then turned to Dennis.

"Valk," he commanded.

Dennis felt his face turn red as everyone's eyes were on him. He hesitated until Domko took a step forward, then he quickly walked to the other side of the room.

"See," Domko said. "I's be tellink you. He's be valkink like it!"

Again he strode across the room, this time exaggerating the movements even more.

Raymond laughed at the sight of his father's silliness, but Norman scoffed. David and Eunice said nothing as they tried to ignore Dennis' embarrassment.

"I's vantink yous to be valkink like I's be," he said, strolling across the room in his usual stiff-legged gait. He stopped then motioned for Dennis to try it.

Dennis looked at him then took a few steps. Since he didn't know what was wrong with his walk, he found it very hard to correct. Stiffening his legs like Domko, he took a few more steps. The sight of him sent the children into a giggling fit. Domko was not amused and continued to criticize Dennis who was so embarrassed that he wished the roof of the house would collapse on them.

For the next hour, Domko sat at the table and scolded Dennis as he practiced walking across the kitchen floor. The other children tired of the spectacle and disappeared upstairs. Tears of frustration streamed down Dennis' cheeks as he tried to walk the way Domko wanted him to.

Domko teased Dennis without mercy for the next few weeks. He tried to change Dennis' walk to resemble his own. If he caught him walking normally, he'd smash him over the head with whatever he could find.

One evening Domko gave Kathy and Raymond each a box of candy-coated popcorn. The children watched in envy as they hadn't had a real treat since they lived in Ashern.

"Ant don't yous be giving the Peeschkes none," Domko ordered.

Kathy and Raymond obeyed and smugly walked past their half-siblings.

Raymond opened his box and stuffed the candy in his mouth. He then turned and clutched the box to his chest.

Dennis watched as Raymond dumped some of his popcorn on the kitchen floor. Out fell a toy whistle. Raymond ate the popcorn as he blew the whistle, sending streams of pink spit out the end. Walking past the twins, he blew the whistle directly at their faces. David and Dennis sat unmoved as the two-year-old tried to elicit a reaction. When they wouldn't do anything, he moved closer and blew harder. The twins ignored him and eventually Raymond tired of the game. He put the whistle on the table and went into the front room.

The twins could hear Eunice and Rosie trying quietly to persuade Kathy to give them some popcorn, but the five-year-old refused. Kathy didn't want to do anything that might anger her father, since she'd lost a lot of his favor after Raymond was born. Raymond was by far Domko's favorite child, and while he treated Kathy well, he was uncomfortable with her handicap.

"No," she whined. "Ta-ta be saying no."

Rosie and Eunice tried to hush the girl as they hurried upstairs, fearing Domko might hear her whining and suspect the reason.

"Ta-ta be saying no," Raymond mimicked.

The twins giggled in the kitchen. "He's just like ol' Satan," Dennis whispered.

"The little bugger even talks like him," David agreed.

The boys moved to the table, and Dennis noticed the whistle. He picked it up and wiped the pink saliva on his sleeve. It was made of bright blue plastic and had a tiny ball inside. Dennis raised it to his lips and exhaled. It tinkled softly, and he watched with crossed eyes as the tiny ball bounced inside.

"Shhh," David warned, as he looked into the front room.

Dennis was enjoying the little toy and whistled again, this time a little louder. Their half brother and sister were making so much noise that nobody could hear the shrill sound of the whistle coming from the kitchen. Dennis played a quiet, unknown tune as he moved his head rhythmically from side to side.

Just then, Raymond came into the kitchen and noticed Dennis playing with the whistle. He opened his mouth as wide as he could and let out a screeching howl that was heard throughout the house. Dennis threw the whistle down just as Domko came flying into the room. It was too late because Domko pulled off his belt when he saw Raymond standing in the middle of the floor pointing at Dennis and crying uncontrollably.

"Vat? You soneebeech bastard," he screamed as he began whipping Den-

Where Children Run

nis. David ran outside to hide, hollering in the secret language that he'd be in the barn.

Raymond continued to cry and feel sorry for himself as he picked up the whistle. Caroline came into the kitchen to see what had happened just as Domko finished beating Dennis.

"He's be hurtink Raymie," Domko sputtered as he picked up his son. The boy's expression by this time had turned from angry tears to spiteful indignation. He pouted and began acting very spoiled as his parents tried to console him.

Dennis waited until Domko was out of the room before he limped out the door. David waited for him near the barn and led him to a stack of hay.

"I'm scared he's gonna break your legs," David said. "And then you won't be no good, and then you know what'll happen."

"I ain't no good already," Dennis sobbed. The past few weeks had been particularly difficult with Domko teasing and hitting him constantly. "I wish I was dead."

"No, you don't," David said. "You don't wanna be dead. Just stay away from him that's all. And run when he comes near you, don't just stand there."

"I told you before, I can't help it," Dennis said, wiping his tears with the back of his hand. "I freeze up."

The boys nestled in the hay, knowing that's where they'd spend the night.

"Did you see Norman watching him?" David asked, his voice thick with admiration. "Did you notice how mad he looked? Norman didn't like him teasing you, and I figure one of these times he's gonna help us."

"Norman can't do nothin'."

"Yes he can," David said. "He'll help us some time, you'll see."

It was Friday morning, and Norman had big plans for the weekend. He approached his mother to ask if she could pay him his owed wages. He'd worked for six weeks and was starting to get anxious.

"Ask him yourself," she said, pointing to the table where Domko sat.

"Can't you just pay me?" he whispered.

"I don't have any money," she said. "You have to ask him."

Norman dreaded the thought of asking Domko for anything. Even though they owed him the money, Domko went out of his way to make Norman feel uncomfortable about his paid position. He tried his best to look confident as he approached the table.

"Hey, I was wondering if I could get paid today," he said.

Domko looked up from his coffee cup. He stared but said nothing.

Norman waited for an answer, then asked again.

"Yeah, I'm going with some friends this weekend and need gas money for my bike."

Domko snickered. He took a long drag from his cigarette then blew the smoke to the ceiling. He pushed his cup to the edge of the table then called for Caroline to fill it.

She quickly grabbed the pot from the stove and topped his cup then went back to peeling potatoes for the soup.

"Yous not be done workink," Domko said as he stirred methodically.

"I know," Norman said cheerily. "But I'll be back and finish up just like I promised."

Domko took a gulp of coffee then sucked on his cigarette again. "If you not be vorkink, you be not gettink paid."

"But I need some money now," Norman said, anger rising. "Nobody else would work for six weeks without getting paid. I'm almost sixteen, and I can get a job any place."

Domko grunted, thinking that Norman was more trouble than he was worth. He looked squarely at the boy in an attempt to intimidate him. But Norman stood his ground.

The veins in Domko's neck and forehead began to throb. The blood began to pool in the depression on his forehead, turning it a bright red color. His eyes became riveted on Norman as his anger rose.

Knowing his stepfather could explode at any minute, he tried not to let his fear show. "I want my money."

"Fraa," Domko yelled, thrusting his right arm into the air as he jumped off the chair.

Norman turned and ran out the door, slamming it behind him. He stopped once he realized Domko was not behind him. His initial feelings of fear turned to frustration, and he began kicking the ground.

"I'm getting outta here," he said as he stormed toward his motorcycle. He needed the twins to help push-start the machine, but neither of them was nearby.

"Figures," he mumbled as he opened the lid of the gas tank and peered in. The bike was low on fuel, and even if he did get it started, he wouldn't get very far.

"Damn it," he said. "I'm trapped here with that sonofabitch and a pile of work. The old bastard is likely never gonna pay me anyway, just like he gypped Walter."

The situation was humiliating and the more he thought about it, the angrier he became. He didn't like being taken advantage of, and while his instincts had told him not to accept his mother's offer in the first place, he'd felt sorry for her. She had begged him to come back and had been very nice, but once he returned, she ignored him like she always had. He'd been tricked, and he knew it.

"Oh yeah?" he spat. "I'll show him."

Turning, he strode to the granary. His mind whirled as he flung open the door. Grabbing his father's old rifle, he pulled back the bolt and looked inside. His hands shook as he grabbed a bullet from a box on the shelf. He loaded the chamber then snapped the bolt in place. He stood for a moment staring out the granary door at the house. He swallowed hard as he thought about the humiliation, not only his but also his siblings', especially Dennis. He recalled the many beatings they had all received and how downtrodden their mother had become. He thought about Bruno lying on the ground and how Domko had shown the dog no mercy.

"I'll show him how it feels," he said as he stepped out of the granary.

Norman's mind was in turmoil as he walked to the house. Just then, Marjorie chased the cattle down the road, waving as she went. He ignored her and hoped the sound of the bawling cattle would muffle the gunshot.

He would confront Domko in the kitchen, and imagined shooting him in the chest. His mother would scream. The police would come and take him away to jail. He knew that nobody would believe his reasons for doing it. Too many people thought the family was lucky that Domko had rescued them from a life of poverty and unhappiness.

He reached for the doorknob but stopped. He'd never killed anything except for a few ducks and rabbits. He didn't know how it would feel to kill a human being. His stomach knotted with frustration, and he couldn't make himself go in the house. He stood on the stoop, holding back tears when Marjorie's dog came sniffing through the bush into the yard. Sandy trotted slowly past the house, on a path to veer back onto the road behind an old lame cow that was having difficulty keeping up with the rest of the herd.

Norman watched the little dog. For no reason except the desire to shoot something that moment, he lifted the gun, took aim and shot Sandy.

Sandy let out a startled yelp as the bullet pierced her heart. The impact sent her flying into the air. Instantly regretting what he'd done, Norman watched the dog whimper then die. The gunshot brought the twins and Eunice running from the barn and Caroline and Domko from inside the house.

"What are you shooting?" Caroline asked.

Norman stood staring at the ground with the gun at his side. It was then his mother noticed Sandy lying just a few feet away.

"Norman," she exclaimed. "What did you do that for?"

He shrugged as Domko grabbed the gun and took it into the house.

"Why did you shoot Sandy?" Caroline asked.

"I dunno," he said. "I just did."

"Well, now we're going to be in trouble with the Harwarts," she snapped. "We don't need any more trouble with the neighbors." Grabbing him by the ear, she pulled him into the house and slammed the door.

The twins could hear the muffled sounds of their mother yelling at Norman.

"Why'd he do that?" Dennis asked.

"I dunno," David said.

"What's Marjie gonna say?"

"We gotta hide her, so nobody finds out."

Dennis nodded. The boys inched over to where Sandy was lying in the grass.

"Are you sure she's dead?" Dennis asked.

"Lemme see," David said. He picked up a small stick and gently poked the dog's side. Then he lifted a limp paw. "Yep, she's dead."

"What are we gonna do?"

David looked around. "We'd better bury her before Marjie gets back."

They picked up the dead dog and carried her into the bush. They dug a shallow grave and covered the body with earth.

"Whaddya think Marjie's gonna do when she finds out Sandy's gone?" Dennis asked.

"I dunno," said David. "But I hope she don't cry too much."

That night David and Dennis covered their ears as they lay in bed. Occasionally David would remove his hands and listen, but the sound of Marjorie calling her beloved dog caused him to cover his ears again. The guilt was overwhelming as they tried to block out the sound of their friend searching for her missing dog.

Over the next few days, the boys avoided Marjorie, especially when she came asking for help to find the dog. Caroline and Domko had warned them to say nothing, so they made excuses that they couldn't help because they had to work.

Another school year began at the end of August. Because Norman was home, the twins didn't have to work as much and were able to start class with the other neighborhood children.

Where Children Run

Mrs. Collier stood at the front of the room and organized the grades on the first day. The older students chuckled, wondering if she would ever retire.

The twins had been promoted to grade four, while Eunice was in grade six and Rosie in grade three. Marjorie didn't attend classes at Bayton anymore since she was taking grade ten by correspondence. This was a relief to the twins who couldn't bear to face her after what had happened to her dog.

Norman's plan to enroll in grade eight was put on hold for a few weeks while he finished some farm work. His mother had promised that as soon as he finished hauling the last stacks of hay closer to home and manure to the garden, he could begin school.

Norman still hadn't been paid but decided to finish the work rather than give Domko an excuse not to pay him.

One Saturday morning in early October, Domko told Norman and the twins to haul manure to the far garden. The potatoes and carrots were already bagged, and a heavy frost had blackened all the remaining greenery. Domko hoped to work the manure into the ground before the snow fell.

The twins followed Norman out to the barn where the horses were hitched to a rickety flatbed wagon made of old planks. They shoveled manure onto the flatbed, then rode out to the far garden to spread it. The boys spent the day working and teasing each other. Since Norman was the oldest, he was able to get away with doing the least amount of work under the guise of being the supervisor. The twins soon caught on to this and began teasing their older brother by calling him lazy and 'goot for nuthink.'

"Hey Schtink Schtank," David laughed, "while you're relaxin' there, don't take off your boots, okay?"

Norman smiled. "You think my feet stink? Smell this," he said farting loudly.

The three laughed as they continued to work and soon the flatbed was empty again.

"This will be the last trip for today," Norman said. "It's getting late, and I wanna go to town."

The twins jogged beside the flatbed as Norman drove to the barn.

"Hey Norman, you drive pretty slow," David teased.

"Yeah," Dennis said. "We can run faster than you can drive."

Norman scowled at them. "Oh yeah? Wanna bet?"

The twins laughed as they ran beside him. They stuck out their tongues and made faces, knowing he couldn't chase and catch them as long as he was driving the team.

"You think you're fast, eh?" Norman said. "Try grabbing hold of the back

Karen Emilson

and running behind. I bet you won't be talking so smart then."

The twins looked at each other and laughed.

"Sure," David said cheerfully. He and Dennis were getting tall, and they were also getting fast from running away from Domko. Sometimes they even out ran him, so holding onto the back of a slow-moving flatbed sounded easy.

"Okay, the rules are that you guys can't let go," Norman hollered. "If you do, then you lose."

"Alright," David yelled. "We'll start now."

The twins gripped the backboards and ran easily behind. Norman looked over his shoulder, then flicked the reins twice. The horses responded by quickening their pace. Norman glanced back to see the boys still holding on. He snapped the reins again, this time harder and the horses began to gallop. Norman laughed as the twins bounded with huge strides through the freshly plowed field.

"Ha!" Norman laughed as he watched. He snapped the reins once more, and the horses jolted the flatbed forward. The twins lost their balance and tumbled to the ground, knocking one of the loose. The board banged into the back of one horse's leg, causing the animal to panic. Without warning, the game had turned serious as the horses pulled the flatbed through the rocky field at a frantic pace.

Norman stood up and pulled the reins back with all his strength, but the horses continued to race through the field creating a huge cloud of dust behind them.

"Runaway!" David yelled as he watched the horses accelerate.

The twins watched as Norman fought to control the team. He pulled the reins, and suddenly the galloping animals turned to the right, running away from the farm toward the bush. Boards from the wagon began to shake loose.

Norman let go of the reins and crawled toward the back of the hay rack as the boards vibrated freely beneath him. Some boards worked their way forward while others skittered back. Norman seemed to be planning to jump off the back of the flatbed, and then two boards beneath his knees shifted forward then dug deep into the ground directly behind the horse's feet. The back end shot up, catapulting Norman into the air. He flew over the front of the team, somersaulting in the air before landing on the ground in the path of the horses. The boys watched in horror as the team and wagon ran over their brother. The horses continued through the field and into the bush where they were forced to stop when they became hung up in the trees.

The twins stared at their brother who lay motionless on the ground.

"Norman, are you okay?" David hollered as they ran to him.

At first, Norman couldn't speak, then slowly he began to groan. The wind was knocked out of him, and he gasped to catch his breath.

"Did the horses stomp on you?" Dennis asked.

In the distance, they could hear Domko yelling. They looked toward the house and saw him storming across the field. He'd seen the horses running out of control and believed Norman had driven them that way intentionally.

"Norman, he's coming, get up," David yelled, pulling at his arm until Domko was just a few feet away. Then the twins turned and ran toward the bush. When they were a safe distance away, they stopped to watch as Domko picked up a piece of board and began beating Norman with it as he lay writhing on the ground.

The twins helped Norman home that night. It took him three days to recover from the accident and the beating. He awoke one morning determined to leave the farm but kept the decision to himself. He avoided Domko's gaze and ignored the sarcastic comments about being 'lazy' as he slipped out the kitchen door. He was able to catch the twins before they went to school.

"Hey you guys, come here," he said as he hurried around the side of the house. "I need your help."

The twins followed, glancing over their shoulders as they went.

Norman stopped near Domko's car, a 1952 Chev, which he'd bought after the other car was wrecked in the accident.

"Here, hold this," he said, handing David a small rubber hose and a tobacco can.

"What's this for?"

"You'll see."

Norman uncapped the gas tank of the car. He took the hose from David and dropped one end inside. He then began sucking on the hose.

"What are you doin'?" Dennis asked. "Drinkin' gas?"

"No, stupid," he said. "It's called siphoning."

The twins watched as Norman sucked the gas up the hose then quickly put the tip in the tobacco can. It had taken four tries and a mouthful of gas before he was able to fill the can.

"Ol' Satan would call this stealin' you know," David warned.

"Yeah, well the way I see it he owes me anyway," Norman said. "The old bastard never did pay me."

David wasn't surprised. He watched as Norman slipped the hose back in his pocket. He capped the tank and the three of them sauntered to the motorcycle.

Norman motioned for Dennis to watch while he and David filled the tank of his bike, then tossed the can in the grass.

"Gimme a push," he said to David.

Since the kick-start was broken, David had to help him push the bike. When it sounded like it might start, Norman jumped on. David pushed Norman down the driveway as the bike backfired then finally started.

"Okay, let go," Norman yelled over the roar of the engine.

David couldn't hear him and continued pushing, making it difficult for Norman to steer. He reached back and trying to loosen his hand, slipped, and accidentally hit him in the nose. David staggered to the house, wiping the blood from his face with his shirt. Norman turned the bike around and drove back to check on David who went inside.

"What happened?" Caroline said, rushing to him with a rag. "Where's the blood coming from?"

"My nose," David mumbled. "I was helpin' Norman start his bike."

"What?" she said.

"Vat he's be doink?" Domko demanded.

Just then Norman walked in the door. The sight of him sent Domko into a rage. He grabbed Norman and pushed him against the wall. Both boys tried to explain what had happened, but Domko and Caroline were too angry to listen. Caroline slapped Norman hard in the face, and David watched in shock as their mother joined Domko in beating Norman.

Later that day, Norman snuck out of the kitchen and pushed his bike to the school where he asked a few of the older boys to give him a push. He drove to Jim's house for help.

Norman had stayed with a handful of people over the past few years on a temporary basis, but now he was looking for somewhere permanent to live. Although the Nachtigalls had been nice to him, they were from his mother's church. Norman feared that if he went there, it would be too easy for his mother to find him and force him back to the farm.

Norman told Jim that he would work hard and be a good kid as long as he was fed and not beaten. Jim decided not to call the police, but to contact people he knew in the Ashern area. Norman ended up in bare feet and with no jacket on the doorstep of Leonard and Emma Geisler. The Geislers were kind, generous people who treated their young workers like family members. They took the boy in, and the first thing they did was buy him a pair of shoes.

DIVIDE AND CONQUER

The twins were finding it difficult to lose themselves in their twin world of make-believe. They could no longer escape the cruel realities of life by daydreaming and wishing Domko would miraculously disappear.

Now they were almost teenagers and understood their circumstances. Still too young to fight back, the boys' lives were made more difficult knowing that Domko wasn't going anywhere. They knew Norman wouldn't return, which made their workload overwhelming as Domko continued to starve, tease, beat and criticize them.

The twins were under further pressure because their mother was beginning to act like Domko. David and Dennis even began quibbling amongst themselves, a sign that Domko's strategy was working.

The twins were always forced to save themselves at the expense of the other, and it was beginning to cause a rift in their relationship. Because Dennis was singled out and beaten more than the others, the twins would never be able to pull together to defend themselves against Domko as long as Dennis was powerless to fight back.

One afternoon Domko attacked Dennis in the kitchen. As Dennis fell to the ground, his leg kicked out, and his foot caught Domko on the shin.

"He's be kickink me," Domko screamed.

Caroline came into the room to see what had happened.

"He's be kickink me, that soneebeech be kickink me!"

Caroline turned to David. "Is that true?"

David looked at his brother huddled on the ground then at his mother's angry face. Domko was shaking his head in disgust, convinced that Dennis had kicked him. David knew it had been an accident, but how could he convince them?

Domko glared at David. Desperate for an excuse to beat either boy, he gave David a look that said that if it weren't Dennis, it would be David the minute Caroline's turned her back.

David nodded then looked away.

Caroline lashed out at Dennis in the same way she had turned on Norman just a month before. Dennis received a horrible beating from both Caroline and Domko. His face was left swollen and bloody.

Without emotion, David dragged his twin up the stairs. Dennis' face was beaten so badly that he was almost unrecognizable.

"Why didn't you tell her it was an accident?" Dennis asked. "You saw."

David was ashamed and stared at the ceiling. "I dunno. I was scared."

Dennis started to cry. His mother and brother turning against him had been the final betrayal. "I'm scared all the time. I can't do it no more. I'm cold and hungry and stiff. I just wanna die."

David gazed at the ceiling. He was cold and hungry too but knew there was a difference between how he felt and the despair engulfing Dennis. Domko was breaking the boy's spirit.

In the days that followed, David noticed how jumpy and irritable Dennis had become. He was inconsolable, and the brothers barely spoke to each other, and when Dennis did say something, it was usually about dying. Domko teased Dennis about his face, calling him ugly and deformed.

Friends from the church came to visit. Outwardly, these people supported Domko, so they were allowed in the house.

Everyone sat at the table through the small talk; then the discussion turned to religion. While the church members were still concerned about the cleanliness of the house, they were pleased that Caroline and Domko seemed to be getting along better.

"Cleanliness is next to godliness, Caroline," the male Witness said. "And your husband would be much more comfortable if the house was kept clean and tidy."

Caroline nodded.

The visitors commended the Domkos for keeping the children under control. They hadn't heard any more reports about the children stealing or running away.

"What happened to Dennis' face?" the man asked.

"He's be fightink ant be losink it some," Domko said. "He's be some goot for sheet."

The boy looked at the floor as his bruised, swollen face turned scarlet.

Friends usually knew better than to initiate a conversation about the Pischke children because it always sent Domko into a tirade of insults that made it uncomfortable for everybody.

"Ant they's not be stealink no more," Domko said proudly. "I's be tellink her they's be stealink, but she's not be hearink."

Caroline fidgeted through the lie as Domko continued to congratulate himself. Everyone but the visitors knew it was an effort to re-direct rumors about himself to the twins.

The boys sat quietly and listened, knowing better than to contradict Domko's interpretation of the truth. It was embarrassing being called thieves, but they accepted that far easier than a beating.

Dennis wondered why their friends from the church never said anything about Domko's personal cleanliness. He stunk horribly, and it was surprising that the neat, clean visitors could stand sitting beside him.

The church members read aloud from the Bible and left a Watchtower magazine. Dennis enjoyed reading the little magazine and snatched it up, running to the bedroom just before the end of the visit. David followed shortly afterward to find Dennis engrossed in the magazine.

"What you readin' that for?" he asked.

Dennis didn't answer.

David reached down and grabbed the magazine from his brother's hands.

Dennis jumped up and shoved him. He took the magazine back and angrily flipped to the page he was reading.

"I don't like readin' the Watchtowers," David said. "They're stupid."

"You're stupid," Dennis argued.

"Well, I ain't that stupid," he said pointing to the magazine.

Dennis turned his back on his brother and continued reading. David climbed in beside him, and the two didn't speak for the rest of the night.

"Where's the ol' bastard?" David asked Eunice the following morning as they sat in the front room.

"Him and Ma went to town," she replied.

"How 'bout Dennis?"

"I dunno," she said. "I made fun of his face, so he got mad and ran out."

David cringed. He knew he should go looking for his brother but didn't want to go outside in the cold. It had snowed a little bit, and he didn't have anything warm to wear on his feet.

Just then the door opened, and Dennis walked in. David looked at him and immediately knew things weren't right with his brother. Dennis walked stiffly into the front room.

"What are you doin'," David asked.

"Nothin'," Dennis said as he walked from one end of the room to the other. "Nobody cares anyhow." His chin began to waver as he shook his head.

"Nobody cares, not you, not Momma and nobody from the church. We don't got no friends, and Momma's family don't like us. Ruby don't care 'cause she left, and we can't go to Emma's no more."

Dennis began to sob. "Momma always says we're gonna die 'cause of Domko, and I keep hopin' he kills me, but he never does. He just smashes me so that I feel dead."

David's heart began to pound as he watched his shaking brother. Eunice stood speechless in the center of the floor.

"It's okay, Denny," David whispered. "Things will get better."

"No they won't," Dennis yelled, stamping his foot on the ground. He shook his head violently as he screamed at his siblings. "They won't, and you know it, too. He's gonna kill us someday."

David had never seen Dennis so defeated. His mind raced to find the words to console his brother.

"No, Dennis," David coaxed. "We can get away. Just you and me. We can go over the beaver dam, you'll see. As soon as winter comes, we'll walk across the ice and never come back. We work good, you and me. We'll find some place to live."

Dennis stared angrily at him. For the first time since he'd come into the room, he looked directly into his brother's eyes. It was like seeing his reflection and the fear he saw there was unsettling. He was so tired of being Domko's victim.

David sensed Dennis' uncertainty and used the moment to his advantage. "We can leave today," he said. "I promise."

Dennis hesitated.

"C'mon," David said cheerfully. "Let's go."

They trudged through the snow in the bush for the rest of the day. David made a makeshift shelter, but as evening approached, it became too cold to sleep outside. They continued walking and circled back, finding themselves in the churchyard. They climbed in through the back window and lit the tall white candles as they had on so many other nights.

Too afraid of what awaited them across the beaver dam, they returned home two days later, hungry and tired but determined to stay away from Domko. They made a pact to resist Domko's attempts to intimidate them. They would stick together no matter what.

One night soon after the boys' return, Caroline poured herself and Domko two small glasses of moonshine from the still they had hidden under the kitchen counter. The boys watched fearfully as their mother and Domko drank and talked, then poured another drink. The couple gossiped about the neighbors, relatives, and friends from church.

David remembered Jim had told him to be wary of people who couldn't handle their liquor. He motioned to Dennis that they should run. Dennis nodded, and the boys crept around the table to the door. Just as David reached for the knob, Domko called out to them.

"David, Dennis," he said. "Coom here."

The boys froze. Dennis grabbed David's arm.

"Don't leave me," he begged. "You promised."

David nodded as they turned around.

"Come here boys," Caroline called. "We want to talk to you."

Reluctantly they went to stand beside their mother. Domko stood up and staggered over. He bent down and put his dirty face a few inches from them.

"Yous not be runnink away no more," he said, raising his finger and pointing it at them. Then his gold tooth shone as he flashed them a wide, sincere smile.

"Now, go on up to bed," Caroline snickered, tapping each boy lightly on the rear end.

Still holding Dennis' arm, David hurried through the front room then up the stairs, pulling his brother behind him.

Astonished, they jumped onto the bed.

"Did you see that?" Dennis asked in amazement.

"Yeah, I hope he drinks moonshine more often," David said.

Domko recovered from his hangover and became his usual, miserable self. The children avoided him and spent as much time in school as he allowed. One December afternoon, the boys were helping him bring home a load of hay from the field. David slipped and fell head first off the wagon, wedging himself between the hay rack and stack. As Domko drove off, David's neck wrenched and he screamed in pain, able to roll away from the hay rack wheels just in time. Domko heard him fall but continued driving, expecting he would catch up later.

David fell unconscious. When he awoke hours later, it was dark outside. He didn't know how long he'd been knocked out. He struggled to stand up, but his arms and legs were stiff from the cold. His neck was so sore that it could no longer support the weight of his head. David cried out each time he took a step as unbearable pain shot through his neck. Clasping each side of his head with his hands, he stumbled home and went straight to bed.

David stayed there for nearly a week. His neck was swollen to double its usual size, and he was plagued with an excruciating headache that throbbed so hard he couldn't stand to be in a room with the lights on. He turned away from the daylight that shone through the bedroom window, praying that Domko wouldn't come upstairs. His mother seemed sympathetic, and this helped David relax.

Caroline came up to check on him and brought some soup.

"Ma, I gotta go to the doctor," he said, voice quivering. "My neck don't feel too good. I think it's broken."

Caroline tried to assess her son's condition. "It's not broken; otherwise you wouldn't be able to walk," she said. "I'll talk to Domko and see if he'll let you go."

David overheard them arguing in the kitchen later that day. Caroline hollered that her son needed to see the doctor while Domko scoffed at the suggestion.

Caroline watched her husband carefully as his eyes narrowed and he scowled in a familiar way. Not wanting to make him more jealous than he already was, she changed the subject. When she had a spare moment, she snuck upstairs to talk to David.

"You can't go but don't worry, it'll be better soon," she said. "Can you lift your head yet?"

David had tried to sit up all day, but the pain was too intense.

"No, it hurts too much."

"We'll see how you're doing tomorrow," she said. "Just be quiet until then, and if it doesn't get better, I'll take you to see Dr. Steenson when Domko's not around."

After staying in bed for a few more days, David was gradually able to sit up and walk around, as long as he held his head in his hands. He came downstairs and noticed how suspiciously Domko was watching him. David decided it would be best to go to school. Dennis helped him put on his boots and coat, and David followed his siblings down the road. He walked delicately, trying not to pound his feet on the ground.

"How come you're walkin' so stupid?" Rosie asked.

"Yeah," Eunice giggled, "you're walkin' like Dennis."

"Shuddup," Dennis said, punching his sister's arm.

"I gotta walk like this 'cause my neck hurts so much," David winced. "I gotta carry my head."

"If we put a metal box on your head it would look like you're carryin' your lunch," Rosie quipped.

The rest of the children laughed, including David who grimaced from the pain. "Yeah, but ol' Satan never let us have a lunch this heavy."

David continued to support his head with his hands until the middle of March. Finally, Domko agreed that since he was incapable of working, he should see a doctor, but he would not drive them to the clinic.

Caroline did not want the neighbors to know about the accident for fear they would tell the social worker, so she contacted her former brother-in-law, Herman Pischke. Herman drove Caroline and David to Grahamdale.

Dr. Steenson examined David, recommending he see a chiropractor.

"A what?" David asked. "He's not gonna give me a needle is he?"

Dr. Steenson chuckled. "No, he'll just adjust your neck back in place. It won't hurt too much."

Steenson opened the door and called Caroline in. She looked worried when she sat down, and he closed the door behind her.

"If you don't do something soon, this boy could end up crippled for life," he said. "David needs to see a chiropractor. Do you know what that is? He has hurt his neck severely, and I believe it's the only way it can be fixed. The procedure is relatively new out here, but quite common in the city. He'll have to go to Winnipeg."

Caroline nodded. Dr. Steenson led them out of the office then instructed his receptionist to make an appointment with the chiropractor.

Caroline told Herman what the doctor had said, and he offered to take them to Winnipeg the following week. David was looking forward to his first trip to the city.

The chiropractor was astonished by the condition of David's neck. He massaged the gnarled lump that had formed at the base of his head.

"It's a miracle that you're still walking," he said as he explained why David's neck had been so swollen.

"That's what Doc S-steenson told me," David stammered.

"You've fractured your neck. Most injuries this serious, leave young men like yourself crippled. You're very fortunate."

David nodded then sat absolutely still as the chiropractor manipulated his spine then once again massaged his neck. It was an odd sensation since it hurt but felt good at the same time.

The chiropractor called Caroline into the room and chastised her for not bringing him in sooner.

Karen Emilson

She nodded but said nothing.

The well-dressed doctor looked at the mother and son and shook his head. It was obvious that poverty was the reason David wasn't brought in sooner. The chiropractor wrote a quick note on David's chart and passed it on to the receptionist.

As they left the office, the man gave David a brief pat on the shoulder. "I expect to see you back in a week," he said.

Caroline paid the fee and was relieved to discover it was a nominal amount. As they left the office, David complained that his neck was still sore. He walked behind his mother and Herman along Winnipeg's busy Portage Avenue, still supporting his head with his hands. Amazed, he looked up at all the tall buildings and was surprised by the number of cars on the street. He was anxious to tell Dennis all about Winnipeg. He liked the chiropractor and looked forward to returning the following week.

Within a few days, his neck began to feel better and soon he was able to do light chores. The headaches started to subside, so Domko would not allow him to go to the second appointment. David still "carried his head" on occasion, especially if he had to run or do anything that jolted his spine.

The older Raymond got, the more of a pest he became. The chubby, dark-skinned, whining three-year-old was the image of his father. The twins, now twelve years old, had a difficult time being nice to a youngster who enjoyed getting them into trouble.

In his father's eyes, little "Raymie" could do no wrong. The child sensed how favored he was and had become quite spoiled as a result.

He followed the twins and spied on them regularly. The older boys soon realized this and that Raymond was reporting their activities to his father. After a few beatings for eating when they weren't supposed to, the twins began avoiding Raymond.

"Do you see how he watches us?" Dennis said one day.

"Yeah, I wish he'd leave us alone."

Disgusted, Dennis looked at the little boy and made a face. "Shoo!"

"Nooooo," Raymond whined. "Raymie wants to come."

The twins walked to the barn carrying milk pails with Raymond close behind.

"He even talks like him," Dennis whispered. "And do you see how black his teeth are?"

"Too much candy," David said as he looked at Raymond who was covered in filth. Dirt stuck to his face, and his hair was grimy and matted.

"He smells like the ol' bastard, too," Dennis laughed as he ran ahead and opened the barn door. David walked in, and Dennis closed the door behind him. "Not you poker, go away," he hollered through the closed door.

Raymond let out a howl and ran back to the house. Dennis was pleased that the name-calling had worked so well. Dennis was also in better spirits since he and David had made the pact to stick together no matter what. It was as if he'd grown up a bit and was determined to find ways to outsmart Domko rather than giving in to him. Thinking of ways to thwart Raymond helped him focus on something other than the bleakness of their lives.

Later that evening, Dennis called Raymond "Poker" again, but this time Domko overheard. He stormed from the front room into the kitchen and smashed Dennis over the head with a broom handle.

"You's not be callink him poker," Domko yelled. He then picked up his crying son and carried him to his bedroom. Raymond emerged a few moments later carrying a chocolate bar, which he waved at the twins.

Dennis stuck out his tongue. David nudged him in the ribs, a signal for him to stop before Raymond started to cry again.

One cold, snowy early April night, just as everyone was preparing for bed, David warmed himself a cup of milk on the stove. He had a head cold and was suffering from the chills that accompanied a fever. Domko was in the front room, and he called Raymond to him.

"Yous be goink to see vat he's be doink," he whispered to Raymond.

The youngster nodded and eagerly went to the kitchen to spy on David, who had just finished pouring milk from a pot on the stove into a mug that sat on the table.

David had just turned his back when suddenly Raymond let out an agonizing scream. David spun around to see Raymond standing stiffly by the table, his face, chest, and arms soaked. He'd reached up to peer into the cup and had spilled the scalding milk on himself.

His screams sent the children running to the door. Eunice and Rosie bolted outside, followed by Dennis. Caroline and Domko ran to the kitchen to find Raymond standing in the middle of the floor pointing at David, who tried briefly to explain what had happened, but ran outside when he saw Domko's anger. His siblings were standing in bare feet about ten yards away.

"Where should we go?" Eunice asked.

They heard Domko screaming as he ran through the house.

"I's be shootink you soneebeech bastards!" he yelled. The children suspected he was getting the rifle from the bedroom, so they turned and ran to the bush. They slowed to a stop as they reached a waist-high snowbank.

A rifle shot echoed in the crisp, clear air and a bullet whizzed overhead. Screaming, they dove over the snow, then crawled into the bush. Domko continued to curse, and another shot whirled by. The children ran in blind panic as far as they could in the darkness. A third bullet came through the trees, as they slid in a heap on the ground.

"Is he coming?" David whispered.

"Shhh," Eunice said. They listened carefully, but all they could hear was their heavy breathing and pounding hearts. Each of them expected Domko to sneak into the bush. Every little sound caused them to twitch in fear.

"He almost got me that time," Dennis whispered.

Eunice started sobbing as she gripped her feet. "My feet are freezing."

"Mine, too," David said.

"Yeah, but not like mine," Eunice argued. "Ever since I froze 'em that time, they've been gettin' cold real easy."

David remembered a frigid January day the year before when he and Eunice had been roughhousing in the bedroom and Domko had flown up the stairs. They had jumped out the window and frozen their feet. Eunice was in terrible pain, and they had begged their mother to protect them if they came back inside. Eunice had screamed all night as the pains shot through her slowly warming feet. The ugly part came when all the skin peeled off, leaving them tender and raw. Of course, Domko had forced her to keep working, so it took her feet months to heal. David didn't want to repeat the frozen feet episode.

"Yeah," he whispered. "We better get to the barn."

"What if he shoots us when we go by?" Eunice asked.

"He won't," David said.

"He might," Dennis added. "Momma says he's gonna kill us all someday."

David interrupted. "How are we gonna get away if you keep talkin' about dyin' all the time?"

Embarrassed, Dennis looked at Eunice's feet. He couldn't help but talk stupid when he was nervous.

"Shhh," Eunice said again.

They listened carefully to the sound of the house door slamming. A few moments later Domko's car started and bumped out of the driveway. It turned south on the road, its lights shining into the bush. The children ducked low, so that they wouldn't be seen, then stood up once the car sped by.

"Where do you think they went?" David asked.

"Probably to the doctor," Eunice said. "I think Raymond was burned pretty bad."

"Did Momma go along?" Dennis asked.

"I think so," Eunice replied.

The children ran to the barn and found themselves a place to sleep in the loft. They expected that when Domko returned he would be calmer. They gambled that he wouldn't check the barn, and they prayed that if he did, they wouldn't be the one he caught.

Domko and Caroline arrived home with Raymond later that night. The doctor had advised them that Raymond would have no permanent scarring. For the next few days, the children avoided Domko, hoping he'd forget the incident. Within a week, Raymond was back to his usual annoying self.

Domko and the twins went to an auction sale in Moosehorn later that spring. While the boys were shy about being seen in public, they were curious about the world outside the farm. They didn't want to run away from strangers anymore, and Norman's comment that they were "bushed" made them want to prove otherwise.

Unfortunately, their reputation had preceded them.

"You have to watch those Pischke twins because they're thieves," a man said as he looked at the items for sale. His companion nodded, not realizing that David could hear them. The comment humiliated David who turned away, hoping they couldn't see his embarrassment.

Later that afternoon when they were back shoveling manure out of the barn, David told Dennis what he'd heard.

"Bein' called a thief is worse than bein' called bushed," David said.

"Yeah," Dennis agreed. "If we are such thieves then how come nobody sent us to jail yet?"

David thought for a moment. His brother had raised an interesting point. Thieves did go to jail. So did people who robbed banks and burned down buildings. The thought of going to jail didn't sound as bad as living with Domko another summer.

The following morning the boys ran down their usual path to school. The snow was all gone, and leaves were beginning to bud on the trees. David pushed his wheelbarrow wheel, affectionately named the "wee-wee," as Dennis ran behind. Suddenly David was knocked slightly off balance when the wheel passed over a bump that he hadn't remembered on the path. Then Dennis let out a scream.

David turned to see Dennis holding his right foot.

"I stepped on somethin'," Dennis winced. "It was real sharp and poked through my foot."

David looked at his brother then at a small mound on the path. He thought it must be a rock that had worked its way to the surface as the frost came out of the ground.

"Hey Dennis, look," he said pointing to the ground. "There's something here."

They knelt beside the small mound and brushed back the leaves and dirt. What at first looked like a stick turned out to be a spike poking straight out of the ground. It took a few moments for them to realize what they had found. Domko had sabotaged their path. David jumped up and grabbing his wee-wee ran toward the church. Dennis ran as fast as he could behind. They expected him to jump out from behind every log and tree along the way. They made it safely to the church, then stopped to catch their breath.

"He did it I just know it," Dennis said as he rubbed his bleeding foot.

"Yeah, 'cause we've walked on that path a thousand times, and it wasn't there before."

"We better go on the road the rest of the way in case he's put some more on the path," David said, leading the way through the churchyard. "And don't you limp or nothin' when we get home. We don't want him to know you stepped on it."

Dennis nodded. Domko was easily discouraged when his plans to hurt them were unsuccessful.

Mrs. Collier reviewed homework with pupils in each grade. The twins had worked late in the barn the night before and hadn't had time to complete their assignments. A few of the older students giggled while they stammered and stuttered as they tried to explain.

"W-we didn't do it," David finally blurted out.

Mrs. Collier looked at them with exasperation, for what must have been the hundredth time. She was annoyed with these boys who were either absent, late or otherwise ill-prepared for class.

"Sit down," she muttered, then called on the next grade.

David's face flushed. He was tired of having to apologize or explain situations he and Dennis were forced into by Domko. For a split second, he felt as if he were in Norman's body. He now understood his older brother's feelings and felt an urgency building in his gut. He was tired of being pushed around and humiliated.

That weekend the twins went on a rampage as only two, twelve-year-olds could. They hid in the ditch and threw rocks at passing cars. They took their dad's rifle and shot at planes passing overhead. David climbed in the

Where Children Run

church window, followed closely by Dennis, then they vandalized the interior, knocking down objects and ripping pages out of the Bible. They broke a few windows then left, chuckling about the damage they'd done.

They finished their weekend spree by breaking into the school.

"Hey Davey, it feels funny bein' in here on a Sunday, don't it?"

David nodded. "Yeah, it's different when there's nobody around."

Dennis picked up a piece of chalk and began drawing insulting pictures on the blackboard. David knocked all the items off the teacher's desk and emptied drawers on the floor. Together, they threw all the books from the library shelves, kicking them across the floor.

They turned over the desks of kids who teased them. Kicking a few books into a pile, David told Dennis to wait outside. Dennis laughed as he pushed over another desk, then went to the cloakroom.

Reaching up to the shelf above the wood stove, David took down a box of matches. He examined one long wooden stick for a minute, then struck it on the edge of the box. A small voice inside his head told him to drop it on the books on the floor.

He watched as the match burned slowly toward his thumb and forefinger. Resisting the temptation, he blew it out. Throwing the box against the wall, he turned and ran out the door.

He grinned at Dennis as they strutted down the road, defiantly hoping that someone would come along. They didn't care if they were caught, not by the teacher, the neighbors or the police. Everyone thought they were bad anyway - so what difference did it make?

They were slightly disappointed when they arrived home. Nobody seemed to care or even know about the things they'd done. As they went upstairs to their bedroom, Dennis tried to re-create the excitement about the damage they'd caused. David played along, daring anyone to try and prove them guilty.

David quietly hoped that the police would come the next day and take them both away to jail. He was a little bit afraid but knew it was their only opportunity to escape the farm.

He thought about the odd looks people had given them that day as they threw rocks. Guilt washed over him as he remembered emptying the teacher's desk onto the floor. He thought of the broken windows in the old church and how that building had never been anything but a friend to them. He knew what they had done that day was wrong. He also knew that the hollow, empty feeling in the pit of his stomach meant it was something he'd never do again.

Halfheartedly hoping the police would be waiting for them, the twins went to school the next day. The entire school room was unusually quiet as Mrs. Collier, and the older students cleaned up the mess. Nobody knew for sure who had committed the crime, but more than a few glances flew at David and Dennis.

When classes finally began an hour later, Mrs. Collier stood at the front of the room and stared at the twins.

I'm getting too old for this, she thought. No doubt the brothers were also the culprits who had dug a deep hole in front of the teacher's cottage outhouse in January. It was the same hole she'd fallen into in the middle of the night.

The Twins avoided her gaze, and their guilt-ridden expressions told her all she needed to know.

The little beggars just don't know any better, she thought as she looked at their manure covered clothing and dirty, bare feet. *In all the years I've taught, I've never seen anything like it. These poor, disadvantaged souls have given me more stories than I care to repeat.*

OFF TO WINNIPEG

Twice a year the twins were given a haircut. This was a frightening experience as Domko ordered them, one at a time, to sit on a chair outside. With a long pair of shears, he snipped their overgrown locks.

The boys sat very still as the scissors clipped close to their ears and throat. Domko seemed to like the job and especially enjoyed the fact that he wasn't particularly good at it.

One afternoon in May he finished cutting Dennis' hair, then stood back and laughed at the sight of him. He was ushered off the chair, and it was David's turn. David dared not say a word for fear that Domko might get angry and purposely slice his neck. He watched as chunks of wavy blonde hair fell to the ground.

"No more hobos," Domko proudly said when he finished.

The Twins waited until he went back into the house before examining each other's haircut.

"What do you think we look like?" Dennis asked.

"I dunno," David said running his fingers through the short, stubbly cut. "But I sure hope I don't look like you."

Domko had promised Caroline that this would be the year he would take her and the children to an annual gathering of Jehovah's Witnesses. This year it would be held at the Winnipeg Arena. Caroline had wanted to attend for years. When the July weekend approached, she was mildly surprised and delighted that he kept his word.

The car was loaded with food and bedding the night before they left for Winnipeg. Early the next morning, everyone in the family except Eunice piled in the vehicle for the trip. Eunice offered to stay home and do the chores.

The twins were excited about going to the city, and Dennis listened wide-eyed as David told him what an exciting place it was.

"There's cars everywhere," he whispered, as Domko sped along the gravel highway. "And there's lights all over the place."

Dennis was anxious to get there and was disappointed when they had to stop for a while in Lundar, a large town about fifty miles south of Moosehorn on Highway No. 6.

They were back on the road by early afternoon, and the children listened to their mother complain about Domko's driving. She told him to slow down and drive straight, but he continued to waver over the center line and then too far onto the shoulder. He became more agitated the further south he drove, and his erratic driving attracted the RCMP who pulled up behind and motioned for him to pull over to the side of the road.

He swore and began to sweat as the officer approached. The policeman asked where they were going and to see a driver's license. Domko pulled the paper out of his wallet and handed it to the officer who examined it as he walked around the car on a quick inspection. He returned, gave Domko his license and warned him about traveling too fast.

Domko nodded sheepishly.

"A stone has knocked out one of your headlights," the policeman said. "You'd better get that fixed. It will be dark before you get to Winnipeg."

Domko cursed under his breath after the officer left. He waited on the side of the road until the cruiser was out of sight before continuing. He didn't want another encounter with the police, so he stopped at the next town to have the headlight fixed.

Embarrassed, the twins covered their faces when Domko argued with the garage owner about the bill, but the mechanic stood firm, so he grudgingly paid and stomped to the car. He gave the mechanic a middle finger salute as he sped away. Caroline grabbed the dashboard and yelled at him to slow down.

When the car hit a small bump, and the ride became smoother, Domko slammed on the brakes and came to an almost complete halt.

"What's wrong?" Caroline asked.

He was now sweating profusely as his hands gripped the steering wheel. He watched the odometer as the car gradually accelerated to twenty miles an hour.

"First you're driving too fast, now too slow. What's wrong?" Caroline asked again.

"I's not be knowink but-a-some road," he exclaimed. He'd never driven on pavement before, and it felt to him that the car was going to slide into the ditch.

"But you can go faster than this," she said.

He shook his head. "I's be drivink ant yous be seetink."

She looked over her shoulder at the traffic nearing from behind.

"You're going to hold things up. The other drivers will smash into the back of us at this speed."

He growled at her, keeping his eyes fixed on the road. The twins looked out the back window in time to see a car come up behind fast. It slowed down, then pull out to pass.

"Where'd you learn to drive?" the man shouted out his open window, shaking his head as he drove past.

"Fraa," Domko yelled.

The same thing happened with many more vehicles and the boys skulked down in the seat as Domko swore and made obscene gestures.

His wavering back and forth caused him to momentarily lose control of the car each time one wheel slipped onto the shoulder. Swearing, he'd spit out the window so David had to roll his up so that the spit wouldn't blow back and hit him in the face.

At one point, a Ford tractor pulled out to pass Domko. Caroline shook her head, and the boys snickered, resigning themselves to a very long ride.

"Look at Domko's window," Dennis whispered.

David peered over his stepfather's shoulder to see the half open window dripping from poorly aimed nose-blowings.

"Blech," David giggled.

"Vat? You's be seetink and sayink nuthink," Domko hollered as he looked in the mirror. He was too nervous to take his hands off the steering wheel to slap either of them, so they giggled even harder.

It was late at night before they arrived in Winnipeg. The boys estimated it took them nearly eight hours to travel the ninety-minute trip from St. Laurent to the city. Caroline was vibrating from a bad case of nerves by the time they arrived, knowing they still had to travel downtown. Her father had moved to Winnipeg a few years earlier, and they planned to stay at his house.

Domko followed Oak Point road into the city. As he drove slowly along and the city emerged the street became congested. Fortunately, it was late, and there wasn't a lot of traffic on the road, but even a little was too much for him.

"Look at all the lights, see how beautiful they are?" David whispered as he and Dennis craned their necks out Dennis' open window. "See Denny, I told you. And see all the cars and houses. They got lots of great stuff here in Winnipeg."

Dennis nodded as he absorbed the activity around him, his stomach churning with excitement.

Domko made a left-hand turn from a right-hand lane as he neared the city's downtown area. He cut off more than one vehicle and continued to drive so slow that honking from the other motorists sent him into a rage. He turned and found himself alone on the street. He drove for two blocks when suddenly a steady stream of cars came straight toward him. The cars veered around Domko's vehicle, and one car slowed long enough for the driver to yell: "You're on a one-way street!"

Domko was stunned. "But she's be goink but-a-some way," he yelled back.

The man shook his head and kept driving.

"I's be goink, but they's crazy bastards be comink," he said to Caroline.

She explained what the man had meant by "one-way," and Domko swore, cursing whoever had designed Winnipeg streets. Suddenly, he turned abruptly to the left and drove over the boulevard and into the traffic going in the opposite direction.

"Stop here," Caroline exclaimed, pointing to a service station. Domko cut off another car, then drove over the sidewalk into the station parking lot. They sat quietly for a moment then Caroline said it would be best if he didn't drive in Winnipeg anymore. She got out of the car and went to the public telephone. She returned to say that Walter would be there soon.

The twins were so excited that they had a difficult time falling asleep on the makeshift beds on the floor of Grandpa Kolodka's front room. The lights and traffic noise kept them awake most of the night.

The next morning, they rose early, and Walter arrived to take them to the meeting. At first, they were quite excited until they noticed the throngs of well-dressed people in the crowded Winnipeg Arena.

David felt humiliated when people glanced at them then veered away. Dennis became suddenly aware of his gangly limbs and clothes that were two sizes too small. He cringed with adolescent embarrassment at the sight of his unsophisticated mother and crude stepfather. Domko carried a flour sack of food over his shoulder while Caroline held Raymond, who shrieked so loud, it echoed down the corridor. His siblings were no better—timid Rosie shrunk from the crowd while Kathy marched along blindly, chatting to no one in particular.

David was the only family member who was not an embarrassment to Dennis, even though he was still recovering from the bad haircut. Dennis looked at the ground in shame as he avoided the gaze of people around him. Their expressions weren't of sympathy nor concern for the bedraggled family. He wondered what had happened to the gentle, loving people that the Bible and Watchtower publication spoke of so often? These people looked at them with disdain, not kindness.

Caroline led the family to a corner near a concession stand where the family set up a makeshift camp while most other people at the gathering filed into the arena auditorium. The family listened to lessons that were broadcast over the loudspeaker. Mostly, the man on the other end talked about how to go door to door, saying that Witnesses should be meek when approaching difficult people. They listened to sermons on how husbands and wives should love each other. They were all encouraged to send money for missionary work.

Caroline and Domko went into the arena to listen for a while, taking Raymond and Kathy along. Occasionally, loud applause and cheers would boom through the building causing the twins to cover their ears. They wandered with Rosie along the cement corridors, returning during the lunch break when the corridors filled with people. While most of the meeting delegates purchased food at the concessions or opened neatly packed lunches, Caroline knelt on the ground and cut slices from a cooked pork hock. The slices were slapped between crookedly sliced bread. Domko scowled as he watched the twins each take a sandwich and disappear silently behind a post to eat.

"Did you see them kids?" Dennis asked, his voice thick with envy. "They got store-boughten hot dogs and pop."

"Shhh," David warned as he looked over his shoulder. "He'll hear you, and then you'll get it. Don't say nothin' or he'll think you're jealous. And remember he hasn't beat anybody for a few days and will be lookin' for an excuse."

Dennis looked at Domko who watched them with distrust. The boys sat quietly watching people stroll by until the meeting resumed. When Domko took Raymond for a walk outside, they were finally able to relax. They edged their way over to a concession stand where a bright, bubbling soft drink machine caught Dennis' attention. "Look," he said.

The machine was divided into two glass sections with a dark pink liquid bubbling on one side and orange on the other. The drinks looked cold and delicious. They stood at the counter and stared longingly at the machine.

"I want to taste it," Dennis said.

David agreed, licking his lips.

The twins watched as people approached and bought drinks for themselves and their children. They hoped that one of the drinks would be abandoned, but none were. They walked around the corridor for a while then back to their mother who was cleaning up from lunch.

"Go get some milk for Raymie," she said, handing them twenty cents and pointing to the concession stand at the end of the hall.

The boys approached the young man in the concession and after a few moments of stammering were told that sales weren't allowed during the meeting. He advised them to return at 2:00 p.m.

"Oh, no," David said as they walked back to their mother. "Ma, they won't sell us nothin' until two o'clock."

"But Raymond needs milk now. Are you sure?" she asked.

"We asked, but he won't sell it to us."

Caroline frowned. When Domko returned, he shot an angry glance at the boys.

"I's be gettink it some," he said.

"What time is it?" Dennis asked.

"I dunno. What if he sells it to him? He'll think we were playing a trick."

The boys crept to the concession stand and hid behind a pole to watch. Just then a loud roar of applause rang over the loudspeaker.

"And there is so much love in the air this afternoon . . ." the male voice boomed.

The boys watched as Domko began talking to the vendor. The young man shook his head no, then pointed to the clock.

"Stand up and greet the neighbors around you . . ."

The twins could see Domko's head shaking and his lips moving. The vendor shook his head again. Domko stamped his foot, then strode out of sight for a moment before re-appearing in the concession. The young man retreated as Domko backed him against the wall. He grabbed the fellow by the front of his shirt and lifted him off the ground.

"With all the love that radiates through the room today, I say to you what an uplifting experience this is!" the voice boomed from the arena, followed by another chorus of applause.

Domko dropped the vendor, then strode to the cooler, opened it and took out a carton of milk. The young man helplessly watched as Domko screamed a few insults then strode back down the hall.

The boys snickered to themselves. It was a relief to see Domko being nasty to someone other than them.

"That was some uplifting experience, eh Davey?" Dennis laughed.

They turned and ran in the opposite direction and soon found themselves outside in the parking lot. They walked between the many cars, trying to guess what sort of job a man needed to afford such luxurious vehicles.

"Look at this one," David called. "It's brand new."

They walked through the parking lot, stepping out of the way as cars entered and left. Bored, they began running after cars that drove by. More than a few drivers looked in their rear view mirrors to see the boys chasing them like dogs. The twins did this until somebody reported them to security personnel. They were told to stop, so they went back inside, and their mother sent them into the arena to listen to the speaker.

That night the twins were billeted by the conference committee to a stranger's house. The people were expecting more affluent visitors and were openly offended that they had to serve their elegantly prepared meal to the twins. As the boys ate happily, the phone rang.

"All of our plans are ruined now," the woman said to her caller as she stood along the kitchen wall with her back to the twins. She didn't even try to hide the disappointment in her voice. "We've got two boys here from some place in the sticks called Moosehorn so we can't come now." She listened for a moment, then continued: "Yes, I thought of that but we just can't." Pause. "Yes, I'm sure." Pause. "Trust me about this," she whispered, winding the cord around her waist as she turned the corner. "You'd have to see it to believe it."

The boys pretended they didn't hear the woman, but as they finished the meal, their faces burned with humiliation. The husband sat coolly at the end of the table asking a few questions and impatiently waited as David stammered his reply. Of course, the man made him terribly nervous which didn't help matters.

The woman hung up the phone. She rolled her eyes.

"Well, we're staying home," she said. "And I really wanted to go, too."

David sat for a moment, then summoned the courage to speak.

"D-don't s-stay 'cause of us," he said. "Me and Denny are g-good at bein' by ourselves."

The adults looked at them.

"No, it's fine," the woman said as she stood to clear the table. Then under her breath: "We want things to be here when we get back."

The next morning the boys went outside to wait for their ride. Walter drove up just before 10:00 a.m. and gave them a vigorous wave. They climbed in the front seat and were excited because this was their first opportunity to speak to him alone.

Walter lived in Winnipeg and worked as a pressman at Union Carbide. He had only visited the farm a few times since moving to the city. He sometimes came if their mother needed help or if Domko wanted to borrow money. Domko still owed him $150 for a bull he bought the spring before.

"G-guess where we're going?" Walter smiled.

"I dunno, where?" David said.

"To the zoo."

The twins cheered since they'd never been to a zoo before.

"Yeah, we're meeting Ma and Domko there," Walter said.

They stopped cheering. "Can't we just go with you?" David asked.

Walter worried that the boys weren't getting along any better than he had. "How are things now? Is he treating you guys good?" he asked.

"No, he works us all the time," David said.

"And he starves us," Dennis added.

Walter looked at the twins. They'd grown a lot.

"Well, you boys talk better now," he said. "Nobody ever understood what you said before. What was that strange language anyway?"

David blurted out a few of their words and Dennis answered back.

Walter shook his head.

"So, whaddya think?" David asked.

"What?"

"What we just said."

"I dunno. I can't understand you."

"Just say yes."

"I'm not gonna say yes to something that I can't understand."

"Please," David begged.

"Okay, then, yes."

The boys cheered.

"What did I agree to?"

"You'll see."

Domko, Caroline, and the other kids were waiting in the zoo parking lot. Domko was pleased to discover that admission to the zoo was free and herded the family in. Excited, the children scattered in all directions. The twins pointed and loudly yelled as they ran between exhibits, enthralled with the monkeys, bears and exotic animals. They sat for a long time in front of the rocky pit where the bears lived. They also watched the monkeys playing in their cages, and after examining them for quite some time, both came to the same conclusion.

"Eunice don't look like no monkey," Dennis said. "Why does he call her that?"

David shook his head. "I dunno. Maybe 'cause she runs slippery."

Walter bought each of them pop and an ice cream cone near the end of the day. As the boys licked the ice cream, they agreed that this was the best day they'd ever experienced.

As the family congregated near the exit, David and Dennis began speaking in the secret language so that Domko couldn't understand them.

"You ask him," Dennis said.

"No, you ask him."

"I can't. You do it 'cause I'm too scared."

David nodded. "As soon as ol' Squeezer ain't lookin'."

Domko told everyone to wait while he went to the restroom and Caroline took the three youngest children in to use the toilet before starting out on the long drive back to Moosehorn.

The boys stood on either side of Walter, looking up at him.

"Hey Walter," David began. "So are we ready to go?"

"Yep, I'm ready."

"Us, too," he said. Then he grabbed Walter's arm and began pulling him towards his car. "We're comin' home with you."

"What?"

"We don't wanna go back to the farm," David said, looking over his shoulder to the men's restroom then back again. "We wanna live with you here in Winnipeg." David equated Winnipeg with heaven, and his tongue wrapped lovingly around the word as he said it.

Walter was stunned. "You guys can't live with me; you're too little. Besides, I only have one room. Where would you sleep?"

"It don't matter," Dennis said. "We'll sleep anywhere. On the floor or in the porch."

"Or in your car," David pleaded. "Do you got a garage? We could stay in there and make it a good spot to live. We've been thinkin' 'bout this. We could get jobs and everything, so we won't even cost you no money."

Overwhelmed, Walter took a few steps back and held up his hands.

"Hold on," he said. "I don't got room for you guys, and besides, Ma and Domko would never let you live with me. They need you on the farm."

David looked at the restroom. "We could go now before they get back," he said, the urgency building in his voice. "C'mon, Walter."

"They'd just come get you and then beat the hell out of us," Walter said.

"Yeah, but you ran away. You're lucky, 'cause we don't got no place to go."

Walter began to soften, just as Domko came out of the restroom. Instinctively, the twins started talking in the secret language, but of course, Walter couldn't understand what they said. They could tell by the look on his face that he felt sorry for them and wanted to help. The sight of Domko approaching with their mother just a few feet behind, caused them to tremble. If he guessed what they'd been talking about, he'd beat them on the spot.

Everyone climbed into Walter's car since he was going to drive them out to the highway where a friend of Walter's would be waiting with Domko's car. The boys sat in the back and watched him carefully. They could tell he was thinking about what they'd said.

When they reached the highway, Walter glanced at the twins, then looked away. He wanted to confront Domko about how he treated the children and also to ask for the money he owed him, but was afraid. He said goodbye to everyone as his friend climbed in beside him, then waved and drove off.

The twins felt as if they'd stepped from paradise into hell. The stark reality that they'd have to leave Winnipeg and return to the farm caused them to begin weeping quietly. They sat in the back seat and daydreamed about how wonderful it would be to live in Winnipeg. No one was looking forward to the slow drive home.

They arrived back at the farm as the sun was rising the following morning. Eunice had done a good job keeping up with the chores, but within a few hours, they were back to their usual schedule.

In mid-July, the health nurse visited the family to discuss education options for Kathy. At six years old she was ready to start school in the fall. Mrs. Burnett brought information about a school in Brantford, Ontario, which had special programs for blind children.

The twins returned home from school to find Domko and their mother in deep conversation with Mrs. Burnett.

"If she's going to manage in the world, she'll need a proper education," Mrs. Burnett said. "They will teach her how to take care of herself and to read Braille."

"But she's so young," Caroline said.

"I know, but the sooner she learns, the better it will be. If you wait too long, she may become stubborn and refuse to learn. Children her age are like sponges - they are eager to try new things."

Caroline glanced at Kathy who sat on the chair listening. She wasn't able to fully comprehend what attending school in Brantford would mean.

Where Children Run

"And there would be a cost associated with this," Margaret Burnett warned. "This type of schooling is not cheap, but you have to remember that her future depends on it. Being blind means her life will be different from all the other children. It will be difficult for her to marry and she will likely never have a job or be able to travel on her own. At least if she learns to read with her hands, it will give her some enjoyment in life."

Caroline nodded. "We'll think about it, and let you know."

"If you decide you want to do this, I can help make the arrangements."

"Thank you."

Domko nodded. He always wanted the best for his children and didn't want to deny Kathy any opportunities. He also felt very guilty about injuring her when she was a baby. He told Caroline this many times, but never admitted what he'd done to others.

Margaret quickly assessed the family's situation before she left. It appeared that Caroline and Domko were no longer fighting and that the children were adequately cared for. While they were still awfully thin, there had been no more reports to the police about Domko.

Stepping outside, she asked Dennis if everything was all right at home.

"Yes, ma'am," he said, his eyes brightening. "We was in Winnipeg and we went to the zoo and saw the animals and Walter bought us pop and ice cream."

Margaret smiled. It was nice to see the twins happy about something. She was satisfied that things had improved and while she didn't believe that men like Domko changed, she wanted to give him the benefit of the doubt.

She made a mental note to review the family's file with the new social worker who had recently been hired to cover the area. She would be unfamiliar with the family and would need some background information in case the situation took a turn for the worse.

Caroline was outside one afternoon when Jim Deighton came for a visit. He had been checking the hay in one of his fields and when he saw her, decided it was time they talked about Ruby's departure. He was embarrassed about the rumors that were circulating and told Caroline his side of the story while they stood in the front yard.

"How's Domko doing anyway?" he asked.

"He's fine," she said brightly. "Things have gotten better since the kids stopped running to the neighbors."

Jim flinched. He knew this was a sore spot with her.

"Well, I'm glad to hear it," he said, although the words didn't sound as sincere as he'd hoped.

They smiled at one another, and Jim got back on his tractor and drove home. Caroline went into the house, slightly buoyed by the visit. Jim always had a way of making her feel like she was worthy. She opened the door to find Domko standing by the window.

"Yous be beechin' around again," he said.

"What?" she said, momentarily flattered by his jealousy. That quickly dissipated when she saw the look of utter hatred in his eyes.

"Me and Jim? What are you talking about? I haven't seen him for a year. We were talking about Ruby and doing a little gossiping."

"Talkink," he roared. "Yous be lazy beech talkink all day. I's be but-a-some seek from work and yous be runnink arount."

"What do you mean you're sick?" He'd been complaining of throbbing headaches since returning from Winnipeg, but he complained so much about even the tiniest of ailments, that she no longer took him seriously.

He turned and went to the table. "I's be readink it," he said lifting her Bible from the table. "You's be goink to heaven? Fraa, murdering beech. She's be goink to heaven?"

"What?" she said.

He strode to the cook stove, still carrying the Bible.

"No," she screamed, grabbing his arm. Holding her back with one arm as she reached across him to rescue the book, he flipped open the firebox door and tossed the Bible on top of a burning log.

"Dat's vere yous be goink."

"Boleslaw, you've got no right," she screamed. "Burning the Bible is a sin, you can go to hell for that."

"I's not be goink to hell, you's be."

"Well, anything is better than being here with you!"

"You's be tryink to kill me like some Bill," he screamed.

She pushed past him and pulled the Bible out of the stove. The cover and a few of the pages were on fire. She pounded the book until the fire was out.

Friends came to visit that night, and in the middle of their conversation, Domko suddenly passed out, his head landing on the table with a thud. The children jumped down from their chairs and ran into the front room. They watched as the visitors and their mother tried desperately to revive Domko. A few minutes later, he woke up as if nothing had happened.

They insisted that he be taken to see the doctor. When he tried to stand, they discovered that he'd lost all feeling on his right-hand side. They loaded him into the car and Caroline sped to the hospital in Ashern.

As they drove down the highway, Domko complained in a child-like voice about the pain in his head. Caroline dreaded the thought of having to care for not only six children, but an invalid husband as well.

They arrived at the hospital, and two nurses rushed to help Domko inside. Dr. Steenson was called, and within a few minutes, he was examined. Domko complained that his illness was Caroline's fault. She stood quietly listening, eyes filled with tears. The doctor calmed Domko, then recommended that he be taken by ambulance to a Winnipeg hospital. She nodded, and within the hour they were on their way south.

Caroline arrived home late the next day to report that Domko had been taken to Winnipeg for x-rays and observation, then sent back to Ashern. The x-rays revealed a blood clot in his head had become dislodged. It was not a stroke as they had originally thought, but he needed to stay in the hospital for a few more days.

EXPANDING HORIZONS

Domko made a full recovery and returned home a few days later. He believed that the blood clot was caused by anger and was frightened that he might have another seizure. He made an effort to control his temper, saying that Caroline and the children were trying to make him angry on purpose.

"You's be keelink me like but-a-some Bill," he said.

Caroline tried to explain that she hadn't killed Bill and that they weren't plotting against him, but her words fell on deaf ears. Eventually, she began ignoring him.

August came, and the twins spent long hours in the hay field cutting and raking hay. Eunice and Rosie helped on stacking and hauling days. One morning while David was cutting and Dennis was raking, Eunice stayed in the house to help her mother.

Domko had been belittling Caroline so much that she refused to get up that morning. Eunice decided to wash the floor to make her mother feel better. The children needed her to be strong since she was their only defense against Domko and his erratic behavior.

A dirty floor makes the whole house look bad, Eunice thought. *I'll wash this up and surprise Ma with how much better it will look.*

"Kathy, you, Rosie and Raymond go outside to play," Eunice ordered, guiding the children out the door. She wasn't concerned that Kathy and Raymond would wander off since she could hear Domko cutting grass near the house and surely he would see them.

Eunice softly hummed as she swept the floor then filled a pail with soap and warm water from the cook stove. She began scrubbing the worn linoleum on hands and knees, starting near the kitchen cupboards then worked her way toward the table. The area around Domko's chair was by far the dirtiest because he never removed his boots when he came inside. She decided to do that spot last. When she had almost finished the floor and was thinking about the next cleaning job to tackle, she heard a scream outside. She ran to the window to see Kathy crying just outside the door. She was holding her finger out to her father who had come to the edge of the house to see what had happened.

Eunice immediately crouched down and began scrubbing the floor hard. Her mind whirled as she wondered what Domko's reaction would be. The door swung open, and he strode inside. As always he was looking for somebody to blame and this time it was Eunice. As he towered over her, he shouted that she should never have sent Kathy outside in the first place. He still carried a scythe in one hand, its sharp, metal blade curved heavily toward the floor. The sight of it caused the blood to drain from Eunice's face. She said nothing as she looked helplessly up at him.

Domko took a few steps forward to stand directly over her.

So this is how it feels to die, she thought, imagining the heavy metal knife slicing through her body, and she understood the utter terror people felt before being murdered. A calm came over her as she stared at him. His arms shook, and his eyes looked confused. She hoped that if he struck her with the blade, she would die instantly.

Everything in his stance indicated that he might lunge and her body tensed, waiting for the fatal blow. Instead, he slowly lowered his arm. Eunice sensed as he stood over her that he knew how he treated the children was wrong but could not stop himself. She was thankful that this time he had.

He grunted at her then stomped out the door.

Eunice relaxed and let out her breath. Closing her eyes, she listened to the sound of her heart pounding. She was still alive.

In that instant, she knew she could no longer tolerate life on the farm unless the situation improved. Domko's behavior was so erratic and violent that she knew he would eventually kill someone. She vowed to make her mother understand before it was too late.

One afternoon in late summer, David fell off the mower seat and almost caught his legs in the blades. He was suffering from heatstroke and afraid he'd faint again, so he tried to drive the team home. Domko saw him and jumping off the tractor, accused David of being lazy and hit him over the head with the large knot in the reins. David hit the ground and fell unconscious. He awoke hours later under the shade of an old oak tree, some distance from where he fell. He must have crawled there but had no memory of it. The shade of the tree helped soothe his sunburned body and was also some comfort to the infected sores on his arms and legs from poison ivy.

Days later, the children went into the bush to find a fencing hammer that they'd lost earlier that spring. Eunice and the twins searched near the place where they had repaired an old strip of barbed wire.

"I think he's gettin' worse," David said as they shuffled along in bare feet, heads bowed, searching the underbrush.

"Worse? I can't imagine it," Dennis said.

"Yeah, he's gettin' worse," Eunice said. "I hear him talkin' to Ma at night. He's complainin' that if Kathy goes to the blind school, he'll only have one kid here matched up against us four. He says it's not fair and we'll get the farm instead of Raymie."

The twins were stunned. They weren't thinking about stealing the farm from anybody. "Well, that's stupid, 'cause I ain't stayin' around here," Dennis said. "How 'bout you Davey?"

"No way, I'm gettin' outta here as soon as I can save up enough and buy a motorcycle like Norman. "Only I'm gonna get one that I can start without runnin' behind it."

They all laughed.

"Well, I'm leaving, too," Eunice said. "Ma's not helping us any when she's lying in bed all the time. Me and her have been fighting a lot lately."

Then she thought for a moment. "Who's her favorite kid?"

Dennis was the first to speak. "Steven."

"Nope, I say, Raymond," David said.

"I say you," Eunice said pointing at David. "She never gives you heck."

"What about Norman?"

"Well, I know it ain't me," Dennis said sadly.

"Me neither," Eunice added.

David thought about his mother and who she seemed to favor. He did get along with her better than Eunice and Dennis, but he never thought of himself as her favorite child.

"Me and Ma get along okay," he said. "She's just stuck that's all. She can't help it 'cause the church says she has to listen to him 'cause he's the head of the house. I'm glad I ain't no girl, 'cause I'm tellin' you right now when I grow up nobody's gonna boss me around."

"Me neither," Dennis said.

"Yeah, well me neither, even if I am a girl," Eunice said.

They continued to search the grass.

"If we're gonna find that hammer, we'd better split up," Eunice said. "Me and David will stay here. Dennis, you go look up ahead."

Dennis nodded. "If I find it, I'll yell back."

The children continued to look in the grass, then Eunice and David sat down for a rest. "How come you haven't left the farm yet?" David asked. "You're fourteen, and lots of kids leave home when they're fourteen."

"They won't let me," she said.

"I hope I'm not still here when I'm fourteen," he said.

"You will be."

"What do you mean?"

"He'll never let you go. Who's gonna do the work?"

"I dunno."

"Not Kathy and Raymond, that's for sure," she said. "How's Dennis doing anyway?"

"You saw him, whaddya think?" he asked.

"He still seems kinda sad to me," she said.

"Yeah," David said. "Sometimes it bugs me when he talks about dyin' and stuff, but he's better."

"He can't help it," she said. "It's worse for him 'cause Domko hates him the most. You gotta keep helping him."

Suddenly, they sensed something was wrong. They stood up and out of the corner of his left eye, David saw movement in the bush. Domko was crouched low, hiding from them. David slapped Eunice's shoulder and pointed at the bush. Her eyes widened, and they took off running down the path along the fence. A hammer flew through the air, just inches over their heads and landed in front of them.

"Fraa, you lazy soneebeech bastards be not workink."

He'd come looking for them and had overheard parts of their conversation and believed once again that they were conspiring against him.

David and Eunice caught up to Dennis who had started walking back toward them. "Run!" Eunice yelled. Dennis stood frozen for a moment, then turned and darted into the bush. They kept going until they were satisfied they were alone.

"That was a close one," Eunice exclaimed.

"What did Satan do?"

"He threw a hammer at us, and it almost took our heads off."

Dennis shuddered. He was thankful Domko hadn't snuck up on him.

The children decided to stay in the bush overnight. They returned the next morning hoping that Domko had cooled off. Eunice tried not to think about Rosie being left alone and hoped that their mother had enough sense to protect her.

One day in late August, Kathy kissed her mother goodbye. Clutching a suitcase of brand new clothing, she climbed into the car with Domko. They were leaving for Winnipeg with friends from the church who had agreed to drive them to the train station so that Kathy could go to the school in Brantford, Ontario. This was a very tough decision for Caroline and Domko, but in the end, they had agreed that sending her away would be the best thing for her.

It was hard for Domko to part with Kathy at the station, and he arrived home later that night in a somber mood. He was also angry that the people who had driven them to Winnipeg had asked him for $15 to cover the cost of gas.

As he went to his room for the night, he complained to Caroline that her friends were "mooney hungry." He fell into a fitful sleep and the next day began behaving very strangely. He was more suspicious and angry than he'd ever been. Caroline and the children avoided him as he paced back and forth, worried about Kathy and the farm. He held Raymond tightly and even mistrusted Caroline where his son was concerned.

Over the next few weeks, he refused to shave and seemed almost to enjoy the stench of his unclean body. Caroline withdrew from everyone as she wondered what was happening to him. She knew that he always became depressed during fall and winter, but it was only early September.

She prayed that he would get better, but nagging thoughts kept entering her mind. She remembered how Dr. Steenson had told her that something was seriously wrong with Domko's mind, but Caroline had refused to believe it. He'd predicted it would get worse if left untreated, but she believed that if she prayed enough, Domko would get better.

Since the blood clot, something had changed in his head. Now, all of the oddities he displayed were magnified. He seemed to be unraveling, and she didn't know what to do. Caroline knew she couldn't go to the church for advice since the blame always shifted from him to her. She felt trapped by his possessiveness and hoped his mood swings would abate. She hated admitting she was wrong and didn't want to face Doctor Steenson again.

The new school year began, and the children were curious to meet their new teacher since Mrs. Collier had retired in June. Although the twins knew she was long past retirement age at sixty-nine years of age, they still felt partly responsible because of their prank the winter before that had sent her into a

Where Children Run

snow-filled hole wearing not much more than a nightgown. They promised themselves that they wouldn't do anything like that to her replacement.

The new teacher, Mrs. Marion Gering, was a tall, dark-haired woman with glasses. At thirty years of age, she had three children and farmed with her husband Roy west of Grahamdale. She was familiar with most people in the area, including the Pischke and Kolodka families.

She had heard rumors that the Pischke children couldn't be controlled and was initially apprehensive about accepting the job at Bayton School. She was pleasantly surprised to find the children polite, helpful and well behaved.

Eunice was now in grade seven. She and her friend Larry Meisner were two of the oldest children at the school. The younger ones liked to call them "Mom & Pop."

Because the twins were regularly attending, they were promoted to grade five and Rosie, who was very smart and seldom absent, was now in grade three.

A couple of months went by, and in late fall Mrs. Gering had the opportunity to meet Domko. He was waiting for the children at the end of the lane when school finished for the day. She introduced herself, pretending she hadn't heard the rumors about him. His crude way of speaking and piercing eyes made her feel uncomfortable. That night while she prepared supper, she told her husband about the encounter.

"Well I spoke to Bob Domko today," she began. "I don't know what you think of him Roy, but I sure don't like him. I think there's something wrong with that man. He's got absolutely no social skills at all."

"Why do you say that?" he asked.

"I don't know. There's just something about him. He grunted at me in a way that made my skin crawl. Now, I know the community is divided over what to think about that family, but I'm siding with those children. You know, I've spent nearly eight weeks with them now, and those twins are just fine. Except for the fact they miss too much school."

"But you know, Roy, I think Domko makes them stay home to work. The only one with perfect attendance is Rosie. She's the youngest one."

"So what do you think is going on?" he said.

"Well, I'm not sure. It's hard to tell because they are such happy-go-lucky kids. They're quite poor, but so are most families in the area. I'm sure the Pischke kids aren't as bad as people think."

Late one afternoon, a family from the church stopped by the house for a short visit. The man was the same one who'd taken Domko and Kathy to

Winnipeg, but he hadn't visited since.

Caroline was always pleased when this family stopped by because they were kind to her. They didn't mind the state of the house or how the children behaved. She invited them in, happy for the company, and called to Domko who was resting in the bedroom. The couple sat down at the table and began making small talk with Caroline. She laughed at a joke the husband told, just as Domko came into the kitchen.

She knew immediately by his expression that something was wrong.

"Yous," he exclaimed pointing to the man.

He turned to Domko and smiled. "Hi Bob, how are you doing?"

"You's be chargink me fifteen dollar. I's be chargink you fifteen dollar for but-a-some coop."

"Pardon?" the man said, bewildered by the comment.

"You's not be comink here no more," he shouted as he went back into his bedroom.

"Boleslaw, what are you talking about?" Caroline said. She could see him pick up his rifle from the top of the bureau and begin searching for bullets.

"You'd better go right now," she said, standing up. "He's got the gun, and he's going to shoot you."

The man and his wife jumped to their feet. "Why? What did we do?"

"Just go," she said.

"Are you going to be all right?" the husband asked but didn't wait for the answer as they ran out the door. Caroline's children followed closely behind then scattered in the bushes.

Domko came out of the bedroom carrying the gun. Caroline tried to stop him, but he pushed his way out the door. He stood cursing in the yard as the visitor's car sped away.

After that, Domko wouldn't drive Caroline to church at Grahamdale or Ashern. Everyone from the church who came to visit were watched with suspicion. Few came, though, since Domko found fault with nearly every single person in the area. He had thrown many people off the farm, telling them never to return. Caroline was so angry that she moved out of the bedroom and slept upstairs with the children.

As another winter set in, the temperatures became frigid, and the snow began to fall. The only respite for the children was school, which they gladly attended now because they were doing better. They noticed that Mrs. Gering took a genuine interest in their well-being.

While Eunice enjoyed the reading period, David and Dennis shone during art class. One afternoon after the lunch recess, Mrs. Gering announced that each student was to draw a picture as an entry in a school art contest. The contest was sponsored by Brooke Bond, a New Brunswick company that made Blue Ribbon tea. She showed the students the location of New Brunswick on the large map that hung on the wall.

Since Mrs. Gering didn't want anyone to be disappointed, she emphasized the fun of entering the contest rather than winning.

David and Dennis looked at each other and smiled. Both boys were anxious to begin and worked hard on their drawings. Over the next few days, pieces of finished artwork gradually appeared on Mrs. Gering's desk. She thanked the students and carefully studied the work, giving each child a fair share of praise.

Some of these children are good little artists, she thought, as she piled the work in a neat stack at the end of her desk. That afternoon during the recess break, Mrs. Gering noticed that two more pictures were added to the pile. She picked them up and saw to her astonishment, that the drawings were excellent. The small signatures on the bottom belonged to Dennis and David.

Studying each one, she couldn't decide which drawing was better. Their work was so much more detailed than their peers that she felt slightly embarrassed for the other students. Dennis had drawn a lovely farm scene that showed farm equipment in detail, and animals along with a farmer who sat high on a tractor while four people worked on the ground below.

David had drawn a picture of a young man sitting at the edge of the bush, by a lake with a dog at his side. It appeared that the young man lived near the lake since he had a little camp set up with a shanty and campfire.

As Mrs. Gering placed all the drawings inside an envelope and carefully sealed the package, she thought it was a shame that the boys would be competing against each other.

Their work is so good I'm certain that one of them will win a prize, she thought.

THE BIRTHDAY PARTY

By the end of January, it appeared that Caroline had given up all hope. The nights were long, and she spent a lot of time upstairs sleeping or hiding with the children.

Dennis was so afraid that he couldn't sleep or eat. It seemed like everywhere he turned, Domko was there, stalking or waiting for him. David helped him escape as often as he could, but mostly just hid in numb shock as his twin received yet another beating.

Most evenings Domko waited in the front room, his chair positioned so that the children had to walk past him to get upstairs. He'd snicker and comment as they skulked to safety. One evening after working late hauling hay, the twins came inside. Freezing rain had pelted them all afternoon, so the felt liners in their boots were soaked. Drenched and shivering, they didn't dare stop by the furnace to warm up but kept their boots on as they snuck upstairs. Once out of his sight, they slipped off their wet clothing and left it on the floor to dry. Climbing into the warm bed beside their mother, Dennis snuggled close to her back. It felt good to have her near, and for the moment he felt safe.

The next morning, they awoke to Domko yelling for the Twins to get to the barn. They'd slept late and were behind schedule. They jumped out of bed, dizzy with hunger, to find their clothes frozen stiff. The hardness scratched against their skin, and the felts were painfully awkward to pull on. Once dressed, they ran downstairs then out the door.

The twins worked in the cold all day with stomachs cramped and intestines turned into knots. Their body functions had slowed almost to a halt. They hadn't had a bowel movement in more than a week and urinated only in the morning and at night.

That evening they waited anxiously for the chance to find something to eat without being caught. When Raymond emerged from his father's bedroom carrying a banana, they watched as he peeled back the skin and began eating it. Raymond was well aware of the twins' hunger and paraded back and forth. When he finished, he tossed the peel onto the floor then laughed as he sauntered to the front room.

The twins lunged for the peel. Dennis got there first, but David quickly wrenched it out of his hands. He picked the remaining knob of the banana off and popped it in his mouth. Dennis nearly burst into tears.

The looks on their faces caused Eunice to start giggling as they began to fight. The noise sent Domko into a rage.

"I's be shootink you some," he screamed.

Eunice saw him go into the bedroom and pick up his gun, so she grabbed Rosie's hand and ran outside. The twins pulled on their boots and sped into the deep snow in the yard. Behind them, Domko was hollering, and then the crack of the rifle sent a bullet overhead.

"C'mon!" David yelled as he cut into the bush with Dennis stepping on his heels. They heard another shot, and the girls began screaming.

"He got Rosie," David groaned as they continued along the snow-packed path. The freezing rain the day before had melted the top layer of snow, and the trees dripped on them as they pushed the branches aside. Eventually, they emerged from the bush and found themselves trudging through knee-deep snow as they made their way toward the beaver dam. They were stiff and exhausted by the time they reached the bank of the frozen lake.

"I can't go no more," Dennis said. "Let's make a fire here."

David reached into his pocket and pulled out a small book of paper matches. They were too wet to strike.

"Maybe we can dry 'em out," Dennis said.

David looked up at the sky. "It's gonna rain again."

Looking out over the dark lake, David could see a row of lights on the other side, about three miles away. He looked back toward the farm and saw nothing but darkness. Raising his eyes to the sky, he saw the silhouette of a full moon shining through light cloud cover. Looking again at the lights, he made the decision for them both.

"C'mon Dennis, we're gonna walk across the beaver dam," he said.

"I can't," Dennis moaned, shaking his head as he sat down on the bank. "I'm tired. Let's just stay here."

David jammed his hands into his pockets and turned his back to the wind. "We're gonna freeze to death."

"I don't care," Dennis said, sitting on the bank. "It's over for us anyhow. Nobody cares 'bout us."

David pushed the truth aside. "There's new people over the beaver dam, and they will help us."

"What if they don't?"

David snorted. "Well we can die then, but I'm sure not gonna die here, not as long as I can see those lights."

David's voice was so full of strength that it gave Dennis hope. He stood up and grabbed his brother's arm. They walked down the lake bank and onto the frozen shore. They stepped onto the ice and Dennis shuddered at the thought of the swirling water that flowed underneath. Fifty feet from shore, they became surrounded by reeds that grew on the lake bottom and stretched up to eight feet above the water.

Dennis looked toward the sky, but the reeds moving with the wind were making him feel dizzy. "Do you know where to go?" he asked.

"Yeah, I'm followin' that light," David said.

Like fleas on a dog's back, the brothers pushed their way through the reeds.

"I can't see nothin'," Dennis said, panicking.

"Me neither," David said, taking a deep breath as they stopped to listen as the wind whistled through the reeds.

"Which way do we go?" Dennis asked.

David strained but felt lost. He looked into the reeds, and miraculously the tall grass parted for him, allowing a tiny glimmer of the light to shine through.

"That way," he said as he began trudging forward.

"How much further?" Dennis asked.

"We're almost there," David said confidently. "Once we get outta these reeds, the house is right there, and the people will let us in. Just think about them givin' us something good to eat and how nice and warm it will be."

Dennis nodded. He thought about days spent at Emma and Ruby's homes and the fun day at the zoo. He remembered stretching out on the pavement in the arena parking lot in Winnipeg and how hot and wonderful it had felt on his arms and legs.

"Just a little bit further, we're almost there," David said, spirits bright.

By the time they crossed the beaver dam, it felt as if they had walked for hours. Their feet, hands, and ears had no feeling, and the same stiffness was beginning to creep into their arms and legs. It began lightly snowing as they climbed the steep edge. They emerged from a small clump of trees to find themselves in a huge hay field. Beyond the field was a thick spruce bluff and beyond that, the light.

Where Children Run

Disappointed, David stared ahead. The light wasn't any closer.

"Where's the farm?" Dennis asked.

"Over there," David pointed.

"That's too far; I can't."

David stared at the light then resigned himself to the bleakness of their situation. They'd never make it through the deep snow in unfamiliar territory to a light that could end up being nothing at all.

"Me neither."

Exhausted, they fell to the ground. Dennis closed his eyes and let himself relax on the frozen ground. He didn't feel cold anymore, and it felt like he was lying on the hot pavement again, and he began dreaming gentle thoughts as he floated in and out of sleep.

When David hit the ground, he landed on a sharp rock which poked into his back similar to the spring on the mattress at home. He closed his eyes and tried to relax, but the rock kept him from falling asleep. Snowflakes fluttered softly on his cheeks, burning as they melted.

In the distance, he could hear a coyote baying at the moon. The call was suddenly answered by series of howls nearby. The closeness of it sharpened his senses, and soon his eyes were open, and he rolled to a sitting position.

Where are they? he thought, as he looked into the blackness. The eerie sound sent a surge of adrenaline through his veins that made his heart pound. It was all he needed to get going again.

"C'mon Dennis," he said, shoving him as he staggered to his feet. "There's coyotes all around."

"I don't care," Dennis mumbled.

"C'mon, get up," David hollered.

"No," Dennis whined, pulling his arms close to his chest. "You go and bring back someone to get me."

David kicked the snow and stomped his foot. He knew in his gut that if he left Dennis now, his brother was going to slip into a deep sleep and die. He looked into the darkness and then gasped.

"Coyotes," he screamed. "They're comin' straight for us,"

Dennis was enjoying the soft dream he'd fallen into and it took a few moments for his mind to work its way back to the frozen field.

"Dennis, they're surroundin' you," David said.

The thought of a pack of frenzied coyotes tearing him apart was enough to make him roll over and stagger to his feet.

"Where?" he asked, frantically.

"Over there!" David hollered, pointing in the direction from where they came. He grabbed Dennis' arm and started running toward the light.

It had taken a few minutes before Dennis realized no coyotes were chasing them, but he welcomed the clarity fear gave him. The light seemed much closer now.

As if reading his thoughts, David glanced over his shoulder.

"We just gotta get through the field and the spruces and then we'll be there," he said, jamming his fists deep in his pockets, squeezing the damp matches in one hand. Once their fear subsided, they started to grow cold again.

"They got electricity, but we don't got electricity," Dennis mumbled.

"Yeah, but we got matches," David said, shaking his head to keep his wits. They stumbled through the field to the edge of the forest.

Confused, Dennis stopped. "Should we make a fire here then?"

"We can't 'cause we need some matches first," David said. "We gotta get some matches."

Grabbing his brother's arm, he pulled him into the dense forest. "This is a good spot, see? We'll come back here once we get some matches and we can hide from everybody."

Dennis nodded and thought for a moment. "Guess what Davey?"

"What?"

"We're over the beaver dam," he said. "It's just like we thought. We never have to go back."

They continued walking, growing sluggish as they went. All David could think about was getting a book of matches, while Dennis kept raving about how much better this forest was than the bush near home.

Finally, they stumbled out of the underbrush and found themselves at the edge of another field. Once in the open, they realized it was snowing hard. The wind whipped their faces and cut through their clothes. David kept his eye on the light, turned a shoulder to the wind and kept going.

"We're almost there," he said.

Too numb to argue, Dennis trudged behind. They walked through another small line of trees, then suddenly found themselves only a few feet from a snow bank.

"What—?" David asked trying hard to focus, rubbing his eyes. The harder he tried, the more abstract it became. The light from the moon cast uneven shadows across a massive wall of snow. "We'll never get over that."

Dennis agreed, looking back at the bush. "Let's go back and sleep."

David focused once more on the huge mound ahead. He'd seen snow piled like this before.

"A road," he said. "We gotta get over it and walk 'til we find a house."

"Huh?" Dennis asked, confused.

"Over there, over the snow. C'mon, let's go."

"No, I'll wait here."

"I won't be able to find you," David said. "You gotta come."

Once they reached the top of the bank, they saw a small farmhouse at the end of a long driveway. A light was shining through the front window, and they could smell smoke from the wood stove.

"We're here," Dennis cried as they slid down the bank.

As they started up the driveway, feelings of doubt crept into his mind. *What if these weren't nice people? What if they called Domko and told him where they were?* David remembered the time Jim told them to be careful where they went in the middle of the night. But his mind was foggy, and he couldn't think straight.

"I'll go and get matches so we can make a fire," he said. "You wait here. If I yell, you run north."

Dennis nodded as he tucked his fists into his armpits.

Slowly, David walked toward the house. Just then the light in the window went out.

His shoulders slumped as he looked back at his brother. He stopped then decided to carry on. The crunching of his boots alerted a medium sized dog that came barking from its doghouse. David extended his hand as he walked by the dog that sniffed him then followed him to the door.

David stood on the stoop for a moment before knocking. He listened for a noise inside, but all was quiet. He unzipped his coat knowing that it was near impossible for an adult to get a good hold on a kid if he could squirm out of his jacket. He took a deep breath, glanced back at Dennis and then knocked on the door.

A few moments later the light came on, and muffled voices gathered behind the door. David was relieved when a woman in her nightdress appeared but gasped when a man came up behind her.

"My goodness," the woman said.

"C-c-can we have s-some matches?" David stammered as he opened his hand to show them the wet, faded matchbook.

"What for?" she asked.

"T-to m-make a fire."

The people were stunned.

"What are you doing outside at night?" the man asked.

"H-he kicked u-us out again."

The woman let out a tiny gasp. She recognized him as one of the Pischke twins. He'd grown since she'd seen him last. They had been neighbors in Ashern, but she hadn't seen Caroline much after she moved back to the farm.

She was shocked by what he wore. He had no toque or mitts and only a thin, spring jacket over what looked like a torn, short-sleeved shirt. His light, cotton pants were too small, and the felt rubbers were not warm enough for winter wear. Somehow he'd gotten wet, and his clothes were frozen stiff. His skin was a ghastly gray, and his eyes were set in dark circles, having lost the bright, inquisitiveness that she remembered. If it weren't for the crazy stutter, she wouldn't have recognized him at all.

"Is there somebody with you?"

David looked back at the road. "D-dennis."

The woman stuck her head outside and saw a shadowy figure standing at the end of the driveway.

"Come in before you freeze," she said. "Tell your brother it's okay."

David stared into the woman's soft brown eyes. She was tall and pretty, and the way her soft German accent twirled around her words was comforting. Her husband seemed gentle as well. He softly agreed with his wife that they should come inside.

Just then, two young heads appeared from behind their father. One was a boy who looked to be a few years older than David while the other was a much younger boy with a bright smile. These people looked familiar, but his mind was still too foggy to think straight. The heat that escaped from the open door felt incredibly good.

"Go call him," the woman coaxed.

David put the soggy matches back in his pocket and called for Dennis. When he got close, David smiled.

"It's okay Denny," he said in their language. "These people are good."

Dennis timidly followed his brother inside. They flinched briefly as the man stepped forward but relaxed once they realized all he planned to do was shut the door behind them. Their cheeks burned from the wave of heat from the wood stove that crackled warmly in the kitchen.

"I'll get you some dry clothes," the woman said as she disappeared into the other room. The husband and boys stood looking at the twins, who stared at the ground as they took off their rubber boots.

"I'm Kenny," the older boy said.

"And I'm Alvin," the little boy said. "Who are you guys?"

"Shhh," their mother said when she returned, carrying an armful of fresh clothes. "Give them a chance to settle in before you start asking too many questions."

She divided up the clothes, fussing, as she wondered out loud what would fit properly. She looked down at their swollen, red feet.

"Where are your socks?" she asked.

"W-we don't got n-none," David said.

They climbed out of their stiff clothes and the woman winced at the sight of their rakish, bruised bodies. She turned away out of politeness as they pulled on the warm underwear, thick pants, and flannel shirts.

"Are you boys hungry?" she asked. They looked at her with such intensity; she knew the answer.

"Well come sit down," she said motioning for them to follow her to the table. "I've got some leftovers you can have."

They skulked to the table and looking out of the corner of their eyes, saw that Kenny and Alvin were watching them closely. They were anxious to hear what brought them to their door in the middle of the night.

"So, how did you boys get here?" the man asked.

The twins ate, and then when David swallowed, he said they walked across the beaver dam.

"Do you mean Pischke Lake?" the man asked.

David nodded.

"You walked all that way, in the dark, by yourselves?"

"Yeah. I kept f-followin' the light and a few times Dennis w-wanted to go to s-sleep, but I wouldn't let him."

"How come you ran away?"

"Ol' Satan got mad and was shootin' at us," Dennis answered.

"Domko?"

They both nodded.

"Shooting?"

"W-we ran in the bush, and the bullets went by our h-head," David said.

Realizing these were people they could trust, the boys began telling more stories as they warmed up. The adults listened in silence as the twins took turns telling them about Domko's violence. Kenny and Alvin were in awe of them.

"And he always comes to get us," David said. "Emma had to hide us, 'cause he came with the gun and said he'd shoot Gus if we went there anymore."

When they had finished eating, Kenny and Alvin were told to take them to the front room.

"What should we do?" the woman asked her husband.

He shook his head. They had heard many stories about Domko but until that day had thought they must be the result of overactive imaginations.

"Should we call Margaret?" she asked, glancing at her watch. It was close to 11:00 p.m.

He nodded. "Someone had better get over to that farm to check on Caroline and the rest of those kids," he said.

She went to the phone and dialed the health nurse's home phone number.

"This is Anna Koch," she said. "It looks as if Domko is up to his old tricks again. We've got the Pischke twins here." Pause. "Just over an hour ago." Pause. "Half-froze. One boy was out of his mind asking for matches. They must have walked four miles across that lake. Leo says it is a miracle that they didn't get lost in the reeds." Pause. "Shot at them." Pause. "Okay, we'll wait."

Anna gave her husband a confident nod. Margaret would be there soon, and she'd know what to do.

The family sat and talked while Alvin brought out his toys. This pleased the twins who pushed the cars along the floor and across the chesterfield. Both had shooting pains in their feet but barely complained as they rubbed their toes. Leo and Anna sat and watched as the twins began to relax and feel comfortable in their surroundings.

An hour after the phone call, a pair of lights shone through the front room window as a car slowly turned in the driveway. Leo stood and looked out.

"Is it Margaret?" Anna whispered.

"I can't tell," he said. "What kind of car does Domko drive?"

Anna turned in time to see terror fill the twins' faces. They jumped up and ran from the front room into the bedroom and in one motion, hit the floor and slid stomach first under the bed. The edge of the quilt swayed for a moment, then stopped. Not another movement or sound came from underneath.

"Is it him?" Kenny asked as his father cautiously went to the kitchen window. Kenny sensed his parents' concern. He envisioned Domko bursting into the house carrying a gun and shooting his parents.

His heart throbbed, and his throat became thick as he wondered what he should do. He wanted to get his father's gun but didn't want to overreact. He thought of the stories and the twins' fear and wondered if overreacting was possible.

Although nobody said anything, little Alvin could sense that something was wrong. His playmates had disappeared under the bed with such urgency that he became frightened by it. He didn't know who this horrible Domko was, but he knew he never wanted to see him face to face. He stood behind Kenny as his parents went to the kitchen door.

Kenny prepared himself for the worst. If it were Domko, he'd sneak around and pick up the gun and load it. Although the thought of a confrontation caused him to shake, he vowed to protect his family. He listened as his father opened the door and began talking to whoever had come. A few moments later Kenny could tell the voices were friendly. He peered around the front room wall to see the health nurse and her driver standing in the kitchen.

"They're in here," Anna said as she led Margaret to the front room, pointing to the bedroom doorway and the double bed. "Under there."

Margaret looked at her and tsked: "The poor little guys."

"You should have seen them, Margaret, it was awful. We didn't mean to scare them," Anna said looking at her husband. "We thought you might be Domko and the boys overheard. Well, they shot off the chesterfield like a pair of scared jackrabbits and slid under that bed so fast—I've never seen anybody so scared before."

Leo nodded. Anna was telling the story well, so he stood back and let her do most of the talking.

Margaret walked cautiously into the bedroom. Kneeling down, she slowly lifted the quilt.

"Boys, it's me, Mrs. Burnett," she said. "You can come out now."

There was still no sound or movement from under the bed.

"Domko's not here, and he won't be coming either," she said. "I'm here to help you, not take you back to the farm, but I need you to come out and talk to me first."

A few seconds passed, and she heard some whispering. They were deciding in their language if this was one of Domko's tricks. They recognized the English accent and knew that Mrs. Burnett always tried to help them. Slowly, they slid out from under the bed.

Margaret's harsh voice softened as she sat down on the edge of the bed. She reached out as the Twins inched toward her, each starting to cry softly.

Anna was watching from the bedroom doorway. As they boys began talking, the floodgates opened and they told her everything that had happened. Dennis lifted up his shirt, and Margaret gently reached out and turned him around. The sight caused a lump to rise in Anna's throat. She turned away, feeling their shame as they described being treated worse than animals.

The Kochs began busying themselves with other things, everyone except Alvin who stood listening curiously in the doorway.

"Come away from there," Anna whispered as she picked him up. "It's time to go to bed."

"Aw, Momma, I wanna play with Dennis and David," he said.

She carried him to his bedroom and said that if the boys were still there in the morning, he could play with them all day if he liked. Alvin continued to protest but worn out from the evening's excitement, soon fell into a deep sleep.

Margaret left the room when the interview was finished, with the boys following closely behind her.

"You boys sit down while I make a phone call," she said. She gave the Kochs a serious look as she picked up the receiver. She took a deep breath then dialed.

"This is an emergency," she said. "Put me through to the RCMP."

They watched as Margaret's call coaxed a tired officer out of bed. She turned away from them in the interest of confidentiality and began explaining the situation to the officer. She listened for a moment, then told him more. Then in an exasperated tone, made the situation and her feelings quite clear.

"I don't care what time it is," she said. "Something has to be done tonight." Pause. "Yes." Pause. "Yes, jail. It's the only way." Pause. "I won't tolerate anything less, and if need be, I'll be on the phone to your superiors all day tomorrow." Pause. "Who knows what's happening in that house this very moment. That whole family could be dead." Pause. "He needs a psychiatric evaluation." Pause. "Thank you."

Margaret's hand was shaking as she hung up the phone.

"Would you mind keeping the boys here until we have everything settled?" she asked, explaining that she'd have to meet the officer at the farm.

"Not at all," Leo smiled. "We'll keep those boys as long as needed."

Margaret smiled. She didn't have to tell the Kochs how pleased she was to hear this and what good neighbors they were.

The twins slept on the Koch's chesterfield that folded out into a bed. They awoke the following morning to the smell of breakfast. Anna insisted they eat their fill and they happily complied and offered to help with chores to earn their keep.

The Kochs brushed off the suggestion, encouraging them to relax and play with Alvin instead. The little boy stuck to the twins like chewing gum on a shoe and asked so many questions about how they escaped that it got to the point that Anna told them to ignore him because the five-year-old was starting to scare himself.

The phone rang early that afternoon. Anna answered and had a lengthy discussion with the caller. When she hung up, she told the twins that their mother, Eunice, and Raymond were fine, but they hadn't found Rosie yet. The police took Domko to jail, but that's all the caller knew. Anna made her promise to call back as soon as she heard more. The boys seemed pleased that Domko was in jail but apprehensive. They'd lived with fear so long they couldn't truly relax.

Early the next morning, the phone rang and Anna was relieved to hear that Rosie was found. She'd been so traumatized by the shooting that she'd burrowed her way into a haystack and had been too afraid to come out. Domko was now at the hospital, and the boys were to stay with the Kochs until it was time to go home.

That afternoon the twins saw a calendar and realized that the following day was their thirteenth birthdays. Alvin told their mother, and the two began secret preparations.

The next day the twins were unaware of the whispers and quiet plans that were being made on their behalf. Everyone was excited, and Alvin looked as if he was going to burst with the secret. Anna and Kenny kept hushing him whenever it appeared he would spoil the surprise.

Everyone rushed to finish the evening chores, and Dennis and David eagerly helped, not understanding the need to hurry.

After supper, while everyone still sat at the table, the lights were dimmed, and Anna carried in a birthday cake. She and Alvin broke into a chorus of "Happy Birthday" while Leo and Kenny, not wanting to draw attention to their singing voices, mumbled softly along.

Anna put the cake on the table in front of the twins, who stared in wonder at the thick icing and beautifully lit candles.

"Make a wish and blow out the candles," she said, sitting down. She watched their faces in the glint of candle light as each thoughtfully closed his eyes tight and whispered a silent wish. Her eyes stung, certain she knew what they'd wished for.

Then they opened their eyes and took in a deep breath.

"Wait for me," Alvin exclaimed as he scrambled up to stand on his chair. Kenny tried to hold him back, but he let out a spit-filled blow at the same time as the twins, causing the candles to go out and everyone to laugh.

"You're not supposed to," Kenny scolded.

"You always let me," he said jumping off the chair. "Can I bring 'em now Momma?"

"Yes, but don't open them," she said.

"I won't," he said.

The twins were surprised when Alvin plopped a present on each boy's lap. Leo got up to switch on the light. His eyes softly glinted as he watched the boy's expression as they fumbled with the gift wrap.

Anna wrung her hands as she watched.

"It's not much and maybe you boys would like something else," she said, voice trailing off.

The twins looked at each other in absolute wonder.

"Davey, look," Dennis whispered. "New socks."

"Yeah," David said examining them carefully. "Store-boughten ones, and look, they still got the tags on."

As Anna reached across the table to hand them the knife, they carefully set the socks down.

"Now, wait," Anna said. "Twins? I wonder who gets to cut first."

"I do," David said almost jumping off his chair.

"No, I do," Dennis said.

Pulling back the knife, she needed a straight answer to this serious birthday question. "Which one of you was born first?" she asked.

"I was!" David said.

"No, I was," Dennis said. "Ma said so, 'member? She said you was in such a big hurry to get out and I was in the way, so you kicked me out first."

Everyone laughed as David pretended to pout.

"Well, it's decided then," Anna said, handing him the knife. "Dennis cuts first."

Dennis stood and slowly cut himself a big, thick piece of chocolate cake then handed the knife to David who looked wide-eyed at how big a piece of cake Dennis took. Never one to be outdone, he cut himself an even bigger piece. The boys began eating the cake as Anna served the remainder.

That night, as the Twins climbed into bed holding their socks, they discussed the day. They agreed this was the happiest day they'd ever had, comparing it to going to the zoo and having Christmas with Deightons.

Dennis put his socks under his pillow while David stroked his gently across his cheek. The socks smelled so fresh and new. He laid them on top of his pillow then fell asleep.

The boys stayed at the Koch farm for nearly ten days. When Anna received a phone call late one morning, she kept the conversation to herself, telling only Leo that the twins would be going home in a few days.

The twins began to notice a change in her—that she seemed distant and they tried to think of what had made her unhappy.

"We musta done somethin'," Dennis said as they relaxed in bed that night. "Whaddya think?"

David thought back to each day, trying to remember something that might have made her angry or upset. Then it came to him, and his face flushed with embarrassment.

"I know what it was," he said, a lump rising in his throat. "I took too much cake."

Dennis cringed. He'd taken a big piece, too. Even Kenny, who was three years older, hadn't cut himself a piece that big.

They eventually fell asleep and spent most of the next day embarrassed by their gluttony. They told Anna that they hadn't had cake since they lived in Ashern and that sometimes they just couldn't control themselves. They skirted around the subject and watched her expression, which didn't change. Anna still looked sad.

When Caroline arrived late that afternoon, the boys tried to hide, begging Kochs to let them stay longer. When Caroline was invited in, the twins were eventually coaxed out of the bedroom. They missed their mother, but the thought of going back to the same wretched circumstances was more than either could bear. They began crying and begging her to leave without them.

"Hush now," Caroline said. "You boys don't have to worry no more. Domko's gone. He's gone to the hospital in Selkirk."

They stopped crying and took a deep breath, looking first at one another then at her.

"Gone?" Dennis asked.

"Yes," she said, voice wavering. ". . . and he won't be coming back."

LIFE WITHOUT DOMKO

Domko was admitted to the Selkirk Mental Health Centre on February 6, 1961, after the Justice of the Peace at Ashern signed an order of committal, supported by a medical certificate from Dr. Steenson. Caroline accompanied her husband to the hospital and stayed until he adjusted to his new surroundings.

After returning home, she contacted the hospital on a regular basis to discover that Domko's discharge date was December 20. In the meantime, she would have to manage financially and supervise the operation of the farm.

Life for the children had gone from unbearable to unbelievably good. While they still had to work before and after school, they did so with enthusiasm. They wanted to prove to everyone that they didn't need Domko, that they could do the farm work themselves.

Margaret Burnett visited the family a few times over the next month, bringing a basket full of food on one occasion. Because Domko had control of the bank account, the only money Caroline had was from the sale of the cream each week. She thanked Margaret for the food and said that once they got on their feet, things would be much better.

The twins had never been happier. They ate regularly, and while their mother complained that there wasn't enough money, this was of no concern to the children who worked, played and went to school.

Caroline had a telephone installed, which the children thought was an excellent idea but later they overheard women in the community complain that Caroline was wasteful with her money, that she made frivolous purchases instead of paying bills. The children didn't care about any of this since all that mattered to them was that Domko was gone.

The months flew by. Kathy returned from Brantford, and everyone was happy to see her. She was anxious to sit with her father so Caroline was forced to explain that he was in the hospital but would be back soon. This seemed to satisfy the little girl who had learned some manners and now spoke clearer than she had when she left.

There were visits from Caroline's church friends who had mixed reactions to Domko's hospitalization. Those who were afraid of him agreed that he needed psychiatric help, but those who sided with Domko believed that Caroline and the children were the ones driving him crazy. This group argued that seeking psychiatric help was evil and that more obedience and patience from Caroline and the children would remedy Domko's condition.

One afternoon a man from the Ashern congregation visited Caroline and the children. He was new to the area and came by to introduce himself. He was of medium height, had blonde hair and a smooth, convincing voice that charmed Caroline. The children sensed there was something insincere about him because when he looked at them, he curled his lip and frowned with disdain.

Caroline politely invited him inside, and they made small talk. He asked her a lot of questions about the farm, Domko, the children and her studies. She soon became uncomfortable, believing he had been sent to spy on her. She worried he would report to the others how unworthy she was.

This made her angry since she wanted to fit in and be accepted by the Witnesses, who were more like a secret club with a set of unspoken rules than a religion. She always felt on the edge of being thrown out and was regularly told that only the best people were rewarded. She had few friends outside the church and an unsympathetic family, so if they shunned her, she'd be alone. To be shunned was a horrible disgrace, so she tried her best, clung to the religious dogma and considered herself a devout Jehovah's Witness even if nobody else did.

One morning in early June, Caroline arranged a ride to Moosehorn and took Raymond with her. Word was sent back to the farm that the twins were to start the tractor, drive it to town to pick them up. Seldom allowed to touch the tractor, they weren't sure how to start it.

"I think it's the battery, whaddya think?" David asked when the engine wouldn't turn over.

"Maybe. It hasn't started for so long. Maybe it needs to be warmed up," Dennis suggested.

Bending over, David unscrewed a little knob on top of the battery and peered in. "I think I know what the problem is," he confidently said as he loosened the clasp that held the battery to the mount near the engine. "I think the battery needs more water. I can see some in there, but it stinks pretty bad. I figure that if we put some fresh water in it will work."

He lifted the battery off the mount and turned it upside down to drain it. A stream of stinky liquid spilled all over the front of his shirt and pants.

He turned his face away as he shook the battery then carried it to the outdoor pump where he filled it. Then he attached it back to the mount, but the tractor still wouldn't start.

"I hope Ma ain't waitin' for us," Dennis said.

"Somebody will give her a ride," David said. "I just can't figure out what's wrong."

Finally, they gave up and began kicking a tin can around the yard. They played until a car pulled slowly into the driveway. At first, they couldn't believe what they were seeing. Domko was sitting in the passenger seat.

"Oh no, he's back," Dennis said.

David groaned.

They watched as their mother got out of the back seat and thanked a neighbor for the ride. Domko stepped out of the car, opened the back passenger door and lifted out his duffel bag. Raymond followed.

Now the last few weeks made sense to the twins. Their mother had been making a lot of phone calls and must have been arranging for Domko's return. Angry and insulted, they vowed to never speak to her again. All their hard work had been in vain. They watched from a distance as she led Domko into the house. He glanced in their direction, but there was no expression on his face.

"She looks happy . . . how can she be happy?" Dennis asked.

David decided as soon as she was alone, he'd speak to her.

"She can't do this to us," he said, gritting his teeth.

The twins crept to the door and listened before opening it slightly to peer in. They could hear them speaking quietly and waited until Domko went to the bedroom for a nap.

"I'm waitin' out here," Dennis said as he sat on the ground and folded his arms as David went inside.

Caroline stood humming softly by the stove as she prepared supper.

"Ma," David said. "How come he's home?"

Caroline turned to face him. "Because this is his farm, too."

"But Ma, we thought he was stayin' in the hospital 'til December. How come they let him out?"

"He's improved so much that they let him come home on probation. He's a lot better now. You'll see, David. He's got medicine that makes his head feel better and the doctor said that as long as he takes it, he'll be okay."

"Are you mad that me and Denny didn't pick you guys up with the tractor?" David asked. "We couldn't get it started. We didn't do it on purpose."

Caroline looked as if she didn't believe him.

David awoke the next morning, and all was quiet in the house. For a moment, he had to think hard to remember if it had been a nightmare or if Domko really was back. He sat up in bed to discover that the clothes he had on when he fell asleep were mostly gone. The buttons from his shirt tinkled from his chest onto the bed. He felt around to discover that he had on only one sleeve and the back of the shirt dangled from the collar. Looking down, he saw the front of his pants were full of holes.

"Dennis, wake up," he said. "Look at my clothes."

Dennis awoke with a start, thinking Domko might be coming upstairs. He looked around but then closed his eyes again after realizing they weren't in danger.

"Look," David exclaimed. "Where'd my clothes go?"

Dennis laughed.

"It ain't funny," David said, "I gotta get some clothes on before Squeezer sees me. You run down and look through the box."

Dennis nodded and climbed out of bed. He crept down the stairs to the box of second-hand clothes that sat on the floor. He searched through it, throwing dirty items on the floor in search of something clean underneath. This was the box that Domko normally filled twice a year, so by now, everything in it was either dirty or too ragged to wear. Finally, Dennis dug out a pair of blue plaid polyester pants and a beige and brown checked shirt.

"They were good pants," David mumbled as he removed what was left of the pants as Dennis tossed the clean ones on the bed.

"What the hell," David said picking up the pants which had big holes in the knees. "I already put these at the bottom of the box a few times. I don't wanna wear this."

"All there was," Dennis said.

David gave him a dirty look as he pulled on the pants. "I gotta go to school like this? And the worst goddamned part is that Flatfoot is gonna say I broke them. You sure there's nothin' else?"

The commotion awoke the girls who had been sleeping on the floor mattress.

"Hey Beanie, look at David's pants," Dennis giggled.

Eunice looked at her brother standing in the middle of the floor and rolled her eyes. "We're poor enough without you wearin' them to school. Where'd your other pants go?"

"I dunno—they just fell off—I think some moths must have ate them in the night," he said. Eunice didn't look like she believed him, so he grabbed the collar and what was left of the pants and held them up for her to see.

She glanced at the rags and laughed. Exasperated, David bunched up the bits of clothes and stuffed them into their hiding place behind the wall. He hurried downstairs and out the door before Domko woke up.

That afternoon the classroom was warm and bright and smelled of little children's sweat. In June it was always difficult keeping the students focused on their lessons since all they could think about was playing outside in the sunshine and fresh air. Anxious for afternoon recess, they all whispered back and forth about who was still on second base in their baseball game which continued over many lunch hours and recesses.

When Mrs. Gering sent the children outside for the last break of the day, she said there would be an important announcement when they came back. This piqued the children's interest as they ran outdoors, so when she rang the bell, they returned promptly and loudly chattered as they took their seats.

Mrs. Gering sat patiently at her desk but said nothing until everyone was quiet. A chorus of "shhh" drifted through the room until there was silence.

"Do you remember the drawings that were sent in for the art contest?" she asked. The children nodded that they did. "Well, I have some excellent news."

Mrs. Gering stood up from her desk holding a large, brown envelope. "One of you has won second place."

The children gasped and looked around, then watched as she opened the envelope. "The winner has won a certificate, a set of encyclopedias and a fifty dollar bond that will be held in trust until he or she finishes grade eight."

The children cheered as the tension built in the room.

"Do you want to know who the winner is?" she smiled.

"Yes!" they cheered.

"All right," she said pulling out the certificate. "It says here that the winner is . . . David Pischke."

It took David a few moments to understand what she'd said, but once he realized that she had called his name, a broad smile broke across his face. Some of the other children sighed, but most cheered and turned to look at him, clapping.

Where Children Run

"Come on up here David to see your new books," Mrs. Gering said.

David stood up and proudly walked to the front of the room. He'd forgotten about the huge holes in his pants, which normally he would have been teased about, but nobody said a word. David was by all accounts a local hero.

Mrs. Gering held out the certificate and told him that when a person receives such an honor, it is customary to shake hands with the presenter. He blushed as he took her hand.

"I have the set of encyclopedias here, and if David agrees, I'd like to suggest that he open up the boxes and give everyone a chance to see the books before he takes them home. Is that all right with you?"

"S-sure," he smiled.

"Well, here you go," she said, handing him the first box. He took the carton to the side shelf and broke open the top, pulling out the books as the children gathered around. He passed them out then opened one. He marveled at the beautiful colored pictures and wonderfully clean, shiny pages.

Mrs. Gering watched closely, scolding the children with dirty hands, telling them they had to wash before they were allowed to open the new books. David noticed this and wiped his hands on his shirt before picking up another one.

The students spent the rest of the afternoon looking through David's encyclopedias. When it was time to go home, everyone had to take the books back to him.

Mrs. Gering dismissed the class then took David aside. She told him to bring the wheelbarrow the next day or have his mother come with the car to help take the books home. Then she reached out and gave his shoulder an affectionate squeeze.

David skipped home that afternoon, recalling how the day had started poorly but had turned out fantastic by afternoon. Drawing had always been his favorite pastime, and now he had been rewarded for his efforts.

He wondered if there were people in Winnipeg who had jobs drawing. At that moment, he decided that if this was the case, it was the job he wanted to do when he grew up. He thought of everything that looked as if it had been drawn—comic books, pictures in the Eaton's catalog and food labels. Even the encyclopedias had drawings in them.

That's what I'm gonna do, he happily thought as he sauntered into the kitchen.

"Ma, guess what?" he beamed.

"What?" she said, sounding distracted.

David looked around. Domko didn't deserve to share this good news, and he was pleased to see he was napping. "I won second place in Manitoba for my art."

"What?"

"A contest. I got second place in a contest and guess what I got? Look, a certificate with my name on it and I got a set of encyclopedia books and fifty dollars that they're gonna give me when I finish grade eight."

"All that for drawing a picture?" she asked.

"Yeah, isn't that great?"

She turned to face him and placed her hands on her hips. She didn't look at all pleased. "Is that why I'm sending you to school? To draw?"

"No, Ma, it's not like that," he said.

"You should be reading and learning arithmetic. What kind of a school is this anyway? And this new teacher of yours, what is she doing wasting time teaching art?"

"But Ma, I won all this good stuff," he said.

"I don't care about none of that. You'd better not let Domko hear about art contests and encyclopedia books. Drawing pictures will never get you anywhere in life, and I don't want to talk about it anymore. Remember what the Bible says: 'Bad associations spoil useful habits.'"

Crushed, David slowly walked to the barn to finish the evening chores without a word. When he came back to the house, Domko was watching him carefully as he went upstairs.

David took the folded certificate out of the breast pocket of his shirt. He pressed it flat on the bed and admired it for a while. Then he folded it again and crawled behind the wall, hiding it in the sawdust insulation of the eaves.

The next morning when he went downstairs, his mother let all the other children go to school, but kept David home to work, saying that he wasn't learning anything useful at school anyway. Domko chuckled as David stormed outside.

Caroline hoped to make an example of David to the other children. She refused to let him go to school for the remainder of the week. She reasoned that he'd been "too full of himself" when he'd won the contest. She felt that his accomplishments should be less selfish so that he could do a better job serving God.

The following Monday, David went to school and Mrs. Gering casually asked him when he wanted to take the books home. He said he would by the end of the week, but too embarrassed to face her again, he skipped Friday's classes. The books stayed at the school and became part of its small library.

To the children's surprise, it appeared that Domko had improved. He now kept himself clean, shaving and washing at the basin every day. He was calm, and almost pleasant, but still regarded the children with suspicion. He didn't swear as much and hardly said anything at all. What surprised them most was that he wouldn't allow Caroline into his bed. He explained that he'd grown accustomed to sleeping alone at the hospital and now enjoyed it very much.

While still leery of him, they no longer lived in constant fear. He was much more subdued, almost childlike as he demanded that Caroline take care of his every need. She did what was necessary, but the older children could see that she was beginning to tire of him. She made a few sarcastic comments about him being "just like Raymie." To escape her sarcasm, he would go outside and putter around the yard.

The children did the haying that year for the first time without Domko watching over them. He complained that he was too tired and had headaches that made it difficult to work. He seemed to enjoy only two things—spoiling Raymond and raising pigeons. He spent hours building roosts and caring for the birds. The twins discovered that he was still an excellent marksman, though, shooting hawks out of the air as they swooped down on his pet birds.

Caroline and the children went to the Jehovah's Witness gathering in Winnipeg again that summer but Domko refused to go, so they rode to the city with a family from the church. He kept Raymond and Kathy at home, saying he'd decided to raise his children as Roman Catholic.

When Caroline and the children arrived home two days later, Domko was walking from the barn carrying pails of milk. When he saw them standing in the driveway, he flew into a rage, dropping the milk as he ran to get his gun. The friends from the church quickly drove away while Caroline yelled for the children to run into the bush. This time she followed, and they walked cross-country to her brother's farm near Faulkner. They slept in his barn for nearly a week before her brother persuaded her to go home.

In early August, Domko became ill and begged Caroline to take him to the hospital. He was admitted with a severe case of bronchitis and while there, became very suspicious of people he didn't know. He was friendly to the nurses, but when they'd leave the room, he demanded Caroline tell him each nurse's last name. If the woman had a German name, he would not listen to her and refused his medication, believing she was trying to poison him.

When he arrived home, he began demanding more of the children and complained that if Caroline didn't stop working him so hard, she was going to kill him. This nonsense caused her to stop talking to him, which made him even more belligerent.

One afternoon late in the month, the Witness from Ashern came to visit. Caroline wasn't pleased to see this man again, realizing that he'd been assigned to her home. Reluctantly, she let him inside and discovered, to her dismay, that he and Domko got along quite well. They joined in criticizing the way Caroline kept the house.

"How can I keep a clean house when I have so much to do around the farm?" she argued.

"You? Vat yous be doink? Nuthink. You ant them lazy keets be doink nuthink. I's be seek ant be doink it all." Domko said.

Caroline tried to argue but soon realized there was little point. It was evident the visitor sided with Domko, so she sat and listened as they criticized her.

Eunice and the twins didn't start school in September; instead, David was kept home to do chores while Eunice and Dennis were sent to a neighboring farm owned by the Gall family to help with threshing. This was hard work, but they didn't mind since they were treated like young adults instead of children. They enjoyed listening to the men tell jokes and grown-up stories during the lunch and coffee breaks.

They brought along Domko's equipment which, by the neighbors' standards, was quite antiquated. They worked for three weeks under the supervision of Arnold Gall who was Robert Gall's oldest son. Arnold was a short, stocky man about thirty years old, with a big face, bushy black hair and jack-o'-lantern teeth.

Neighborhood children called him names because his thinking processes were a little slower than everybody else. As a youngster, Arnold was trampled by an enraged bull and afterward was left fighting for his life. When he eventually recovered, he was never quite the same.

It didn't take Eunice and Dennis long to discover Arnold's weaknesses, and they began teasing him, and he was equally nasty in return. After three weeks of working together, a friendly hate had built up between Arnold and his two helpers who would throw dried cow manure at him whenever he turned his back. This infuriated Arnold who would chase them, but he never caught the quick teenagers because of his lumbering size.

Near the end of September, Caroline saw that Domko's moods were worsening. She recognized the same pattern of paranoia building that she'd seen the autumn before. An empty pill bottle on his bureau revealed that he had finished all his medication.

"How long have you been off your pills?" she asked one morning.

"I's not be know," he said. "Two, maybe tree weeks."

"We have to get you more," she said. "You're still on probation."

Domko shook his fist in anger. "Yous not be tellink me," he said as he strode out of the house.

Caroline contacted Margaret Burnett and explained the situation. She said that Domko was beginning to lose his temper with the children again, but didn't mention that he had beaten one of them the night before—the first time since his return. Caroline also said that Domko had bought himself another gun to replace the ones the police had confiscated. Margaret arrived the next day with the police. They persuaded him to go back to Selkirk for a check-up. He handed them his gun and went willingly.

With Domko gone again, the children were beginning to have more faith in their mother and the justice system. Excited, Eunice and the twins made a plan to go to town. They had never been to Moosehorn by themselves and thought it would be an adventure. They asked their mother for permission to go, and she said that if they found themselves a ride, she would give each of them enough money for a hamburger and coke.

Elated, Eunice ran to get Marjorie and dragged her back to the house. They needed her experience to help arrange the details. After quite an animated discussion at the kitchen table, they decided to persuade Arnold Gall to give them a ride.

Marjorie was skeptical. "Why would he want to take you guys to town?"

"He's the only one we can think of who can drive and isn't working," Dennis said.

"Yeah, and because he's so slow, it's like he's our age," Eunice said.

"I don't know," Marjorie said. "What will you say?"

"Maybe if we just ask him nice, he'll take us," David said.

"Not a chance," Eunice said. "We tease him too much. He hates us."

Then they all looked at Marjorie.

"If you come along, he'd take us for sure," Eunice said.

"Me? No way, I'm not going to pretend to be his girlfriend," she said.

"Oh, come on Marjie, it'll be fun," Eunice said.

"Fun? For who? Sorry, but you will have to find somebody else."

Since the bait had refused the hook, they had to think of another girl.

"What about Eunice?" David suggested. "She's a girl, sorta."

Karen Emilson

"Me and Arnold Gall? You can go lay an egg," Eunice laughed.

"C'mon Eunice, you heard the men teasin' him that he's never had no girlfriend," Dennis said. "If you call him, he'll take us."

"Yeah, and you're beautiful, too," David said.

"Shuddup," Eunice said, punching him in the arm.

"C'mon Eunice he won't take us without you," Dennis said, but Eunice refused. They thought for a while longer, then David came up with an idea.

"Too bad we don't have some cousin that we could bring along," he said. Then they turned to look at Dennis who was thinking very hard about who could be Arnold's girlfriend.

"Dennnis," David sang. "I've got an ideeea."

Dennis suddenly saw all eyes were upon him. Once he realized what they were thinking, he jumped back.

"No," he said, shaking his head. "Not me, I'm not gonna go nowhere as Arnold's girlfriend."

"C'mon Dennis, you can do it," Eunice said.

"How about David?"

"I got a deeper voice than you. He'll know it's me. Besides, you're taller. You can be our cousin from Winnipeg," David said. "It'll be fun."

Eunice and Marjorie laughed as they looked Dennis over.

"Hey, stop that," he said trying to cover his face. Eunice reached out and pulled his hands away. He blushed and started to laugh.

"Come on Dennis. He'll never know."

"Never know? Of course, he'll know, I don't look like no girl."

"You will when we finish with you," Eunice said. "And besides ol' Arnold is as dumb as a post. He'll never know the difference."

It took some persuading, but finally, Dennis agreed after they reminded him how good the hamburger and pop would taste.

Caroline, who was listening to the bantering from the front room, let out a howl of delight. The girls jumped up from the table and ran into Domko's bedroom where Caroline kept her clothes. Much to the children's delight, she joined in, and for the first time in months, Dennis noticed his mother smile.

"Okay, but before I put all that girl stuff on, make sure he'll come," Dennis said, enjoying being the center of attention.

The children giggled. "Ma, you gotta make the call for us," David said.

"Yeah, Ma, please," Eunice begged. "It'll sound better if it comes from you."

Caroline dropped a dress and brassiere on the table.

Where Children Run

"Okay," she giggled, "but you all be quiet."

The children spun with excitement, muffling laughter with their hands over their mouths, as Caroline summoned her courage and picked up the phone.

"Could I talk to Arnold, please," she said, smiling as she turned her back to the children. There was a brief pause. "Hello Arnold, it's Caroline Domko." Pause. "I'm fine. I am calling to see if you would be interested in coming to the farm to meet my niece." Pause. "Her name? Umm—Mary Maxwell." Pause. "Yes, and if the two of you like you can go to town for a while." Pause. "The cafe would be nice." Pause. "How about two o'clock?" Pause. "Yes? All right we'll see you then."

The teens held back their laughter until Caroline hung up the phone, then they cheered loudly.

"Well, we'd better hurry," Caroline said. "We've got less than an hour to make Dennis look like a girl."

"Hey, Ma how did you get the name, Mary Maxwell?" David asked.

Caroline held up a small catalog. "It's the name of a pattern company."

The girls gathered around Dennis and told him to take off his clothes.

"Take off my clothes?"

"Yes, you've got to put these on," she said holding up a pair of stockings. "And you have to wear this, too."

Dennis and David blushed as Eunice smiled, stretching out the wide, ample cupped bra. Marjorie laughed as Dennis began stripping off his shirt and pants.

"Lift up your arms," Eunice said.

"I'm not puttin' that on," he said.

"We can't have a cousin Mary with a flat chest," she said.

Dennis shrank from her while David and Marjorie laughed so hard they could barely catch their breath.

Dennis squeezed his eyes shut and stuck his arms straight out as Eunice slipped the bra over his arms and fastened it in the back. She stood back and giggled at the sight of the bra over his thin white chest. She told David to find something to stuff inside.

The girls pulled the stockings over his skinny legs just as David returned with an armful of potatoes. "How 'bout these?" he asked.

The girls took the potatoes and stuffed them inside the bra. They adjusted each side to make sure they looked even. Then they helped Dennis pull on a full slip, followed by Caroline's favorite dress. They slipped her high heels on his feet, which were about the right size.

Caroline lifted up an old, blonde wig that had come home accidentally in the clothes box. She pulled the wig onto Dennis' head and adjusted it.

As the girls covered his face with make-up, Caroline combed the blonde hair into a bouffant style, and Marjorie strung fake pearls around his neck.

"This don't fit so good," Dennis complained as he adjusted the wig. "It'll fall off if I bend over."

Caroline went to the bedroom and returned with a scarf. She folded it and put it on top of Dennis' head, tying it tightly under his chin.

"Ma, it's too tight," he said, his cheeks puffing out from under the scarf. "It's makin' my lips stick out."

"Here, I'll fix that," Eunice said, slathering thick red lipstick across his puckered lips.

Then they all stood back to admire their new cousin, Mary Maxwell. Everyone bent in laughter except Dennis who hadn't yet seen himself in the mirror. "What's so funny?" he asked innocently.

By two o'clock, Dennis looked very much like a girl as he practiced walking across the floor in his mother's shoes. It took some coaxing, but he tried to wiggle his hips, and he even agreed to carry a purse. Dennis wasn't as scared as he thought he might be, feeling wholly unrecognizable in the dress and make-up. For once, he enjoyed being on the other end of a joke.

Caroline gave each of them fifty cents to spend. Arnold drove into the yard at five minutes past two. The children watched from the window as he got out of the car, dressed in clean clothes and slapped a hand over his slicked-back hair.

The children frantically whispered as Caroline opened the door. She invited Arnold in and introduced him to Mary, who stood shyly between David and Eunice.

Arnold's eyebrows shot straight up, and he smiled. Caroline choked back a giggle and hurried them out the door.

Eunice and David followed close behind Dennis, giving him little nudges since it appeared he was changing his mind. When they got to the car, Arnold scowled at Eunice and David.

"We have to come," Eunice said. "Mary barely knows you."

He smiled at Mary and opened the passenger door. Dennis got in.

"Get in the back," he grunted at Eunice and David, who climbed quickly in and stifled a laugh as they stared at the back of Dennis' head. Arnold started the car and put his arm on the top of the seat as he backed up, leaving it there as he drove toward town, chatting quietly.

Where Children Run

David and Eunice began to giggle.

Arnold shot them an angry glance in the mirror then continued to tell Mary about his farm and how many cattle he had.

"Yes, uh-huh," Dennis replied sweetly. He stared straight ahead to avoid looking him directly in the eyes.

The car bumped along, and Eunice and David began giggling when the back of Dennis' babushka-covered head started bobbing up and down.

"What you laughing at?" Arnold said over his shoulder to them. Then shaking his head, he looked back at Mary.

"There's two of them little bastards somewhere," he said pointing a thumb at David. "But I don't know where the other one is."

David and Eunice broke into fits of laughter. The sight of Dennis' shoulders convulsing, caused them to laugh even harder. They were all thankful to finally arrive in Moosehorn.

"Where do you want to go?" Arnold asked Mary, but Dennis pretended to be too shy to answer.

"The café," Eunice said.

Arnold drove into town and pulled up beside the small restaurant. He hollered at David and Eunice to get out, and they scrambled out of the car. Dennis reached for the door handle, but Arnold said they had another stop to make. He yelled out the window that he'd be back in a while, then pulled away.

"Where's he goin'?" David asked.

Eunice shook her head. They watched until the car was out of sight then, with nothing more to do, went into the café. They sat down, ordered a hamburger and coke, expecting Arnold and Dennis to be back in a few minutes.

"I'm hungry," Dennis said as Arnold stopped in front of the hotel.

"I'll be back in a minute," he said. "You wait here."

Dennis nodded. Once Arnold had gone inside, he relaxed and adjusted his clothing, hair, and bosom. About ten minutes later, a group of men came out of the bar and approached the car. They bent down and looked inside at Dennis, who stared straight ahead. Some peered through the front window, then all of them shook their heads and laughed as they left.

Arnold appeared about ten minutes later. He smelled of alcohol and carried a small case of beer. He apologized for the wait, then drove back to the café. By then, Eunice and David were waiting impatiently outside. Afraid that Arnold had discovered who his date was, they were relieved to see that Dennis was still intact and unharmed. Stomachs full, and with no more money left to spend, the pair were anxious to end the charade.

Dennis made a faint indication that he was hungry, but David and Eunice vetoed the idea of going into the café. While waiting on the sidewalk, they had agreed that he looked far more convincing at home than he did in town. They imagined their made-up brother trying to eat a hamburger, with a chest full of potatoes—and it became too embarrassing to risk getting caught.

Arnold shrugged that it made no different to him. He'd had a few beers and had long since forgotten that he'd promised to buy Mary a meal. Dennis didn't dare protest because that would mean saying more than two words at a time. They left for home, and once they arrived back at the farm, Eunice giggled at David. "We made it," she whispered.

Arnold stopped the car and turned around.

"Get out," he said. Anxious to get away, Eunice and David opened the door and slid out, but Dennis fumbled with the door handle a little too long. In an instant, Arnold had the car in reverse and was turning around. He drove quickly out of the driveway.

Eunice ran into the house. "Ma, Arnold took Dennis!"

Caroline ran outside in time to see nothing but dust.

"Oh no," David said. "If he finds out, he's gonna kill him."

Dennis tried to stay calm as Arnold drove to a quiet spot where he said they could talk. Dennis looked around, gauging they were about three miles from home when Arnold pulled off the road into the bushes.

"So, how long have you been living in Winnipeg?" Arnold asked, handing him a bottle of beer.

"All my life," he squeaked, refusing the beer.

"You don't drink?"

"No."

"So, what do you do in Winnipeg?"

"Go to school."

"What kind of school?"

"A big one."

Arnold thought for a moment. "You're very shy, aren't you?"

"Y-yes," he stammered.

He moved closer, sliding his arm across the back of the seat. The weight of his forearm caught the wig and tugged it back.

Giggling softly, Dennis adjusted the wig and tried to move closer to the door. Arnold made small talk for a little longer then reached across. Dennis closed his eyes and tried to slouch on the seat as Arnold pressed his body against his. Then Arnold puckered his lips and gave him a big kiss on the lips. His hand reached gently for his knee.

"Oh No," Dennis said. "Not on the first date."

Arnold reluctantly backed away, and they sat chatting for a few more minutes while he finished his beer. An hour had passed before Arnold slowly drove back to the farm.

David and Eunice were waiting outside when Arnold's car slowly pulled into the yard and came to a stop. This time, Dennis quickly jumped out. Arnold got out of the car and grabbed Dennis' arm, insisting that he walk him to the door. A potato dropped to the ground, which Dennis casually kicked aside.

"Well, I'll see you tomorrow Mary," he said, pulling him close and planting another kiss on his lips. Dennis squealed.

Relieved, Caroline opened the door, and she tried not to laugh at the sight of Dennis, obviously frightened and slightly disheveled. She knew better than to invite Arnold inside.

Once he'd left, everyone gathered around Dennis, whose bosom was now quite lopsided and his face was smeared with lipstick.

"Where did he take you?" Eunice asked.

"D-down the road into the b-bushes," Dennis stammered. "I was never so scared in all my life. Arnold kissed me and—he touched my potatoes!"

Dennis' re-enactment of the afternoon sent waves of laughter throughout the house, lasting well into the night. It had been a fun time for all, including Arnold, who was never the wiser.

"Well, Dennis," Caroline said, remembering her teenaged years, "You're very lucky that Arnold was a gentleman."

THE LAME LEADING THE BLIND

THE PLEASANT ATMOSPHERE IN THE HOUSE WAS SHORT-LIVED ONCE Domko came back to the farm. He took his pills long enough to convince the hospital to discharge him, then quit immediately after arriving home. His moods got progressively worse as each week passed.

Margaret Burnett left her job as health nurse when she and her family moved out of the area. Caroline was sorry to see Margaret go because she was so well-versed on the family's problems. And while Caroline found it difficult to confide in people she knew she could still count on Dr. Steenson.

The social worker who replaced Martha Jeske had left and been replaced twice since then. The new workers had no first-hand experience with the family, and since Domko's mental condition was the main problem, it was now the responsibility of the police to take him into custody when he became violent.

At almost fourteen years old, the twins had grown taller than Domko and were starting to mature. They now knew the difference between boys and girls and no longer worried about Eunice in the same way. They were curious about girls and looked at the ladies' underwear pictures in catalogs until they blushed.

One day while David was daydreaming during class, he began sketching a picture from his imagination of what a woman must look like without her clothes. He worked on the drawing for a long time while Mrs. Gering gave a history lesson. She noticed his preoccupation with his art book and slowly inched her way over to see what he was doing. David continued drawing until he could sense someone standing beside him. He looked up to see Mrs. Gering's shocked expression. Fumbling, he tried to cover his work.

"We're doing history, Mr. Pischke," she whispered. "And next time, could you put some clothes on me?"

Where Children Run

David looked at the drawing and flushed. While daydreaming, he hadn't realized that he'd drawn Mrs. Gering's face on the woman. He quickly lifted up his desktop and put the book inside.

Later that week the school inspector visited the classroom. He spoke with the teacher, talked to the students, examined the register book, and wrote things down on a small notepad he carried in his breast pocket. Before he left, Mrs. Gering called him aside and talked to him for a long time. Soon the superintendent was standing in front of David's desk.

"David, could I have your art book please?" he said.

Embarrassed, David reluctantly reached into his desk and took out the book. It was thick with the many drawings and caricatures he'd drawn since the beginning of the school year.

For the next few days he expected to be punished for drawing the picture of Mrs. Gering, but nothing came of it. Soon he forgot the incident.

Just when the boys thought that Domko had tormented them in every conceivable way, he thought of something new. That winter he bought a television.

It was the most fascinating, world-expanding invention they'd ever seen and desperately wanted to watch it, but weren't allowed. The magical box was bought with money given to the family by Grandpa Kolodka. It sat in the corner of the front room and was only turned on in the evening so Domko could watch the news. The children weren't even allowed to watch that and were sent to the kitchen or upstairs. They listened through the thin walls as a stranger's voice blared out information about world events like the Cuban Missile Crisis. The twins tried hard to grasp what the world was like away from the farm.

Domko sat on the chesterfield and muttered to himself, calling anyone he disagreed with a communist. He seemed to like watching the news, but it always made him angry afterward.

Sometimes, the boys would sneak a peek at the television by turning it on when Domko was away, but Raymond reported them the moment his father returned. The five-year-old even snitched when he overheard Dennis bragging that he was going to be just like "Little Joe" when he grew up. The twins had been sneaking into the teacher's cottage to watch *Bonanza* on Sunday nights. Once caught, they received a beating for it. Domko wasn't mad they were in the teacherage, he didn't like that they'd watched the television instead of working.

One night in March while the twins sat on the floor after receiving a beating, Raymond came into the kitchen carrying a bag of treats. The boys had heard Domko tell him not to give them any, and by now, Raymond knew it was fun to tease them.

Taking a candy bar out of the bag, he pulled back the wrapper. He began walking back and forth, holding the bag in his dirty fist, taunting the twins. He had a spoiled, mean look on his face that the twins had grown to loathe.

"We gotta think of new words so poker can't understand us," Dennis said in their language.

"Yeah," David answered. "Satan's always makin' him spy on us. I hear him askin' the little bugger where we go and what we do. He's tryin' really hard to understand what we're sayin'."

"We'll just have to trick him," Dennis said slyly.

From that day on, the twins baited Raymond. They discussed where they would be hiding in front of their younger brother but then would go to a different place. Raymond would tell Domko where the twins were, and he would stalk off in the wrong direction.

The twins pretended they were going to sneak out to watch television but hid in the church instead. They'd look through the windows as Domko crept up to the teacherage and walk in, only to walk home confused and disappointed a few minutes later. They changed their words so often that both Raymond and Domko had no idea what they were saying.

Spring arrived in April. Except for the occasional cold day, winter was virtually over. Domko was watching the twins continually now, never accomplishing anything on his own, preoccupied with stalking and spying on them. They became nervous and irritable, never knowing what to expect next, and matters were made worse by the fact their mother had spent the past two months confined to her bed. Her condition was something the twins didn't understand, except that she was no help to them. David and Dennis agreed that this was by far the lowest point of their lives.

One chilly, misty morning after a meager breakfast, the twins were sent out to shovel manure. Domko told them to take pitchforks and clean out the small lean-to attached to the east side of the barn.

The twins nodded and hurried out the door.

"He can't think of nothin' else for us to do so he makes us shovel shit," David said. "I'm sick of all this work, and I wanna get outta here."

"Yeah, me, too."

"He's nuts you know," David explained. "That's what the kids say 'bout goin' to Selkirk. That's where the police send all the crazy people. They told me that it's just full of crazy people there."

Dennis shuddered. "I ain't never goin' there."

"Me neither."

The Twins opened the barn door and picked up the forks. They walked around the side of the barn to the lean-to and opening the small door, stepped into the dank room. Their eyes quickly adjusted to the darkness as thin rays shone through cracks on the wall. They'd shoveled enough manure to know this was going to be a long, difficult job.

After tapping his pitchfork on the hard earth, David's shoulders slumped. It had been a cold night, so the eight inches of manure that had accumulated since the last shoveling was frozen to the earthen floor.

"Hey Denny, we'll start here 'cause it'll be softer," David said banging his fork again and pointing to the southeast corner. Together they dug their pitchforks underneath.

"Lift when I say," David said.

Both grunted as they lifted a big chunk of manure and tossed it in the corner. Steam rose from underneath where the ground had thawed the afternoon before.

"That looks easier," David said, heartened by the warmth underneath. "This won't be so bad." He stuck his pitchfork under the pile, and as he lifted, two prongs broke off and the manure and fell to the ground. Both he and Dennis gasped.

"Oh no," David said. "Where's the other pitchfork?"

"I don't know."

Just then, the light shining through the door suddenly dimmed. The boys knew why and cringed, not wanting to turn around.

"Vat? Yous be playink again?" Domko said as he strode into the lean-to. When he saw the broken pitchfork in David's hand, he went berserk.

"Yous be breakink it some," he screamed as he strode toward them. They braced themselves as Domko spun around and threw his right leg in the air in a karate-style kick, catching David on the face. The impact knocked David's feet out from under him and sent the pitchfork flying through the air. Instinctively, David curled his legs and rolled onto his side as he tried to cover his head. His face was in such excruciating pain that he barely noticed the heavy work boots kicking his arms and the front of his legs.

"I's be givink you some," Domko grunted each time he kicked.

Dennis tried to run, but Domko caught him before he reached the door. He slammed his fist into Dennis' face, sending him crashing into the lean-to wall. Too frightened to fight back, he curled against the wall as Domko alter-

Karen Emilson

nated between kicking David in the arms and knees and him in the legs and back. Eventually, he began to tire, and with one final blow to Dennis' legs, he left them groaning and weeping on the cold ground.

David was the first to struggle to his feet. He wiped the manure from his face and tried to open his eyes but couldn't see anything. He staggered toward the brightness of the open door

"Dennis, we gotta get out of here," he choked, as he tried to clear his mouth of the blood that trickled down his throat. He was beginning to panic.

"Get up; I need you to come look and see if he's out there."

Dennis tried to stand, but couldn't. He crawled to where David stood, then pulled himself up high enough to see through a crack in the wall.

"I don't see him nowhere," he panted. "I think my legs are broke, this time for sure."

"I can't see," David rasped, voice rising in panic. "Denny, I can't see no more. I think he poked out my eyes!"

Dennis looked at his brother's face, still covered in manure. Blood was flowing from a gaping wound just over an eyebrow. His eyes were puffed out so far that all he could see were tiny slits.

"Your face is so beat up I can't see your eyes."

"I think I'm blind," David cried. "Get me outta here before he comes back."

Grabbing David by the arm, Dennis pulled him to the door. He lost his balance and landed heavily on the ground.

"Where are you?" David whispered. "We gotta go."

Dennis struggled but couldn't stand up. "I can't," he said.

Aside from the horrible stinging on his face from the manure, David was physically fine. "Climb on my back, and I'll carry you, but I can't see nothin' so you gotta tell me where to go."

Dennis climbed on his brother's back, wrapping his legs around David's waist. David leaned slightly forward and grabbed Dennis' arms.

He trudged toward the bush behind the barn, visualizing the cattle trail that would take them east to the beaver dam.

"There's a big rock so you gotta go to the left," Dennis said. "Okay, now keep goin'. We're almost at the fence, so you're gonna have to turn to the right."

"He's not comin' is he?" David asked.

Dennis looked back over his shoulder. "He's not comin' yet."

David continued to plod along as Dennis guided him back onto the trail when he veered off.

"How far we gonna go?" Dennis asked.

"We gotta go to the beaver dam, 'cause he'll never walk that far," David said. "You gotta keep lookin' around in case he does come."

Soon they arrived at the lake bank. Exhausted, David dropped to his knees, and Dennis rolled off his back onto the ground. They both shivered uncontrollably on the cold, wet ground. Dennis rolled onto his side and began to weep.

David crawled over the small ridge to the water's edge. The ice was still thick but mushy on top from the previous week's warm weather, and the ice had melted along the shore. Cupping his hands, he splashed handfuls of water on his aching face. He tried to rub the manure out of his eyes but the harder he tried, the more it stung. He wiped his face and hands dry with his shirt, then stumbled back to his brother.

"Are you really blind?" Dennis asked.

"I dunno. Are you really crippled?"

"I think so. I still can't walk. Can you see anything?"

"No, nothin'," David cried.

They sat on the cold lake bank for a long time without speaking.

Frustrated, hungry, beaten and now likely crippled, Dennis started to cry again. "What are we gonna do, Davey? Where are we gonna go? We can't walk across the beaver dam 'cause the ice is too soft. Domko's gonna find us, and if we're blind and crippled, he'll shoot us and throw us in the bush. Nobody will ever find us. He'll just say we ran away."

David listened, and for the very first time, he agreed with his brother. He also believed they would be shot if they couldn't work. If they recovered, then Domko would never let them leave the farm. No matter how hard they tried, they'd never escape him.

The words of the chiropractor rang loudly in his ears: "Most boys your age with this type of injury would end up in a wheelchair."

While David sat on the soggy ground, he wondered why they had been chosen to live such a horrible life. He knew that not all children lived like this—only them. Life seemed so unfair and not worth living.

Tired of listening to Dennis, he got up and stumbled along the lake bank. A feeling of utter hopelessness washed over him. He groped his way along, grasping tree branches as he went. When he could no longer hear Dennis crying, he found a spot that was relatively dry and curled up on the ground. He decided that if he were going to die, this would be a good place.

David decided that he would no longer look for food or water. He would not go home, would stay away from Dennis and hopefully die a peaceful

Karen Emilson

death among the trees. His heart ached for all the things he'd longed to do, and then he started to cry.

At first, he sobbed softly, then gradually large tears began to flow from his swollen eyelids. He cried long and hard as he remembered every incident from his childhood, every time he'd received a beating, and every disappointment and embarrassment. His empty stomach ached as he thought about the few good days he'd had—remembering Ruby's bright smiling face and Mrs. Koch's kindness. He thought of Emma fussing over him and remembered the trip to Winnipeg. Oh, how he wanted to live in Winnipeg and be a professional drawing person! He thought of the cars he'd never own and the friends he'd never meet.

He begged for an answer. Why him? Why Dennis? What could they do except die? The hours went by and his body, wracked with sobbing, began to ache. He drifted in and out of sleep, awakening suddenly, with a feeling that someone was standing near him. He mumbled softly for Dennis to go away.

A hand reached out and gently squeezed his shoulder. David was too weak and dazed to move. He knew instinctively not to be afraid. This was a familiar hand, one that hadn't touched him in more than ten years. Then as if his mind was being read, a voice spoke softly.

"Tush, be strong," it echoed. "Don't give up. You've got to look after him; Dennis. Remember—I'll always be with you."

As quickly as it had materialized, the voice and pressure on his shoulder vanished. David lay in awe of the experience for a long time and then rolled onto his back.

Whether his father's presence had been real or imagined, David didn't care. He opened his eyes, and through tiny slits, he could see the fuzzy image of branches overhead. Sitting up, he looked at the ground and the faint sprouting of new grass around him. His tears must have washed the dirt from his eyes.

Ashamed that he had almost given up, he pounded the ground with his fist. He knew how silly and useless his ravings had been. Now he felt older than his fourteen years. He stood up and with a renewed sense of energy, walked back to where Dennis was sitting.

Dennis had cried for hours, and it seemed to clear his mind and ease his frustration as well. They looked at each other and said nothing but a deep understanding passed between them. Nobody else would ever fully understand the hell they lived with each day. Dennis gave him a timid smile.

"Can you see okay?"

David nodded. "Can you walk?"

"Unless I wanna sit here 'til I die, I'd better."

David grabbed him by the arm and supported him as they walked to the bush. He decided not to tell Dennis about his experience.

"C'mon, we gotta find us some place to sleep," David said. "There's a good spot in the bush over here. Remember when the ol' bastard took our cooked rabbit? I bet that spot is still clear."

Maybe there was no God, but David felt a renewed sense of hope, believing that his father might be nearby.

And that's all the strength he needed.

The boys went home two days later. Domko sensed the change in David immediately. Normally, he would have taunted him about his swollen face and blackened eyes, but not this time. He stood back and said nothing as the twins came into the house. He didn't even ask where they'd been when they picked up milk pails and went to the barn.

Raymond came strolling in behind them carrying a pail.

"What are you doin' here, poker?" Dennis asked.

"Don't call Raymie poker," he yelled.

"Well, what do you want?"

"I's be showink you how to milk but-a-some cow," he said. He strode up and down the aisle looking for a cow to milk.

The twins made fun of him which caused Raymond to screech again. He stuck out his tongue, then stopped in front of the biggest animal in the barn.

"Uh, Raymie . . ." David began.

"Shhh," Dennis whispered. "Let him, since he thinks he's so smart."

The twins watched as Raymond stood directly behind Domko's big Brahma bull. He gave them a naughty glance, sticking out his tongue again, then put the milking stool on the ground and reached in behind the bull's tail.

The bull, startled, shot his leg back, sending Raymond, the stool, and the milk pail into the air. Raymond landed with a thud and then howling, jumped to his feet and ran to the door. He gave the twins an embarrassed look before running to the house.

"The bull almost killed him," Dennis laughed.

"Yeah, 'I's be showink you how to milk,'" David mimicked. "That was a close one. It's a lucky thing for us he landed on his fat Pollack head and didn't get hurt."

That evening they went quietly upstairs.

"Guess what I'm gonna do," Dennis whispered.

"What?"

"I'm gonna build a boat so that we can float across the beaver dam. The water's too deep to walk across, and I don't think we can wait until winter again."

David thought this sounded like a good idea.

The following morning, they finished chores and then after school, Dennis disappeared into the bush beside the church while David went home and did chores with Eunice. It took nearly two weeks for him to finish the boat.

"You gotta help me get it to the beaver dam," he said. "We can try it out and then hide it in the bushes where Squeezer won't find it."

"When?"

"Tomorrow, when he takes the cream to town."

The next day they waited until Domko left and then ran to the bush on the far side of the churchyard. Dennis beamed as he pulled the branches away he'd used to camouflage the hiding spot.

"See, I told you I was gonna build a boat," he said.

David looked at the odd-shaped vessel. It was a flat, wide-bottomed boat with small sides. He'd made it from tin and wood, and while it didn't look like it would survive the waves, Dennis was confident it would float.

David was surprised by the meticulous work and how good it looked considering it was made from old, used lumber and scraps of tin.

"Let's test it out," he said, grabbing an end.

They strained and groaned as they carried the boat across the swampy field. They laughed about how stupid Domko would feel standing on the shore helplessly watching as they paddled across to the Koch farm.

They arrived at the lake to find how much it had changed in the past three weeks. The water was flowing freely now, and the trees had tiny buds forming on their branches. Life felt so much brighter than it had the last time they were there.

Dennis was anxious to set the boat adrift, so they pulled it right up to the water's edge. He found two sticks and handed one to David.

"We'll both push and when I say, jump in," he said, climbing in and sitting down in the front. "You can be in the back."

"I guess you get to be the pilot," David said.

"Not pilot, that's for planes. I get to be the Captain."

"And what do I get to be? The pirate?"

"Shuddup and push," Dennis said.

David pushed the boat and stepped into the cold water, letting out a howl.

"Give one more push and jump in," Dennis said.

David heaved and then jumped into the boat. They floated for a few seconds and then water started flooding in at every joint.

"Oh no," David hollered as he jumped out.

Dennis, who was so shocked and dismayed that his boat wasn't going to float, after all, stayed sitting long enough that technically, he went down with the ship. He jumped up when he was waist deep. They scrambled out of the water and stood dripping on shore.

"What happened?" Dennis cried. "I built it so good, how come it didn't float?"

David started laughing. "Good? You built it too good. Too many goddamned nails in the bottom. It didn't float 'cause it was too heavy."

"No," Dennis argued.

"It almost busted our arms off bringin' it here," David said. "C'mon Denny, admit you put too many nails in."

"I'm not sayin' that."

"C'mon say it," David teased.

"I had to put them nails in so the water wouldn't get in," he said.

"Nails don't stop water, stupid," David said. "Only rubber stops water—and whoever heard of a tin boat anyway?"

"Lots of boats are made of tin."

"No, they ain't."

"Yes, they is. I know 'cause I saw some in the encyclopedia books. One was called the TIT-anic."

"TIT-anic?" David said. "Do you mean TI-tanic?"

"Yeah. It was made of tin."

"Denny, the Titanic sank all the way to the bottom of the lake," David laughed.

Dennis thought for a moment. "Well, I don't care. It still might float. Help me pull it out."

David complained that he didn't want to go into the water again, so Dennis called him a chicken. Neither complained about the cold as they pulled it onto the shore. They stood staring at it for a few minutes then started dragging it back to the churchyard.

"I'm gonna help fix it, so it's done right this time," David said.

"How?"

"Rubber," David said. "Wrap rubber around it, and it'll float for sure."

Once the boat was safely hidden again, they scrounged through a pile of junk near the granary and found an old tire that they carried to the boat. David sliced the tire into long strips using a sharp kitchen knife while Dennis happily nailed rubber on all the seams.

"Don't use too many nails," David warned.

The following morning, they were back at the lake, but not as optimistic as the day before.

"You go first," David said. "You're the captain."

"I ain't the Captain," Dennis said. "It's too cold a job."

They decided to wait and see if the boat floated before getting in. They gave it a push but because it was even heavier now, could barely get it off the pebbly shore. They waded up to their knees and watched helplessly as the boat sank again. They dragged it back onto shore and sat down.

"Are you gonna make me carry it back to the church again?" David panted.

"Well, we can't leave it here," Dennis said. "I'll take out some of the nails."

David shook his head. "We gotta make it out of just wood and rubber—like a raft."

"Okay," Dennis said hopefully. "It's gonna float, you'll see."

Groaning, they dragged the boat back to the church.

"Float," David mumbled. "That's what all them people on the Titanic said."

NARROW ESCAPE

ONE AFTERNOON IN EARLY MAY, THE TWINS CAME IN FROM OUTSIDE TO find Kathy alone in the house. She stood in her usual place between the kitchen and the front room, jogging on the spot and humming a made-up tune. She wrapped her knuckles on the wall the entire time, an annoying habit that the twins despised.

"Will you quit doin' that?" David said. "You're buggin' us."

Kathy continued as if she didn't hear them. She'd started the strange ritual soon after returning from Brantford.

"How come it don't bug the ol' weasel when she does that?" Dennis asked.

"I dunno. It sure bugs me."

"Hey Kathy, where's Ma?" Dennis asked.

"Walter came, and she went to Winnipeg with him," she said, not breaking her stride. "She's comin' back later."

"Later?" David asked. "When?"

"Don't know," she said. "Maybe two or three weeks."

The twins groaned. Domko was always worse when their mother was gone.

"I'm not stayin' here with him alone no more," Dennis said. "I'm leavin' as soon as I can get away."

They watched Kathy for a few more minutes, then David pointed to the kitchen cupboard. Dennis knew he wanted to sneak some food, so he went to the door to make sure Domko was not around. Then he grabbed a raw potato and took a big bite.

"Where's Raymie?" David asked, distracting Kathy who always seemed to know what was going on and often reported back to Domko.

"He's with Ta-ta," she answered. "They're outside."

Dennis finished chewing and swallowed. He coughed a little bit, then began talking to Kathy while David took a bite.

"Where did Eunice and Rosie go?" he asked.

"To school."

They filled the front pockets of their pants with rolled oats. They planned to run into the bush, but Domko returned sooner than expected. Their pockets bulged, and they hoped he didn't notice.

He told them to open their mouths. The boys did, but by this time they had swallowed all they'd eaten. Domko was already frustrated that Caroline wouldn't be back for a few weeks and worried that they would run away. He sent them upstairs for the rest of the evening.

As the days passed, he became increasingly irritable, and the children knew he was looking for an excuse to beat somebody. Now slightly afraid of Eunice and David, Domko singled out Dennis who avoided him, doing the chores perfectly and staying out of arm's reach.

One afternoon Dennis decided to sneak into the house and try some of the soup Rosie was making. He walked through the yard and was almost at the door when he saw Domko coming, so he swerved back around the edge of the house and ran to the barn. He climbed into the loft and found the deepest pile of hay along the far wall. He was able to squeeze between the hay and the wall by digging a small hole and burrowing inside. He hoped Domko hadn't seen him escape.

The damp, moldy hay caused him to cough lightly. He listened, stiffening at every noise in the old barn. He'd been hiding for about fifteen minutes when he heard footsteps coming up the ladder. Parting his lips, he tried to breathe as shallowly as possible, hoping he was well covered. As Domko came closer, he could hear the floor creaking under his weight.

Dennis squeezed his eyes tight and prayed as Domko poked the hay with a pitchfork.

"Dennnnis," he cooed. "Yous be comink out."

Dennis laid still, his mind racing as he tried to decide what to do, knowing the beating would be less severe if he showed himself right away. He could hear Domko inching his way closer, moving from one side of the barn to the other, kicking and stabbing the hay. Just when Dennis thought he'd be discovered, Domko stopped. Someone had driven up the driveway, and he left to see who it was.

Dennis stayed in the hiding spot for more than an hour, and once it appeared Domko wasn't coming back, he brushed off the hay and crept to the ladder. On his hands and knees, he poked his head through the loft opening and seeing nobody around, climbed down the ladder. He went to the door and peered through a crack before slipping outside. Not seeing anyone in the yard, he realized this was his best chance to escape.

As fast as he could run, Dennis took off through the barnyard toward the road. He was over the fence in an instant, then into the thick bush northwest of the house. He couldn't bring himself to look over his shoulder, so he kept running until he was far from home.

He'd done it. He had used his wits to escape, and Dennis was finally free.

Nobody's ever gonna hurt me again, he thought as he walked through the bush. *Not ol' Satan and not anybody else.* He thought about how many times Domko had nearly killed him and knew nobody would ever treat him worse than that.

As he walked through the bush, his confidence soared. He'd recognized a change for the better in both himself and David since they were beaten so badly in the lean-to. David seemed different after they had slept along the lake bank. He was stronger and had more patience, and his confidence inspired Dennis to be stronger, too. His stepfather would never catch him again.

Dennis walked for nearly two hours through bush and fields before stopping at the first farmhouse he saw. By then, it was early evening, and he was becoming desperate to find a place to stay before it got dark. He didn't want to sleep outside alone, so he went to the door.

I can do this, he thought as he knocked.

A tall woman answered. Puzzled, she looked at his feet.

"Yes?" she asked.

"C-can I c-come in?" he stammered. "Ma is gone, and Domko chased me out." It was the best explanation he could come up with since usually, David did most of the talking.

The woman seemed to know who he was and opened the door to invite him inside. A man sat at the kitchen table reading a farm paper, and when he looked up, he was surprised to see Dennis.

"You're one of Bill Pischke's boys, aren't you?" he said with a Scottish accent. "You're a heck of a long way from home."

His wife recounted what Dennis had said, and invited him to sit and have something to eat. They introduced themselves as Mr. and Mrs. Stewart "Scotty" Brown. They had a lovely, clean home and Dennis felt comfortable there.

"Would you like to stay a few days until your mother comes back?" Mrs. Brown asked.

Dennis nodded without hesitation. That night while lying under crisp,

Karen Emilson

clean sheets and a thick quilt, he said a silent thank you to whatever had guided him to the Brown house.

Dennis stayed for three days then Mr. Brown suggested that he'd better go to school or they might all get into trouble. Dennis reluctantly agreed and rode to school the next morning with their daughter Ruth. But when Dennis came out of the schoolhouse that afternoon, his heart sank. Domko was waiting in front with his arms folded across his chest. Dennis walked home sideways, refusing to turn his back on Domko. Now that they were older, and harder to catch, he usually hit them from behind.

That night when he and David were hidden behind the wall, Dennis asked how Domko found him.

"He was listenin' in on everyone's phone calls," he said. "He's makin' sure that me and Beanie don't run away. He got Rosie real bad the other night, so I guess you're safe for another day."

Dennis lay quietly for a moment. Aware that Domko resented the fact he'd run away, he decided he'd be gone before Domko decided to teach him a lesson. "I'm gonna go where he can't find me," he said before falling asleep.

Dennis woke the next morning and walked to school with the other children. He only stayed until the noon hour, then disappeared into the bush across the road. He walked to Jim's house where he spent the afternoon. He didn't feel comfortable without Ruby there, so he left before dark, staying overnight in an abandoned building.

The next day he continued walking, arriving at a farmhouse near Grahamdale. He knocked on the door, and this time a tall, thin bachelor named Henry Sherbert answered. Dennis repeated the story he'd told the Browns and was invited in. Henry quietly listened as Dennis told him about Domko's beatings and lifted his shirt as proof.

Henry prepared supper, and then in the early evening, his brother Louis came inside from working in the field. Louis was a short, chubby man who initially seemed unfriendly. Henry explained the situation and the brothers agreed that Dennis could stay overnight.

As Dennis rested on the chesterfield draped in a woolen blanket, he looked around the room. He could hear Henry and Louis whispering in the kitchen and wondered what they were saying. He looked around at the many antiques and interesting things that the bachelors had collected over the years.

It was then that Dennis speculated how many different types of people there must be in the world. He was glad that he and David had started venturing further from their farm, meeting people like the Kochs, Browns and now the Sherberts.

For the next few days, Dennis shadowed Henry. He helped peel potatoes, wash dishes and cook. He enjoyed helping the man who listened patiently and offered the occasional consoling pat on the back.

"Would you like to come to town with me today?" Henry asked.

Dennis said that he would, and they drove together to Grahamdale to buy supplies. Henry took Dennis to the store where they stood for a while talking with a group of Henry's friends. They were invited to sit down, and after the usual small talk about the weather and cattle prices, one of the men asked Henry who his young friend was.

"This is Dennis Pischke," Henry said. "One of Caroline's boys from across the lake."

The men nodded. Some of them recognized Dennis from auction sales.

"How come he's with you?"

Henry bought Dennis a chocolate bar and coke, then turned back to the men. Henry started explaining Dennis' situation, and the longer he spoke, the angrier his voice became.

Dennis looked at the chocolate bar in wonder—it was an *Oh Henry* bar. Then he looked at Henry. He had no idea that somebody had named a chocolate bar after him!

Dennis felt all eyes on him as Henry acted out what he'd told him.

"Stand up and show them," he coaxed.

Dennis looked at him, then glanced around the store. There were only a few people there, and none of them were watching. Shyly, he stood up and lifted his shirt.

"Turn around, son," Henry said, voice softening.

Keeping his eyes on the floor, Dennis slowly turned his back to the men.

"See what I'm saying?" Henry said.

Dennis dropped his shirt and sat down, opening the chocolate bar package.

One man admitted he hadn't believed Gus' stories but was convinced now that Domko was unstable.

"Selkirk, that's where he belongs," another man said as he lit a homemade cigarette. "Jim has been saying that for years."

The others nodded in agreement.

Dennis finished his drink, and he and Henry left soon afterward. They drove back to the farm where Henry told Dennis to go inside and wait because he needed to go to Ashern. Dennis started supper and puttered around the house until Henry's return.

The next morning, Henry told Dennis it was safe for him to go home. "Your mother is there, and Domko was taken by the police."

Dennis smiled. He missed David but until then had pushed thoughts of him out of his mind. He became excited about the prospect of going home, but refused Henry's offer for a ride, saying he'd rather walk.

As Henry stood at the door, he told him that he could come back for a visit anytime. Dennis waved then jogged to the road. He arrived home two hours later to find the house quiet, except for the noise Kathy was making, jogging in her usual spot.

"Where's Ma?" he asked.

Kathy pointed to the upstairs bedroom.

Dennis cautiously went up. "Are you here?" he whispered.

Caroline was sitting at the far end of the room on the bed. It took Dennis' eyes a few moments to adjust to the darkness. He was shocked to see a newborn baby at her breast.

"Why did you bring another baby home?" he asked.

Instead of answering his question, she became angry, asking why he'd run away. "Now the police have come and taken Domko away again," she said.

"I couldn't stay here without you," he cried.

"Well, what am I going to do now? I can't be working in the barn all day," she said.

"We'll do the work, me, Davey and Eunice," Dennis said. "Us kids can do all the work."

The baby fussed and began to cry.

"Shhh," Caroline scolded as she transferred her attention to the tiny, wiggling baby. She moved the infant from one breast to the other and soon it was content again.

"Ma, why'd you bring another baby home?" he asked again.

"I had to because he was at the hospital waiting for me," she said. "His name is Mark."

Dennis shook his head as he went back downstairs. He knew that storks brought babies to the hospital but didn't understand why his mother kept bringing them home. Why couldn't another woman take her turn? Now they were doomed to have another sibling like Raymond.

Maybe Domko will be gone for good this time, he thought as he went outside to find David.

Where Children Run

One afternoon in mid-June when Caroline was washing diapers, there was a rap on the door. She dried her hands on her apron and opened it to find Emma standing there.

"Emma," she said. "How are you?"

"I'm fine. I thought I'd come for a little visit."

"You must come in," Caroline said stepping back. "Ignore the mess. The new baby has kept me up all night, and there is just no way I can get everything done."

Emma smiled as she stepped into the kitchen carrying a big box. She and Caroline had barely spoken the past few years since disagreeing about the children. Emma pushed the bad memories aside, hoping to focus on the new start she hoped to forge that afternoon.

"Would you like to see my washing machine?" Caroline nervously asked as she motioned for Emma to follow her to the laundry area. "I thought this would be the best spot for it. It's the place where the kids throw all their clothes anyway."

Emma nodded as she looked at the shiny round white tub with ringers on top. "It's very nice," she said. "Gus and I have been talking about getting some of these new appliances, but we just hate to go to the expense of putting hydro in the house. We're probably going to retire and move to town in a year or so."

For a moment, Caroline wasn't sure which one of them was getting the better deal. She would love a solid reason to move to town.

"Hi Emma," Kathy called out from the front room. She had an excellent memory and a knack for recognizing voices.

"How are you?" Emma said. "Did you like the school in Brantford?"

As Kathy explained some of what she'd learned, Raymond came bursting into the front room, awakening the baby who was sleeping in his crib. Caroline sent Kathy and Raymond outside to play as she picked up little Mark.

"Things haven't changed much around here," Emma laughed.

Caroline smiled. "That's for sure. One of these days I'm going to have to find out what's causing all these babies."

Emma forced a smile. She disliked the idea that Caroline was still in a relationship with Domko, but knew better than to say so. Instead, she spoke of safer subjects, and they made small talk for a while, their conversation punctuated by the occasional awkward moment. Soon they fell into a pattern that each of them remembered so well. Caroline made coffee, and they chatted as old friends do.

"I brought you some canning," Emma said. She had heard that Caroline was having a difficult time financially, but didn't want to injure her pride. "Like I said, we'll be retiring soon, and the girls keep telling me that I don't need to do so much canning, but you know me. I just can't help myself. I can't stand to see anything go to waste. Those boys must be eating a lot by now, and all I can say is, I'm sure thankful I didn't have a whole mess of boys instead of girls."

Caroline laughed. "The twins can eat their weight, I'm sure. And Raymond, well, he's growing, and I figure he's going to eat just as much if not more when he's their age."

"The children are fine then?" Emma asked.

"Yes. We're all good. Walter has the same job in Winnipeg, and Steven is working on a ranch in Alberta. He's coming home for a visit next week. Norman is still at Geisler's farm; and Domko, well, he's away right now on account of his episodes. I'm not sure when he's coming back."

Emma smiled, not sure what to say and so she changed the subject.

"I've heard Marion won't be teaching school here next year," she said. "Sounds as if we'll have to find a new teacher."

Caroline was surprised by the news. Her estrangement from Emma had isolated her from the goings-on in the community. She was her only friend now that Ruby was gone.

The women chatted until the children came rolling into the house after school. They were all surprised and pleased to see Emma. The twins each drank a glass of milk and had a piece of fresh bread while peering into the box that Emma had brought. Eunice asked Caroline if she would make some cornstarch pudding for dessert.

"Well, I can see you're busy, it's time for me to go," Emma said, pleased to see the children looking so content. "I have to get home and get supper ready for Gus."

The women smiled at one another. "Thanks for the canning," Caroline said. "I'll send the boys over with the jars when we're finished."

"Don't bother," Emma said, waving her hand. "I have no more use for them, really."

The children soon began to sense that something was bothering their mother. She began speaking quietly on the telephone and hung up when they came in the house. Their suspicions that Domko would be home soon were confirmed when she called them together to say that he would be back July 3.

"I'll run away," Dennis said. "I'm not gonna stay here no more when Satan's around."

"Don't talk like that," Caroline said. She despised the names the children called him but couldn't break them of the habit.

"He smashes us, and if he does it again, I'm gonna tell some more people," Dennis said.

Of all her ten children, Dennis was the most stubborn, and she believed what he said. Now it seemed like the right time to send the twins to live elsewhere. It was an idea she'd been considering for a while.

"All right," she said. "I'll see what I can do."

A few days later, she told the boys of a family living near Lundar willing to take them in. They would have to work on their farm in exchange for room and board, and she asked if they wanted to go there.

Both nodded vigorously. "When can we leave?" David asked.

"Tomorrow. Steven's coming for a visit, and he'll take us there."

They packed their belongings and waited eagerly, anxious to begin their lives away from the farm as their older brothers had. When Steven arrived, they slid into the back seat of his car and rolled down the windows. Faces turned to the sun; the warm breeze overwhelmed their senses as they rode along. Their mother enjoyed the outing as well—talking and laughing over the blare of the radio as they sped toward the highway, a huge cloud of dust rising behind them.

They arrived in Lundar by early afternoon and drove to a lovely farm just south of town. The house was modest but nicely painted, and the yard was tidy. A stately barn stood out back, and it appeared to Caroline that these were wealthy farmers by the day's standards.

She told them to wait by the car while she went to talk to her acquaintances. They were an older Jehovah's Witness couple she had met on a few occasions. They had been friendly to her on the phone when she'd called about the boys, explaining that her sons from her first marriage "just didn't get along" with their stepfather. They'd been sympathetic and said they needed help milking their large dairy herd.

The Twins unloaded their belongings and stretched their long legs.

"Do you think these people are nice?" Dennis asked as they watched their mother talking with a man and woman on the front porch.

"They'll be good," David said. "And they can't be no worse than the ol' black bastard anyway."

They sensed something was wrong when the man and woman went back inside, and their mother came hurrying toward the car.

"What is it Ma?" David asked.

"Just get in the car," she said. "You're not staying here."

"What happened?" he asked. "We gotta stay here. We don't got no other place to go."

"Get in," she said.

Steven asked what was wrong as they all climbed back in and slammed the doors. Caroline sat for a moment staring at the lovely house. The boys knew it would take her a bit of time to sort out her thoughts.

"They said they don't need help after all," she finally said. "They tried calling this morning, but we'd already left."

"How can they need help one day and not the next?" Steven asked. "Everyone will be haying soon."

Caroline's jaw tightened. She knew the truth was going to hurt the twins.

"I know what happened," she said.

"What?" the boys chorused.

"They think you boys are liars and thieves and don't want to work."

"Did he say that?" Steven asked.

"He didn't have to. He said he changed his mind about taking the twins after talking to people from the church. What else could that mean?"

Steven backed out of the driveway, churning dust and stones as he sped away. The twins sat quietly in the back.

"What are we going to do?" Dennis whispered.

"I dunno. Lemme think a minute."

David felt heartened by his mother's attempt to find them a place to live.

"We'll do somethin'," he said. "We'll be okay for a few days. By the time Squeezer's nice-ness wears off, maybe Ma will find us some other place."

Two days later, Domko arrived in Moosehorn by bus, then rode the local taxi home. He seldom spoke, napped often, ate less, and continued to watch the twins with suspicion.

The boys had grown a lot, and it was as if Domko was seeing them for the first time. They were now lanky teenagers with hands and feet like adults. Adolescent muscles were beginning to develop on their arms and legs, and while their strength and skills were still youthful, they wouldn't be for much longer.

When Domko noticed the jars of preserves and vegetables that sat in a box beside the cupboard, he let everyone know he was not pleased that Caroline had accepted charity from Emma. She tried to reason with him, but he picked up the box and flung it out the door. The twins darted out after the preserves, and as soon as Domko shut the door, they ran to see what could be salvaged.

"We can still eat this," Dennis said.

"Yeah, Ma shoulda known," David said as they stood over the broken jars. "We shoulda hid it sooner."

David picked up the box, and they tossed large pieces of glass inside. The saskatoons and raspberries were too small to save, so they ate as many from the ground as they could. They put two jars of jam aside, then making aprons out of their shirts, began scooping up the vegetables.

"You do the beets, and I'll pick the beans and carrots," Dennis said.

When they had saved all they could, and eaten what they couldn't, they went to the chicken coop to hide. When Domko went to the barn, they ran to the house, they took a bowl from the kitchen and went upstairs. They put the vegetables into the bowl and hid it along with the two jam jars behind the wall.

Domko complained that he was too tired to work, so he and Caroline decided to bring in outside help. They were already weeks late with seeding but decided it would be better to do it late than not at all. If the oats were too immature to sell once harvested, they could be fed to the cattle.

Caroline called a bachelor friend named Henry Harliss who lived near Grahamdale. Henry had known Caroline for many years and became friends with Domko. He also raised pigeons, so this was something the men had in common. Henry had always liked the family and agreed to work for them for a few weeks and arrived the following day. He was a tall, quiet man who always saw the good in people. He refused to take sides between Caroline and Domko and for the most part, discouraged Domko's posturing. He preferred to talk about the weather, current events and community matters rather than how much Domko disliked the children.

While Henry and the children worked, Domko stood nearby and complained about his health. He said the medicine he took while at the hospital made him feel lethargic, so he stopped taking it. Henry told him he didn't think that was a good idea. Domko argued that he was "but-a-some goot man." To that Henry said nothing, turning to the children to talk about their schoolwork and friends.

Henry's thoughtfulness encouraged the children who seldom found an adult that took an interest in them. They began looking forward to Henry's arrival each morning and knew that as long as he was there, Domko would be on his best behavior.

But it didn't take long until Domko became irritated as he watched the children working under Henry's supervision. They were not slouching and fearful, and Henry allowed them to take water breaks. He ate lunch and supper with the family, so the children were also eating regular meals.

The children were trying to think of a way to keep Henry on longer, while Domko wanted to hasten his departure. It bothered him that it was his suggestion to hire help; which as it turned out, made him feel threatened on his own farm. He was starting to unravel again.

The children were working nearby when they heard Domko lose his temper and began arguing with Henry.

"I's be shootink but-a-some keets ant killink Carlorka," he said, patting the breast pocket where he kept his knife. "They's be goot for sheet. She's be killink me like but-a-some Bill."

Henry was shocked by the outburst, but then his eyes narrowed, and he took a step toward Domko.

"That's a terrible way to talk," he said. "You should be ashamed of such thoughts—how can you say those things? If you choose to have evil and wicked ideas then fine, but don't tell them to me again."

Domko took a step back.

"I have nothing against your wife and kids," he said. "I won't stand here and listen to you talk about them. It's disgusting, plain disgusting, and I am embarrassed that you might call me a friend."

Domko had never seen mild-mannered Henry so angry, and the twins thought Domko looked afraid of him. The children stared at Henry with admiration when Domko turned and went back to the house. They wished other people, especially those from the church, would also stand up to Domko.

Dennis thought of the *Oh Henry* chocolate bar again. Now he wasn't sure which man it was named after.

The following week they began haying. Rather than starting on their land, Domko sent the twins to a piece of land leased by Jim, saying that he had permission to hay it that year. When they protested, he chased them with a shovel.

"Do you think Jim said this is all right?" Dennis asked as they hitched the horses.

"Jim hates Domko. He'd let the hay rot before giving it to him."

With no choice, they drove to the field and began cutting anyway. The following morning Dennis began raking while David continued to cut. On the third day, they pushed it into stacks. Later that afternoon, Domko drove out to the field and told them to haul the stacks home. Usually, they waited until all the hay was up.

"See?" David whispered. "He wants us to hide it. Pretty tricky, eh?"

"Yeah, and people think he's got no control over himself," Dennis whispered back. "Just like how he never hits Raymie or Kathy."

They drove the horses home to hitch them to the hay wagon. They were able to haul one stack home that night. The following morning, Domko told them to bring the others. They arrived at the field, loaded a stack and then drove the team home. Domko pointed to an area behind the barn and told them to unload it there.

As they stood on top, forking the hay off the wagon, an unfamiliar vehicle came up the driveway. A man got out and began talking to Domko. The boys jumped off the stack and snuck around the barnyard fence so they could overhear the conversation.

"I's not be doink it, they's be," Domko said raising his hands helplessly in the air. "I's be seek ant tellink them to hay. Vat? They's be hayink in Jim's but-a-some field?"

The man nodded. The boys recognized neighbor Rudy Metner, and it was evident that he didn't believe Domko's explanation. Rudy shook his head angrily. He decided that Domko could keep the hay already hauled home, but he would take what was left in the field. After Rudy left, the twins ran back to continue unloading the stack.

"Now we gotta ask him what to do next," David said. "You do it."

"I'm not gonna ask him. You do it."

"No way. He's gonna be pissed off for sure and is gonna find some way of blamin' us for this."

So they hid in the back of the barn.

"Why don't we just go to the south quarter and start?" Dennis said.

While they fretted over what to do next, another vehicle drove into the yard. They recognized it was Domko's friend from the church who came by for weekly visits.

Domko approached the man and shook his hand.

"C'mon," David said. Feeling safe with someone else there, they walked boldly up to Domko to ask where he wanted them to start cutting hay. The visitor shot them a distasteful look.

Domko guessed the boys had overheard his discussion with Rudy and looked embarrassed. He told them to go to the south field.

"That was easy," David said.

"Yeah, I never thought I'd be glad to see that ol' Devil from the church visiting," Dennis laughed.

FREEDOM

Domko's condition continued to deteriorate, and as another summer came to an end, he returned to his habit of beating one of them each day and taunting them with chocolate bars. The children fled to the neighbors when they could, but nobody realized that Domko was still on probation and that the police would pick him up if he violated the terms of his release.

Caroline spent the early part of September depressed and confined to her bed. When school began, the older children were not allowed to attend since they had run away so often during July and August, that the haying still was not done. Wet weather did not help matters so on the dry days, they had to stay home to finish putting up the hay.

The children came in one night to find their mother screaming and sobbing uncontrollably after yet another fight with Domko. The following afternoon Eunice sat outside along the south side of the house. The sun was warm on her face as she let her head fall gently back against the rough wall. She watched the pale yellow and orange leaves blow gently in the early autumn breeze. They were just starting to turn and looked beautiful.

It's not fair, she thought. *Life has been so unfair.*

She remembered being thirteen years old and her daily desire then was to escape the confines of this God-forsaken place that she called home. The days, months, and years had crept by, and now, at sixteen, she was still on the farm and had lost all hope of ever leaving.

Eunice alternated between feeling sorry for her mother and despising her. They'd been fighting a lot lately, and she remembered one particularly bad argument. Domko had wanted to knock her down a few notches, so he forced her to sit on a chair. He had grabbed her soft, long brown hair and cut a huge chunk from the back of her head right at the scalp.

He had stood back and laughed, calling her "the queen," for a reason she never understood. She'd tried to hide the bald spot, but it was impossible, so her mother cut her hair short, except for a piece at the front that she pushed back to cover the bald spot. She'd been so embarrassed that she confronted her mother and demanded to know why she put up with Domko. How could she let him do this to her children day in and day out?

Eunice shook her head at the memory. The fights escalated after that as Eunice tried to make her mother see what was happening to the family, but she seemed lost in her own world and only concerned with herself. Eunice said some hurtful things during their fight, and afterward, her mother had taken a handful of pills in a half-hearted suicide attempt.

What if she does it again but dies? Eunice thought. *Then I'd be here alone with him.* She shuddered. There was nobody to talk to about this—the boys wouldn't understand. They didn't know what it was like for her and Rosie.

Eunice believed that her mother didn't like her much because she was too much a "Pischke." Her mother said this all the time, and Eunice hated the way the word rolled off her mother's tongue like a swear word.

As she leaned against the wall, she began to weep. Her tears were interrupted by the sound of a car turning into the driveway. She quickly wiped away her tears and stood up.

A man stepped out of the car and introduced himself as Henry Schedler. He told Eunice that his wife Irene was not well and that they needed a live-in housekeeper. He said that they lived in Spear Hill, a small hamlet near Moosehorn. The job paid $75 a month and asked if she would be interested.

Stunned, Eunice quickly accepted. Henry told her he needed her to begin work after the weekend. She agreed and ran to the house to tell her mother. Caroline was not surprised about the job offer, and Eunice wondered if she had arranged it. She was too excited to ask and couldn't believe her good luck. This was the best day of her life.

The following day they went to Moosehorn, and her mother bought her a few new pair of underwear. She knew that her mother was embarrassed by the condition of the clothes she had packed, but didn't have enough money to buy her anything else. As it was, Domko would be mad once he discovered Eunice was gone.

Her mother drove her to the Schedler's home that afternoon. It was one day early, but the Schedlers didn't seem to mind.

"I'll start workin' today, and you don't even have to pay me," she said. Caroline waved good-bye then drove away.

Eunice's departure was difficult for the twins and Rosie. They missed her mothering, and she'd been a diligent worker. Without her, their workload almost doubled. They slept in the bush the night Domko found out Eunice was gone.

The twins began school a few days later. The new teacher, 21-year-old Miss Leah D'Hoore, was surprised to see them. She told the other students to start their lessons, then found a place for the boys at one of the larger desks at the back of the room.

"I thought maybe you weren't coming this year," she said as they settled in. "Where's Eunice?"

"She's got a good job at Schedlers, keepin' care of the house," David said.

"Well, you boys can start at the beginning of grade seven. You'll have to do some work at home to get caught up because you've already missed a whole month."

The twins nodded and watched Miss D'Hoore as she returned to the front of the room. Dennis was smitten. She was, without a doubt, the most beautiful woman he'd ever seen. Leah had long red hair and lovely clear skin, with a spattering of freckles across her nose and cheeks. Her eyes were bright, and she had a very womanly figure, which made Dennis blush. He and David agreed that attending school would be a lot less painful with Miss D'Hoore as their teacher.

For the next two weeks, they found themselves trying to catch up with their lessons. There was no time before or after school, so they stayed in during recess to complete their assignments.

One afternoon during the lunch break, Miss D'Hoore sat at the front of the room and watched the boys discussing a math problem. They seemed sincere in their attempt to learn, and this surprised her. She'd heard that these boys were troublemakers and initially she was thankful that they hadn't started school. When they did, she was nervous that she wouldn't be able to control them. So far, they'd been well-behaved and helpful.

Her thoughts were interrupted when a student burst through the door.

"Miss D'Hoore, come quick," he yelled.

She jumped from her chair and ran to the door to see a huge, black bull standing in the schoolyard. It was the biggest, meanest looking thing she'd ever seen and was terrified. She'd heard horrible stories about people being killed by bulls and had no idea how to get him out of the schoolyard.

Just then David and Dennis pushed past her and stepped onto the porch.

"That's our bull, Miss D'Hoore," David said. "Sorry if he scared you."

The bull watched solemnly as the twins split up and walked slowly toward him. He let out a long, low bellow.

Where Children Run

"We'll get him outta here," Dennis said.

"Be careful," she said.

"It's okay, we're not scared of him," David grinned.

They waved their arms gently and coaxed the bull to turn around. As soon as they had it lumbering toward the road, Miss D'Hoore called the rest of the children inside. The twins returned fifteen minutes later and began working on their math problems as if nothing had happened. They smiled at Miss D'Hoore who at that moment decided that she liked these boys despite what others said.

Caroline called David and Dennis into the kitchen. "Go and see what those two devils are talking about now," she said pointing out the window. "Then come back and tell me."

They looked out to see Domko talking with the man from the church. He had been coming every week to see Domko since he arrived home from the hospital. They went out and stood by the door.

"You're a good man, Bob," the man said, patting him on the back as they walked toward the barn.

The boys cringed. Now they understood why Domko's confidence soared after every visit.

"Why are they going behind the barn instead of coming in the house?" David whispered.

Dennis shook his head. "Maybe they're talkin' about Ma."

"I think he gets her in trouble with the Witnesses."

"He looks at us in a mean way," Dennis said.

"One of us has to go listen," David said. "You understand the church talk better than me."

Dennis thought for a moment then agreed. He wanted to help his mother and was very curious about what they were saying.

Creeping around the west side of the barn, he climbed over a fence and moved like a cat through the tall grass. He hoped to listen from the back of the barn but as he rounded the corner, expecting the men to be on the far side, found them sitting right there. They turned around, and Domko glared at him. Dennis wheeled in a full circle and ran back in the direction he came, slipping into the barn to catch his breath. He could see David and Rosie walking out to the pasture to get the cows. It was his turn to pump water into the trough.

He decided to run to the pump house and hide. Once inside, he began pumping furiously, hoping to finish the job then hide in the bush. He worked for about ten minutes then Domko was there. Dennis looked up just as Domko's boot came up and slammed into his face. The inside of the pump house began to swirl as he was slammed against the wall and floor over and over again until everything went black.

Dennis awoke some time later choking and gagging. He turned on his side and vomited blood, struggling to breathe through his nose which was throbbing and too tender to touch. When he was finally able, he got up and staggered to the house, crying out to his mother who was sitting at the table.
"What happened?" she asked, jumping up from the chair.
Dennis pointed at Domko who stood between the kitchen and the front room.
"Vat?" he said innocently. "Vat I's be do?"
"You could have killed him," she screamed. "Look at his face."
Dennis waited until Domko came into the kitchen, then staggered past and crawled upstairs. From the hiding spot behind the wall, he could hear the two of them arguing.
"What happened to Dennis?" she demanded.
"He's be fallink off but-a-some lean-to roof," he said.
"You don't expect me to believe that, do you?" she said. Caroline knew that Dennis must have been caught spying and she began swearing and threatening to call the police. They fought for hours about Dennis, their relationship and everything else that came to mind. It abruptly ended when Domko left, slamming the kitchen door.

"Where's Dennis?" Miss D'Hoore asked the following morning.
David hesitated. "He's not feelin' too good this mornin'."
"Tell him I hope he's better tomorrow."
David nodded.
The next morning Dennis looked at his face in the mirror. "Can I go to school like this?"
David told him to turn around so he could examine his blackened eyes and swollen lip. "Halloween's not for a few more days," he joked.
"Thanks a lot."
"Just kiddin'. But if you go to school like that, everyone's gonna know."
"Everyone knows anyway."
"Yeah, but Miss D'Hoore don't know," David said.
"Then we can say I fell off 'but-a-some roof,'" he said.
David laughed, and they hurried off to school. Dennis kept his eyes low

most of the morning. At noon, when their classmates went running outside to play, Miss D'Hoore called the twins to her desk.

"How come you boys don't bring a lunch?" she asked.

"I dunno," David said.

"Do you forget to bring it?"

"No. We don't got none to bring," he said.

"You don't have one," she corrected. And then eyeing Dennis, she asked what happened to his face.

"I h-had an accident," he said.

"What kind of accident?"

He fidgeted but wouldn't answer.

Miss D'Hoore saw how uncomfortable he was and decided not to push too hard.

"I have to go make my lunch, how would you boys like to come with me?" she asked.

The twins looked at each other then nodded. They followed her across the schoolyard to the teacherage. Miss D'Hoore opened the door, and they followed her inside.

"Ever been in here before?" she asked.

They were left speechless for a moment.

"When Mrs. Gering was the teacher she went home at night, so this place was empty," David said looking around. "We used to come in here to get away from Squeezer, but then Raymie started tellin' on us, so we had to stop."

"Who's Squeezer?"

"Our stepfather."

"Would that be Bob Domko?" she asked as she took a jar of peanut butter and bag of bread from the shelf.

"Yeah."

"I've heard a little bit about him. What's he like?"

They watched as she took ten slices of bread from the bag and put them evenly on the table. She opened the peanut butter and with a knife, spread a thick layer on every other slice.

"He's nuts," David said.

"Nuts?"

"Yeah. He goes to Selkirk, and they give him pills and Ma lets him come home. After a couple weeks, we gotta run away again."

"Where do you children run?"

"Any place where he can't find us. We run in the bush and to Gus and

Jim's place. We go over the beaver dam. We just run 'til we can't run no more."

"What about the police? Do you go there?"

"No, ma'am. The police don't believe us."

"Are you sure?"

"Yeah, they just bring us home and then it's worse."

Miss D'Hoore handed them two sandwiches each. Then she went to the refrigerator, took out a bottle and poured each of them a glass of milk.

"I don't have anything but peanut butter," she said.

"That's okay; we like peanut butter, don't we Davey?" Dennis said.

"We sure do."

They bit into the bread and were astounded by the taste. Except for the ice cream they'd had at the zoo, this was the best thing they ever tasted. They quickly ate the sandwiches and drank the milk.

Miss D'Hoore's conversation with the twins bothered her for the rest of the week. She went home to visit her parents for the Thanksgiving weekend and hoped that the twins would go to the teacherage if they needed somewhere to hide. She left the door open just in case.

"Eileen, you're a more experienced teacher than me," she said to her older sister. "I need to ask you a question. Have you ever had a family of kids that you've worried about?"

"Yes, a few times. Why?" Eileen said.

"You're never gonna believe what I heard earlier this week. I've got these students named David and Dennis Pischke. They're dirt poor, and they've got a crazy stepfather, and when I say crazy, I mean he's been to Selkirk. Anyway, when he's home, I'm convinced he beats them . . . ."

MARCH 1963

The cold March wind whipped through the bare trees near the beaver dam. The twins sat huddled around a small fire, nursing their injuries. So far, it was their worst winter yet.

"How much longer can we keep livin' like this?" David asked.

He and Dennis had been outside since the day before and planned to spend at least one more night in the cold before going home.

"I dunno," Dennis said. "Do you think he hopes we just freeze to death?"

David shrugged. "Maybe, but who'd do the work?"

"Not Raymie that's for sure. He'd never make his son work like a slave." David tossed the small stick he'd been playing with into the fire and watched as flames slowly consumed it. "Yeah, he always gets mad when we run away 'cause there's no one there to work. But he's just as mad when we go back, and he finds out we're not dead."

"I've never been able to understand the ol' bastard," Dennis said. "How 'bout you?"

"He don't make no sense. What does 'but-a-some' mean anyway?"

Dennis laughed. "I think he means 'the.'"

"How can Ma stand him?"

"I dunno. I guess she can't smell him."

The brothers laughed. Dennis reached for another log to put on the fire. A small wisp of smoke rose up, and within a few minutes, it was burning.

"Is he gonna kill us?"

David looked at his hands draped across his knees. He'd been thinking about their future a lot lately.

"He's gettin' worse, and if we don't go some place soon, we're not gonna."

"Where should we go?"

"We'll go over the beaver dam again, but his time we'll stay," David said. "We'll find good jobs and make lots of money."

Dennis nodded. They would have to wait until the snow melted and the farmers needed hired hands. If they went too soon, they'd just be sent home.

David put his feet in front of the fire and unwrapped the rags he had tied around them, old shirts he found after Domko took away his felt boots because his toes poked through the end.

"Hey Davey, have you ever noticed how people look at us when we tell them about him?"

David laughed. "Yeah, like they can't believe it."

"When we get away from here, are you gonna tell people?"

"I dunno," David said. "Will anyone believe us?"

Dennis stared at him. "Why would we lie?"

David shrugged. "Who knows. People are stupid. Squeezer's got friends, and they won't never believe us. I think I'm gonna just try to forget," he said, shifting his weight, trying to get comfortable on the cold ground.

"You can't forget."

David looked into the dark bush. "It don't matter."

"Yes, it does. You gotta promise that if he kills me first, you'll tell people."

David shrugged as a tiny lump rose in his throat. He thought it was odd that telling people the truth seemed more important to Dennis than surviving. He became lost in his thoughts until Dennis broke the silence.

"If we was gone, do you think anybody would miss us?" he asked.

David looked at him, and his chin began to waver. He stared deeply into his twin's eyes and wished he could tell him that they were loved. David tried hard to think of somebody who'd miss them. Ashamed, he looked at the ground.

"No," he choked, "nobody would."

The boys woke the next morning mildly surprised that they were still alive. It had been a cold night, and while they had refueled the fire many times, it was now reduced to ashes.

"Well, we ain't dead yet, so we better find somethin' to eat," David laughed, his spirits now brightened by a new day and the prospect of a good meal in Emma's kitchen.

"I've been thinkin'," David said as they trudged through the deep snow. "You're right, Denny. We gotta tell people."

Dennis was pleased to hear that he agreed with him after all. "Yeah, I'm gonna tell everybody how Domko treated us and how some people helped us and some didn't."

"Someday when we're big," David said, vowing that they would not hide behind the shame. "We'll find somebody who'll help us tell the whole world."

Emma invited the boys inside and fussed over them. Gus was outside working, so she welcomed the company and was interested to hear what had been happening at their house. Unfortunately, her reconciliation with Caroline had been brief since Domko no longer allowed her to socialize.

Emma fried three eggs for each of them and sliced fresh bread until it was piled high on the plate. The twins slathered thick gobs of jam on the bread and ate heartily.

"Have some more," she said as she poured them another cup of cocoa.

They had chatted for a while before the twins raised the serious subject on both their minds. It was another reason they'd come to see Emma.

"Auntie Emma," David began, "If we freeze or drown goin' across the beaver dam to get away from Squeezer, then it's his fault, right?"

Emma looked puzzled. "I suppose so, why do you ask?"

"And if he kills us some day, even if it looks like an accident, will the police know?" Dennis asked.

Emma stopped sipping her coffee to stare at him. She was left speechless by their matter-of-fact tones. David could sense they'd upset her but finished what he was saying.

"'Cause Ma always sticks up for him 'cause she's scared," David said. "If he kills Dennis then I'm gonna tell everybody. But if he kills us both, then will you?"

"Don't talk like that," she said. "He's not going to kill you boys. You're almost grown now. Soon you'll get off the farm, and things will be better."

They stared at her, waiting for an answer.

"Well, will you?" Dennis asked.

Emma felt a pang of regret. She wished that she and Gus had been more help to the family. Honestly, though, she didn't know what more they could have done.

"Well, I know one thing for sure," she said. "I'll never forget you boys, and I'll never forget what he's done to you. And I swear to God, if you boys turn up dead, I won't rest until people know the truth."

The twins smiled. That was the answer they needed to hear.

"But that doesn't mean I want you to give up, you hear?" she said, getting up from the table and disappearing into the front room, her words trailing behind her. "And I want you to know I've been thinking about you."

She reappeared a short time later carrying two white toques.

"I'm ashamed I didn't give these to you sooner, but Domko chased me off when I brought them over. I thought he might take it out on you boys, so I just put them away," she said, handing them the toques. "I haven't seen much of you lately. Where have you been hiding?"

They pulled the identical toques over their heads and smiled at each other. "We've been in the church and the barn, and we've been in the bush," Dennis said. "Sometimes we stay in the school cottage on the weekends when Miss D'Hoore is gone. Please, don't tell nobody 'cause we don't want to get in trouble."

"I won't," Emma said.

"We're smarter now, so we know how to trick the ol' bast . . . I mean, ol' Satan," David said. "We know how to sneak food when he's not lookin' and Miss D'Hoore makes us samiches."

"That's SANDwiches," Dennis corrected.

"I know, that's what I said—SAMiches."

Emma laughed.

"Is it a school day?" Dennis asked. They hadn't attended for a few days and weren't sure.

"Hmmm," she said glancing at the calendar. "It's Wednesday the 13th. Are you boys going to school today?"

They nodded and stood to leave. The twins thanked Emma for breakfast and waved goodbye.

"Puck puck Muchtork!" David yelled as he swung his legs out the bedroom window then let himself fall to the ground. He landed hard on his feet and rolled onto his side. He jumped up and ran to the edge of the house. It was nearly dark outside, and he could hear Dennis' screams as Domko whipped him with the belt. When he couldn't listen to the sound any longer, he ran to hide in the chicken coop.

That's what he'd hollered in their language—that he'd wait in the chicken coop, but if Domko came, then he'd run to the beaver dam and wait there. David hoped that thoughts of going to the Koch's house would give Dennis strength.

David waited anxiously behind the chicken coop door. He heard the house door opening. He held his breath to the sound of footsteps in the yard. The crisp sound of a gun bolt clicking in place caused him to stiffen. He could hear Domko's unmistakable grunting as he scoured the yard. Soon it was quiet, and David emerged from behind the door and peeked outside. Domko was walking slowly down the driveway, gun in hand.

He watched until Domko strode down the road to the teacherage. Just then, there was movement at the window, and Dennis leaped out. He landed hard on the ground.

"Are you okay?" David asked as Dennis rolled onto his feet.

"Yeah, I pretended I was dead," he said.

"Let's get outta here, he's lookin' for me, and he's got the gun."

They ran into the bush and kept going until they found themselves on the lake bank. In the darkness, every sound caused them to turn as they looked across the dark water. They shivered at the sight of tiny waves lapping against the shore. Twinkling lights on the other side seemed so far away.

"How are we gonna get across?" Dennis asked.

"We gotta go around," David said. "But it's a long ways."

They walked along the lake bank to its southern-most tip. They came to a fortress of logs and sticks with a mud hut in the center. They knew they were nearing the wide drainage ditch that channeled water from Pischke Lake into Lake Manitoba. They could see the expanse of water become narrow and shallower as rocks broke the surface in places.

The thought of walking through the cold water did not appeal to either of them. "Why don't we just go to the road?" Dennis asked.

David looked in that direction and listened. He could hear a vehicle somewhere in the distance, and there was a chance that Domko had gone back for the car. "We can't. He's wild 'bout us goin' to the neighbors. He's scared 'bout the police comin' and takin' him back to Selkirk. Hear that? I bet it's him."

Dennis' eyes widened. Twice before they had run down the road and Domko had easily caught them.

"Yeah, it won't be so bad," he said, eyeing the glassy water. It was early May, and although it had been a warm spring, the water was just above the freezing point.

Hearing a noise behind them, David grabbed Dennis' arm and pulled him to the ground. The rustling abated as David slowly turned and strained to see into the dark bush. A moment later, the still air was penetrated by the sound of footsteps in the underbrush, coming directly toward them.

They jumped up and stepped into the cold water. They waded in up to their thighs and tried not to splash as the water rippled against their legs. Dennis glanced nervously over his shoulder but saw nothing along the shore.

"Do you think it's him?" he whispered.

"I wasn't gonna stand there and find out," David said.

"I'm freezin' my legs off—are we almost there?"

"It'll get shallow soon," David said, but the water continued to get deeper.

Ruts in the ditch made the bottom slippery and difficult to walk on. As they neared the other shore, they discovered the holes were even deeper and soon they were up to their waists.

"C'mon we'll walk further south," David groaned, as Dennis followed closely behind. Dry ground was less than one hundred yards away, but their legs were cramping, slowing them down.

"Keep goin'," Dennis said. "I can see the shore."

"Yeah, but it's getting deeper."

"But it's too far to go back."

David took a deep breath as he continued. One more rut plunged them in up to their chests. They cried out from the throbbing cold.

"Keep going," Dennis yelled. "We're almost there."

Gradually, the water began to lower, and soon they were standing on dry land. They shivered uncontrollably in the cold night. The only light came from the brightness of the moon. The wind was beginning to blow.

"You got any matches?" Dennis asked through chattering teeth.

"No, the old bastard keeps 'em in his bedroom now. We're not far from Kochs. It won't take long to get there."

They hurried through the field then into a bluff of trees. They followed the same light they'd seen the time they came through the reeds. They kept their minds busy by pointing out trees, rocks and other landmarks that looked familiar. Soon they found themselves on the same road they'd traveled the last time they crossed the lake, but this time the Koch's house was nowhere to be seen.

"Where'd the farm go?" Dennis asked.

"I dunno," David said looking around. "Where do we go now?"

Dennis pointed north. "We probably came out there last time. Maybe we're all turned around?"

They trudged along the road expecting to arrive at Koch's house after rounding each unfamiliar bluff of trees. The wind picked up slightly and a pelting, cold rain added to their misery. As they got closer to a distant light, they realized this wasn't the Koch house.

"Should we ask?" Dennis asked.

"We better," David said. "We'll freeze if we don't."

They stood together rapping on the door. A man answered, and David recognized him immediately. He was the same man who had caught Dennis feeding Domko's cows in his grain field. A huge fight had erupted between him and Domko.

"C-can we c-come in," David asked.

The man looked at them suspiciously.

"You boys go back to where you came from," he said. "I don't want to get involved."

The door shut and the twins were left standing on the stoop in the pouring rain.

"Come on, Denny," David said. "Let's get outta here."

They walked down the driveway and along the road until they noticed a small building and decided they should spend the night. Dennis opened the door, and David followed him inside. There was nothing in the shed except a few rusted iron rails and an old red can. The shed was reasonably dry, so they found themselves a place in a corner. Pressing their bodies together, they listened to the patter of rain on the roof and the skittering of mice across the floor.

"Tomorrow it'll be easier to find our way around," David said. "We'll go to Schedlers and find Eunice. She'll know what we should do."

The next morning, they emerged from the shed stiff and hungry. They headed in the general direction of Grahamdale and walked through the sloppy wet fields. They found themselves on the road and asked a motorist for directions. Soon they were standing in front of Schedler's house. They knocked on the door and were happy when Eunice answered. She was surprised and pleased to see them, but slightly embarrassed by their appearance. They explained what had happened and told her that they didn't want to go home ever again.

After discussing their plight with Mr. Schedler, Eunice washed and dried their clothes. The boys were fed lunch while Mr. Schedler made a few telephone calls.

"Don't tell Ma where we are," David whispered to Eunice.

Eunice nodded in understanding. She had a wonderful life with the Schedlers and shuddered at the thought of having to go back to the farm. She didn't want that for her brothers either.

Later that afternoon, Mr. Schedler arranged for the twins to work for Fred and Mary Buztynski who agreed to keep them for a few months since they needed two farm hands. The boys could work in exchange for room and board.

Fred and Mary were kind people who fed and treated them well. There was a lot to do, but they were strong, capable, and willing workers when they weren't being beaten.

They began work the next day. They shoveled manure and picked stones from the fields. Near the end of the month, they seeded a field of oats. Occasionally they went to visit the Kochs who lived nearby.

"Do you think Ma knows where we are?" Dennis asked one Sunday afternoon as they walked from the Kochs house back to the Buztynski farm.

David thought for a moment. "No, or she woulda come to get us. She and Domko probably think we died somewhere and are too scared to phone the police in case they get blamed."

Dennis laughed. "I don't care, just as long as they don't come."

The twins worked for the Buztynskis for nearly two months. Caroline must have somehow heard where they were because she and Walter came for a visit one Sunday afternoon. It became awkward when she tried to persuade them to go back to the farm, and the twins refused. Eventually, she and Walter left. The boys fell back into a routine but knew that the Buztynskis wouldn't need them much longer.

One day while they repaired fences along the road, a car slowly pulled up beside them. A man got out and introduced himself as Herman Bray from Grahamdale. He had heard that the Buztynskis wouldn't need the twins anymore and wondered if one of them would like to work for him. They nodded eagerly, until they realized that the man only needed one worker.

Herman looked both boys over and offered Dennis the job. He was quick to say that he'd find a place for David, too. The twins agreed, and Herman came back to get them the following day. They thanked the Buztynskis and soon were on their way, each to new homes.

Except for the time Dennis had run to the Brown and Sherbert homes, the brothers had never been apart. They understood that not everyone needed two growing boys who ate a lot, but it didn't make their separation from one another any easier.

They sat quietly in the back seat of Herman's car as he drove toward Highway No. 6. David was upset and jealous that Herman had chosen Dennis over him. They said their good-byes when David was dropped off at a farm on the highway at the Grahamdale curve. His new boss was a man named Mr. Whipper. After a minimal introduction, David was put to work immediately. He became discouraged when he was sent to shovel manure out of the barn and saw that it hadn't been cleaned out in so long that the manure was almost high enough for the cows to walk into the loft.

"It would be easier to pick up the barn and move it," David muttered to himself as he began shoveling.

Dennis settled in nicely at the Bray home. Herman's wife Crystal was a lovely woman who treated Dennis like a son. She was an excellent cook and kept a clean, beautiful home. Herman was a little rough around the edges, but a kind man who was always good to Dennis.

It was here that Dennis saw Nick Skleparik once again. Nick worked part time for the Brays and was kind enough to teach Dennis the social skills he'd never learned at home.

Nick was a Jehovah's Witness who, in Dennis' mind, was the epitome of human kindness. Nick had been thrown off the farm by Domko years before, and Dennis wished that all the Witnesses who came to visit were as principled as Nick. Dennis began studying the Bible and watched as Nick slowly converted Herman to the truth according to the Jehovah's Witnesses.

David stayed at the Whipper farm for only a few weeks. He was overwhelmed by the workload and depressed that he wasn't allowed to see Dennis who was only three miles away, so he accepted his mother's next offer to go home. He arrived back on the farm and immediately began haying. Rosie was happy to see him since she and her mother had been doing all the chores by themselves.

Domko was as belligerent as ever but dared not ridicule David for fear he might run away again. It had been difficult getting the work done without the twins. He was beginning to realize how valuable they were to the farming operation.

One afternoon in September, David was called to the kitchen, and Domko surprised him by giving him a watch, saying it was payment for the work he'd done in the hay field. Domko was very pleased with himself, and David accepted it gratefully, even though he suspected it was stolen. He put the watch on his wrist and liked how it looked. He'd never received a gift before and treasured it, taking it off carefully each night and putting it on a shelf in his room.

David began grade eight near the end of September but was only able to attend nine days of classes in October because there was so much work on the farm. As time wore on, he missed Dennis terribly, but kept busy and accompanied Rosie to school whenever he could.

David got dressed one morning in early December and reached for his watch but found it was missing. He looked all over the house but could not find it. Domko soon noticed.

"Vere's be but-a-some vatch?" he asked suspiciously. "Yous be trowink it in the bush?"

David said that he didn't lose the watch, that he'd misplaced it, but would find it soon. Domko berated him all winter while David looked everywhere. Suspecting that David wouldn't run into the cold night by himself, he stopped beating Rosie and started attacking David again.

One afternoon in early spring, David was sitting at the kitchen table and glanced into his mother's purse that sat open on the chair beside him. He noticed his battered watch inside and took it out, and seeing it no longer worked, stuffed it in his pocket.

"Ma, I found my watch in your purse," he whispered, the next time they were alone. "Why didn't you tell me you found it?"

Caroline flushed. "You must have left it in your pocket," she whispered. "I put it through the ringer on the washing machine."

"Why didn't you tell me?" he asked. "How could you let him torture me all winter?"

Caroline began crying softly. "I was too scared. I hoped that he would forget, and I was hoping to buy you a new one just like it, but he never lets me go to town."

David sighed. He was angry but understood.

"He's getting worse," she said.

"Then why don't you call the police to take him back to Selkirk?"

Caroline said nothing. "If he found out it was me, he'd kill me."

"Then get someone else to do it," David said.

Caroline turned away, refusing to say anything more.

During the next few weeks, Domko continued to berate David about the missing watch while he and his mother sat in silence.

One early April afternoon, David was shoveling manure beside the barn where the horses were kept over the winter. He was thinking about Dennis, wondering how life was for him in his new home. David hummed softly to himself as he shoveled chunks of half-frozen manure onto the wagon. He chuckled as he thought of the huge manure pile in Mr. Whipper's barn, wondering who the next unsuspecting farmhand might be.

Standing with his back to the house, suddenly he had an uneasy feeling pass over him. A tiny voice inside his head told him to turn around. He smelled Domko's foul stench and turned quickly, and in that second, a pitchfork came like a bullet through the air, and its prongs stuck into the barn just inches from his stomach. David looked in shock at the fork that protruded from the wall, the prongs deep in the weathered wood. Domko was less than three yards away, and he lunged at him.

Where Children Run

David dropped the shovel and darted around the edge of the barn, his boots slipping on the wet manure as he ran toward the bush. He heard the footsteps behind him stop and realized he'd outrun Domko, but continued down the path at top speed.

He assumed that Domko must have found the watch. Or maybe he saw him eating lunch, or smiling when he thought of Whipper's manure pile.

He went to the lake and walked along the shore for a while. He turned and meandered back into the bush until he came to an old campfire that he and Dennis had shared many times the winter before. He gathered wood, made a fire with matches he'd managed to steal from Domko's bedroom and sat down. It was then he realized how much he missed Dennis. While he hoped that his brother had a good life at the Bray house, he wished that he'd been chosen as well.

What's wrong with me? he thought. *I'm a good worker. Boy, is Dennis ever lucky! When am I gonna get outta here anyway? I wanna go to Winnipeg and do some drawing, but I don't know who to ask for help.*

David snared and cooked a rabbit for supper then sat for hours after his meal, mulling over his life, wondering how to get off the farm. He promised himself that the next time he left, he wouldn't return.

The next afternoon David was daydreaming when he heard someone coming along the bush trail. He immediately crouched down behind his small pile of wood and flared his nostrils, hoping to smell whatever might be coming. The rustling continued, then somebody called his name. David recognized it was Norman.

"Hey Norman," he said, standing up. "I'm over here."

Norman waved as he left the trail and pushed his way through the bush.

"I've been looking for you all morning," he smiled. "Ma phoned me. I guess the ol' bastard came in yesterday and told her that he'd stabbed you with a pitchfork."

David shook his head. "He missed me by that much," he said pressing his thumb and index finger a half inch apart. "If I hadn't turned around, he woulda killed me for sure."

Norman snorted in disgust. "What's wrong with him anyway? Who keeps letting him out of Selkirk?"

David shrugged. "He sure is nuts. He thinks I'm gonna take the farm away from his kids, but he needs me to work. It don't make no sense."

"Why did he try to stab you?"

"I don't know," David said. "I was just shovelin' when he did it."

"Does he still beat the hell outta you kids?"

"Yeah. Poor Rosie, he's gotten her good a few times. I was listenin' to him beatin' her the other night and she finally just gave up screamin'."

"Bastard," Norman said as he kicked his black boot into the ground. Then he reached into his breast pocket. "Guess what I got?"

Norman smiled as he brought out a small, silver handgun. He grinned at David. "You can use it if you want."

David's eyes widened. "No, I can't. Me and Denny already tried that once, and I'm too scared to do it again."

Norman laughed as he gave his brother a shove.

"C'mon, let's go back to the farm. I'm staying there tonight and tomorrow we're going to Moosehorn. You can come live with me."

David's mouth dropped open. He could hardly believe his luck. To live with Norman was a dream come true. He was fun, exciting and he had a motorcycle and a car. David kicked out the fire then they both started walking to the trail.

"I'm sleeping with it," Norman said showing David the gun again before shoving it in the waistband of his jeans. "And if the old bugger comes upstairs tonight, I'm gonna blow his head off."

THE GUN

THAT NIGHT, NORMAN SLEPT WITH THE GUN IN HIS JEANS JUST AS HE'D promised. David sat awake for a long time, wondering if Domko would come upstairs. He had mixed feelings about Norman's threat, believing that if provoked, Norman would do it. He worried that if Norman did that, though, he'd end up in jail and it would spoil their plans to live in Moosehorn together.

The next morning, Norman seemed mildly disappointed that he wasn't given an excuse to shoot Domko, who sat at the table watching them as they finished their breakfast. Once outside, they began making plans.

"Do you got any money?" Norman whispered.

"No, I'm just workin' for room and board," he said, but then remembered the fifty dollar bond he'd won in the art contest.

"Do you think you can get it?" Norman asked.

"The teacher said I can cash it when I finish school," David said.

"Well, if you're moving to Moosehorn with me," Norman chuckled, "then I guess you've finished school."

David nodded.

"I guess so."

"Do you have your driver's license yet?" Norman asked as they crouched around the corner of the house.

"My driving license? No. Domko wouldn't let me."

"Christ, man you're missing out," Norman whistled. "We gotta get you a driver's license. You'll never get a job without one."

"What do I gotta do?"

"You'll need your birth certificate. Do you have it?"

"I can look through Ma's papers and see if I can find it," David said.

"Okay, you go do that, and I'll distract them in the barn," he said punching David in the arm. "We'll leave after lunch."

David nodded. They waited outside until everyone went to the barn. Domko came out and ordered them to follow him.

"What if he sees me go back inside?" David whispered.

"Don't worry," Norman said. "He ain't never gonna beat you again, not while I'm here."

David's heart swelled with pride. He snuck back into the house and into his mother's room. He assumed she kept all her important papers in the cardboard box that sat on top of her bureau. He took the box down, sat on the bed and pulled back the flaps. There was a huge stack of papers inside, and for a moment finding the birth certificate seemed like a daunting task. He lifted out a handful of documents and letters. He felt uneasy looking through his mother's personal things but reasoned he'd never get the birth certificate otherwise.

He began flipping through the papers and saw Mark and Raymond's birth certificates, plus a clipped stack of official looking papers from the blind school. He was careful to put everything in the same order he'd found it, piling letters and pictures of the Kolodka family on top. There were invoices and the deed to their land. The further down he dug, the older and more interesting the documents became.

Near the bottom of the box, he found a folded paper and when he opened it, discovered a picture of his father. He recognized him immediately. The prominent nose, wide grin, and laughing eyes—how he'd longed to see that face over the last twelve years. He stared at the photo then read the marriage certificate it was wrapped in. David stared at the picture for a long time, suddenly feeling apprehensive about the changes coming in his life.

Was he ready? Could he live in Moosehorn and get a good job? What about Dennis? David thought about his mother and wondered if leaving was the right thing. He wondered what his father would have wanted him to do. He asked out loud if he should stay and take care of his mother and Rosie. He listened for the voice to answer his question, but heard nothing.

Would his father think he was a coward for running away?

Carefully, he set the picture and certificate aside. He reached into the box and brought out a handful of papers, and in this bundle, he found his birth certificate as well as Dennis'. He also found the bond.

Still feeling uncertain, he tucked his father's picture near the bottom then put the rest of the papers on top. He hoisted the box overhead and placed it back on the bureau. He stood back to see if it looked as if it had been disturbed and it was then he saw a brown envelope folded into an exposed rafter in the ceiling. Curious, he stood on the edge of the bed and pulled the envelope down. It was addressed to him and had been opened.

David read the letter in disbelief. Apparently, an application had been sent on his behalf, and he'd been accepted to a Winnipeg art school. All he had to do was fill out the enclosed enrollment form and a bursary to pay the associated costs, would be forwarded to the school. The Brooke Bond company was mentioned as well as the Manitoba Department of Education. The letter ended by saying that he was a very talented young man and that the school administration looked forward to having him as a pupil in their drafting-commercial art program for the 1963-64 school year. The letter was dated April of 1963. He glanced at the calendar on the wall - April 20, 1964.

David had known many disappointments in his life, but until then had never experienced a hurt of such magnitude. His chest pounded heavily, and his mind whirled as he realized the opportunity he'd missed. The chance to go to art school for free. It was almost more than he could stand to know that his dream of becoming a professional artist had been dashed by his own mother.

How could she do this to me? he thought as he tossed the envelope on the bed and stormed out of the bedroom. He ran upstairs and packed a few clothes in a bag. He fell on the bed and cried, yelling in frustration as tears streamed down his cheeks, vowing never to draw anything, ever again.

David stayed upstairs until he heard everyone come inside. Norman dashed up the stairs.

"What's the matter?" he asked as he lifted David's bag.

"Nothin'," David said rubbing his eyes with the cuff of his shirt.

"Did you get it?"

"Yeah," he sniffled. "I gotta talk to Ma before we go."

"You're not gonna tell her are you?"

"I'm gonna tell her all right, but not what you think," David said. "Where's Flatfoot?"

Norman shrugged. "He's feeding his stupid birds."

David got up from the bed and followed Norman, who whispered that he'd be waiting in the car.

David nodded as he went into the kitchen. The sight of his mother serving Kathy's lunch made him even angrier. She'd sent Kathy to the blind school but had refused the opportunity offered to him.

"Ma, I gotta talk to you," he muttered.

Caroline turned to look at him and saw that his eyes were bloodshot from crying.

"What's wrong with you?" she asked.

"What's wrong with me?" he said, slapping himself on the chest. "What's wrong with you, Ma? I found the envelope about the art school in your room. How come you never told me about it?"

Caroline flushed then turned away as she poured the fresh milk into the separator. "What were you doing in my papers?"

"Your papers? Ma, that letter was 'sposed to be for me."

"I'm your mother, so I can read it if I want," she said. "Art school. What would you want to go there for?"

"What for? What *for*? So I can get a good job," he said.

"What kinda job can you get from learning art? Nothing, that's what. All they do is take your money, and you end up with no job."

"It was free! I read the letter, and it said that 'cause we got no money some rich people were gonna pay for me to go. If you don't think school is good, then why'd you send Kathy?"

"That's different," she said. "Kathy's blind."

"And she's Squeezer's kid, right? Dad's kids got nothin'. That was my chance Ma, and you wrecked it for me."

Caroline poured herself a cup of tea. "Domko would never let you go anyway."

"He wouldn't have been able to stop me. I woulda went, Ma, I'm tellin' you that right now."

"And then when it didn't work out, what would you have done?" she said. "Come back home?"

"Back here? To shovel shit for the rest of my life? It was my dream, and now I'm never gonna get the chance. You wrecked it, just like you wrecked everything else in our lives."

Caroline's shoulders slumped, and she turned her back on him. Then she began to sob, rubbing her hand across her abdomen. Her eleventh child was due in a few months.

David watched her for a moment, a lump rising in his throat.

"Bye, Ma," he said as he closed the door behind him.

Herman Bray had experienced financial difficulties that summer and told Dennis he'd have to go home because there was no money to pay him what he was owed. Dennis had been very frightened by this and told Herman he could keep the $150 in back pay and Dennis would work for free as long as he was allowed to stay. Herman was agreeable, and the deal was made.

A relative of Caroline's came one day to visit Dennis and took him aside. The farmer convinced him that he'd been swindled and said that if Dennis

Where Children Run

went to work for him, he'd pay him $2 a day—double what Herman said he'd pay before he ran out of money.

Dennis thought about this for a few days and decided to accept the man's offer. The Brays were very upset to see him leave.

Dennis arrived at the man's farm and soon found that there was double the amount of work and that he had to work with one of Domko's old miserable horses, Darby. Dennis labored for three days then realized he'd made a mistake. He packed his clothes and climbed out of a bedroom window in the middle of the night and returned to the Brays. They were happy to have him back.

"You have to be careful who you trust," Crystal warned. "People will take advantage of a naive boy like you."

Ashamed that he had not paid Dennis for working that summer, Herman bought Dennis a motorbike and began paying him an allowance. Dennis also noticed that Herman referred to him as "Mine Dennis" when he spoke of him. His kind words, the allowance, and the motorcycle put Dennis on top of the world.

Dennis decided to visit his mother one Friday afternoon. He phoned first to be sure that Domko would not be home. He told Crystal he'd be away for awhile, jumped on the motorbike and drove to the farm. He arrived to find his mother and Rosie working harder than ever.

Caroline was pregnant, and Rosie was suffering so badly from malnutrition, that she had festering sores on her legs. Dennis felt sorry for them, but self-preservation kept him from offering to return. They sat in the kitchen making small talk and drinking tea. Kathy jogged on the spot in the front room while Mark played with toys on the floor. Raymond was at school.

Dennis looked at little Mark with jealousy. Domko had never allowed him and David to have toys.

"Ma, I was wonderin' if I could have Dad's old gun," he asked.

"What for?" she asked as she refilled his mug.

"I'd just like to have it," he said. "Satan's got his own guns, and I don't got nothin' to remember dad."

Caroline thought for a moment. "Don't tell Domko I gave it to you."

They visited a while longer then Caroline handed him the gun as he was leaving. Dennis waved goodbye, climbed on his motorcycle and drove back to Grahamdale. He told Crystal he was back and went to the garage.

"I'll call you when it's supper time," she said.

Dennis walked confidently to Herman's garage and set the rifle on the workbench. A flood of memories returned as he looked at the old, somewhat rusted .22 caliber rifle. He remembered how his father would carry the rifle over his shoulder when he went hunting. He and David had learned to hunt with that gun, and it was the one Norman had used to kill Sandy.

It was the gun that jammed the day he had tried to shoot Domko, sealing their fate for the next eight years. It was the gun that Domko had pointed at them so many times in anger, and had laughed at how ironic it would be to shoot the twins with their dad's gun.

It was up to Dennis how it would be used in future. He found a hacksaw and changed the blade before placing the gun in a vise and started sawing the rusty barrel. The blade squeaked back and forth as Dennis put all his strength into it. Tears of frustration streamed down his cheeks.

Dad wouldn't have wanted his gun used against his kids, he thought. *Never again will this gun be used to scare anybody.*

David had been right—things were better over the beaver dam, and he'd kept his promise to take him there. In a way, his mother had been right, too. For him, justice was right around the corner. He now lived with wonderful people who loved him. He'd waited, and suffered, and now his life was just beginning. Dennis was glad he hadn't given up and had chosen the right path. He'd learned how to survive, and it had made him a stronger person.

The blade continued to squeak through the steel. Dennis sawed faster, and a piece dropped to the ground.

I'll never shoot anything again, he vowed as he measured another six inches and began cutting again. An hour later when he had finished, and the barrel was in many pieces, he disassembled the stock and held the smooth bolt in his hand. He examined it then dropped it in his pocket. He picked up the rest of the gun and tossed it in Herman's scrap pile in the corner of the garage.

When Dennis stepped out of the garage, it felt as if a twelve-year weight had been lifted from his shoulders, as if he'd already lived a thousand lives. He walked confidently to the house, knowing he was no longer the frightened little boy whom Domko loathed. Dennis felt like a man.

Later that summer David went to visit Dennis, and the twins had a cheerful reunion. David had been managing on his own in Winnipeg but was consumed by loneliness. He missed Dennis and hoped to lure him to the bright lights of the city.

"Do you ever come to Moosehorn?" David asked.

"Yeah," Dennis said. "I stopped at Norman's trailer once, but you weren't there."

"I'm in Winnipeg workin' now and only come out on weekends."

"Where are you workin'?" Dennis asked.

"I got this great job with Ramsey-Bird Construction," David said. "You should see me, Denny, I'm drivin' these big road construction machines, all different kinds, and it's great work."

Dennis was impressed. "How much money do you make?"

"A hundred and fifty bucks, every two weeks," he said.

Dennis' mouth gaped wide; then he slowly repeated the figure.

"That's right and guess what the best part is? I asked the boss, and you know what he said? He said, 'If your brother works half as good as you do, then he can start on Monday.' Hear that Dennis? You can come work for Ramsey-Bird, too."

"I can?"

"Sure, I can take you back with me today," David said. "We can stay in Moosehorn tonight then go to Winnipeg tomorrow."

Dennis was speechless. He didn't think he'd be leaving the Brays so soon and knew that this time, it would be for good.

"I gotta talk to Herman and Crystal," he whispered. "They're gonna be sad I'm going."

"Sure, I get it," David said. "Oh yeah, do you got your license yet?"

"Driver's license?"

"Yeah."

"No, not yet."

"Christ, man you're missin' out," David said, imitating Norman. "We gotta get you a license. I've got your birth certificate in my wallet—I took it when I got mine."

Dennis nodded cheerfully and asked David to wait outside while he told the Brays. His friend Nick was there which also gave him the opportunity to say good-bye to him.

Dennis packed his bag and climbed into the car beside David. As the vehicle slowly backed out the driveway, Dennis waved goodbye to the Brays who stood together at the living room window.

Looking back one final time, Dennis saw that Crystal was crying.

ONE LAST VISIT

February 8, 1965

Two years later while visiting friends in Moosehorn, the twins heard rumors that things were deteriorating at the farm.

They weren't surprised by this news and even chuckled. They had been saying for years that Domko didn't do a stitch of work and that he'd never manage without them. They were concerned about their mother and Rosie, though. Deciding they should visit, David phoned to see if they would be home.

The twins climbed into David's cream-colored pickup truck.

"Happy Birthday to us," David said. "We made it Denny. We're eighteen today."

"Yeah," Dennis said as he looked solemnly out the window as David backed out of the driveway. "Remember how we never thought we'd make it out of the bush?"

David shook his head in disbelief. With two years gone by, it felt like a whole other lifetime. "There were lots of times we almost didn't."

They drove to the edge of town and pulled onto the snow-packed highway. Just north of Moosehorn, they turned on the Township Line. The sun was just setting on what had been a beautiful day, sending streams of pink and gold across the sky.

"I couldn't go back to those days again," David said thoughtfully, enjoying the beautiful sky. "I think it would kill me."

"Me, too," Dennis said. "We've got it so good. I sometimes have to think hard to be sure it's real. We lived through hell, and I know it was hell 'cause the Devil was standing there the whole time."

David laughed. "You got that right."

"Those times, when we were kids, seems so far away," Dennis said dreamily. "And sometimes it feels like yesterday. Remember our birthdays? Remember the time Squeezer got in the car accident on the road right around here—and how you smashed your teeth?"

David laughed. "Yeah, and remember how stupid he was driving right into that guy like that?" David made an ugly face, gripping the wheel, pretending he was Domko. He growled as he drove toward the ditch.

Dennis laughed as he grabbed the dashboard and pretended to be their mother. "Slow down, slow down," he screamed in his best woman's voice.

Then they laughed.

"And remember our best birthday ever?" David asked. "At Kochs' and you got to cut the cake first?"

"Yeah, and you took the biggest piece."

"Yeah, but Denny, remember—it was chocolate cake. Remember what I'd do for chocolate cake?" he joked.

"And the socks," Dennis said. "Five years ago today, we got the nicest presents ever. What happened to them anyway?"

"I never wore mine," David said. "I didn't wanna take them nice tags off. I hid them upstairs and I think he took wore them to Walter's wedding. How about you?"

"They were too nice to wear. I just saved them and then they disappeared."

They sighed as they continued down the road. Out of habit, Dennis looked to his right when they came to the small bluff of trees that shielded Jim's house from the east. David slowed down almost to a stop and craned his neck.

"How's Jim doing?" Dennis asked.

"Good, I think."

"Anybody ever hear from Ruby?"

"Yeah, she's got a new husband named Harry Ratz," David said. "I heard she's happy and I sure hope so. I'll never forget the time she kissed me."

"Kissed you?" Dennis exclaimed. "She never kissed me."

"Yes she did, but you were asleep. She kissed me right here," David said gently touching his cheek.

"Jim was the bravest guy I ever saw," Dennis said. "And he tells it like it is."

"That's for sure. Everyone else just kisses the old bastard's ass, or they stay the hell away from him," David said. "Except for Jim. And Gus—he fought with him more than anybody. Poor old Gus, do you remember?"

"Yeah, after Satan kicked him that time I never wanted to go to Harwart's house again."

"Me neither."

David slowed, and the truck slipped a bit as he turned toward the farm.

"Too bad Ma wasn't more like Emma," David said as he slowed down. "She loved her kids and never woulda put up with Satan's crap."

"That's for sure," Dennis said.

They drove slowly past the abandoned barn, then Harwart's house, which had sat empty since Gus and Emma moved to Moosehorn in the fall of 1964. A warm feeling washed over Dennis as he looked at the old log home.

"I never told nobody, but I used to wish that Emma and Gus were my parents," he said, voice cracking.

David looked at him and smiled softly. "You and me, both."

They drove in silence for a moment, then Dennis shivered as he looked toward the thick bush.

"Turn the heat up high," David laughed. "We got lots of heat now."

They looked at the fields and trees. The bush had an ominous appearance that made both boys quake a little inside. They had no fond memories of their childhood and only a feeling of foreboding for the place they once called home. Instinctively, they knew what the other was thinking.

"I couldn't sleep in the bush again," Dennis said sadly. "Davey, how did we survive?"

"I don't know," he said, forcing a smile. "I think it was some of that tough German blood that the old bastard hated so much."

They drove in silence until they came to the church that sat as it always had, calm and unwavering in the bitter wind.

"Do you ever talk to other people about what happened to us?" Dennis asked as he stared at it. Nothing about it had changed except there were a few more headstones in the cemetery.

"Sometimes I do, but mostly just try to forget," David said as he stopped in front of the church. Looking to his left, he could see his mother's house through the bare trees. A flood of bad memories returned, and he had to look away. He wondered how long it would be before he could look into that bush and not be propelled back to his childhood. His eyes were still drawn every time to the place where he'd seen the Collie dogs hanging. The stick that had been used to hang the dogs was still there, wedged in the naked trees.

Looking away, he put the truck in reverse and turned to face the direction from where they came. The sun had completely set now, and he wondered how long it would take before his mother would be able to sneak out of the house.

"Was the church a good or bad place?" Dennis asked.

"That church?" David asked pointing back over his shoulder.

Dennis nodded.

"It was a good place," he said. "I figure the church and the Harwarts are what saved our lives."

They sat remembering for a moment, then Dennis broke the silence.

"How do you think Rosie is?"

A pang of guilt stabbed David in the gut. He'd heard that Rosie had suffered more than any of them.

"She's not good," he said. "We gotta get her out of here. I heard that her legs were so bad that she couldn't keep the bugs out of the sores. Lucky Doc Steenson gave her some medicine and cleared it up. Otherwise, they would have had to cut her legs off."

Dennis shuddered. He remembered how they'd come to visit soon after moving to Winnipeg. Domko was inconsolable that the boys were not coming back and had threatened to shoot them all. Dennis was thankful that he'd escaped but felt horrible about his sister.

"How come the social workers don't take her away?" Dennis asked.

David shrugged. "Same reason they never came to get us, I guess. They're probably scared of old Satan."

"Yeah, everyone except Mrs. Patterson," Dennis laughed. "Boy, I wouldn't want to fight her."

David laughed as he remembered how frustrated Domko had been with her.

"Maybe Rosie can come live with us?" Dennis suggested. "We'll have to sneak her out, so he doesn't know."

David glanced in his rear view mirror and saw his mother approaching the back of the vehicle.

"Ma's coming," he said.

Dennis looked out the back window. "Oh no, she's bringing Poker."

David laughed, opening his door and stepping out onto the road. "How are you doing Ma?" he asked in a quiet voice.

"About the same," she said weakly. "I don't know what I'm gonna do."

Inside the house, Domko was sitting on the chair listening to the radio.

Where is she now? he wondered. *Carlorka is always going places without me. She shouldn't be going anywhere since there is still cooking and cleaning that needs to be done.*

He was the head of the house, and it was his responsibility to make sure things ran smoothly on the farm but didn't know how that was possible now that there was nobody left at home to work.

Baby Jenny started to cry. He called for Carlorka, but she didn't answer. The baby, who was only eighteen months old, cried even louder. He liked to rest each evening after a hard day of work but now had to get up to find his wife. He called her name again, but she still didn't answer.

He went to the kitchen to look out the window. It was starting to get dark, and he saw nothing. He glanced at his watch.

Where could she be? Maybe she's found another man, he thought. She was always looking for a new husband, he believed. That is why she didn't care when he was sent to the hospital. *She likely wraps herself around another man when I am gone.* The thought of it made him angry, and he pulled on his boots. *Carlorka never gives me enough love and attention. She always sides with the children instead of me. There is only one way to control that woman, and it is through her religion. As long as I keep the members of the church on my side, she has to do as I say.*

He believed that she was trying to kill him. Because divorce is not permitted, she was trying to work him to death—the same way she killed Bill.

She had bought a box of rat poison the other day, so he now checked his food before eating. He believed she wants to take the farm away from him and give it to the Pischke kids.

Those boys are going to come back and kill me like so many people have said they would. I'm not afraid of Steven, Walter or the girls, but Norman cannot be trusted. And those twins! They are always conspiring against me. They are waiting for their chance to kill me and take the farm. That's why they talk in that language—right from the very first day I arrived. Everyone understood them except me.

He knew he was brutal to the children. People said that beating children was wrong, but his father had beaten him and he turned into a good man. How else did you discipline children? And that's all he wanted the Pischkes to be—hardworking and obedient.

Nothing he tried had worked. *They are good for nothing little German bastards who hate me because I am Polish. They'll be nothing but punks some day, living off the government.*

He thought of the labor camps he'd been in—where he'd learned to survive. He had watched how the guards beat the strongest of the Polish soldiers and starved the rest. It became a habit, a way of survival. They taunted and exposed the weak and vulnerable then destroyed them one by one. This was a method that worked; it had broken many men's spirits. And it was the only way he knew to keep the twins under control.

The baby was still crying. He pulled on his coat and stepped outside into the cool air. His gun was loaded all the time now.

Somebody followed me the other day, probably one of the twins, he thought as he tiptoed down the driveway, looking in the direction of the church. He could see a vehicle parked there. Moving closer he squinted then recognized the truck. It was David's, and he could see Dennis there, too.

He took a few more steps and saw Carlorka sitting between them. Then he noticed Raymond on the seat beside her.

They are talking about me, likely planning how they are going to kill me. They are telling Raymie lies and then will send him spying. He began running toward the truck. *I'll shoot them before they kill me.*

David stiffened. Dennis also sensed the old but still familiar feeling of danger nearby. They shot a quick glance at each other, then, swinging around in the crowded cab, caught sight of a dark figure running toward the back of the truck. It was Domko, shaking a fist in the air while clutching a rifle in the other. For the twins, it was as if they had been propelled back in time.

"It's that crazy bastard," David said as he yanked the truck into gear, slamming the gas pedal to the floor. The tires spun instead of gripping the slick, snow-packed road. Staring intently into the rear-view mirror, he could see Domko stop in the center of the road and raise the rifle to eye level.

"He's gonna shoot," he yelled, "everybody down!"

Instinctively Dennis' arms came up over his head as he slid low on the seat. Caroline pulled Raymond down and covered him with her body.

Got to get out of here, David thought, clenching his jaw tight. His heart raced as adrenaline surged into his bloodstream. *We don't deserve to die like this, not after what we've lived through. If only I can get out of range . . .* Moments seemed like hours as the truck slipped sideways down the center of the road.

Domko could barely see into the crowded cab. He took aim at what he thought was Dennis' head but hesitated thinking it might be Raymond. He looked over the barrel, squinting in the fading light.

The back wheels finally caught on a bare piece of road, straightening the vehicle and propelling it forward. David pushed the gas pedal to the floor, and within seconds, the truck was speeding toward the Township Line. He glanced in the mirror and could still see Domko standing on the road, but now he was just a speck in the distance.

"We made it," David gasped, struggling to catch his breath. He hadn't felt fear like that in nearly two years.

Dennis and Caroline, both still shaking from the ordeal, complimented his driving and reached across the cab to hug and congratulate him.

"David, will you take us to the police?" his mother asked. "We gotta send him back to Selkirk, but this time for good."

Both boys looked at her, at first skeptical, but then as they studied her, realized that she meant what she was saying this time.

"I'm going to leave him and get a legal separation," she said. "We just can't live like this anymore."

The boys didn't ask any further questions as they drove to Ashern. Each silently wished that their mother had done this much sooner, but they knew that was not her way. It took her a long time to make up her mind, but once she finally did, she never changed it.

It was the first time the twins had been at the Ashern RCMP office since they were youngsters. They rang the bell then stepped inside.

The officer who came to the front seemed much friendlier than the men they remembered in the past.

"Can I help you?" the officer asked.

They stood silent for a moment, then David looked at his mother. She nodded at him, and he knew it was his signal to speak for her.

"Y-yes, you c-can," David began. "We w-want to report that our s-s-stepfather just tried to sh-shoot us. We were t-talkin' with our M-Mother out by the farm, and he snuck up behind the t-truck and pointed his rifle at us. If I hadn't saw him coming, we'd all be dead r-r-right now."

The officer looked stunned. It took him a few moments to decipher through the stutter. "Who's your stepfather?" he asked.

"Bob Domko," David said without hesitation. It was then he realized how strange those words sounded coming from his mouth. Never once in his life had he consciously uttered the man's name, never in anger and certainly not in fondness. The man had been nothing but their tormenter, and he'd always addressed him as such.

"Domko should have been locked up a long time ago," the officer said. "It's a miracle he hasn't killed somebody already. He should never have been released from Selkirk."

David was prepared for an argument, and the officer's words nearly knocked him backward. He looked at Dennis who also stared in amazement.

Where was this man when we were kids?

"H-he tried to kill us many times and more than once he almost did,"

Dennis said firmly. "W-we were beaten and starved for twelve years, and the police did nothing about it. We w-want you to do s-something about it now."

Caroline explained that her youngest children were still in the house.

The officer called in a constable, and after a short discussion, Caroline and Raymond were asked to ride back to the farm with them. As the cruiser sped along the highway, the twins followed behind in the truck.

"Remember how we would ride like that," David said, pointing at his mother's silhouette illuminated by his headlights.

"And he'd beat the hell out of us when we got home," Dennis added. "But this time, they're gonna take him away."

"Do you think he'll be gone for good?"

"I don't know, but if he comes back we'll just keep calling the police," Dennis said. "That is if Ma keeps her word this time."

David thought for a moment then nodded. "This time, she means it. You know Ma when she makes up her mind."

Dennis leaned his head back against the window and sighed.

"Do you think that dad knows we made it?" he asked.

David looked at his brother and felt a warm strength flood over him.

"I know he does."

Then, as they had so many times in the bush, the twins shared their thoughts without speaking. They knew instinctively that never again would there be a reason so urgent that they'd run screaming into the cold, windy night. They knew that whatever lay ahead could be no worse than what loomed behind; that no threat could ever be more severe than what they had already endured.

At that moment, David and Dennis knew they would never run again.

DAVID PISCHKE
1948 – 2004
Rest in Peace

EPILOGUE

THE RCMP ARRIVED AT THE PISCHKE FARM SHORTLY AFTER THE TWINS and their mother went to the police station in Ashern. Domko was taken to jail that night and during questioning admitted that he had planned to kill Caroline and the twins. He said during the interview that he did not shoot because he feared that he might hit his son Raymond. Domko was held overnight then taken to the Selkirk Mental Health Centre where he was admitted once again as a patient.

Caroline, Rosie and Domko's four biological children stayed at the farm until he was discharged on June 6, 1966. Caroline left the farm and obtained a marital separation shortly afterward.

When Domko realized he was unable to do the farm work alone, he re-admitted himself to the hospital on July 6, 1966. Caroline returned to the farm and managed it until the fall of that year. After selling the livestock, the land was leased to Hugo Russell. The house still stands on the Pischke property, now owned by Arden and Barb Weigelt of Moosehorn.

DAVID PISCHKE

David continued working for Ramsey Bird Construction in Winnipeg as a heavy equipment operator during the summer months. He spent the winter working in sawmills in British Columbia, Canada. In 1969 he married Bonnie Shiells of Steep Rock, and they had two sons, Dale and Ian. David and Bonnie divorced in 1984.

In 1968 David became employed by Winnipeg Fuel & Supply in Spear Hill, Manitoba. The company now operates under the name Graymont (before that, Continental Lime). In 1985 David married Lynne Jensen of Ashern. They lived in Moosehorn until 1995, then moved the log home they built to Steep Rock. David had three step-children, Bill, David, and Sherry. His wife Lynne said: "My children were extremely fond of David. He certainly didn't inherit any of Domko's stepfather traits. If anything, he is the exact opposite. My children thought the world of him."

On June 13, 2004, David died in his sleep from a massive heart attack, stunning the community and forever altering the lives of all who knew him. His remains are interred at the cemetery in Faulkner, Manitoba.

AUTHOR'S NOTE

Reflecting on the past twenty years are particularly poignant for me. Reading over the epilogue in the 1996 printing of *Where Children Run*, I can say that David stayed true to himself until the day he died.

When this story was first published, it propelled the Twins into the public eye. They expected to face a lot of criticism but instead, were congratulated by most people. Some said: "I understand. It happened to me, too."

David said that he and Dennis had been plagued by rumors and misunderstanding their whole lives. He described writing the book as "letting the monster out." It helped him get a lot of issues out in the open, and it helped him come to terms with his past. David said that it was nice to be believed and was comforted to know that so many people cared.

When asked why he and Dennis decided to tell their story, David said that while he'd tried to forget the abuse and seldom discussed his childhood, gradually the memories started creeping back. He'd told friends some of the stories in the book but always glossed over the details, throwing an amusing spin on it by making fun of Domko. He didn't tell his wife Lynne how abusive his childhood was until 1995, so she had no idea what he'd lived through until then. During the interview process for this book was the first time she heard most of the stories.

David described himself as a workaholic. He suffered from nightmares for many years, mostly images of Domko stalking him and not being able to escape. He was a very tidy man who kept himself and his surroundings immaculate. He always worried about not having enough food to eat so he and Lynne canned hundreds of sealer jars of vegetables and fruit every year. Winter was his least favorite time of year, so he always had plenty of wood cut and ready for the stove, and they started taking an annual winter holiday to Mexico.

David feared the sight of blood and refused to take a blood test and was deathly afraid of snakes. He admitted to having a bad temper and often found himself frustrated because it was hard to express his feelings or anger. He consciously decided to avoid disciplining his children and grandchildren, knowing he'd never learned the skills to do it properly.

Many people telephoned or wrote asking how their mother, Caroline, had allowed such abuse to take place. David fluctuated between resenting his mother and feeling sorry for her. He never understood why she left them alone with Domko, but also acknowledged that she received beatings while trying to defend them. He admitted that his mother was a very private person who he did not understand very well. In later years when he'd ask her questions about the past, she would cry and become upset. He visited her up until her death and was always very kind to her.

Before his death, David came to understand that his mother was trapped in a cycle of abuse that began in her childhood. But his feelings toward Bob Domko never changed.

"He meant absolutely nothing to me," David said, explaining that he only saw Domko on a few occasions after he became a permanent resident at the Selkirk Mental Health facility. Sometimes his mother would ask him to take her to visit Domko, and David would agree. He never understood why Domko treated them so badly and never forgave him, but he did attend his funeral.

"But only to be sure that the SOB was really dead," he said.

David had no interest in the Jehovah's Witness religion and as an adult did not attend church. He had no respect for the senior members of his mother's church for turning a blind eye to their situation. He resented the fact that there was no enjoyment in their childhood, made worse by the fact their mother's religious beliefs further deprived them of special occasions such as birthday celebrations and Christmas. "It gave people no opportunity to get to know us," he said. "We were different than the rest, shunned by people in our religion and people outside."

However, David did believe in an afterlife. He was confident that he would see his father again and was not afraid to die.

"I've been to hell already," he laughed. "Nothing can be worse than that."

On May 6, 2000, David embarked upon an adventure that saw him walk from Banff, Alberta to Steep Rock, Manitoba. For three months, he and Lynne spread the word about the effects of child abuse, collecting donations along the way. One of David's proudest moments came the day he received notice from his employer, Continental Lime (now Graymont), that they would endorse the walk by paying his full salary while on the road.

Although "Walk with Me" was not a huge financial success, David returned home with an even clearer perspective on his life that helped him come to terms with his past. Everyone who knew him agreed that the experience benefitted David in ways none of us could have anticipated and he carried with him those memories and a tremendous feeling of self-worth for the few remaining years of his life.

Most of the money raised was donated to children's foundations, and the remainder became the "David Pischke Scholarship," awarded annually in his memory to a deserving student at the Ashern Central School graduation ceremonies.

David's dream was to help children in need. He wanted to raise awareness worldwide about the prevalence of child abuse. His legacy is *Where Children Run*.

LYNNE PISCHKE

After David's death, Lynne sold their home in Steep Rock and moved to Teulon, Manitoba to be closer to her daughter Sherry and son-in-law John. On February 17, 2012 she passed away in the Teulon hospital following a brief illness.

DENNIS PISCHKE

The twins continued to mirror one another into adulthood. Dennis worked for Ramsey Bird Construction as a heavy equipment operator during the summer months and along with David, spent the winter working in the sawmills of British Columbia.

In 1970, Dennis married Robynne Shiells of Fort Whyte, Manitoba and together they raised twin daughters Deanna and Dawn; and a son, Ryan. In 1968 Dennis left Ramsey-Bird Construction and became employed at Winnipeg Fuel & Supply in Spear Hill, Manitoba. The company moved operations to Steep Rock and now operates under the name Graymont (formerly Continental Lime).

Dennis and Robynne lived on the outskirts of Steep Rock for many years. Dennis credits Jack McInnis and George Rentz from Ramsey-Bird for giving him and David each a job. He also offers thanks to John Brown, who hired them to work at the limestone plant. Dennis recently retired, and he and Robynne now live in Selkirk, Manitoba.

Dennis says that for many years he blocked out many of the incidents that happened to him when he was a child. He tried to forget but found that living in the area where he grew up and associating with the same people brought back many memories.

What many people don't realize is that it was Dennis who initiated the newspaper article that resulted in *Where Children Run*.

"There were people who wouldn't let us forget," he said. Former friends of Domko and members of the Ashern Jehovah's Witness congregation even accused him of being a thief.

"Once a thief, always a thief," he said. "This was said in front of a group of people and once the situation was resolved, and it was discovered that it wasn't I who was the thief, there was no apology - nothing."

Dennis also remembers a senior member of the congregation making a derogatory comment about his sister, based on past events. When Dennis demanded an apology on her behalf, he was refused again.

"They are the ones who opened the old wounds," he said. "I want to forget, but that is impossible as long as they continue to judge my siblings and myself unfairly."

Dennis believes that because a church is made up of families, they have a moral obligation to help members in need. He acknowledges that there were some people in their church who helped, but only if they weren't considered "involved." The remainder turned a blind eye. In some instances, church members made the situation worse by befriending Domko and blaming their mother for his wrongdoing.

"They even said, 'Domko made you into good men,' and that makes me so angry," he said, adding that they became the men they are not because of Domko but in spite of him.

"We were struggling every day to survive and they were worried if my mother kept a clean house," he said. "Now that shows you the priorities of that particular church." Dennis added that in the late 1970s there were others within the same church who were experiencing similar problems. He brought it to the attention of the church elders and was told: "Mind your own business."

"And that is my point," he said. "If it isn't the church's business then whose is it? And what is the purpose of organized religion then? Just for show? To gather around and pretend to be wonderful Christians while others are suffering?"

Dennis said that he was a member of the Jehovah's Witness religion through his teens and adult years. In the early 1980s he began to question some of the beliefs and when he realized the hypocrisy, stopped associating with them in the fall of 1994.

The residual effects of the abuse he endured are everlasting. He is a workaholic who is obsessed with cleanliness. While he will take a needle in the arm, he also becomes ill at the sight of blood. Like David, he suffered from nightmares for years. Dennis also has back problems and arthritis, both ailments he attributes to the beatings and having to be outside in the cold while not warmly dressed.

Dennis vowed that Domko would never hurt his wife and children and made a concerted effort not to mimic Domko's behavior. He did not physically discipline his children and would "clap my hands behind their rear ends" instead.

He said that writing *Where Children Run* helped him come to terms with his past. It unlocked some of the pent up frustration, particularly towards members of the church, who'd he'd watched through a child's eye, virtually ignore his suffering family.

He feels vindicated that so many readers have written to thank them for telling their story; that so many people believe in him.

"Now I can make friends with people and not feel like my past is hanging over my head," he said. "People understand."

Dennis was thrilled with the idea of updating and reprinting *Where Children Run*, saying that it is important that book stays in print so that their story is never forgotten.

BOLESLAW DOMKO

Medical records show that after re-admitting himself to the Selkirk Mental Health Centre on July 6, 1966, Domko was diagnosed as a paranoid schizophrenic with violent tendencies. These records also show that he stayed in the hospital until September 27, 1967, when he was released under the supervision of a farmer in Petersfield, Manitoba as a farmhand. Domko was brought back to Selkirk by that farmer on October 3, 1967. The files show that on his release he arrived in Moosehorn and began harassing Caroline once again. She called the police and he was re-admitted to the hospital.

On May 14, 1968 he was released into a work situation once again, this time to the Gmitzyk family in Faulkner, Manitoba. He was returned to the hospital by his employers because he was unable to work, was depressed, and had suicidal thoughts. In August, Domko begged to be sent back to Caroline, and while she previously refused, she decided to give him one last chance. He arrived in Moosehorn August 29, 1968, but the police were again called, and he was returned to Selkirk September 7, 1968. He had one other short stint as a farmhand in East Selkirk in early December of that year but was again returned to the hospital.

Schizophrenia is a mental disorder that has the following symptoms: In the early stages, people with schizophrenia may find themselves losing the ability to relax, concentrate or sleep. They may want to shut long-time friends out of their lives. Work or school begins to suffer; so does their personal appearance. These symptoms persist for at least six months. During that time, there will be one or more episodes where they talk in ways that may be difficult to understand and/or start having unusual perceptions. Once it has taken hold, schizophrenia tends to appear in cycles of remission and relapse. When in remission, a person with schizophrenia may seem relatively unaffected and can more or less function in society. During relapse, however, it is a different story. People with schizophrenia may experience one or all of the following: delusions, hallucinations and thought disorders. Most people who are schizophrenic are not violent.

Since Domko was diagnosed with this mental condition, it could explain some of his irrational behavior. He did have an agreeable side, which might explain why there were people who liked him. It is entirely possible that Caroline fell in love with one part of his personality and felt sorry for him.

There were people who knew Domko who told us (after reading the book) that Domko had confessed that he was unable at times to control himself and even appeared remorseful about beating the children. The twins never remember him showing any remorse, except after injuring Kathy but only after he realized that she was indeed his biological daughter.

Written details from recorded interviews during a psychiatric evaluation in his hospital file show that he felt no remorse, blaming the children for his ills and complaining about them constantly. A search by the psychiatrist into Domko's childhood revealed that he was severely abused as a child by his father and that one of Domko's brothers also suffered from a mental illness.

The records also showed that Domko's biological children visited only once or twice during his stay in Selkirk; and that no one from Caroline's church or his friends from Moosehorn and Grahamdale visited him during his stay in the hospital. Steven Pischke and Caroline did visit occasionally.

Domko's military record obtained from the Ministry of Defence in England shows that he was a single, Roman Catholic who worked as a butcher before enlisting. He was deported from Poland to the former USSR in 1940 and spent time as a POW in a prison camp. On the basis of the Sikorski-Maisky pact of July 30, 1941, he was released for the purpose of joining the Polish Armed Forces which were being organized in 1941-42 on the former Soviet territories. He enlisted in the Polish army on February 1, 1942 and was posted to the 7th Heavy Artillery Regiment. With his unit he crossed the Soviet-Iranian frontier, was evacuated to Iran and thereby came under British command with effect from August 15, 1942. On the re-organization of the Polish army in the Middle East, he was posted to the 8th Heavy Anti-aircraft Artillery Regiment. He served in the Iran, Iraq, and Palestine until

1944 and then was sent to Italy.

His theatre of operations included: Italy, February 1944-May 1945 with action on the rivers Sangro and Rapido February 1944-April 1944; battle for Monte Cassino/Gustav-Hitler line of enemy defences April 1944-May 1944; battle for Ancona and Goths line of enemy defences June 1944-September 1944; rearguard of the 8th British Army September 1944-October 1944; Northern Apennines October 1944-January 1945; action on the river Senio January 1945-April 1945; battle for Bologna/Lombardy Plain April 1945-May 1945. Private Domko was honorably discharged in December 1947 from the Polish Resettlement Corps. His conduct while in the army was classified as good. He received the following medals: Polish Cross of Monte Cassino No. 36473. British 1939-45 Star, Italy Star, Defence Medal and The War Medal 1939-45.

At some point in his life, Domko suffered a serious skull injury, and a steel plate was inserted in his head. Based on what he told Caroline's family, the twins always believed that he'd acquired the injury during the war. However, relatives of his who still live in Europe contradicted that story, saying that as a young man Domko got into trouble of some kind, was beaten and left alongside the road to die. Someone took him to the hospital and he recovered. These same relatives also say that when Domko enlisted in the Polish army he was married and had children. Growing up, the twins were not aware of this.

In 1976 while a permanent resident at the Selkirk Mental Health Centre Villa, Domko suffered a stroke that left him impaired on his right-hand side. He had another series of strokes that left him almost totally impaired until his death on November 19, 1983. Although not a baptized Jehovah's Witness, his memorial service was held at the Kingdom Hall in Selkirk. Later, his cremains were buried by Caroline and Eunice under a fence post at the farm.

CAROLINE DOMKO

After leaving the farm, Caroline lived in Moosehorn until the 1970s, then moved to British Columbia, returning to Moosehorn, then Ashern in the early 1980s where she bought a house for herself and daughter Kathy.

Caroline maintained a good relationship with all of her children and was remembered by her grandchildren as a kind, loving person. She seldom spoke about the past and seemed to have the attitude that the hardships they'd all endured were simply a fact of life. She remained a devout Jehovah's Witness until she died in March 1987 from complications related to Diabetes. She was buried in the Grahamdale cemetery.

WALTER PISCHKE

Walter worked for years as a printing press operator in Winnipeg. He and his wife Lorie moved to Amaranth, Manitoba and raised three children - Kimberly, Rhonda, and Eugene on their cattle ranch. In the winter months, they fished commercially on Lake Manitoba. Walter is now retired, and he and Lorie now live in Portage la Prairie, Manitoba.

STEVEN PISCHKE

Steven spent his younger years on the rodeo circuit in Western Canada. He had little contact with his siblings until his later years. Steven attended David's funeral then passed away from cancer in 2006.

NORMAN PISCHKE

Norman worked as a truck driver and married Sharon Russell of Moosehorn. They had two sons, Lee and Trevor. Norman obtained his pilot's license and soon afterward purchased an airplane. He operated a crop spraying and charter business "NormAir" in Estevan, Saskatchewan. Norman died on a mountainside on May 5, 1979, after the plane he was piloting crashed on its way to Boise, Idaho. The story was documented in a book, *The Sacrament* by Peter Gzowski. Norman was 35 years old when he died.

EUNICE PISCHKE

In 1965 Eunice married Mel Bullerwell who was stationed at the Canadian Armed Forces base in Gypsumville. They raised three children - Marlo, Melissa and foster daughter Dreena, and now live at Spear Hill, Manitoba.

ROSE PISCHKE

Rosie left the farm soon after Domko was arrested in 1966 and lived with her brothers until she married Al Gardner. They moved to a farm at Moosehorn and raised three daughters - Theresa, Tiffany, and Vanessa. Al passed away in 2005; after that Rose moved to town and takes care of sister Kathy.

KATHY DOMKO

Kathy spent another year in Brantford's school for the blind then lived with her mother until Caroline's death. After her mother's death, Kathy was taken to a specialist in Winnipeg to investigate if there was anything that could be done to restore her eyesight. It was determined that her optic nerve was severed at some point in her young life, likely from a severe blow to the head, confirming the twins' remembrances of the time Domko threw

Kathy against the wall. Now she lives in Moosehorn with Rose.

RAYMOND DOMKO
Raymond stayed with his mother until be began working with Norman in Estevan, Saskatchewan. In 1975 when he was 18 years old, Raymond was involved in a car accident on the highway between Moosehorn and Ashern, suffering severe injuries that left him a quadriplegic. He died in 1987 at the age of 30 years.

MARK DOMKO
Mark is married and lives in Winnipeg. He has had little contact with the twins over the years.

JENNY DOMKO
Jenny is married and lives in British Columbia. She had an amicable relationship with the twins.

GUS AND EMMA HARWART
Gus and Emma retired to Moosehorn in the fall of 1964. Gus died October 21, 1981. Emma died April 25, 1984. Both are buried in the St. John's Cemetery behind the church where the children sought refuge so many nights.

MARJORIE HARWART
Marjorie obtained her Grade 12 education then moved to Winnipeg where she still resides. Marjorie still spends time in the Moosehorn area and kept contact with Eunice and the twins over the years. She strongly supported the research efforts of *Where Children Run*, contributing much of what was written about herself and her family.

LEON AND ANNA KOCH
Leon and Anna Koch retired and moved to the senior citizen's home in Moosehorn. The Twins paid a visit to the Koch's shortly after *Where Children Run* was released and the Kochs are featured in the CBC documentary about the twins' lives, written and produced by David Gerow.

Leon and Anna were married for 76 years. Leon died October 6, 2011, at the age of 96 years; Anna died August 26, 2014, at the age of 93. They are buried in the Peace Lutheran Cemetery. Their son, Ken, remained friends with the Twins over the years. He passed away in 2016.

JIM DEIGHTON

Jim eventually sold his farm to a group of Americans who used the house and land for hunting purposes. Jim stayed in the house until the early 1980s then moved into the senior citizen's home in Moosehorn. His stepsons, Harold and Charles Boutilier kept in close contact with him over the years.

An emotional interview with Jim in 1996 confirmed the authenticity of many stories in the book. Jim died on March 13, 1997. The house at the farm was eventually torn down.

RUBY DEIGHTON

After leaving the farm, Ruby married Harry Ratz and moved to Radium Springs, B.C. She died peacefully in her sleep of an apparent heart attack on October 31, 1991, at the age of 73 years.

THE PISCHKE FARM

In 1995 an inspection of the rafters in the attic of the old house revealed tin cans, cutlery, books, school work and notes. The bush where the newborn infant had been buried was bulldozed. Inspection of the area turned up eating utensils, broken cups and hundreds of nails from the makeshift houses the twins had built together.

Many readers wondered what happened to Dolly, the horse. The twins say that shortly after they left home, Domko became frustrated that the horse kept running away from him and that he could not catch her. He chased her down with the tractor until she became exhausted and then killed her.

Strange sights and happenings on that particular parcel of land have led people in the area to believe that it is either cursed or haunted. While researching the book and after its release in 1996, a number of people came forward to offer many unsettling remembrances about the farm, the family, and Domko.

THE LUTHERAN CHURCH

When research on this book began the Lutheran Church was standing in an almost perfect state, with the exception of a few broken windows in the bell tower. Shortly afterward, the roof began to leak. The twins volunteered to repair and re-shingle the roof, but an agreement was never reached with the local committee. The building quickly deteriorated and was demolished. The brothers believed that the Church stood long enough to provide a haven when they were young and then later as a testament to their survival.

To honor the legacy of the building, Dennis built a replica that now stands on the Moosehorn museum grounds. On August 14, 2010, Dennis and Robynne's son Ryan and his fiancé, Suzi Menezes were married in the church.

WANT TO READ MORE ABOUT DAVID AND DENNIS PISCHKE?
In June 1997, six months after the release of *Where Children Run*, rumors began circulating that David and Dennis Pischke were responsible for the disappearance and subsequent murder of an acquaintance, Mike Kalanza. *When Memories Remain* is the continuing story available on Amazon, in bookstores or at: www.karenemilson.com.

The remains of the boat Dennis built. It was found when we went looking through the bush on a trip to the churchyard in 1995.

The brothers digging through the attic of the old house. They found cans, utensils, jars, and school notes.

Walter, Dennis, and David in front of the house. Taken in 1995.

The church where the children slept many nights to escape Domko.

Inside the church. In 1995, it looked much like it did when the Pischkes were children.

David, Dennis, Lynne, and Robynne with Majorie Harwart (left) and her sisters, Evelyn (kneeling) and Violet (right). Taken in 1995.

Family and friends held a 50th birthday party in their honor in 1998. They received a number of phone calls from strangers who'd read the book, plus a few pair of socks.

At one of their last book signings together in September 2003, Dennis, David and Karen with the staff at the St. Vital Chapters store.

Dennis and Robynne    *David and Lynne. Taken 2001.*

The last known photo of David taken with Tracy Hill on the church steps, May 15, 2004. He died a month later.

The church replica built by Dennis after David's death.

Friends and family gathered to celebrate Ryan Pischke's marriage to Suzi Menezes.

Dennis and Robynne's family, including Walter and Lorie; daughters Deanna, Dawn, their partners, and children.

WHEN MEMORIES REMAIN

The continuing story of the
Pischke Twins
available in stores and at Amazon

ACKNOWLEDGEMENTS

It is said that it takes a community to raise a child and I believe it takes at least that to create a book. I would like to express my sincere gratitude to the following people who contributed to the creation of this timeless, important story. I will start with Roger Newman, a very talented editor and to Fred Edge and Lorne Reimer for reading the initial manuscript. To Melanie Matheson who designed the original cover in 1996 and to Lisa Friesen for the current design of the book, now in its 21st year of publication.

To Arden and Barb Weight, present owners of the former Pischke farm, who allowed us to spend as much time there as we needed during the interview phase; and to Iver & Amanda Bankert, Doug Becker and Dave Greene for their efforts.

Readers sometimes wonder if this story, told by David and Dennis to me over the span of a year, is an accurate recollection of their childhood memories. Many others were interviewed and they include: Marjorie Harwart and her sisters Evelyn, Violet and Linda; Jim Deighton, Leon & Anna Koch, Ken Koch, Alvin Koch, Walter Pischke, Jackie Richter, Leah Gasper, Bernie Gmitzyk, Eunice Bullerwell, Marion Gering, Louise Collier, Margaret Harvey, Mary Burnett, Nina Kiesman, Ida Townsend, Henry Kort, Robert Jeske, Harold Boutilier, Marlene Emilson, Robert Gunnlaugson, Sophie Kolt, Len Kaminsky, Donna Murphy, Vera Johnson, Ken Rutherford and Michael Leitold. There were others, who for personal reasons, asked to remain anonymous.

Special thanks to our family, friends, neighbors and all the readers, who through their unwavering support, have kept *Where Children Run* alive all these years.

And finally, I will remain forever indebted to Peter Warren, former host of the CJOB Action Line radio show in Winnipeg, Manitoba. He believed in the twins and gave us the needed encouragement to proceed with this book.

KAREN EMILSON lives and writes full time from her home in Grunthal, Manitoba. She is the author of the narrative non-fiction bestsellers, *Where Children Run* and *When Memories Remain*. She recently completed her first novel, *Be Still the Water*.

www.karenemilson.com

Made in United States
North Haven, CT
16 May 2025